The Homeless Channel

The Homeless Channel
by Matt Silady

published by
Larry Young and Mimi Rosenheim
AiT/Planet Lar, LLC
2034 47th Avenue
San Francisco, CA 94116

First Edition: May 2007
10 9 8 7 6 5 4 3 2 1

cover photo and design by Matt Silady
book design and production by Matt Silady and Josh Richardson
lettered in WildWords by Comicraft

ISBN-10: 1-932051-49-X
ISBN-13: 978-1-932051-49-0

Printed and bound in Canada by Imprimerie Lebonfon, Inc.

The Homeless Channel

Matt Silady

San Francisco

for Serena

1

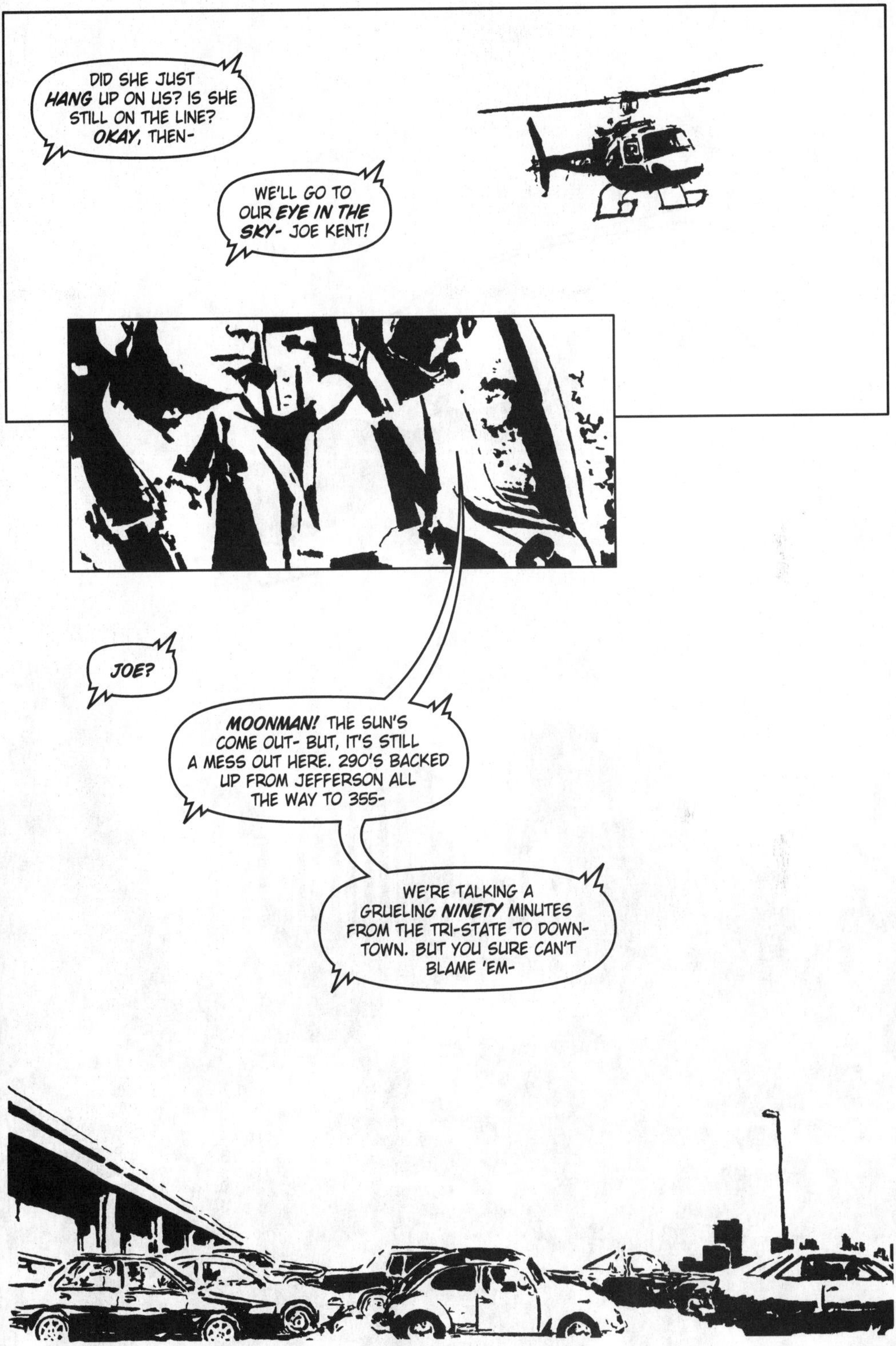
DID SHE JUST HANG UP ON US? IS SHE STILL ON THE LINE? OKAY, THEN-
WE'LL GO TO OUR EYE IN THE SKY- JOE KENT!
JOE?
MOONMAN! THE SUN'S COME OUT- BUT, IT'S STILL A MESS OUT HERE. 290'S BACKED UP FROM JEFFERSON ALL THE WAY TO 355-
WE'RE TALKING A GRUELING NINETY MINUTES FROM THE TRI-STATE TO DOWN-TOWN. BUT YOU SURE CAN'T BLAME 'EM-

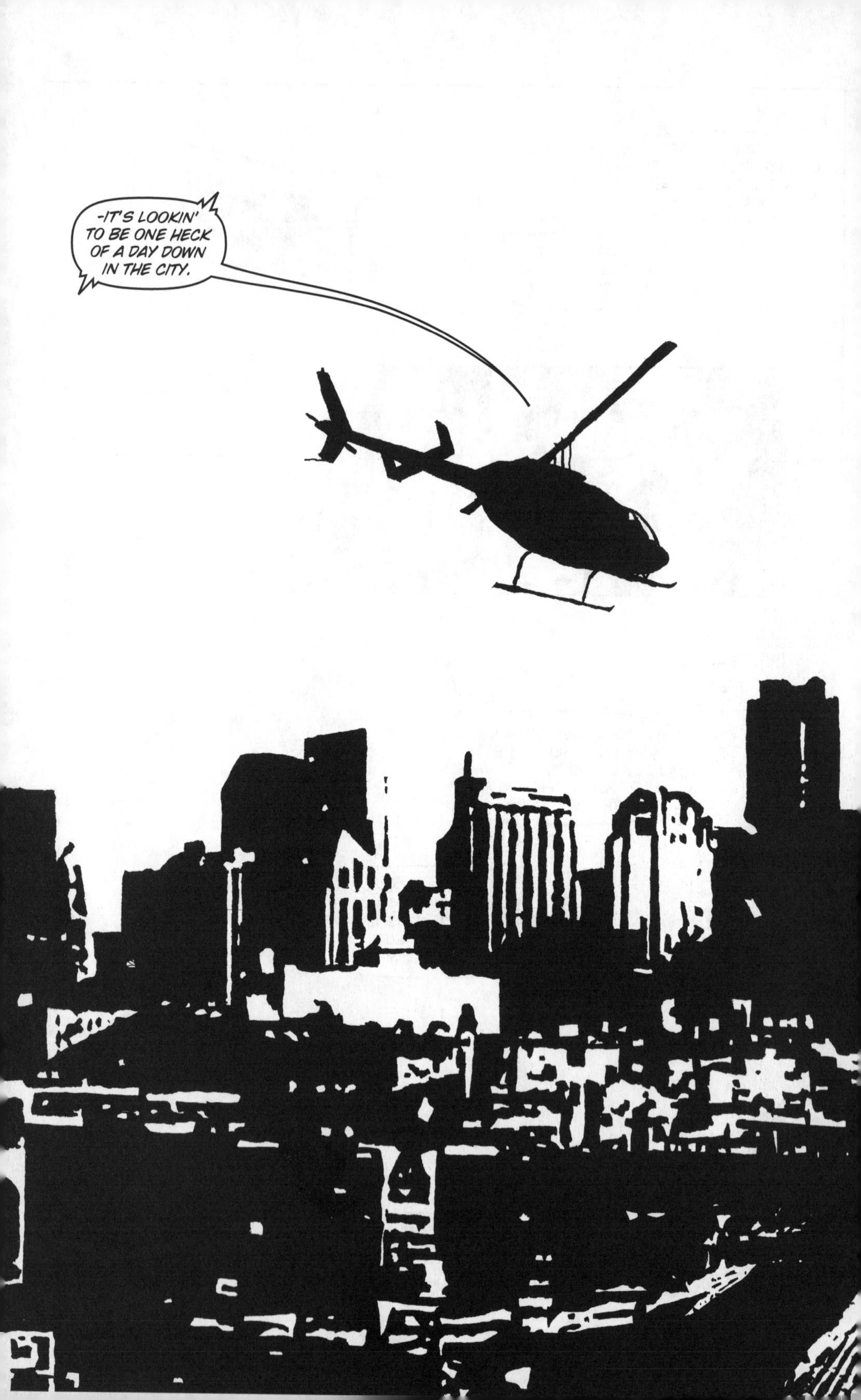
-IT'S LOOKIN' TO BE ONE HECK OF A DAY DOWN IN THE CITY.

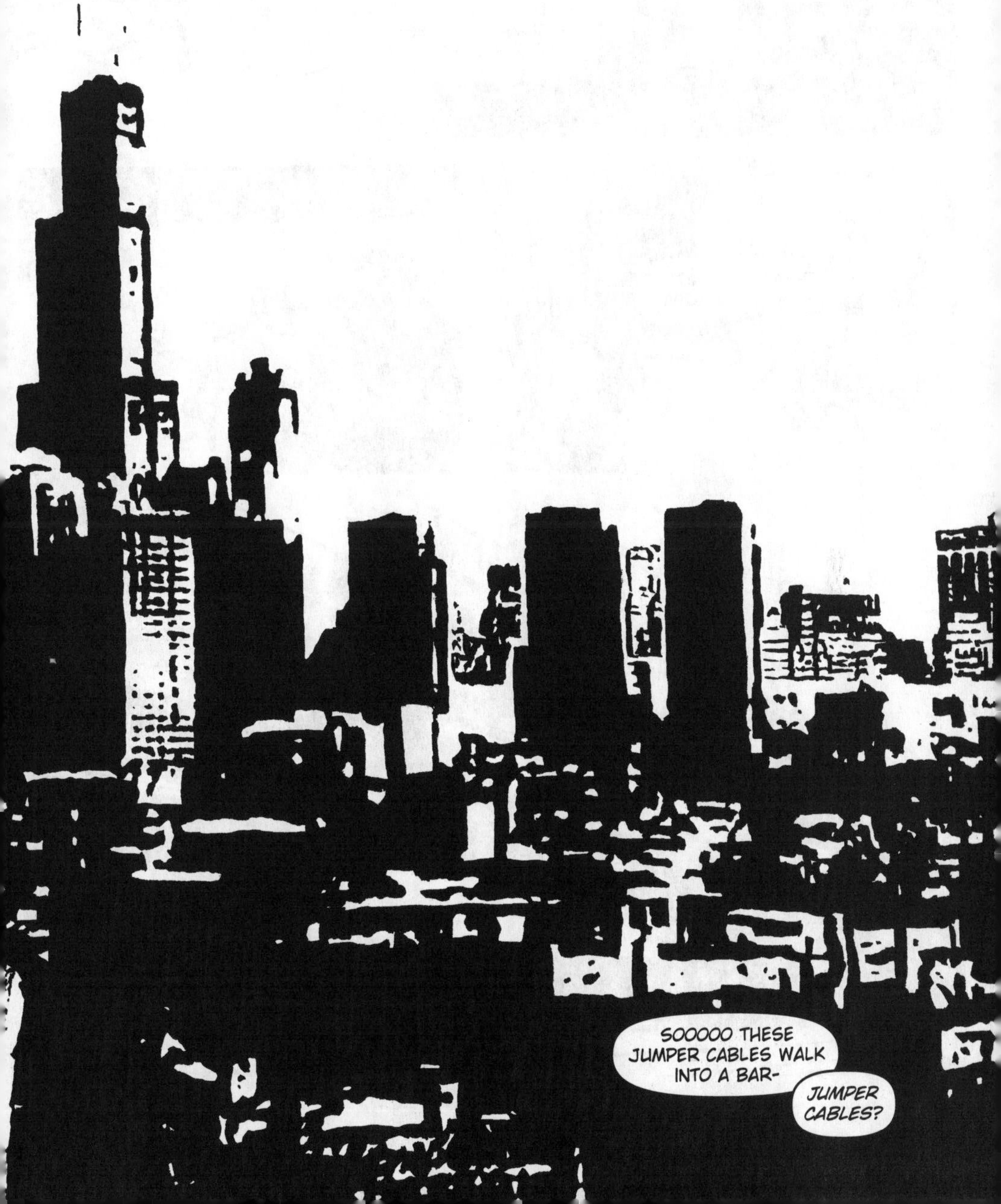
SOOOOO THESE JUMPER CABLES WALK INTO A BAR-
JUMPER CABLES?

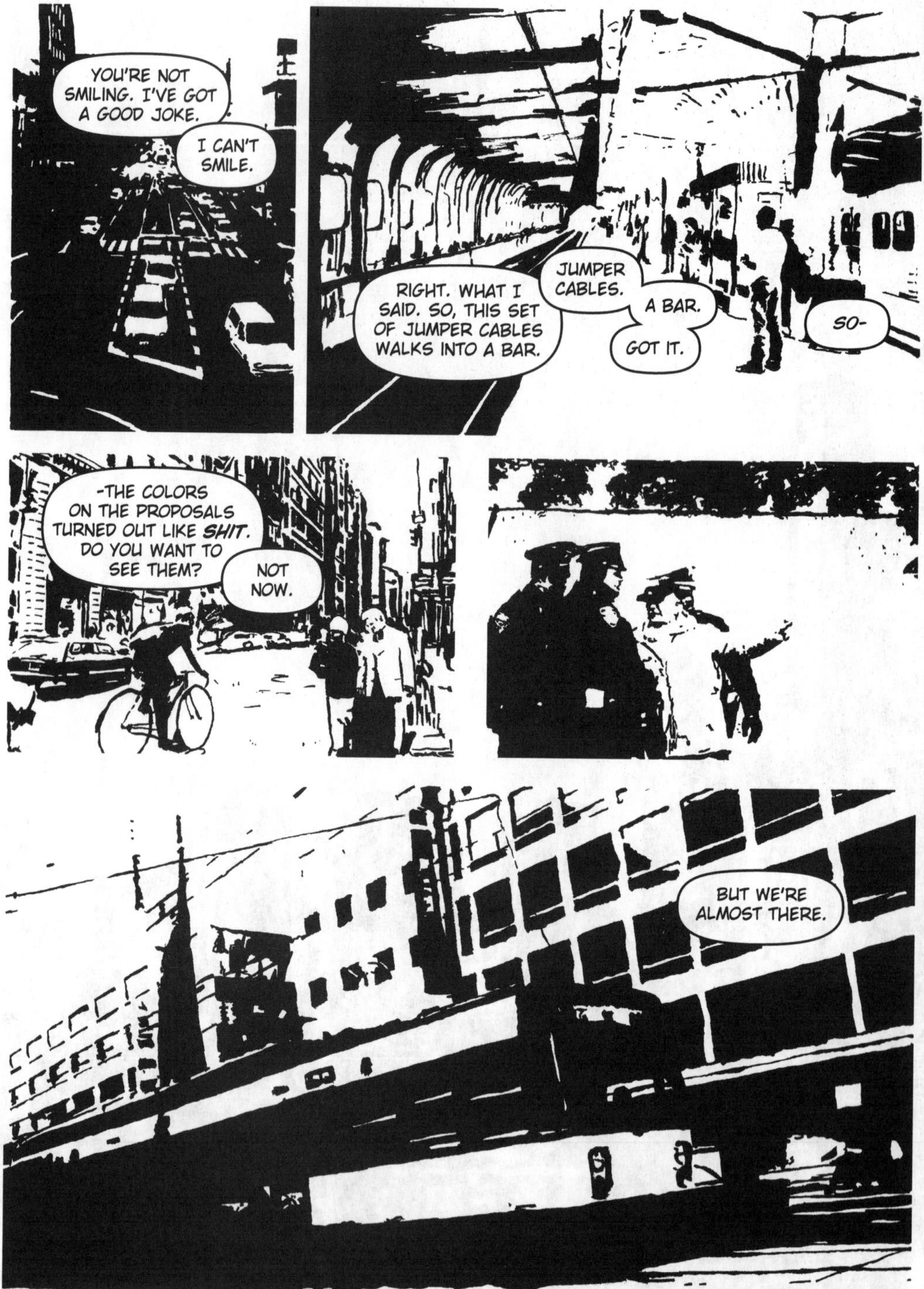
YOU'RE NOT SMILING. I'VE GOT A GOOD JOKE.
I CAN'T SMILE.
RIGHT. WHAT I SAID. SO, THIS SET OF JUMPER CABLES WALKS INTO A BAR.
JUMPER CABLES.
A BAR.
GOT IT.
SO-
-THE COLORS ON THE PROPOSALS TURNED OUT LIKE *SHIT*. DO YOU WANT TO SEE THEM?
NOT NOW.
BUT WE'RE ALMOST THERE.

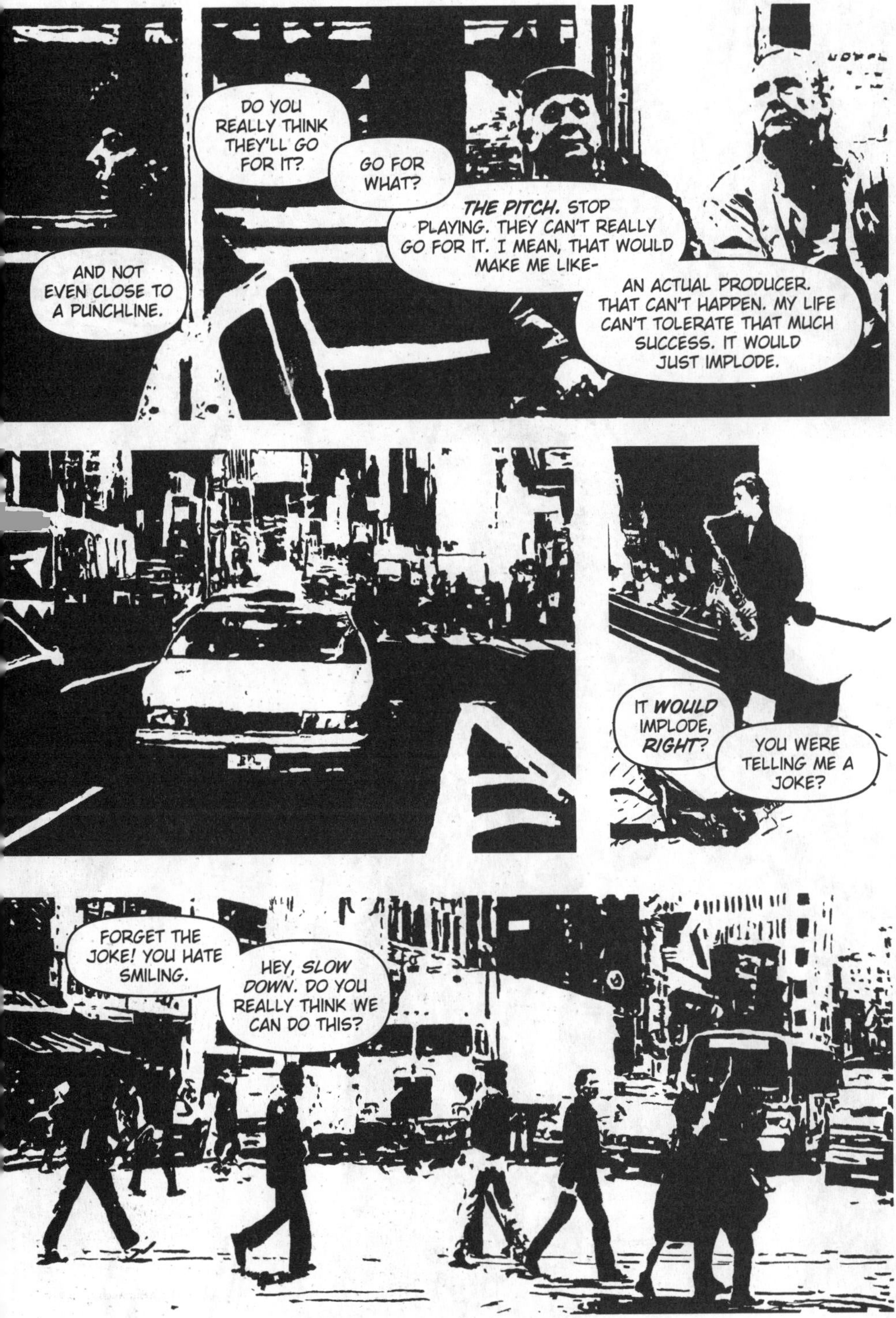
AND NOT EVEN CLOSE TO A PUNCHLINE.
DO YOU REALLY THINK THEY'LL GO FOR IT?
GO FOR WHAT?
THE PITCH. STOP PLAYING. THEY CAN'T REALLY GO FOR IT. I MEAN, THAT WOULD MAKE ME LIKE-
AN ACTUAL PRODUCER. THAT CAN'T HAPPEN. MY LIFE CAN'T TOLERATE THAT MUCH SUCCESS. IT WOULD JUST IMPLODE.
IT *WOULD* IMPLODE, *RIGHT*?
YOU WERE TELLING ME A JOKE?
FORGET THE JOKE! YOU HATE SMILING.
HEY, *SLOW DOWN*. DO YOU REALLY THINK WE CAN DO THIS?

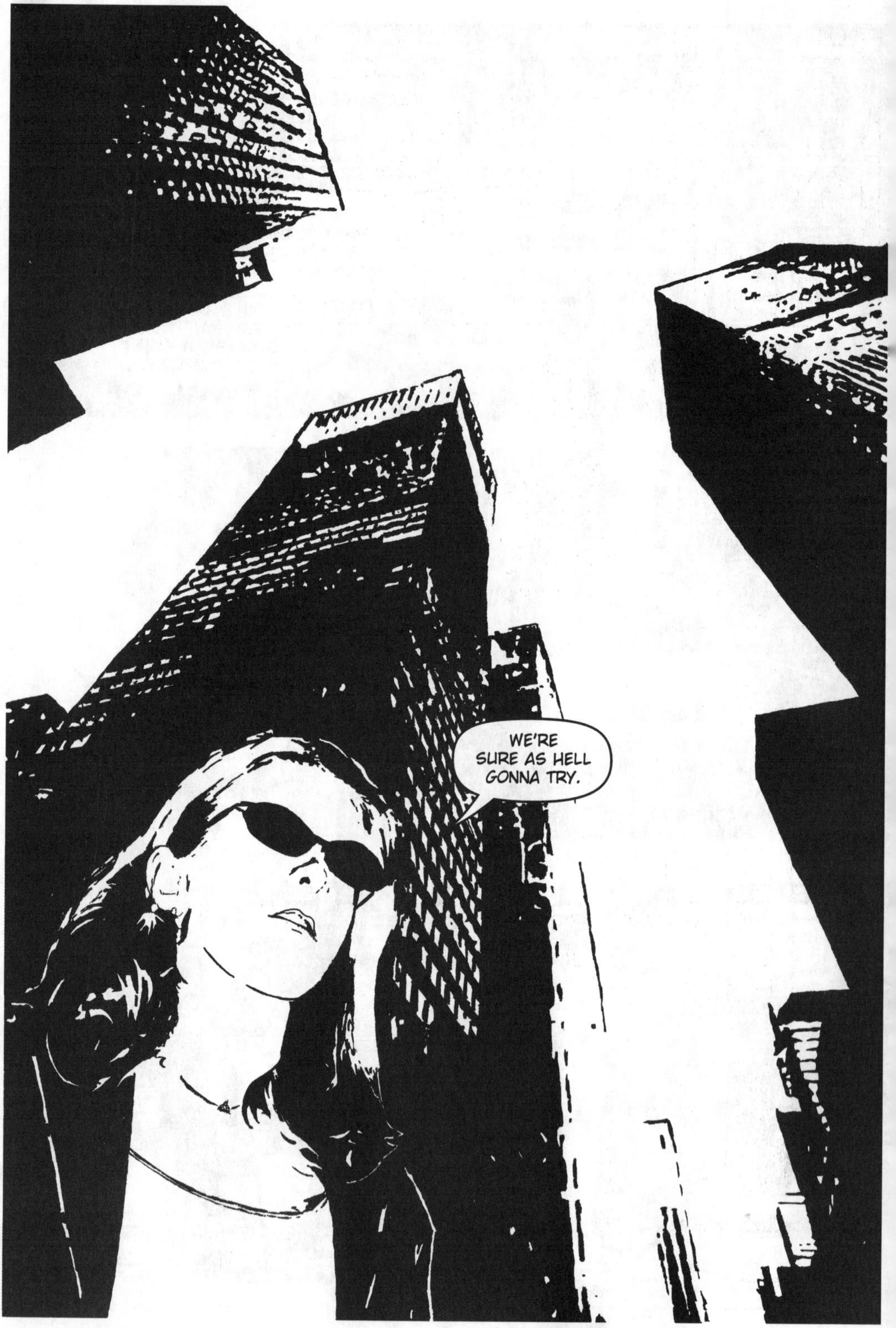
WE'RE SURE AS HELL GONNA TRY.

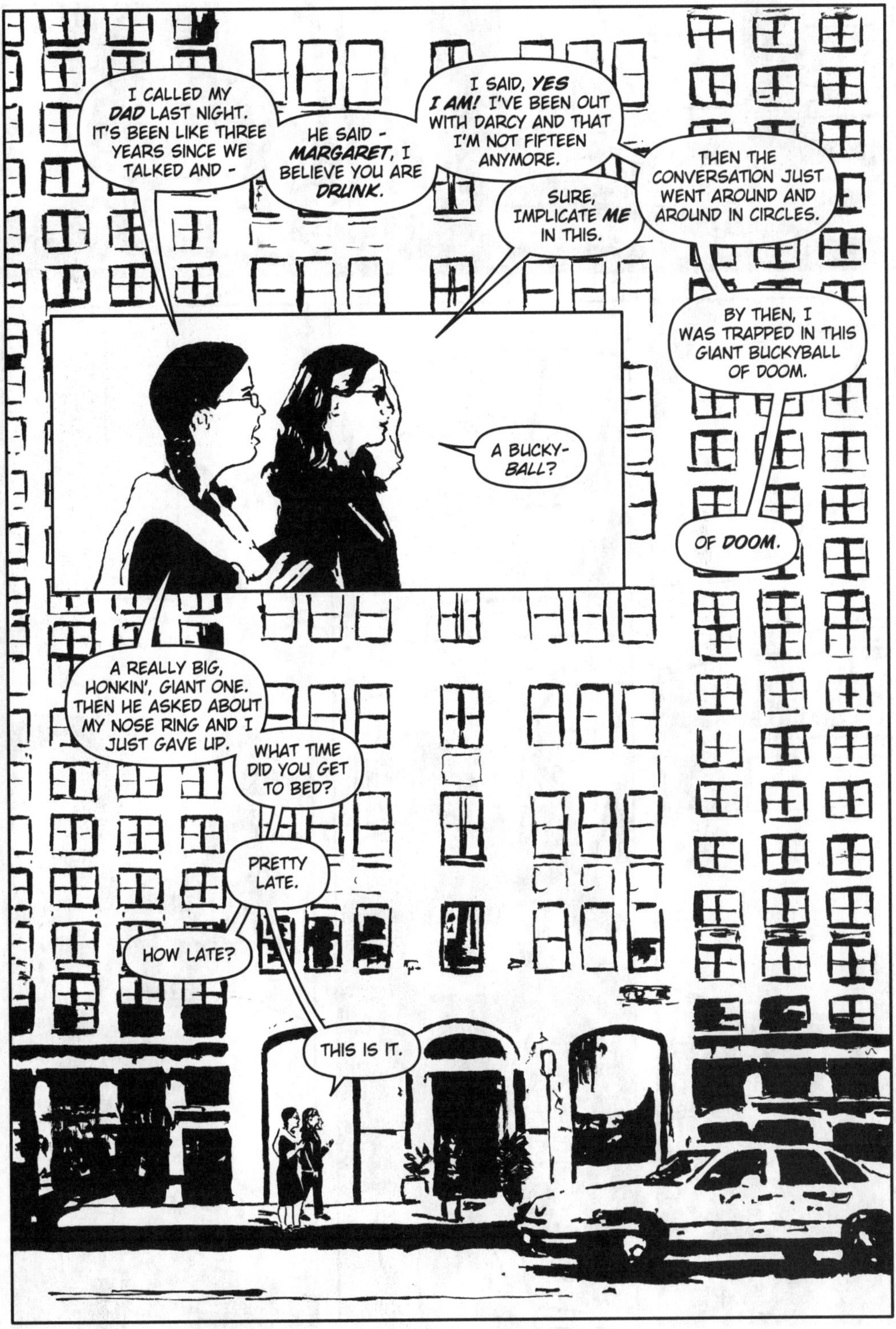
I CALLED MY DAD LAST NIGHT. IT'S BEEN LIKE THREE YEARS SINCE WE TALKED AND -
HE SAID - MARGARET, I BELIEVE YOU ARE DRUNK.
I SAID, YES I AM! I'VE BEEN OUT WITH DARCY AND THAT I'M NOT FIFTEEN ANYMORE.
SURE, IMPLICATE ME IN THIS.
THEN THE CONVERSATION JUST WENT AROUND AND AROUND IN CIRCLES.
BY THEN, I WAS TRAPPED IN THIS GIANT BUCKYBALL OF DOOM.
A BUCKY-BALL?
OF DOOM.
A REALLY BIG, HONKIN', GIANT ONE. THEN HE ASKED ABOUT MY NOSE RING AND I JUST GAVE UP.
WHAT TIME DID YOU GET TO BED?
PRETTY LATE.
HOW LATE?
THIS IS IT.

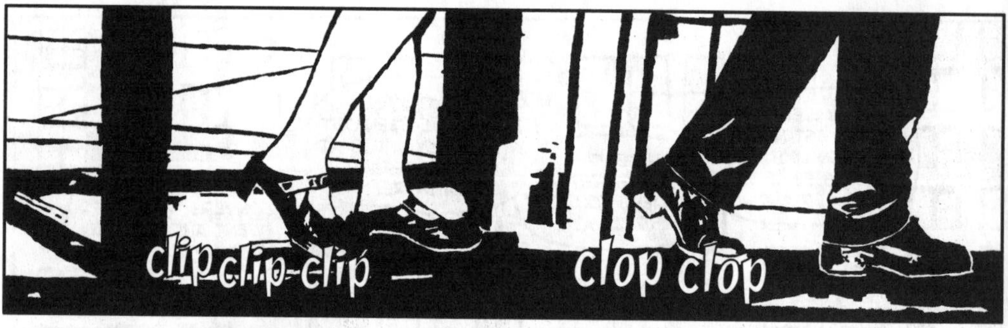
clip clip-clip
clop clop

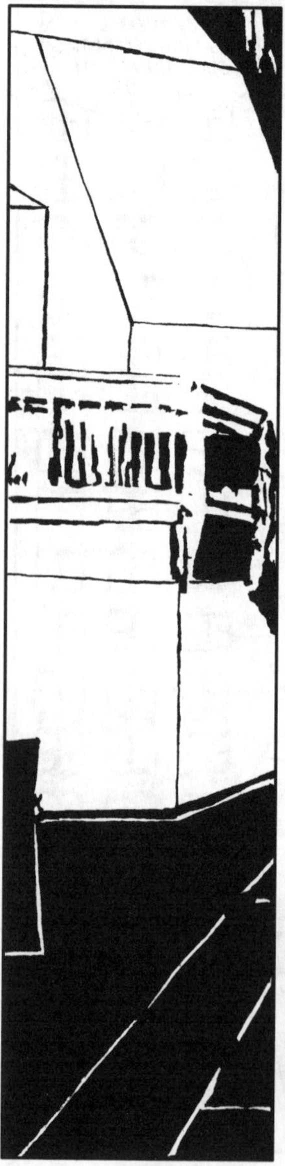

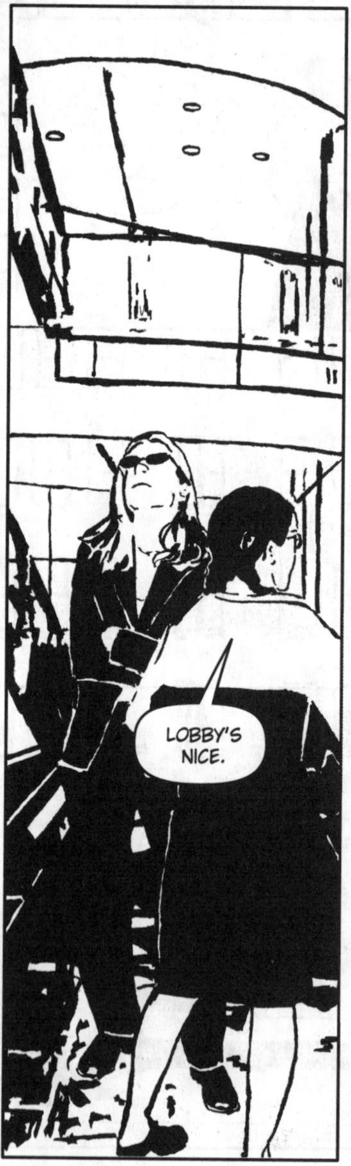
LOBBY'S NICE.

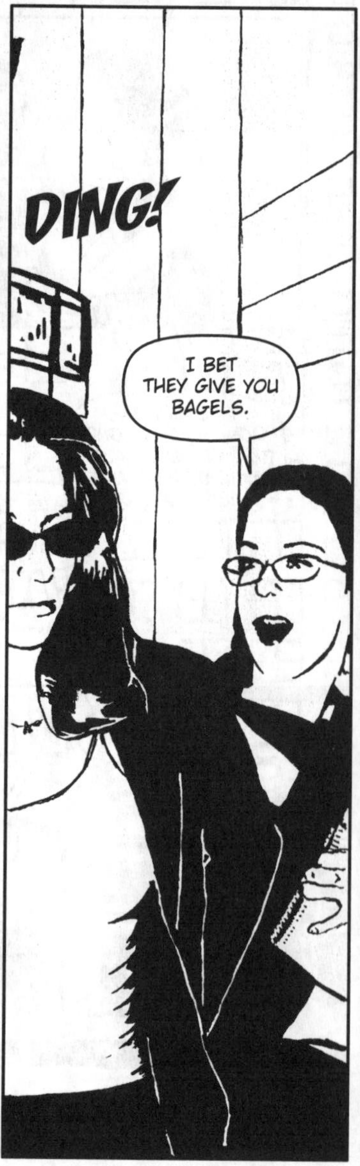
DING!
I BET THEY GIVE YOU BAGELS.

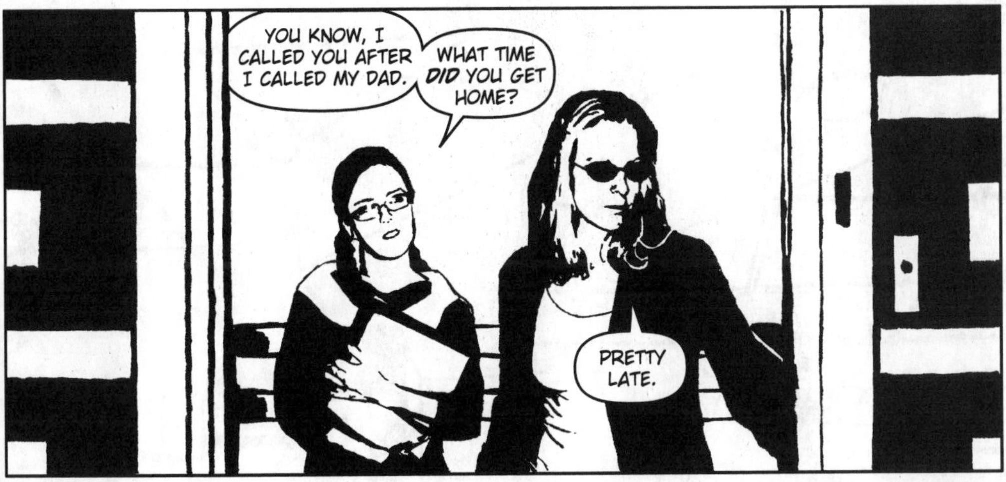
YOU KNOW, I CALLED YOU AFTER I CALLED MY DAD.
WHAT TIME *DID* YOU GET HOME?
PRETTY LATE.

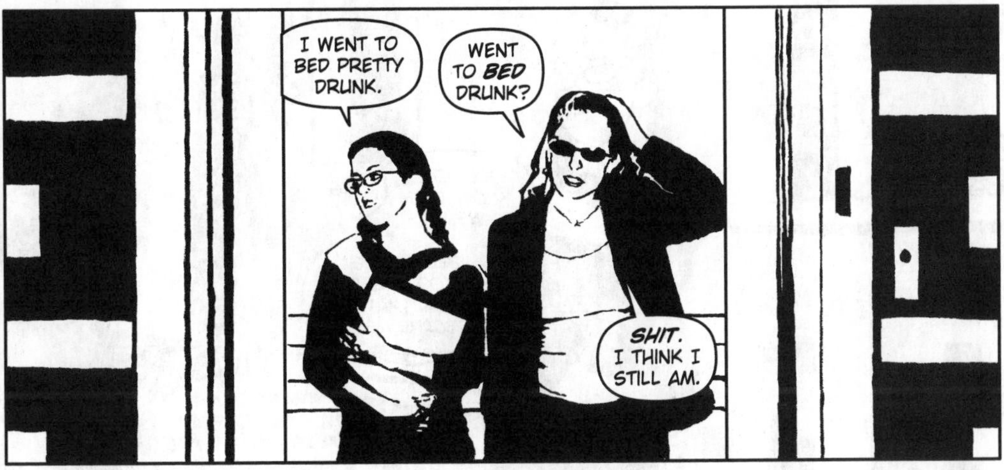
I WENT TO BED PRETTY DRUNK.
WENT TO *BED* DRUNK?
SHIT. I THINK I STILL AM.

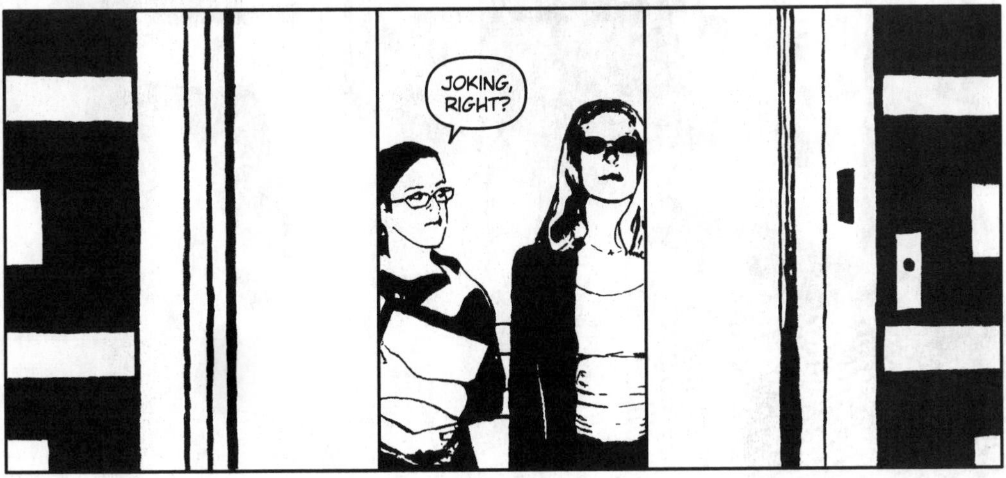
JOKING, RIGHT?

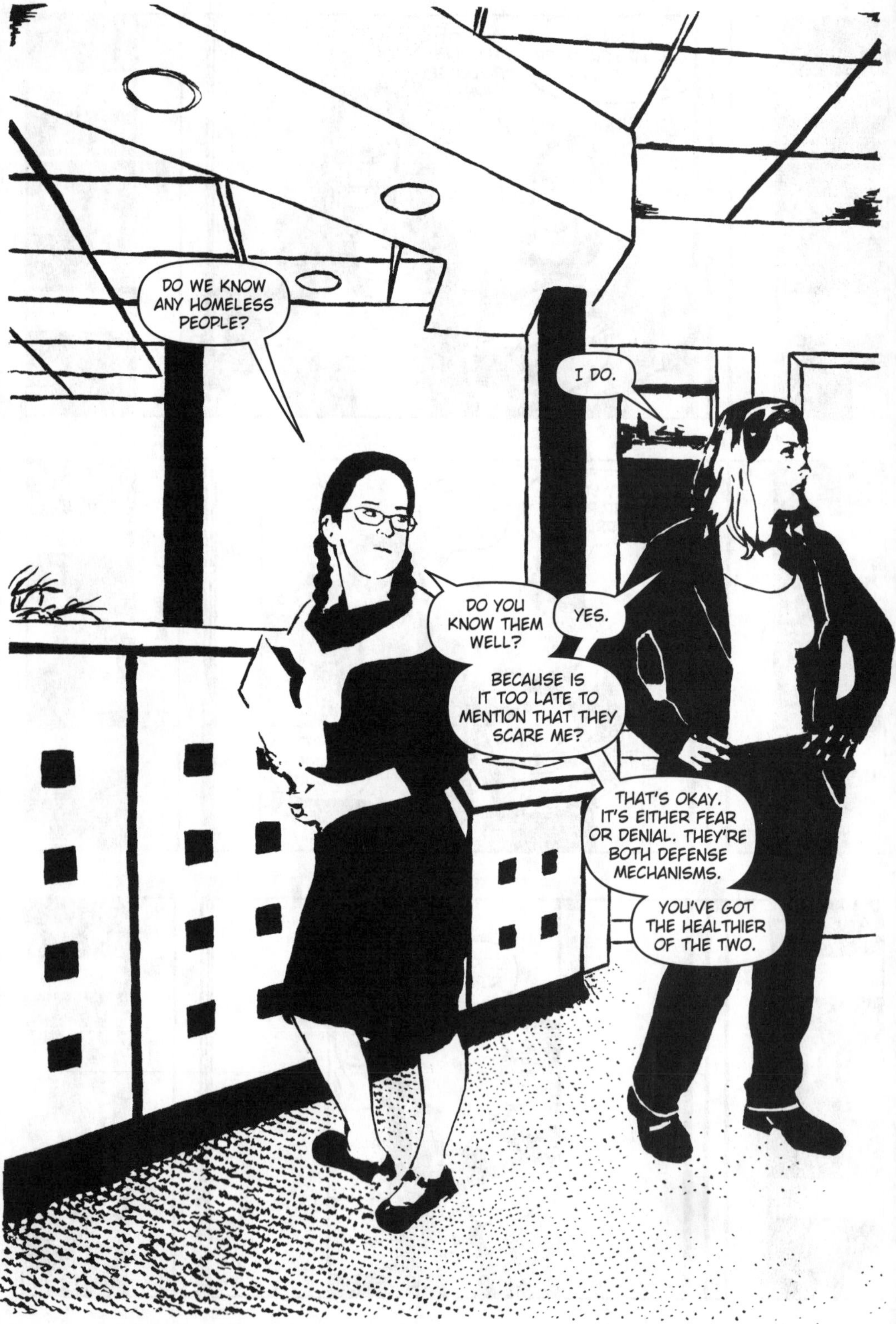
DO WE KNOW ANY HOMELESS PEOPLE?
I DO.
DO YOU KNOW THEM WELL?
YES.
BECAUSE IS IT TOO LATE TO MENTION THAT THEY SCARE ME?
THAT'S OKAY. IT'S EITHER FEAR OR DENIAL. THEY'RE BOTH DEFENSE MECHANISMS.
YOU'VE GOT THE HEALTHIER OF THE TWO.

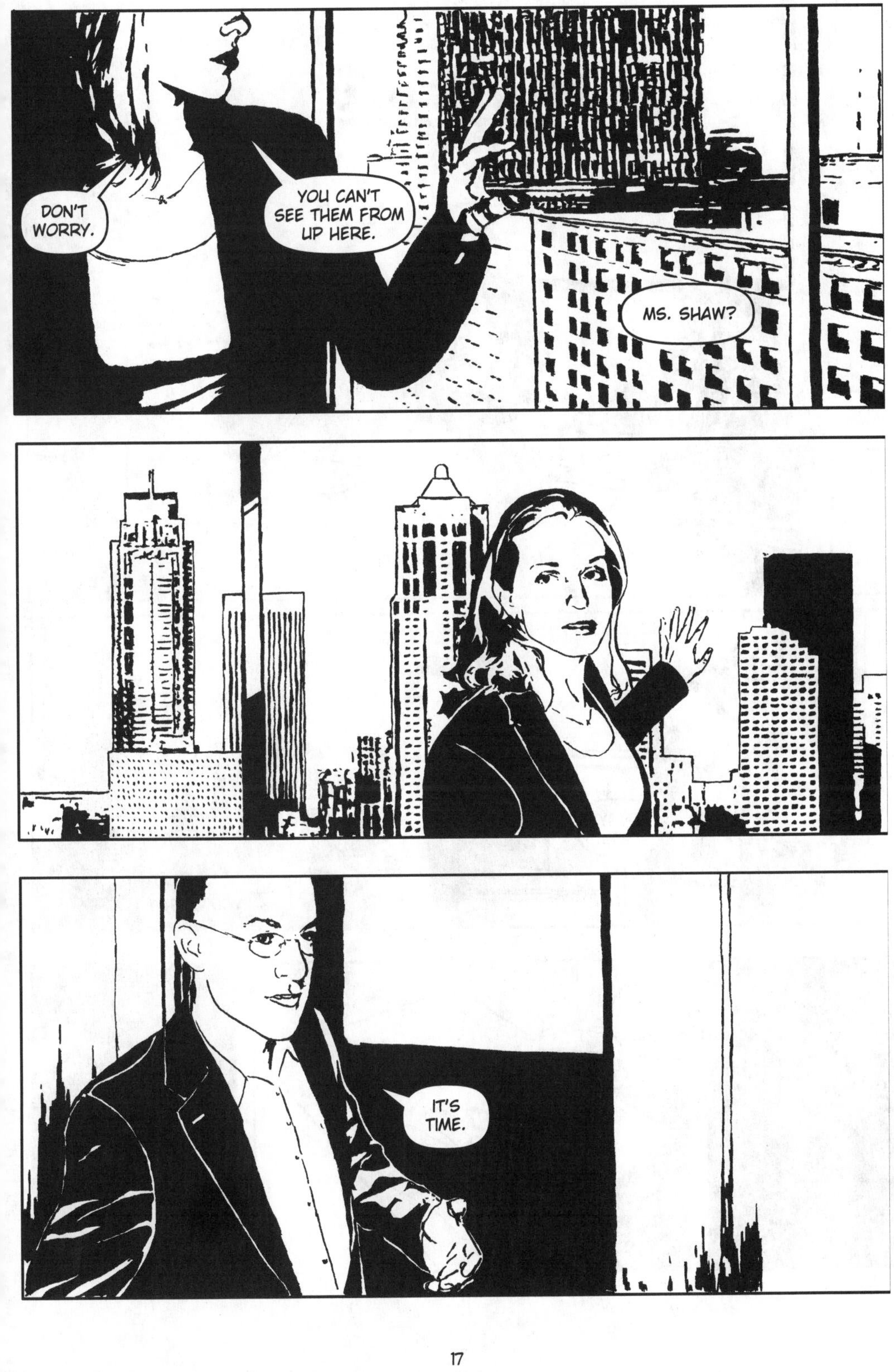
DON'T WORRY.
YOU CAN'T SEE THEM FROM UP HERE.
MS. SHAW?
IT'S TIME.

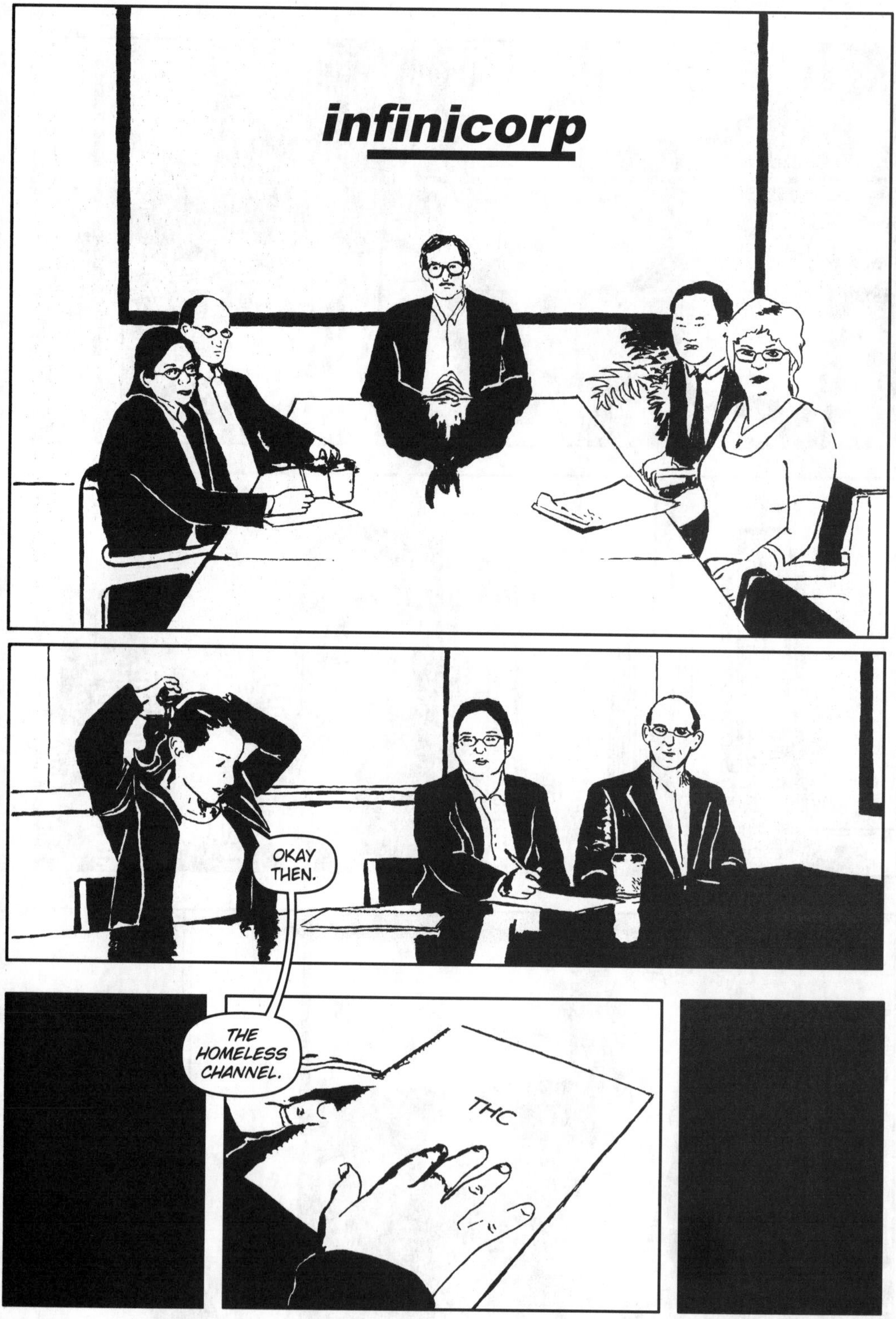
infinicorp
OKAY THEN.
THE HOMELESS CHANNEL.
THC

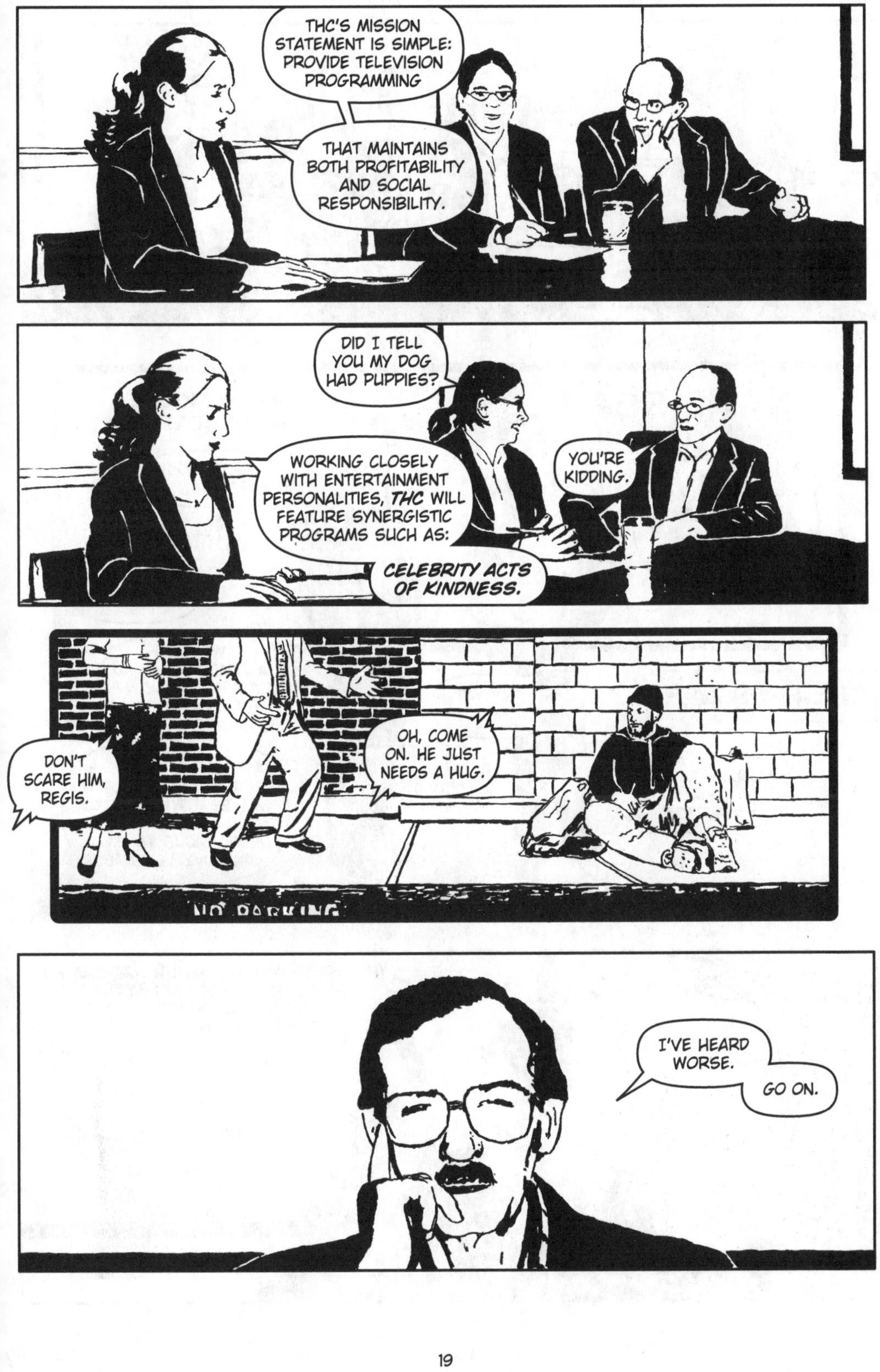
THC'S MISSION STATEMENT IS SIMPLE: PROVIDE TELEVISION PROGRAMMING
THAT MAINTAINS BOTH PROFITABILITY AND SOCIAL RESPONSIBILITY.
DID I TELL YOU MY DOG HAD PUPPIES?
WORKING CLOSELY WITH ENTERTAINMENT PERSONALITIES, *THC* WILL FEATURE SYNERGISTIC PROGRAMS SUCH AS:
YOU'RE KIDDING.
CELEBRITY ACTS OF KINDNESS.
DON'T SCARE HIM, REGIS.
OH, COME ON. HE JUST NEEDS A HUG.
NO PARKING
I'VE HEARD WORSE.
GO ON.

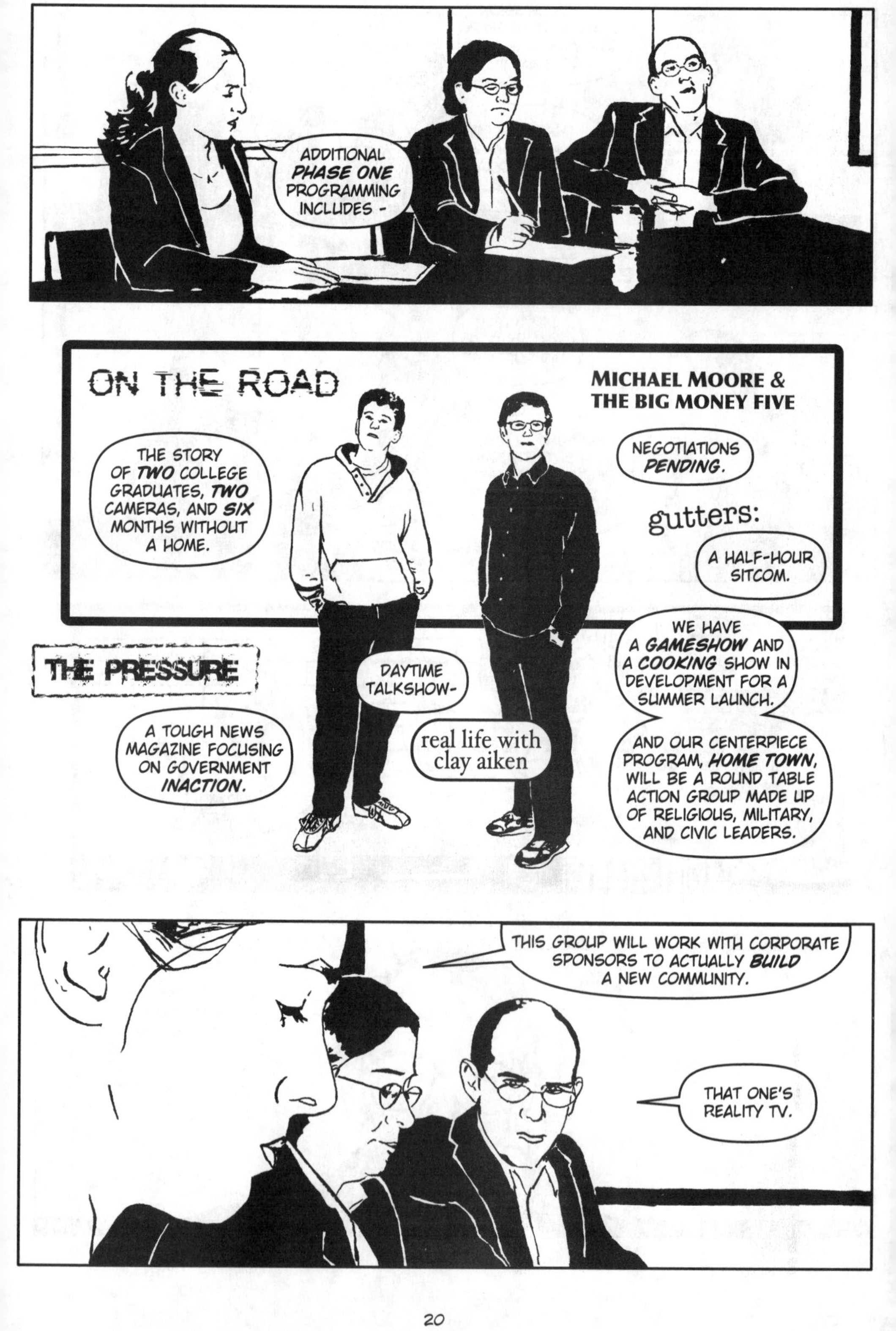
ADDITIONAL PHASE ONE PROGRAMMING INCLUDES -
ON THE ROAD
THE STORY OF TWO COLLEGE GRADUATES, TWO CAMERAS, AND SIX MONTHS WITHOUT A HOME.
MICHAEL MOORE & THE BIG MONEY FIVE
NEGOTIATIONS PENDING.
gutters:
A HALF-HOUR SITCOM.
THE PRESSURE
A TOUGH NEWS MAGAZINE FOCUSING ON GOVERNMENT INACTION.
DAYTIME TALKSHOW-
real life with clay aiken
WE HAVE A GAMESHOW AND A COOKING SHOW IN DEVELOPMENT FOR A SUMMER LAUNCH.
AND OUR CENTERPIECE PROGRAM, HOME TOWN, WILL BE A ROUND TABLE ACTION GROUP MADE UP OF RELIGIOUS, MILITARY, AND CIVIC LEADERS.
THIS GROUP WILL WORK WITH CORPORATE SPONSORS TO ACTUALLY BUILD A NEW COMMUNITY.
THAT ONE'S REALITY TV.

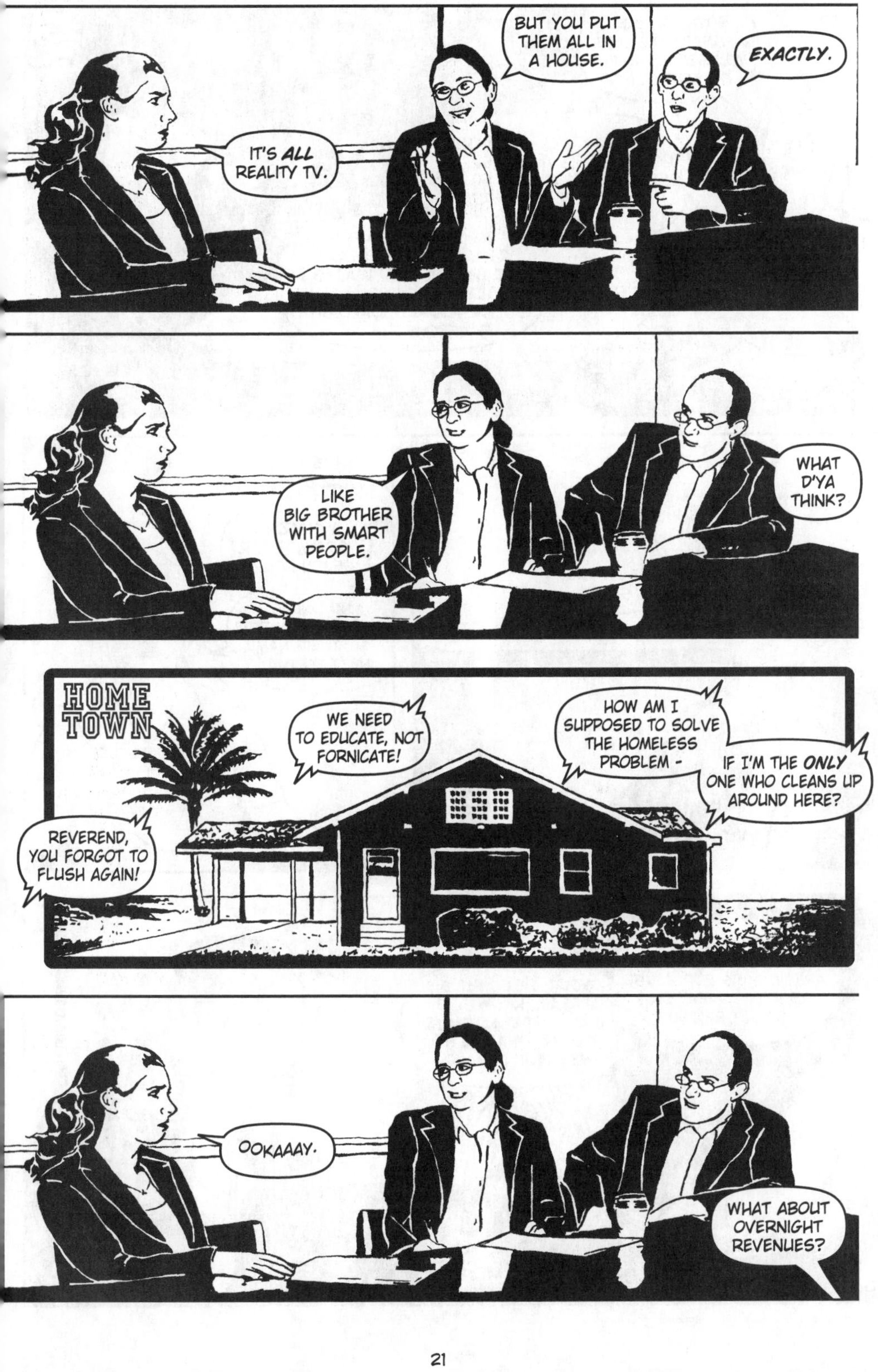

BUT YOU PUT THEM ALL IN A HOUSE.
EXACTLY.
IT'S ALL REALITY TV.
LIKE BIG BROTHER WITH SMART PEOPLE.
WHAT D'YA THINK?
HOME TOWN
WE NEED TO EDUCATE, NOT FORNICATE!
HOW AM I SUPPOSED TO SOLVE THE HOMELESS PROBLEM -
IF I'M THE ONLY ONE WHO CLEANS UP AROUND HERE?
REVEREND, YOU FORGOT TO FLUSH AGAIN!
OOKAAAY.
WHAT ABOUT OVERNIGHT REVENUES?

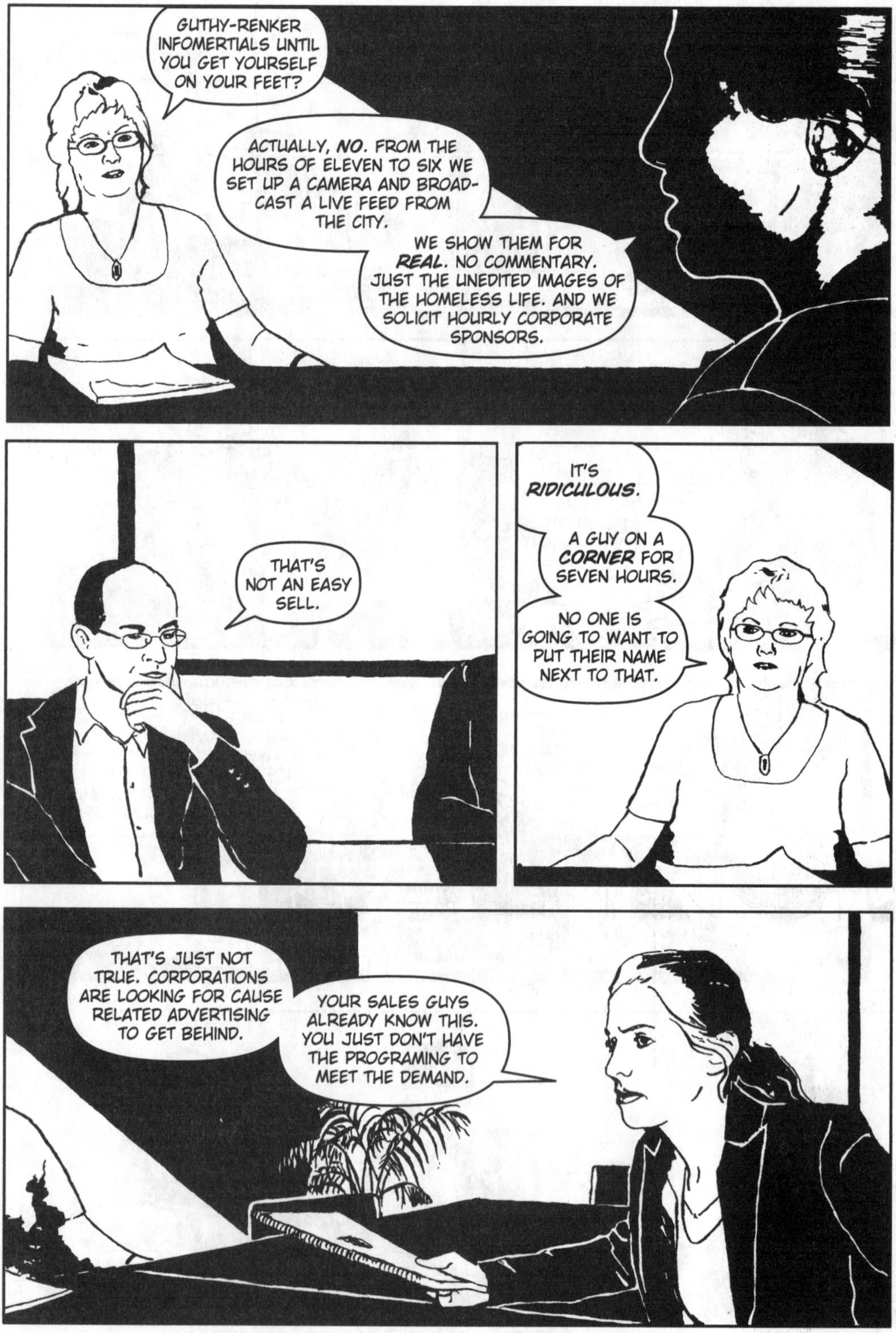
GUTHY-RENKER INFOMERTIALS UNTIL YOU GET YOURSELF ON YOUR FEET?
ACTUALLY, **NO**. FROM THE HOURS OF ELEVEN TO SIX WE SET UP A CAMERA AND BROAD-CAST A LIVE FEED FROM THE CITY.
WE SHOW THEM FOR **REAL**. NO COMMENTARY. JUST THE UNEDITED IMAGES OF THE HOMELESS LIFE. AND WE SOLICIT HOURLY CORPORATE SPONSORS.
THAT'S NOT AN EASY SELL.
IT'S **RIDICULOUS**.
A GUY ON A **CORNER** FOR SEVEN HOURS.
NO ONE IS GOING TO WANT TO PUT THEIR NAME NEXT TO THAT.
THAT'S JUST NOT TRUE. CORPORATIONS ARE LOOKING FOR CAUSE RELATED ADVERTISING TO GET BEHIND.
YOUR SALES GUYS ALREADY KNOW THIS. YOU JUST DON'T HAVE THE PROGRAMING TO MEET THE DEMAND.

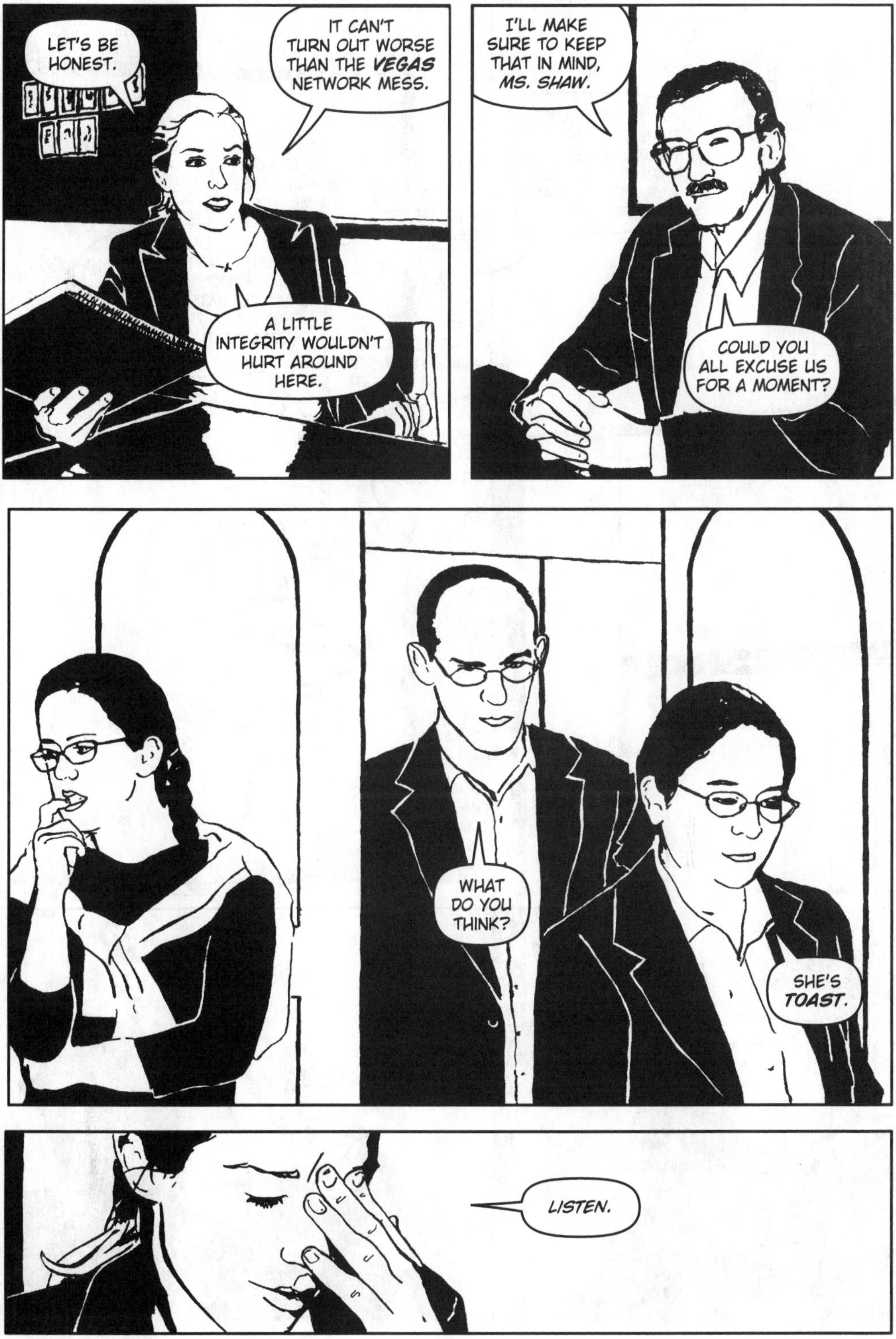
LET'S BE HONEST.
IT CAN'T TURN OUT WORSE THAN THE *VEGAS* NETWORK MESS.
A LITTLE INTEGRITY WOULDN'T HURT AROUND HERE.
I'LL MAKE SURE TO KEEP THAT IN MIND, *MS. SHAW*.
COULD YOU ALL EXCUSE US FOR A MOMENT?
WHAT DO YOU THINK?
SHE'S *TOAST*.
LISTEN.

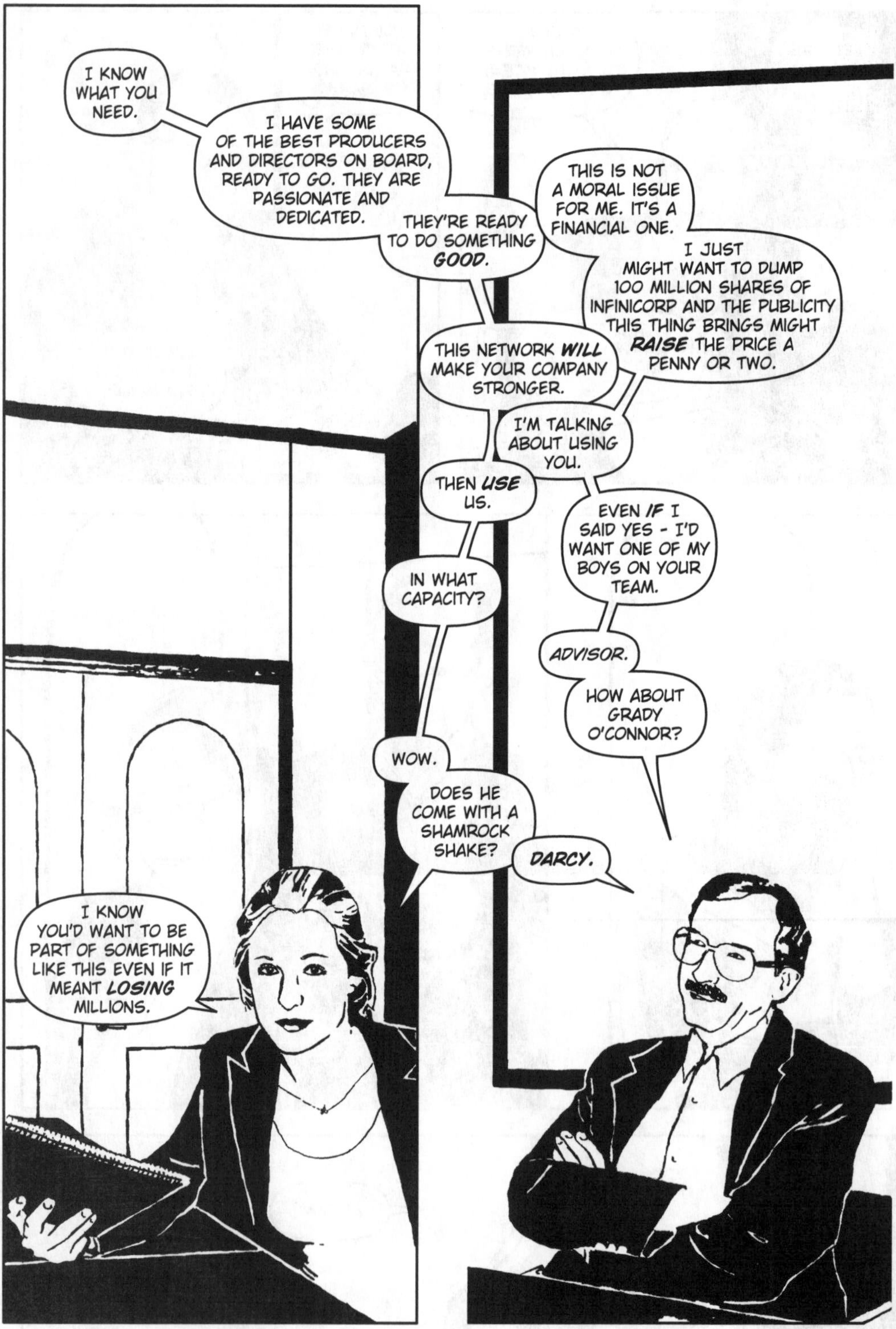
I KNOW WHAT YOU NEED.
I HAVE SOME OF THE BEST PRODUCERS AND DIRECTORS ON BOARD, READY TO GO. THEY ARE PASSIONATE AND DEDICATED.
THEY'RE READY TO DO SOMETHING *GOOD*.
THIS IS NOT A MORAL ISSUE FOR ME. IT'S A FINANCIAL ONE.
I JUST MIGHT WANT TO DUMP 100 MILLION SHARES OF INFINICORP AND THE PUBLICITY THIS THING BRINGS MIGHT *RAISE* THE PRICE A PENNY OR TWO.
THIS NETWORK *WILL* MAKE YOUR COMPANY STRONGER.
I'M TALKING ABOUT USING YOU.
THEN *USE* US.
EVEN *IF* I SAID YES - I'D WANT ONE OF MY BOYS ON YOUR TEAM.
IN WHAT CAPACITY?
ADVISOR.
HOW ABOUT GRADY O'CONNOR?
WOW.
DOES HE COME WITH A SHAMROCK SHAKE?
DARCY.
I KNOW YOU'D WANT TO BE PART OF SOMETHING LIKE THIS EVEN IF IT MEANT *LOSING* MILLIONS.

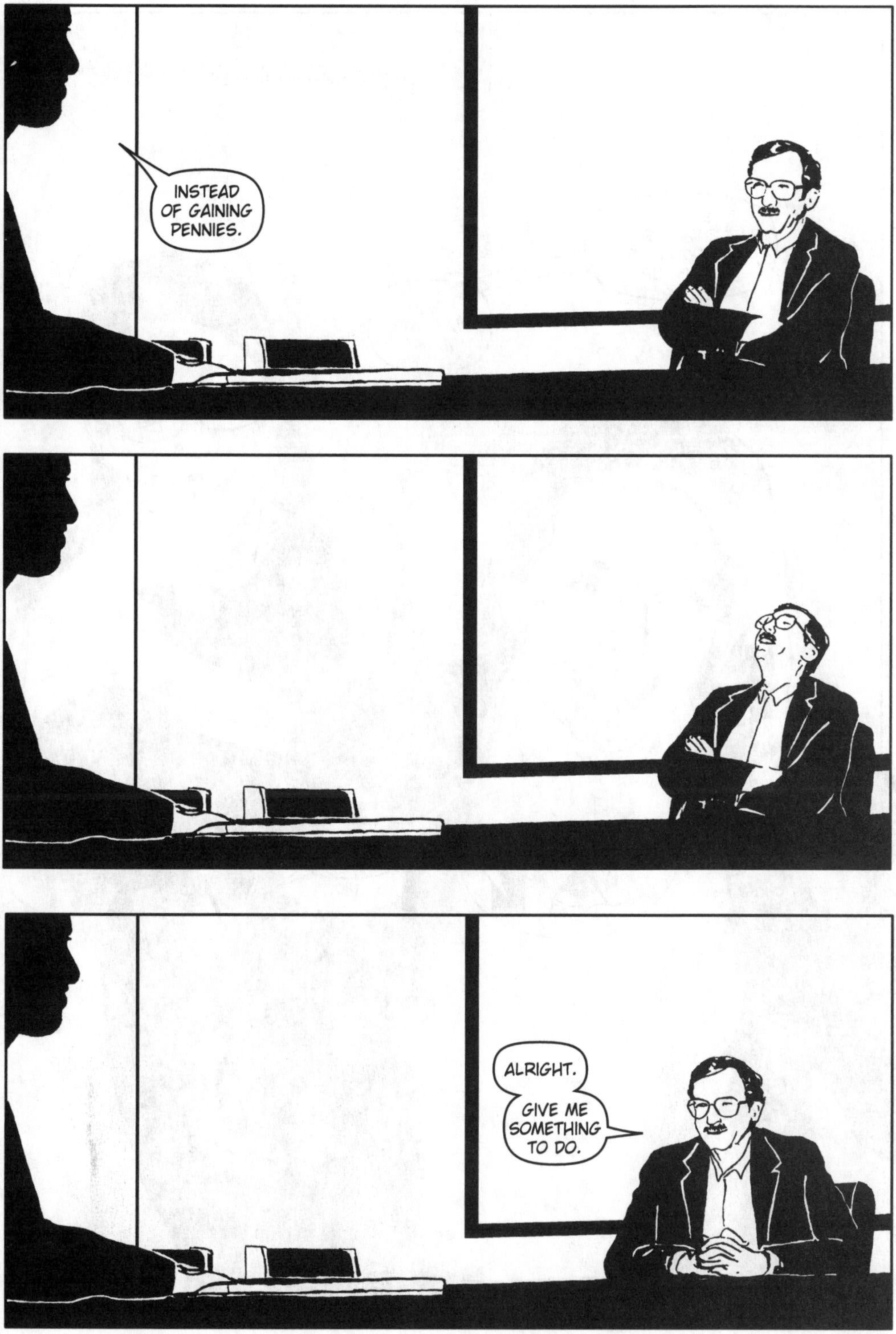
INSTEAD OF GAINING PENNIES.
ALRIGHT.
GIVE ME SOMETHING TO DO.

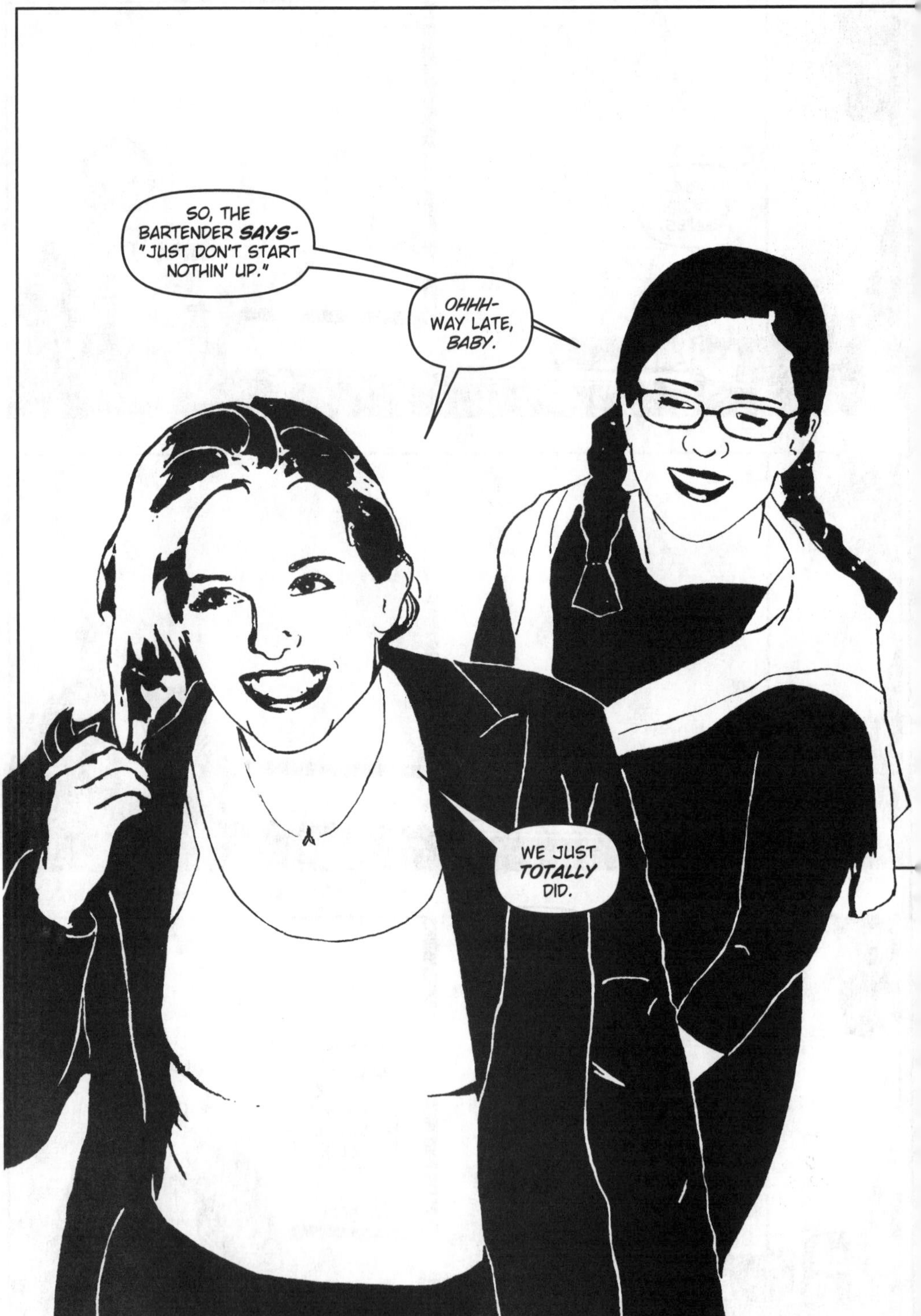
SO, THE BARTENDER **SAYS**- "JUST DON'T START NOTHIN' UP."
OHHH- WAY LATE, *BABY*.
WE JUST **TOTALLY** DID.

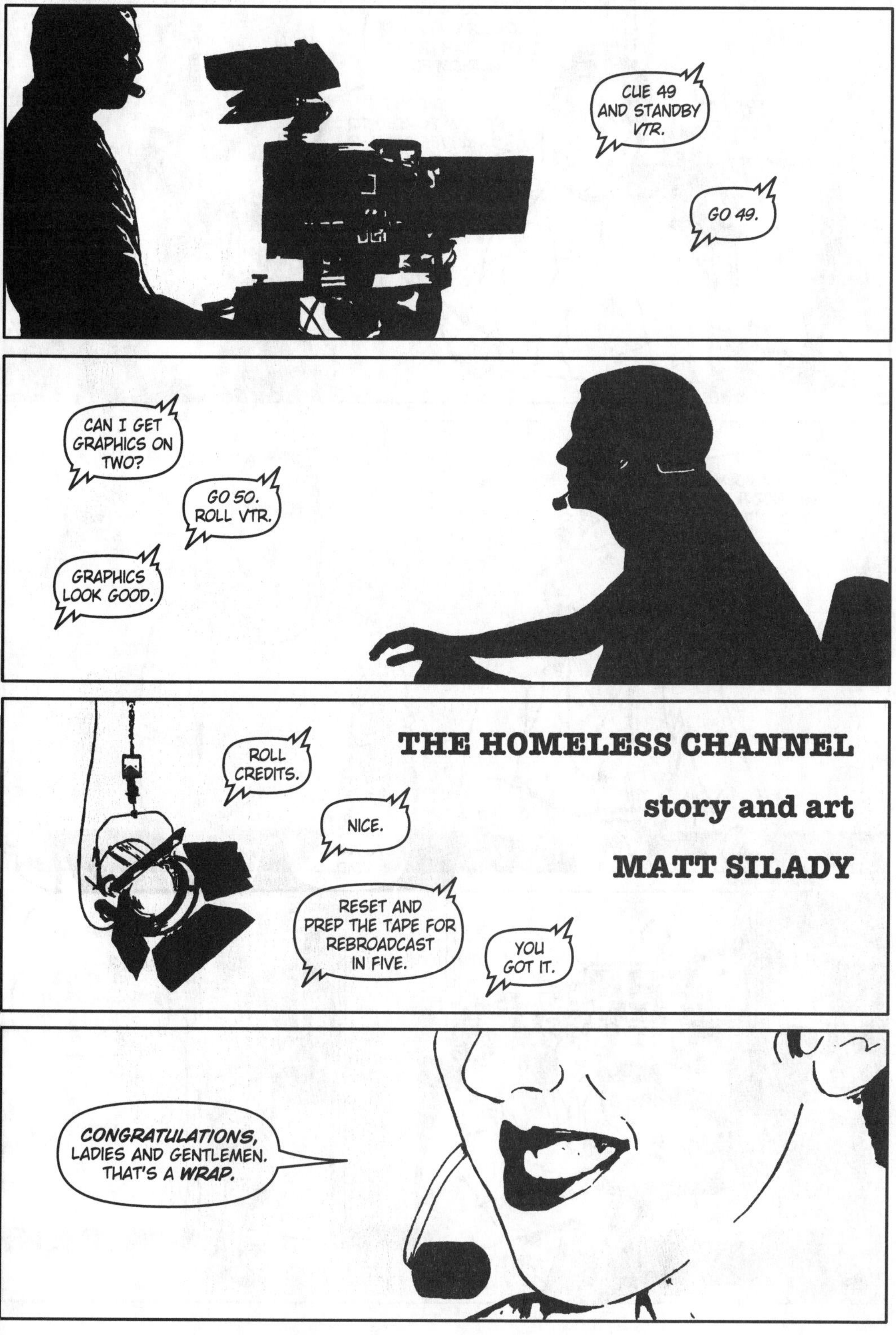

CUE 49 AND STANDBY VTR.
GO 49.
CAN I GET GRAPHICS ON TWO?
GO 50. ROLL VTR.
GRAPHICS LOOK GOOD.
THE HOMELESS CHANNEL
story and art
MATT SILADY
ROLL CREDITS.
NICE.
RESET AND PREP THE TAPE FOR REBROADCAST IN FIVE.
YOU GOT IT.
CONGRATULATIONS, LADIES AND GENTLEMEN. THAT'S A WRAP.

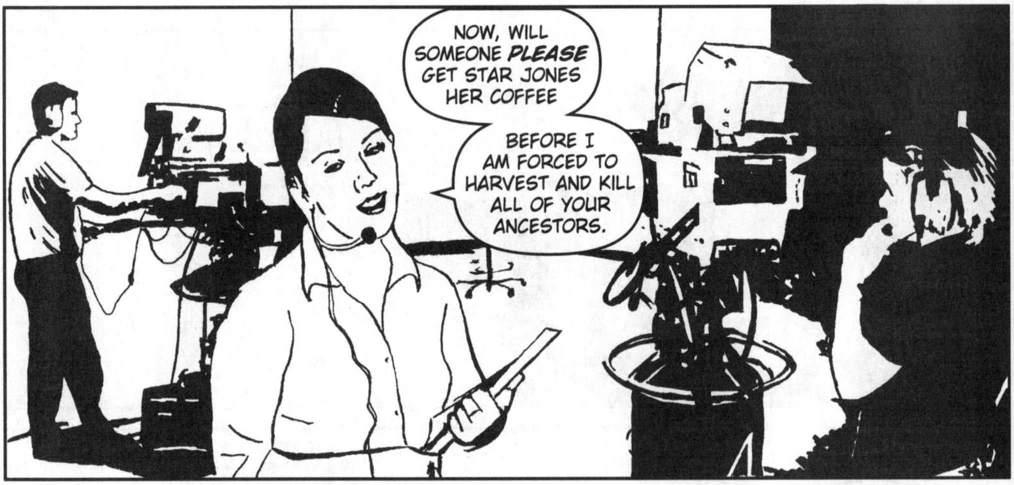
NOW, WILL SOMEONE *PLEASE* GET STAR JONES HER COFFEE
BEFORE I AM FORCED TO HARVEST AND KILL ALL OF YOUR ANCESTORS.

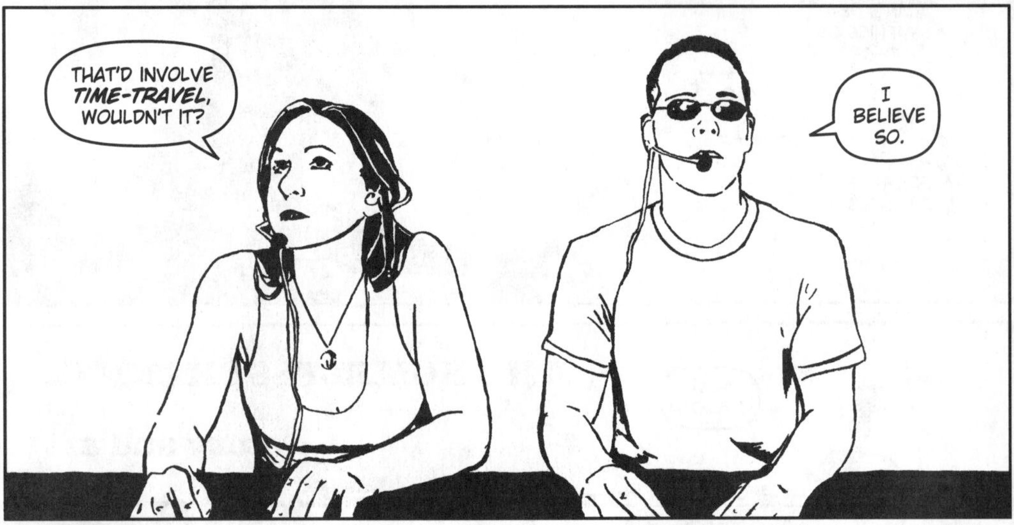
THAT'D INVOLVE *TIME-TRAVEL,* WOULDN'T IT?
I BELIEVE SO.

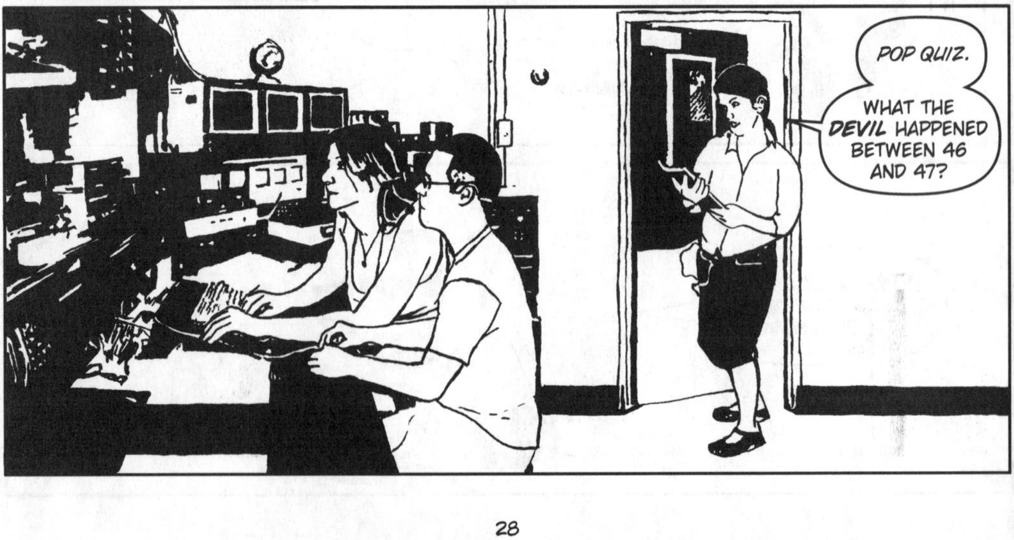
POP QUIZ.
WHAT THE *DEVIL* HAPPENED BETWEEN 46 AND 47?

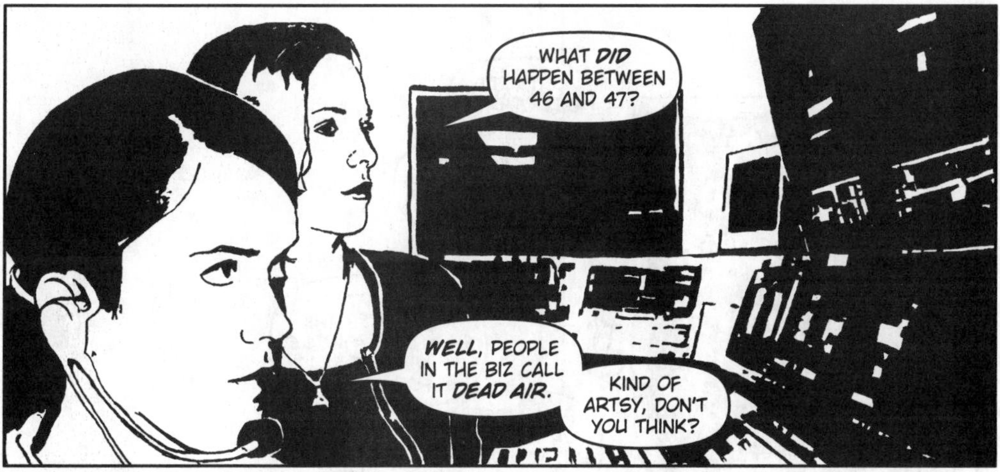
WHAT DID HAPPEN BETWEEN 46 AND 47?
WELL, PEOPLE IN THE BIZ CALL IT DEAD AIR.
KIND OF ARTSY, DON'T YOU THINK?

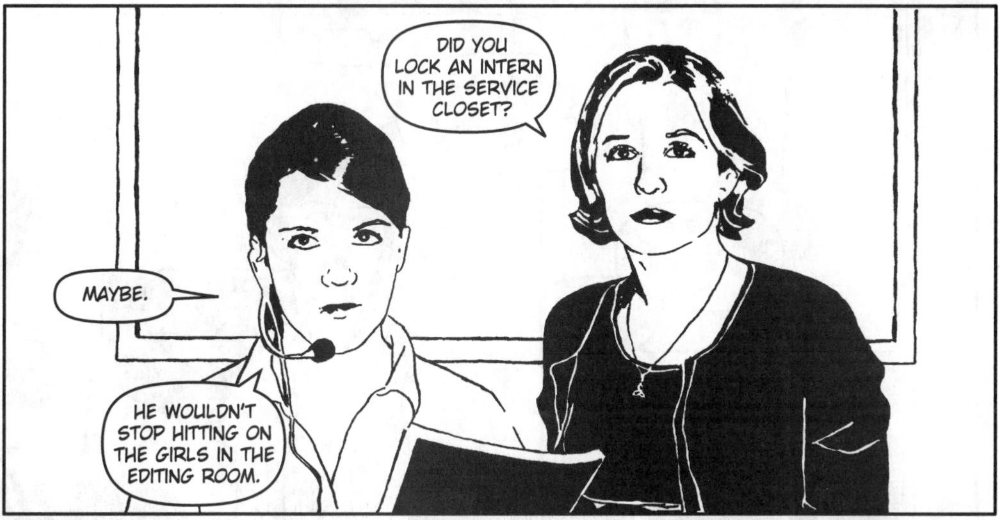
DID YOU LOCK AN INTERN IN THE SERVICE CLOSET?
MAYBE.
HE WOULDN'T STOP HITTING ON THE GIRLS IN THE EDITING ROOM.

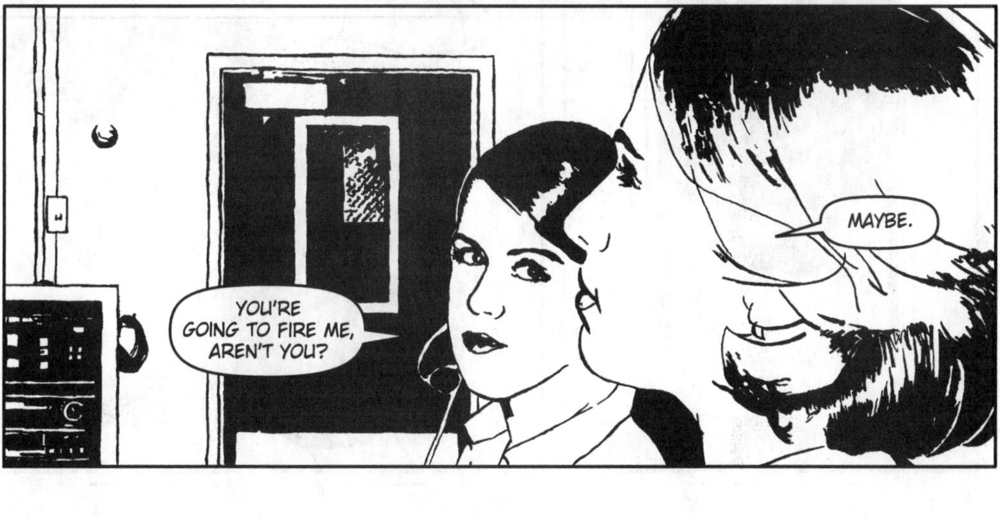
YOU'RE GOING TO FIRE ME, AREN'T YOU?
MAYBE.

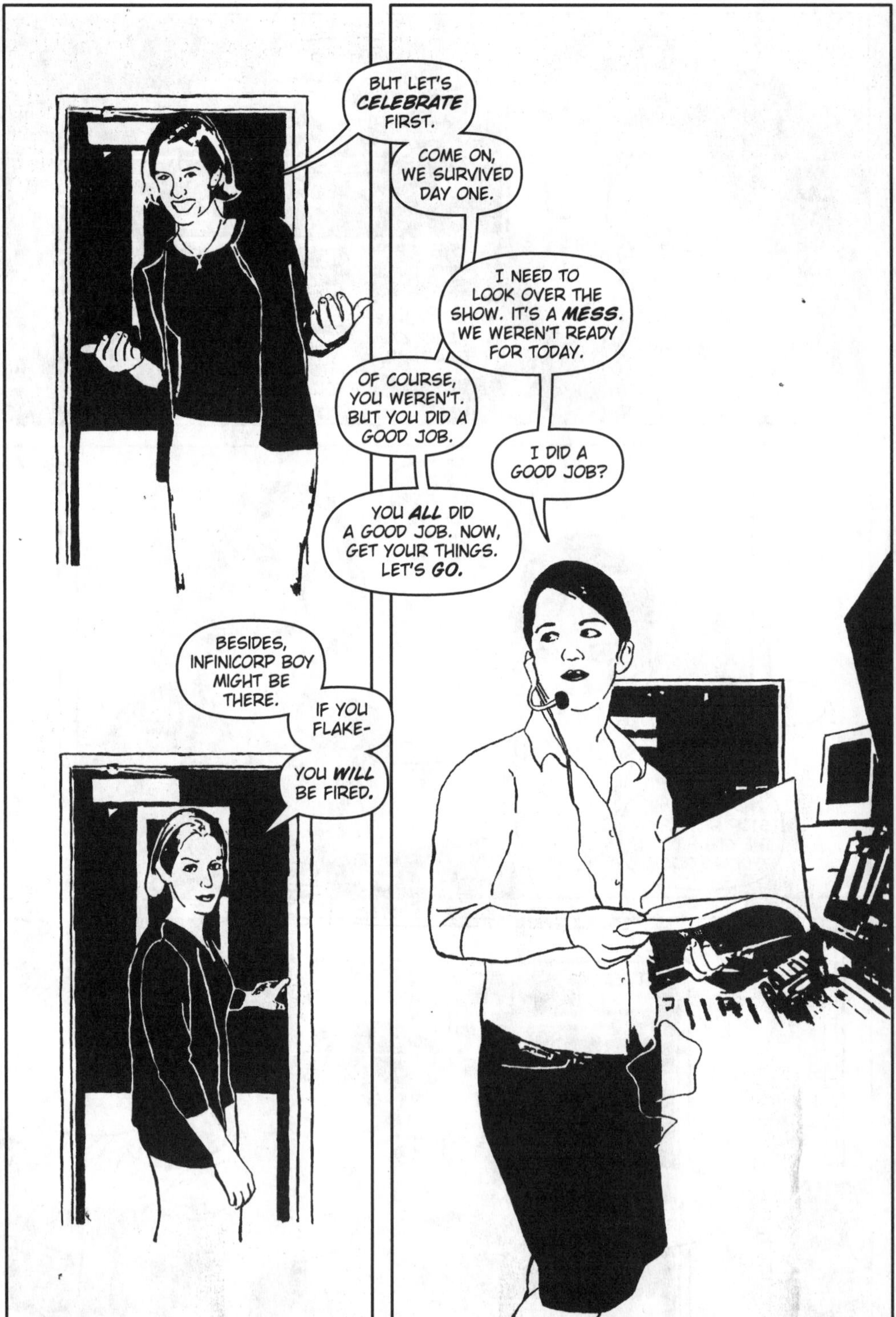
BUT LET'S CELEBRATE FIRST.
COME ON, WE SURVIVED DAY ONE.
I NEED TO LOOK OVER THE SHOW. IT'S A MESS. WE WEREN'T READY FOR TODAY.
OF COURSE, YOU WEREN'T. BUT YOU DID A GOOD JOB.
I DID A GOOD JOB?
YOU ALL DID A GOOD JOB. NOW, GET YOUR THINGS. LET'S GO.
BESIDES, INFINICORP BOY MIGHT BE THERE.
IF YOU FLAKE-
YOU WILL BE FIRED.

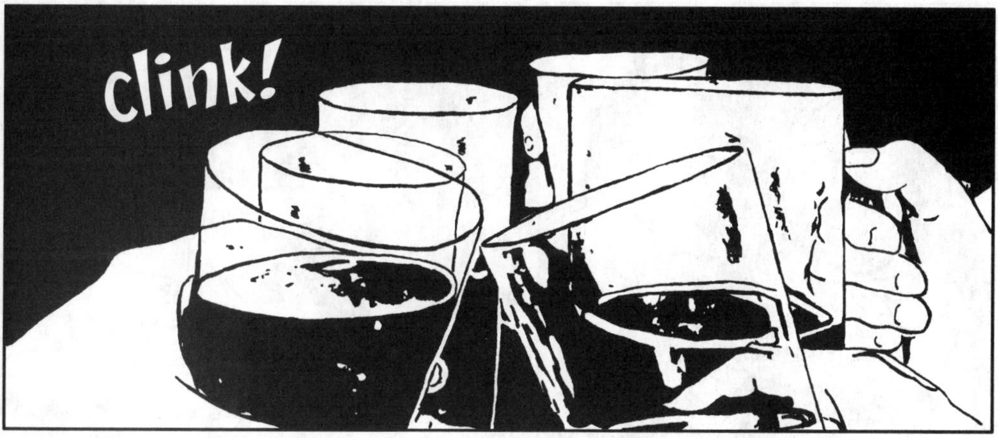
clink!

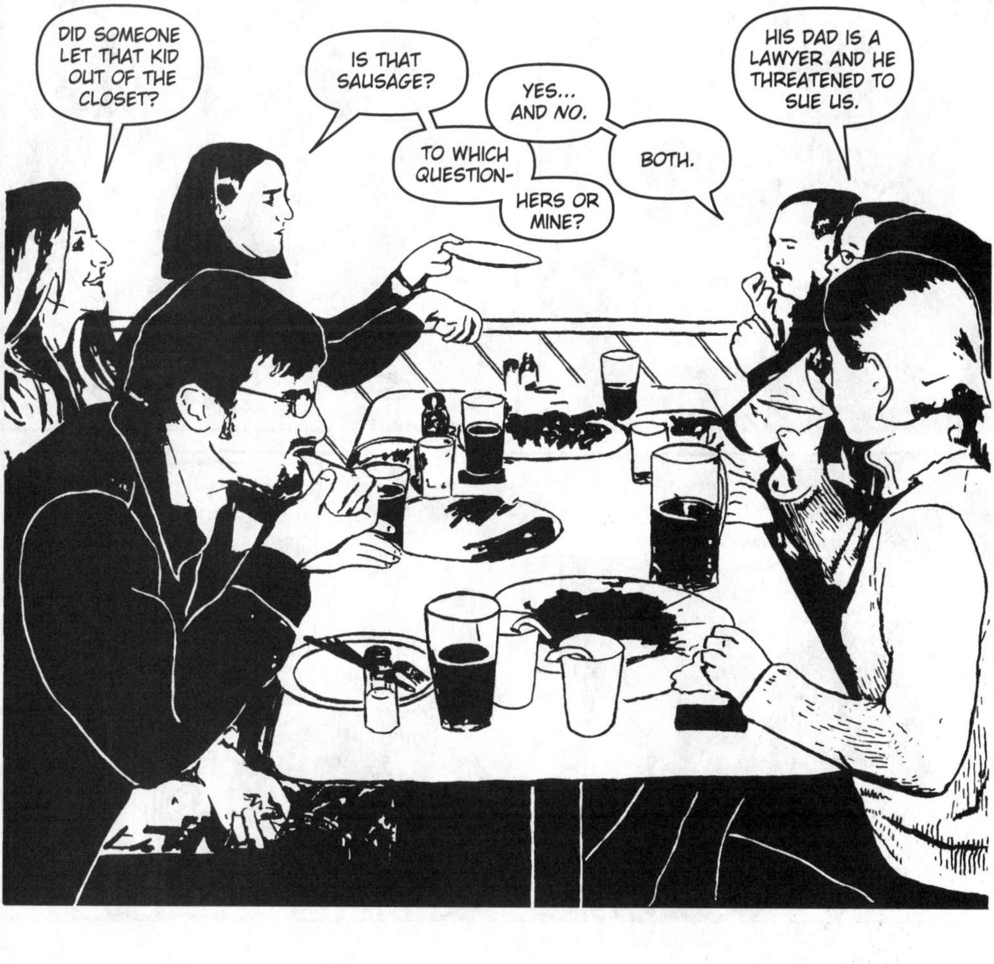
DID SOMEONE LET THAT KID OUT OF THE CLOSET?
IS THAT SAUSAGE?
TO WHICH QUESTION-
YES... AND NO.
HERS OR MINE?
BOTH.
HIS DAD IS A LAWYER AND HE THREATENED TO SUE US.

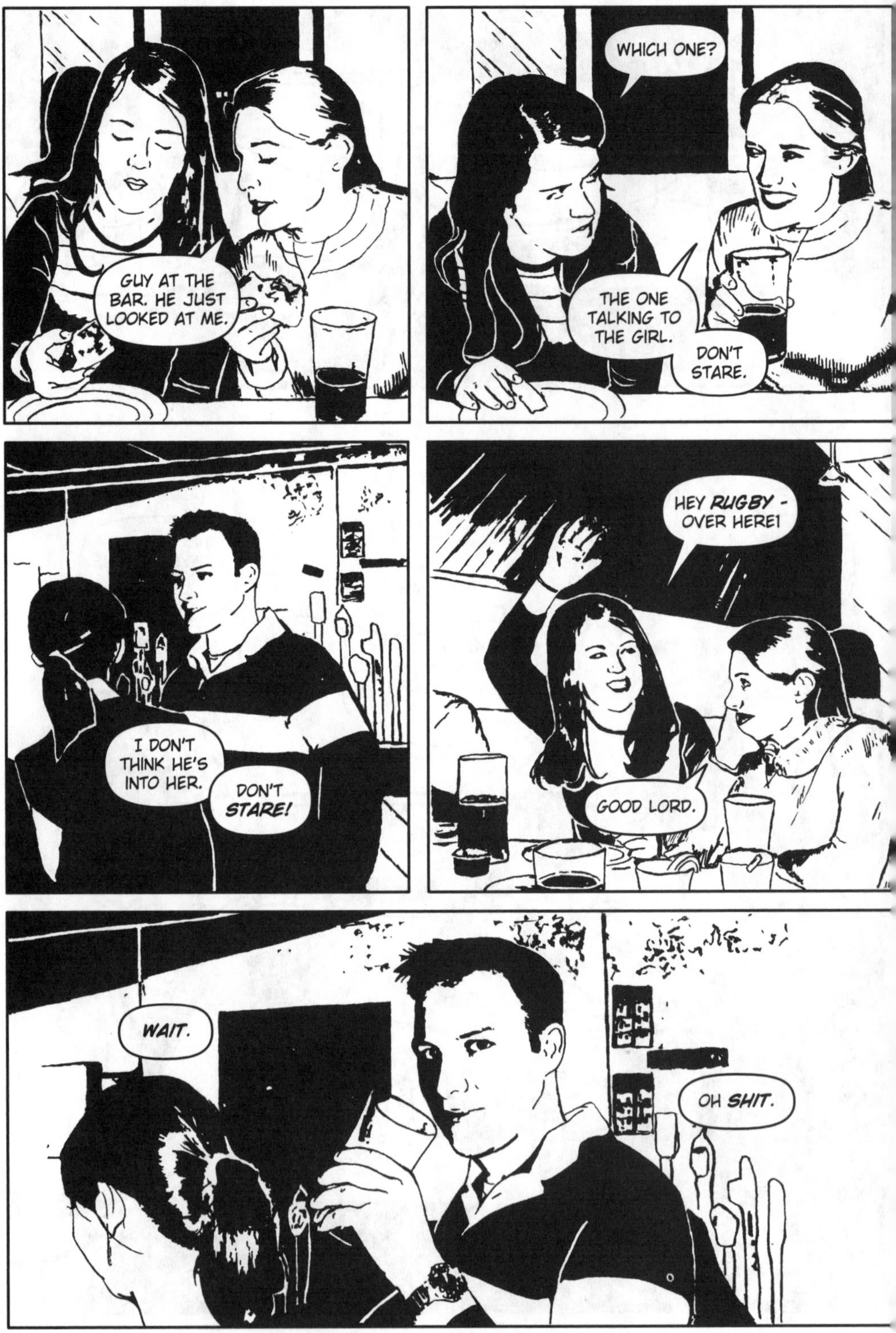
GUY AT THE BAR. HE JUST LOOKED AT ME.
WHICH ONE?
THE ONE TALKING TO THE GIRL.
DON'T STARE.
I DON'T THINK HE'S INTO HER.
DON'T STARE!
HEY RUGBY - OVER HERE1
GOOD LORD.
WAIT.
OH SHIT.

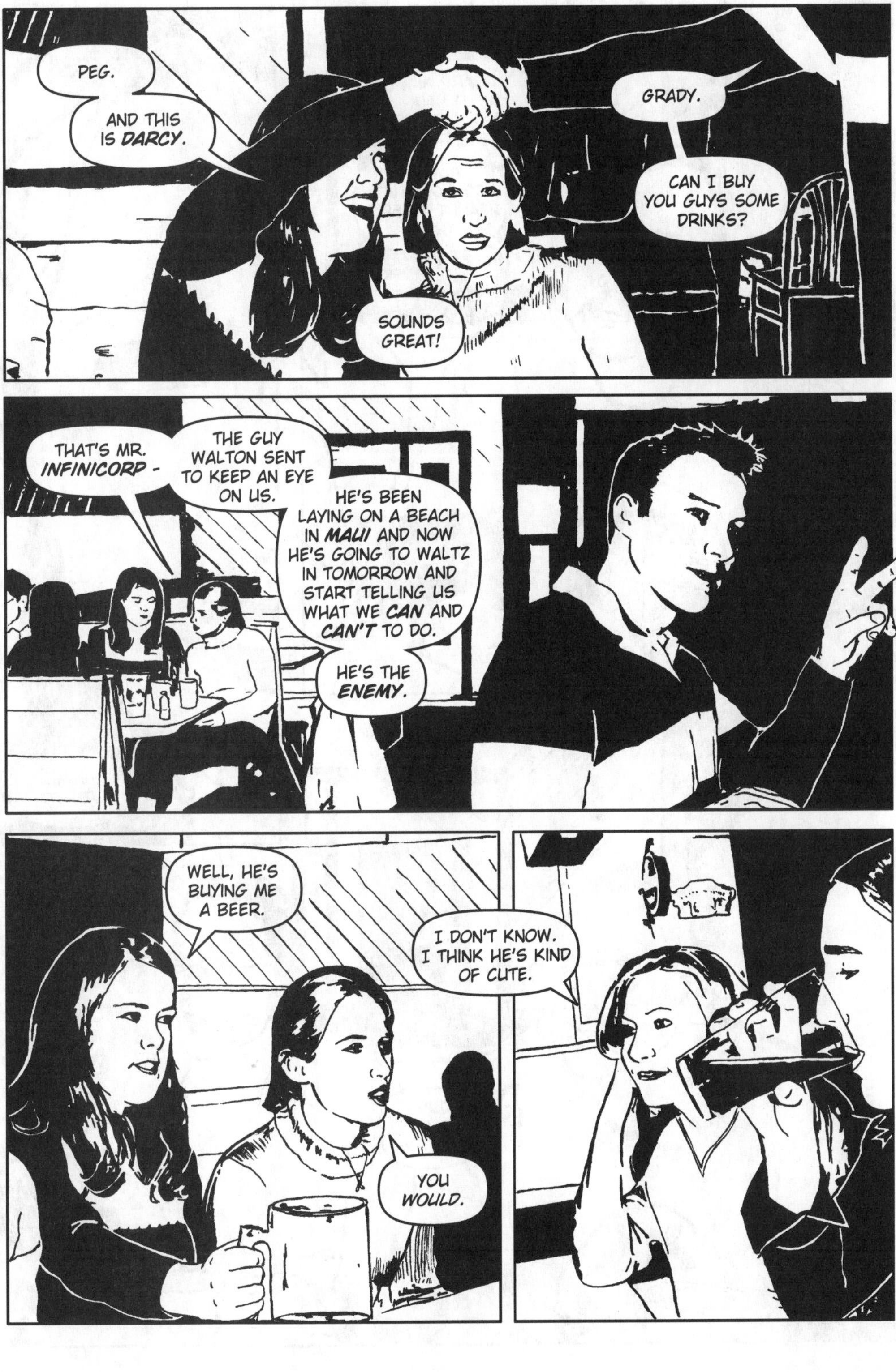
PEG.
AND THIS IS DARCY.
GRADY.
CAN I BUY YOU GUYS SOME DRINKS?
SOUNDS GREAT!
THAT'S MR. INFINICORP -
THE GUY WALTON SENT TO KEEP AN EYE ON US.
HE'S BEEN LAYING ON A BEACH IN MAUI AND NOW HE'S GOING TO WALTZ IN TOMORROW AND START TELLING US WHAT WE CAN AND CAN'T TO DO.
HE'S THE ENEMY.
WELL, HE'S BUYING ME A BEER.
YOU WOULD.
I DON'T KNOW. I THINK HE'S KIND OF CUTE.

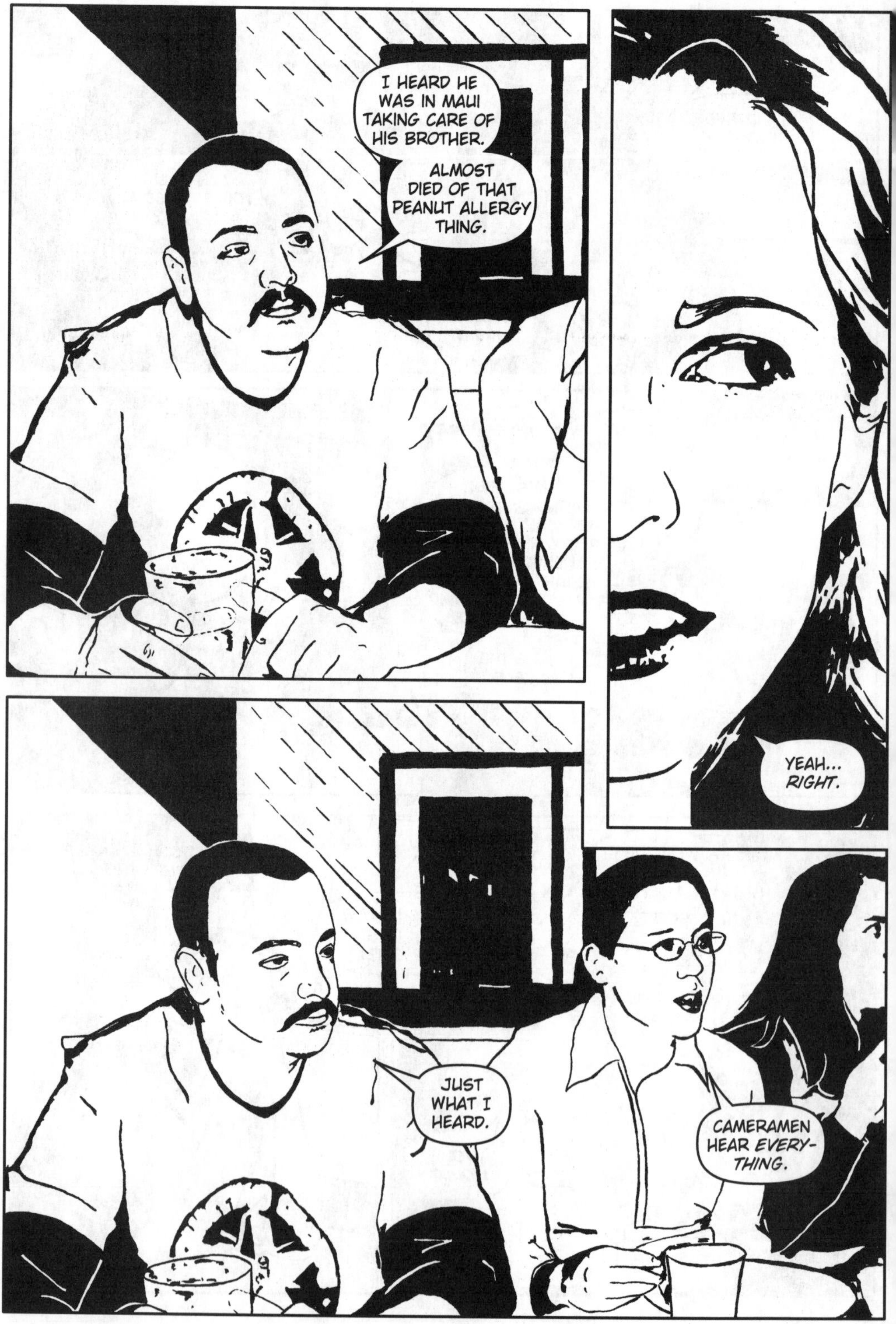
I HEARD HE WAS IN MAUI TAKING CARE OF HIS BROTHER.
ALMOST DIED OF THAT PEANUT ALLERGY THING.
YEAH... RIGHT.
JUST WHAT I HEARD.
CAMERAMEN HEAR EVERY-THING.

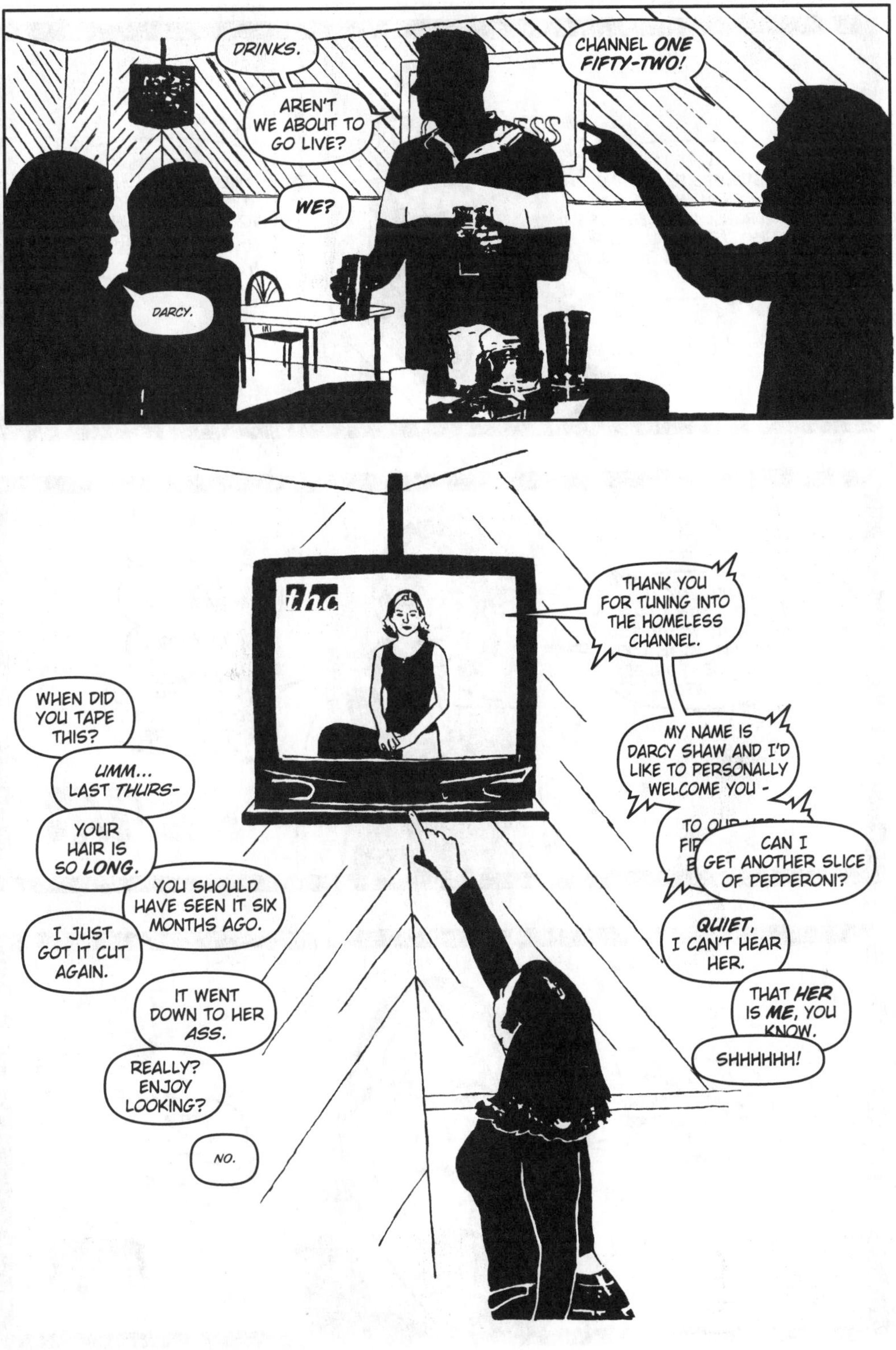
DRINKS.
AREN'T WE ABOUT TO GO LIVE?
CHANNEL ONE FIFTY-TWO!
WE?
DARCY.
THANK YOU FOR TUNING INTO THE HOMELESS CHANNEL.
WHEN DID YOU TAPE THIS?
UMM... LAST THURS-
MY NAME IS DARCY SHAW AND I'D LIKE TO PERSONALLY WELCOME YOU -
YOUR HAIR IS SO LONG.
TO OUR
CAN I GET ANOTHER SLICE OF PEPPERONI?
YOU SHOULD HAVE SEEN IT SIX MONTHS AGO.
I JUST GOT IT CUT AGAIN.
QUIET, I CAN'T HEAR HER.
IT WENT DOWN TO HER ASS.
THAT HER IS ME, YOU KNOW.
SHHHHHH!
REALLY? ENJOY LOOKING?
NO.

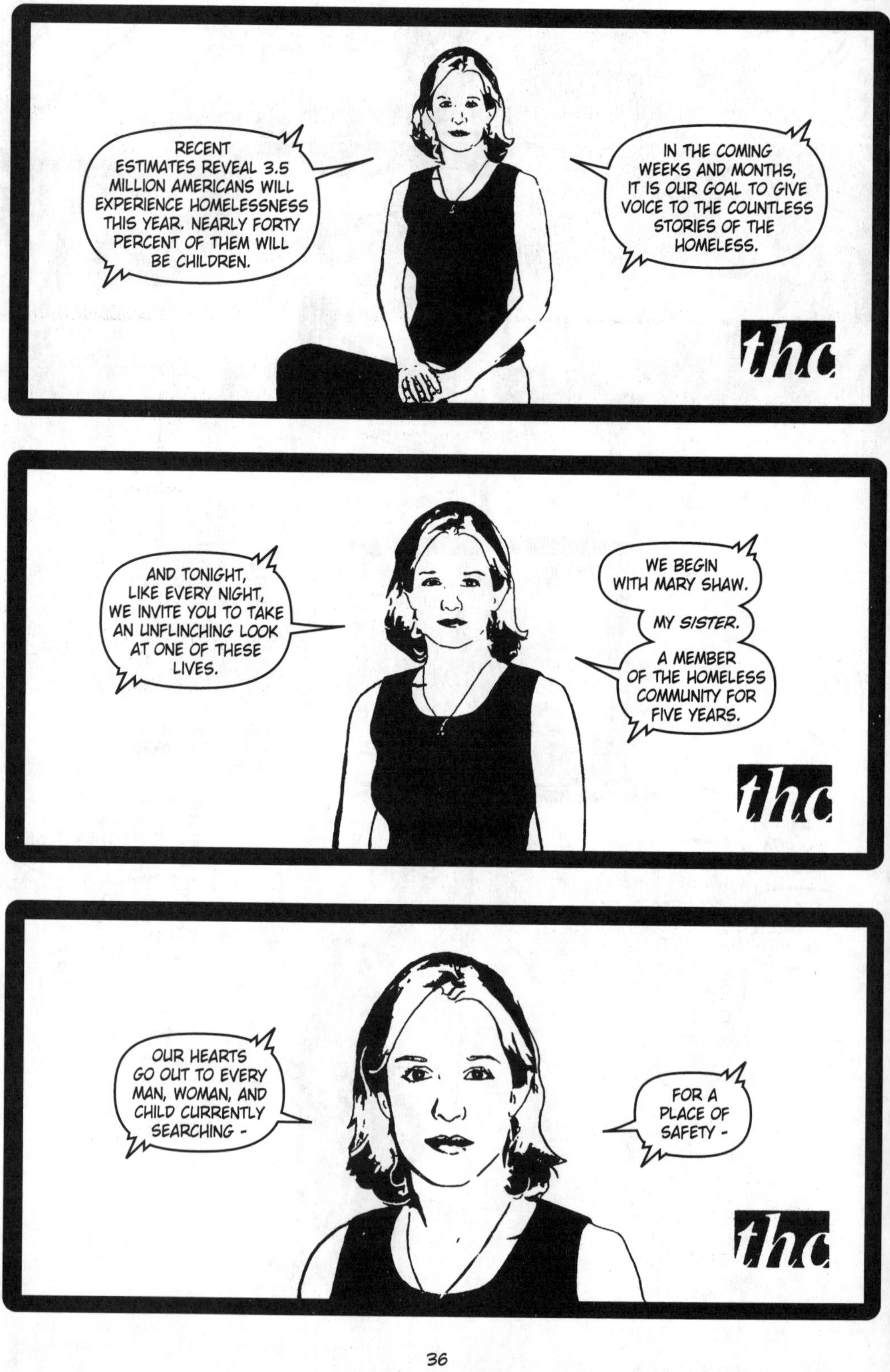
RECENT ESTIMATES REVEAL 3.5 MILLION AMERICANS WILL EXPERIENCE HOMELESSNESS THIS YEAR. NEARLY FORTY PERCENT OF THEM WILL BE CHILDREN.
IN THE COMING WEEKS AND MONTHS, IT IS OUR GOAL TO GIVE VOICE TO THE COUNTLESS STORIES OF THE HOMELESS.
AND TONIGHT, LIKE EVERY NIGHT, WE INVITE YOU TO TAKE AN UNFLINCHING LOOK AT ONE OF THESE LIVES.
WE BEGIN WITH MARY SHAW.
MY *SISTER*.
A MEMBER OF THE HOMELESS COMMUNITY FOR FIVE YEARS.
OUR HEARTS GO OUT TO EVERY MAN, WOMAN, AND CHILD CURRENTLY SEARCHING -
FOR A PLACE OF SAFETY -

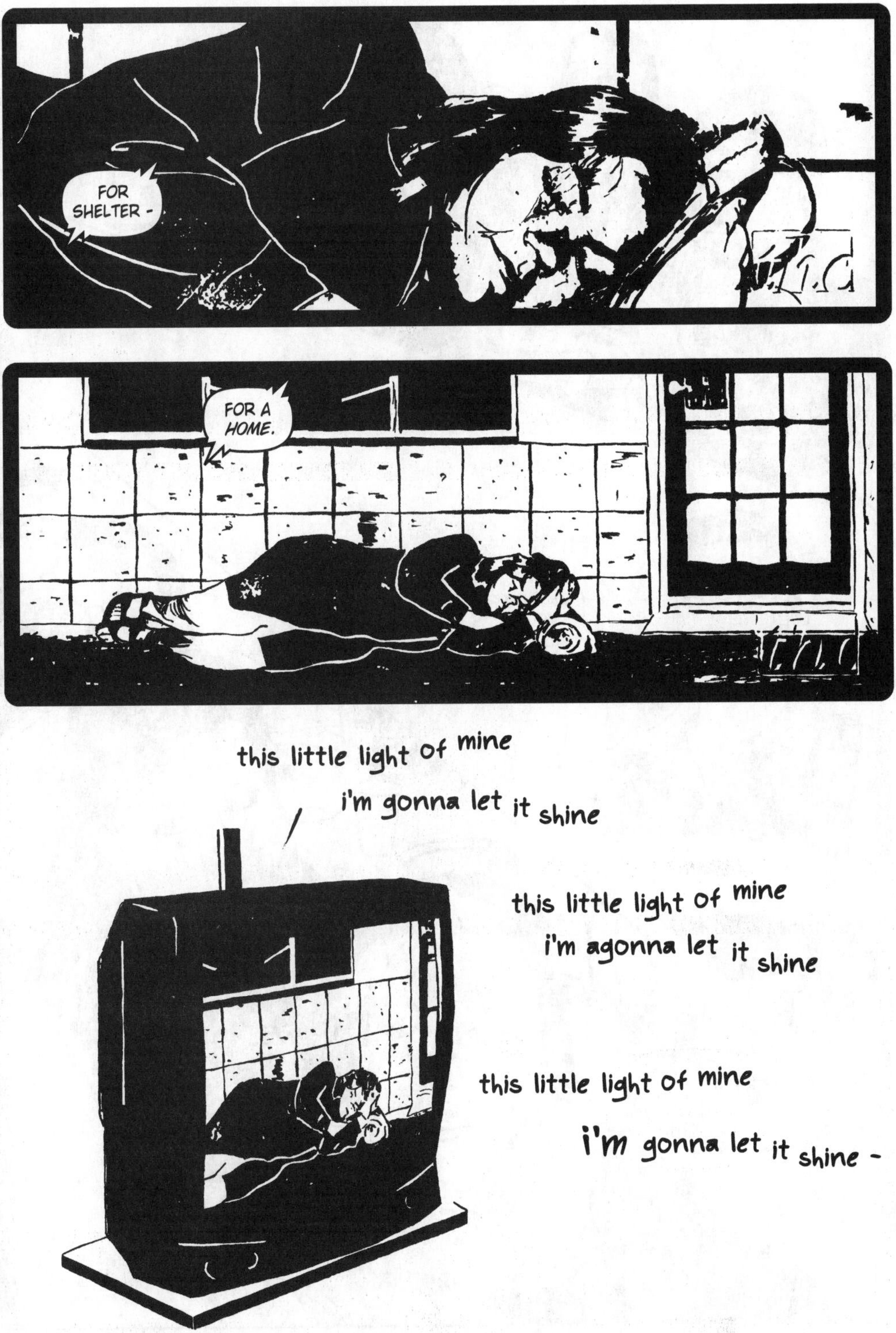
FOR SHELTER -
FOR A HOME.
this little light of mine
i'm gonna let it shine
this little light of mine
i'm agonna let it shine
this little light of mine
i'm gonna let it shine -

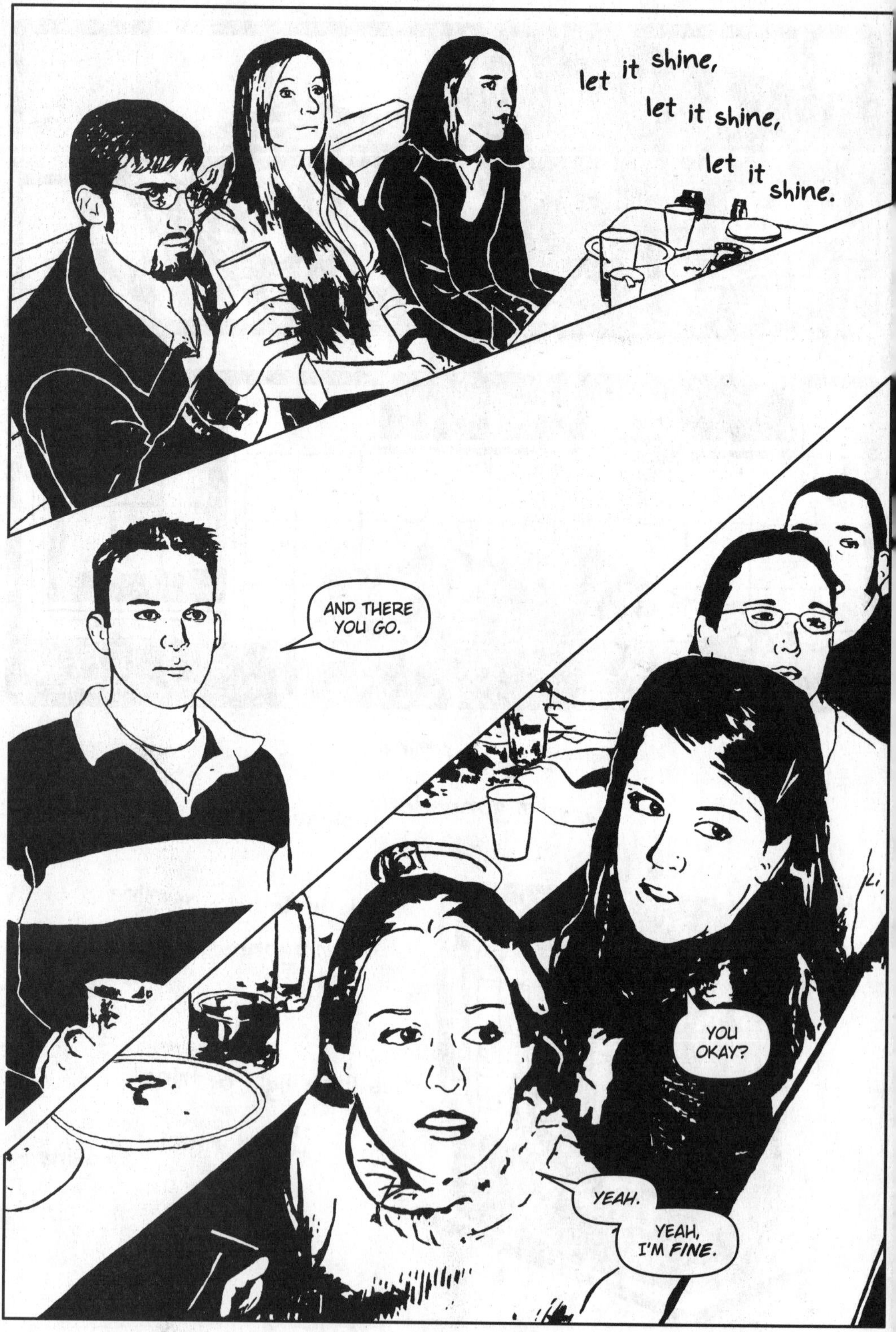
let it shine,
let it shine,
let it shine.
AND THERE YOU GO.
YOU OKAY?
YEAH.
YEAH, I'M FINE.

2

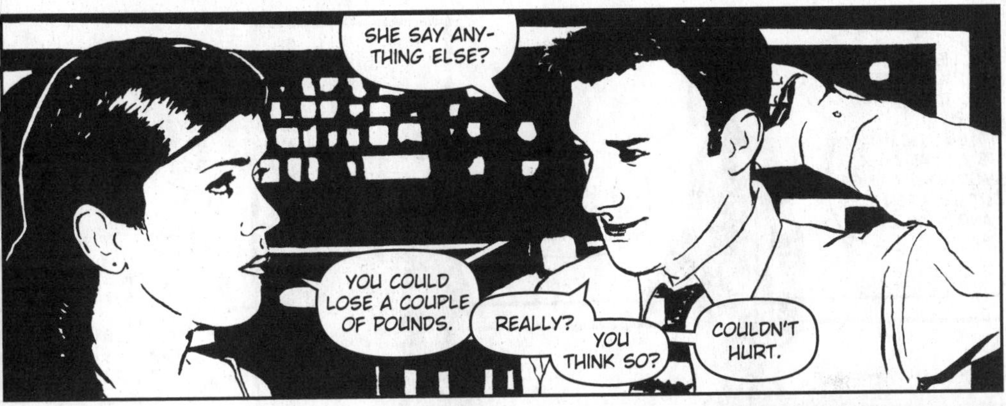
SHE SAY ANY-THING ELSE?
YOU COULD LOSE A COUPLE OF POUNDS.
REALLY?
YOU THINK SO?
COULDN'T HURT.

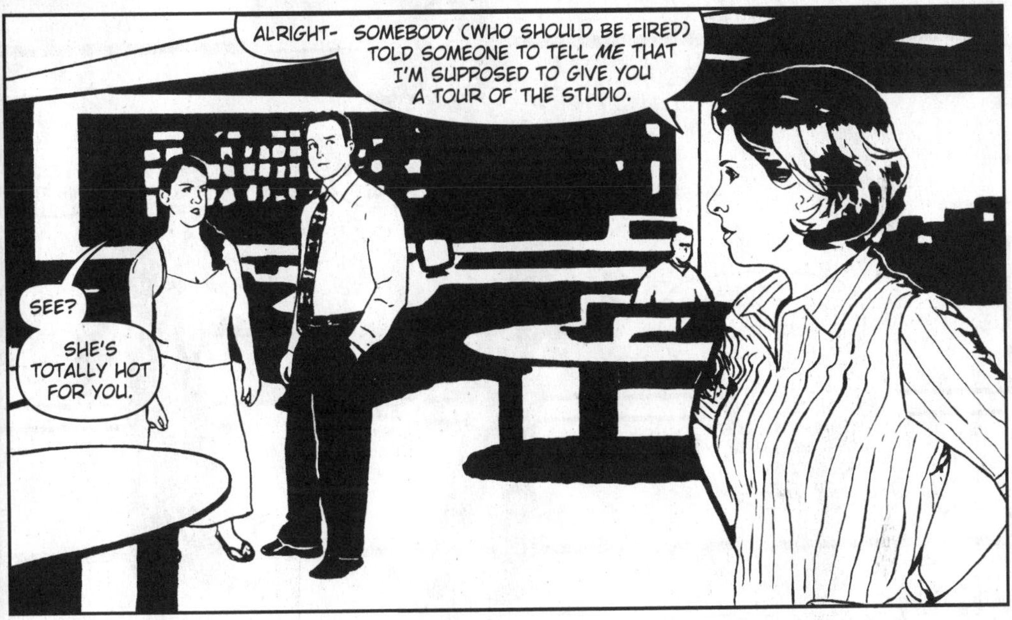
ALRIGHT-
SOMEBODY (WHO SHOULD BE FIRED) TOLD SOMEONE TO TELL *ME* THAT I'M SUPPOSED TO GIVE YOU A TOUR OF THE STUDIO.
SEE?
SHE'S TOTALLY HOT FOR YOU.

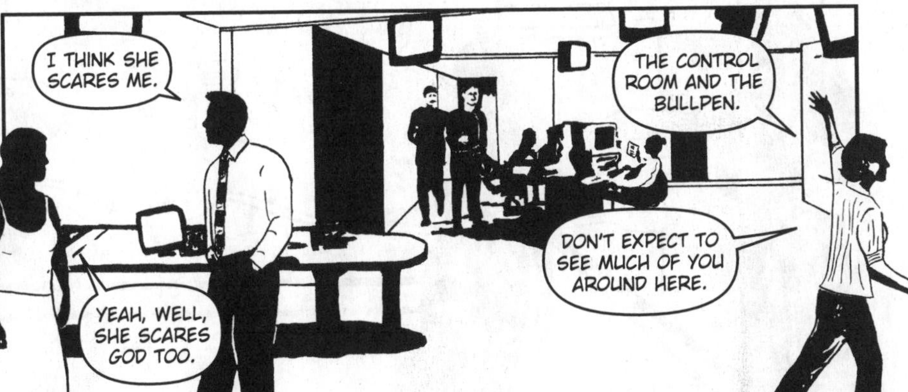
I THINK SHE SCARES ME.
THE CONTROL ROOM AND THE BULLPEN.
DON'T EXPECT TO SEE MUCH OF YOU AROUND HERE.
YEAH, WELL, SHE SCARES GOD TOO.

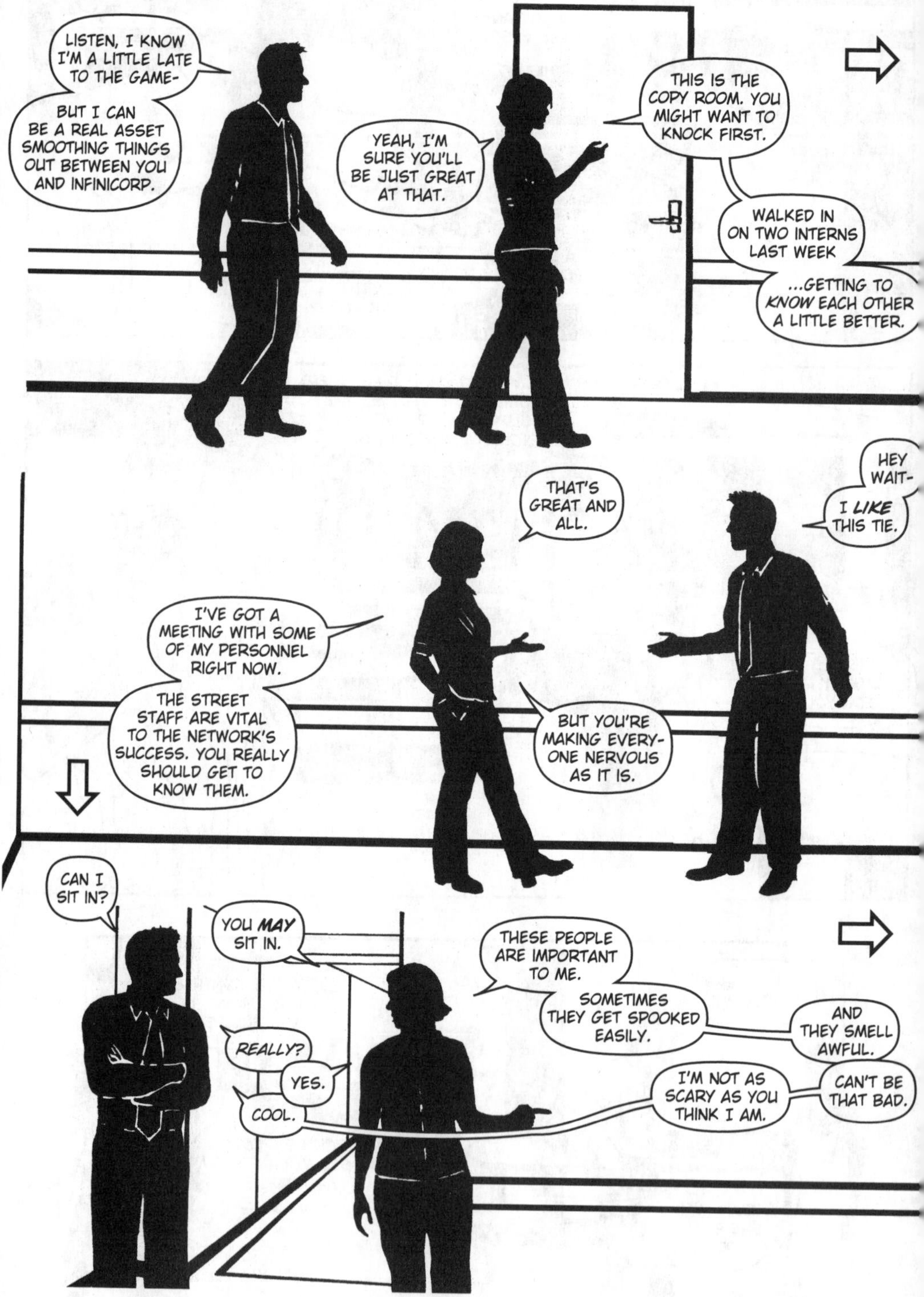
LISTEN, I KNOW I'M A LITTLE LATE TO THE GAME-
BUT I CAN BE A REAL ASSET SMOOTHING THINGS OUT BETWEEN YOU AND INFINICORP.
YEAH, I'M SURE YOU'LL BE JUST GREAT AT THAT.
THIS IS THE COPY ROOM. YOU MIGHT WANT TO KNOCK FIRST.
WALKED IN ON TWO INTERNS LAST WEEK
...GETTING TO *KNOW* EACH OTHER A LITTLE BETTER.
THAT'S GREAT AND ALL.
HEY WAIT-
I *LIKE* THIS TIE.
I'VE GOT A MEETING WITH SOME OF MY PERSONNEL RIGHT NOW.
THE STREET STAFF ARE VITAL TO THE NETWORK'S SUCCESS. YOU REALLY SHOULD GET TO KNOW THEM.
BUT YOU'RE MAKING EVERY-ONE NERVOUS AS IT IS.
CAN I SIT IN?
YOU *MAY* SIT IN.
THESE PEOPLE ARE IMPORTANT TO ME.
SOMETIMES THEY GET SPOOKED EASILY.
AND THEY SMELL AWFUL.
REALLY?
YES.
COOL.
I'M NOT AS SCARY AS YOU THINK I AM.
CAN'T BE THAT BAD.

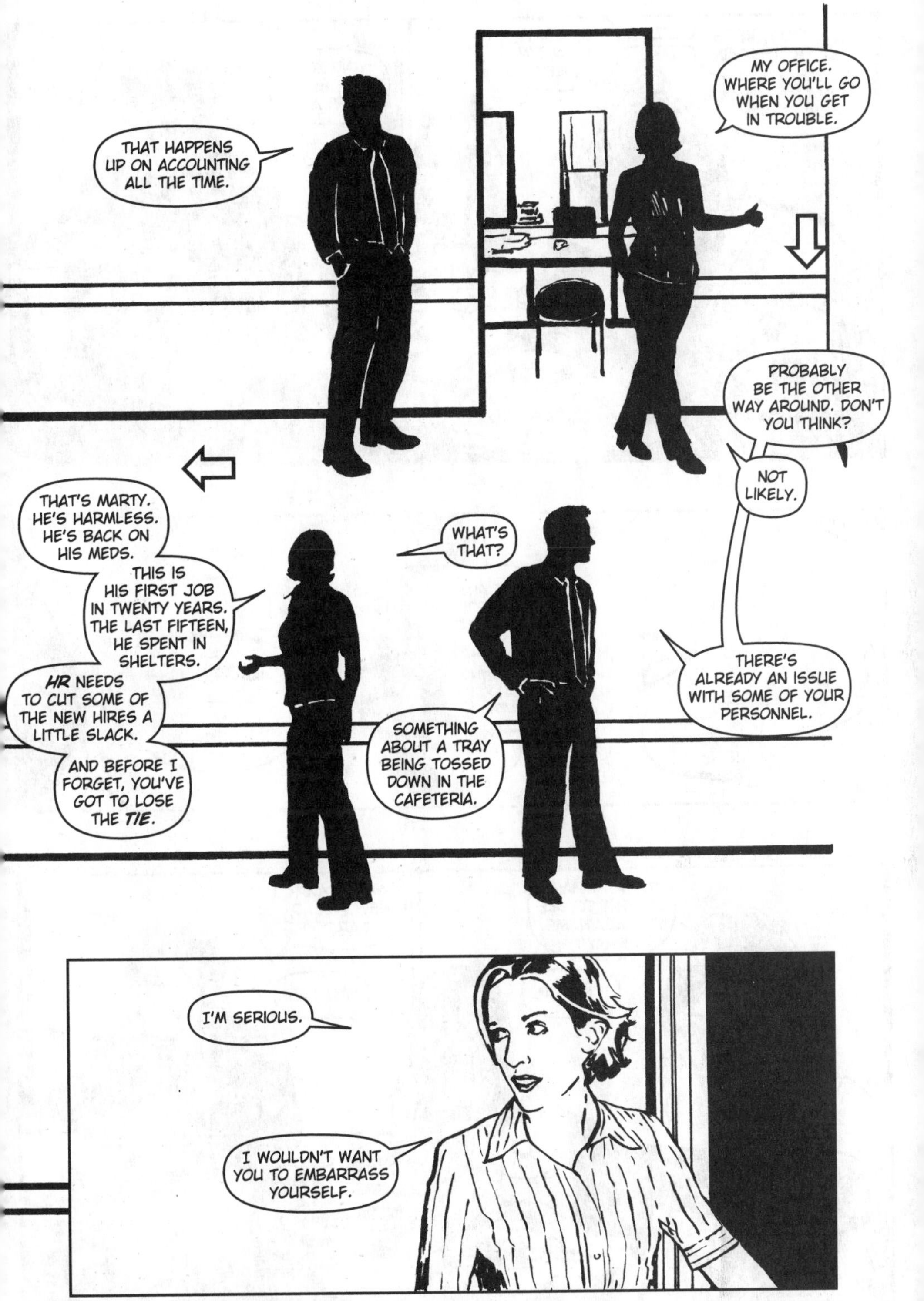

MY OFFICE. WHERE YOU'LL GO WHEN YOU GET IN TROUBLE.
PROBABLY BE THE OTHER WAY AROUND. DON'T YOU THINK?
NOT LIKELY.
THERE'S ALREADY AN ISSUE WITH SOME OF YOUR PERSONNEL.
WHAT'S THAT?
SOMETHING ABOUT A TRAY BEING TOSSED DOWN IN THE CAFETERIA.
THAT HAPPENS UP ON ACCOUNTING ALL THE TIME.
THAT'S MARTY. HE'S HARMLESS. HE'S BACK ON HIS MEDS.
THIS IS HIS FIRST JOB IN TWENTY YEARS. THE LAST FIFTEEN, HE SPENT IN SHELTERS.
HR NEEDS TO CUT SOME OF THE NEW HIRES A LITTLE SLACK.
AND BEFORE I FORGET, YOU'VE GOT TO LOSE THE *TIE*.
I'M SERIOUS.
I WOULDN'T WANT YOU TO EMBARRASS YOURSELF.

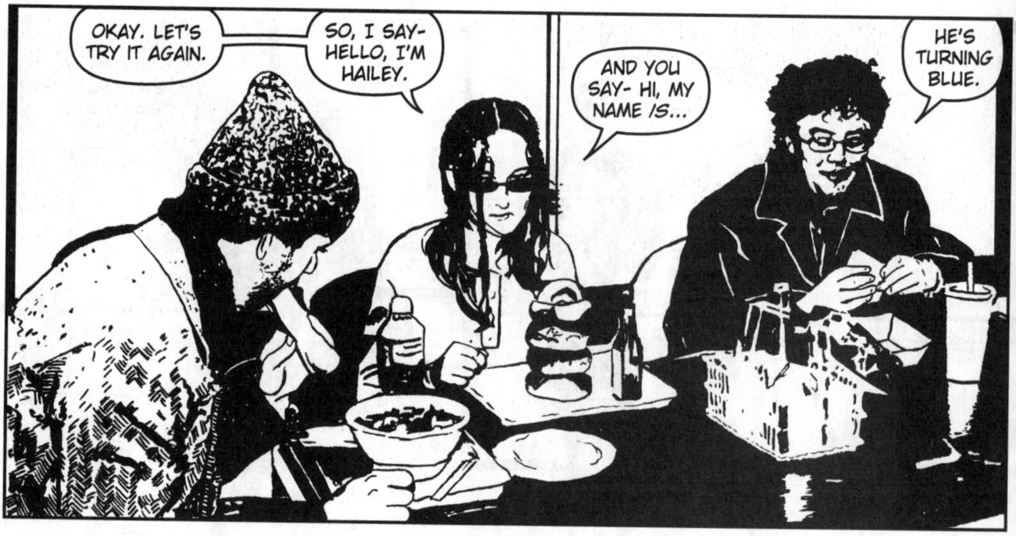
OKAY. LET'S TRY IT AGAIN.
SO, I SAY- HELLO, I'M HAILEY.
AND YOU SAY- HI, MY NAME *IS*...
HE'S TURNING BLUE.

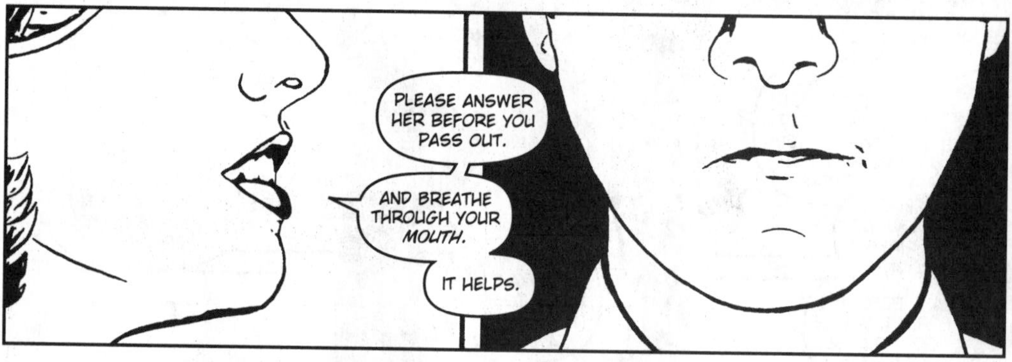
PLEASE ANSWER HER BEFORE YOU PASS OUT.
AND BREATHE THROUGH YOUR *MOUTH*.
IT HELPS.

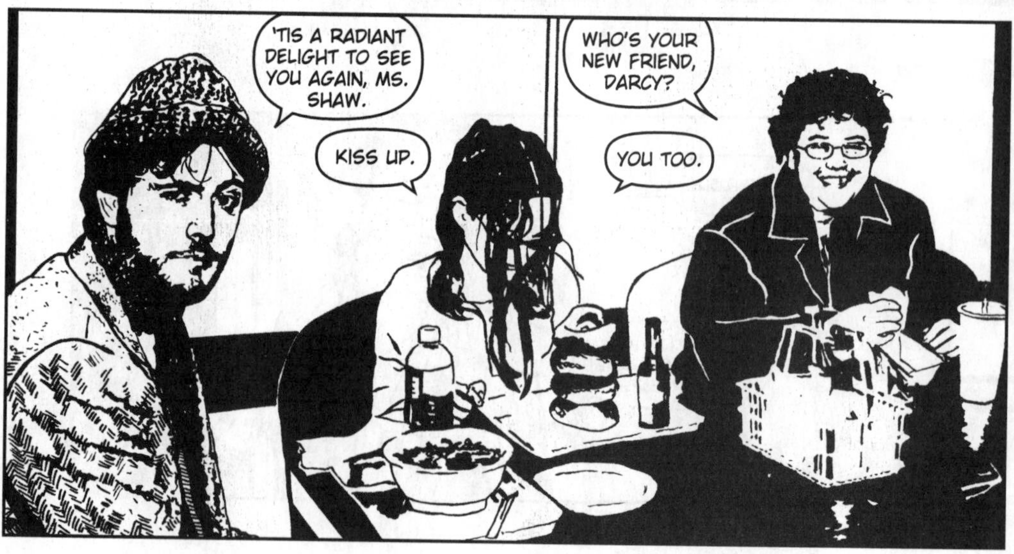
'TIS A RADIANT DELIGHT TO SEE YOU AGAIN, MS. SHAW.
KISS UP.
WHO'S YOUR NEW FRIEND, DARCY?
YOU TOO.

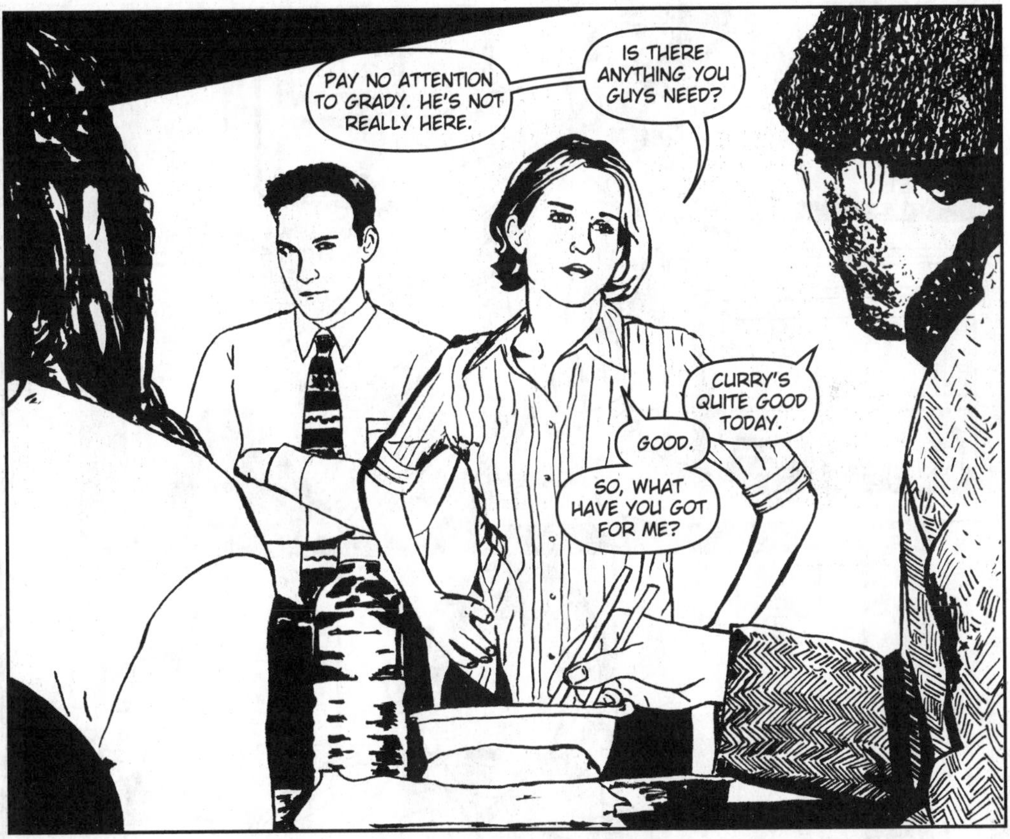
PAY NO ATTENTION TO GRADY. HE'S NOT REALLY HERE.
IS THERE ANYTHING YOU GUYS NEED?
CURRY'S QUITE GOOD TODAY.
GOOD.
SO, WHAT HAVE YOU GOT FOR ME?

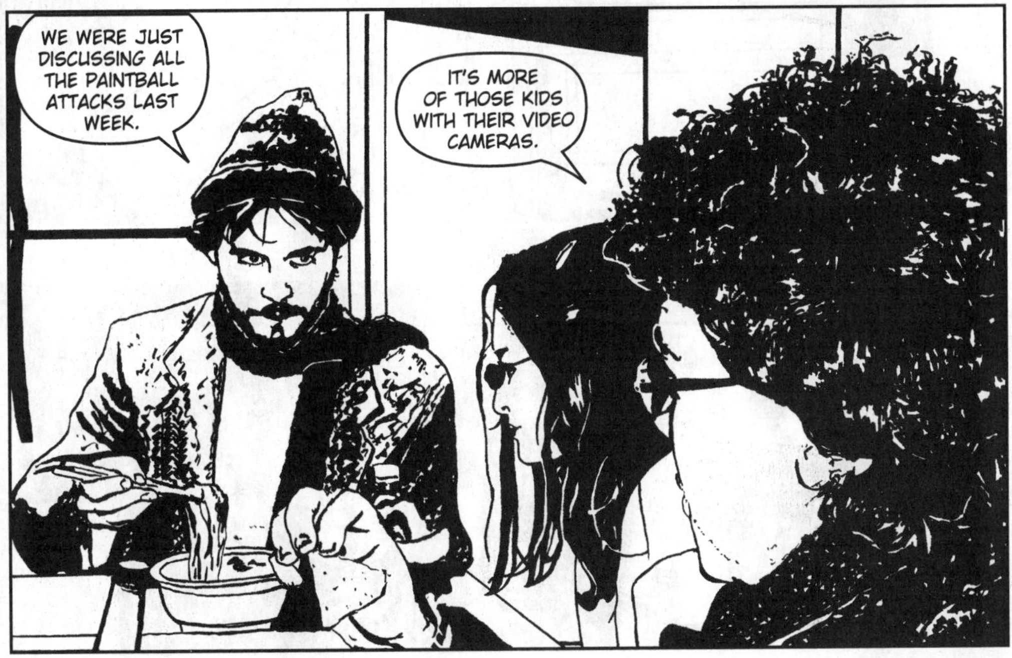
WE WERE JUST DISCUSSING ALL THE PAINTBALL ATTACKS LAST WEEK.
IT'S MORE OF THOSE KIDS WITH THEIR VIDEO CAMERAS.

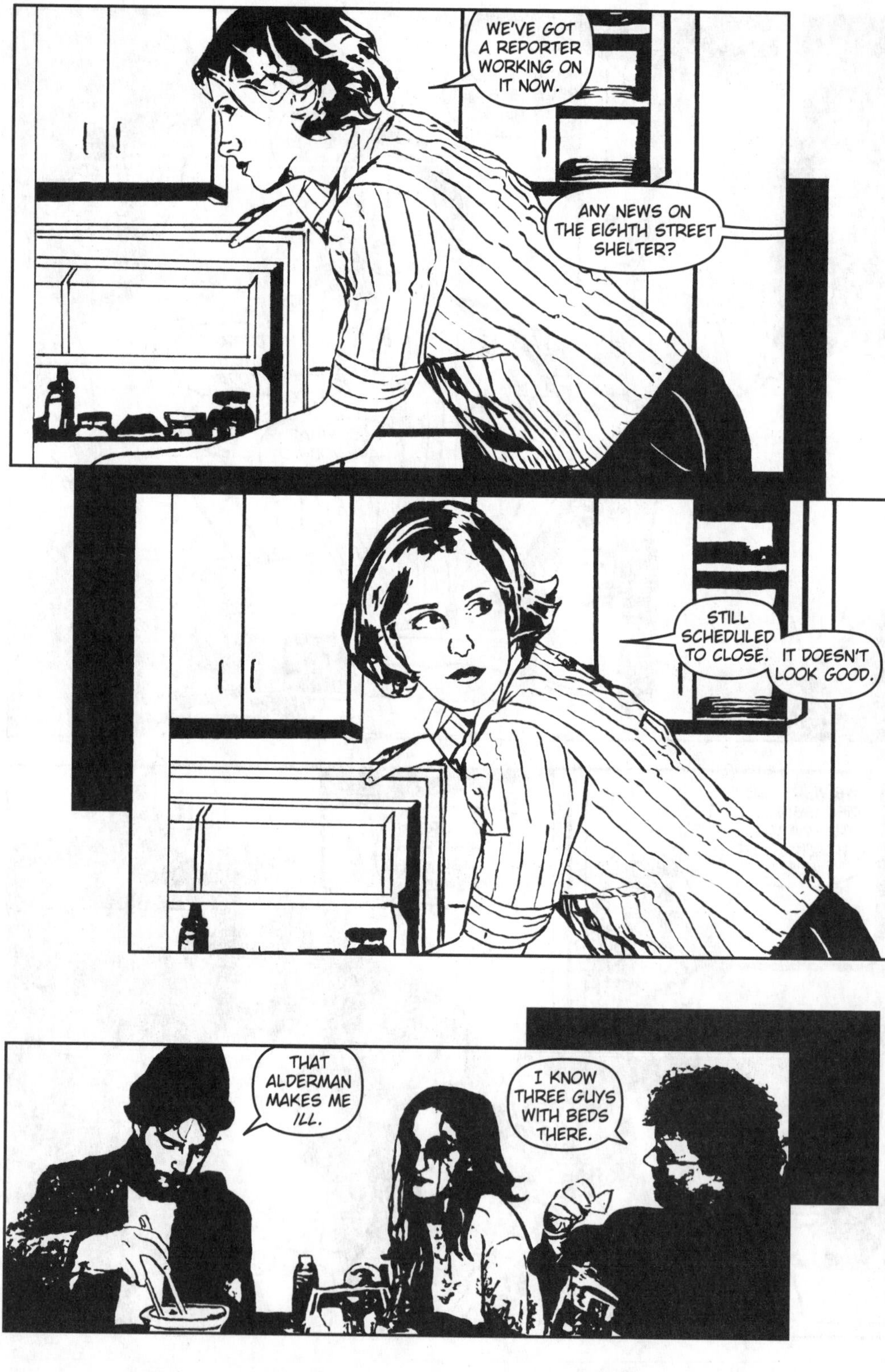
WE'VE GOT A REPORTER WORKING ON IT NOW.
ANY NEWS ON THE EIGHTH STREET SHELTER?
STILL SCHEDULED TO CLOSE.
IT DOESN'T LOOK GOOD.
THAT ALDERMAN MAKES ME *ILL*.
I KNOW THREE GUYS WITH BEDS THERE.

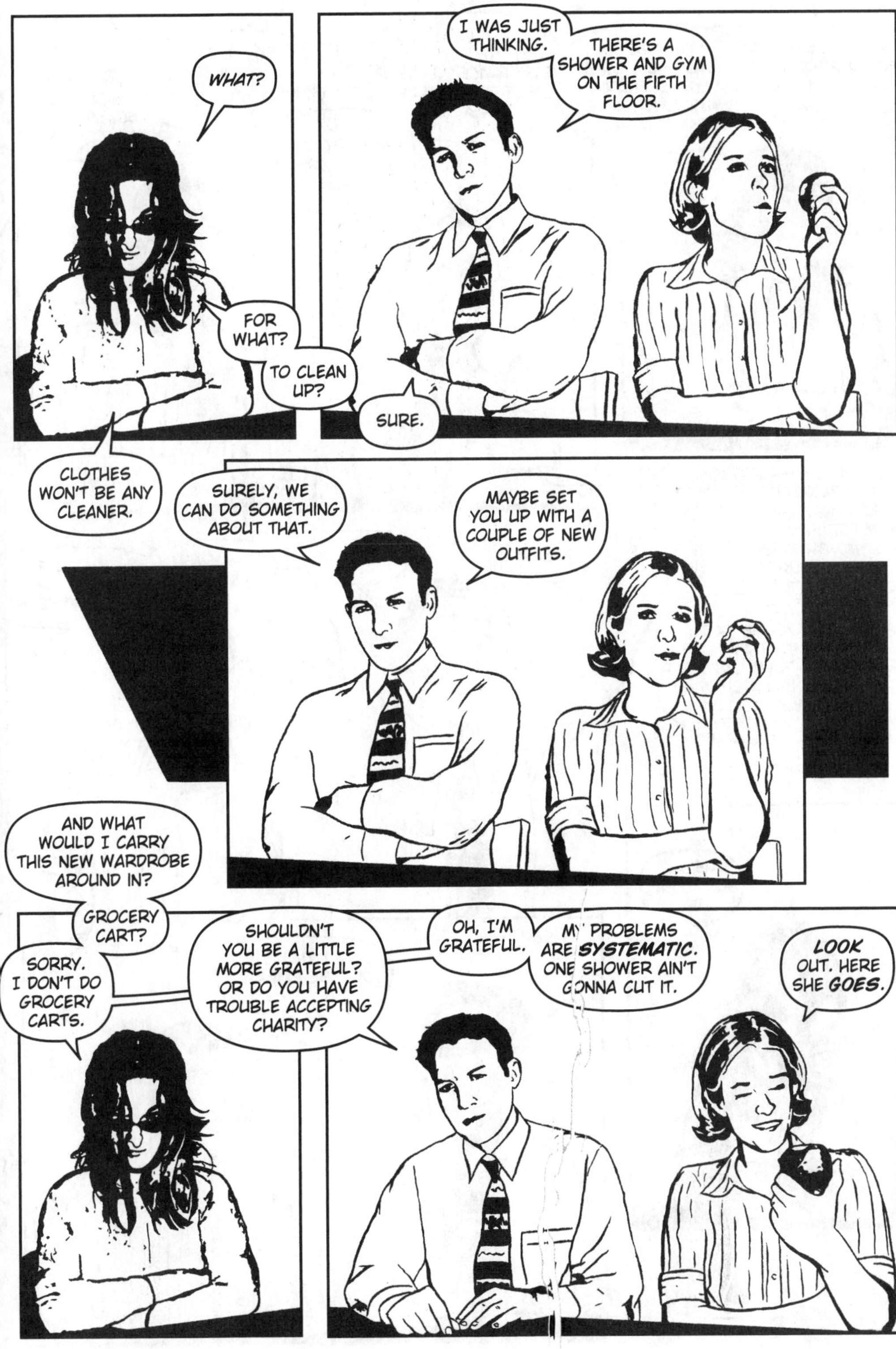
WHAT?
I WAS JUST THINKING.
THERE'S A SHOWER AND GYM ON THE FIFTH FLOOR.
FOR WHAT?
TO CLEAN UP?
SURE.
CLOTHES WON'T BE ANY CLEANER.
SURELY, WE CAN DO SOMETHING ABOUT THAT.
MAYBE SET YOU UP WITH A COUPLE OF NEW OUTFITS.
AND WHAT WOULD I CARRY THIS NEW WARDROBE AROUND IN?
GROCERY CART?
SORRY. I DON'T DO GROCERY CARTS.
SHOULDN'T YOU BE A LITTLE MORE GRATEFUL? OR DO YOU HAVE TROUBLE ACCEPTING CHARITY?
OH, I'M GRATEFUL.
MY PROBLEMS ARE SYSTEMATIC. ONE SHOWER AIN'T GONNA CUT IT.
LOOK OUT. HERE SHE GOES.

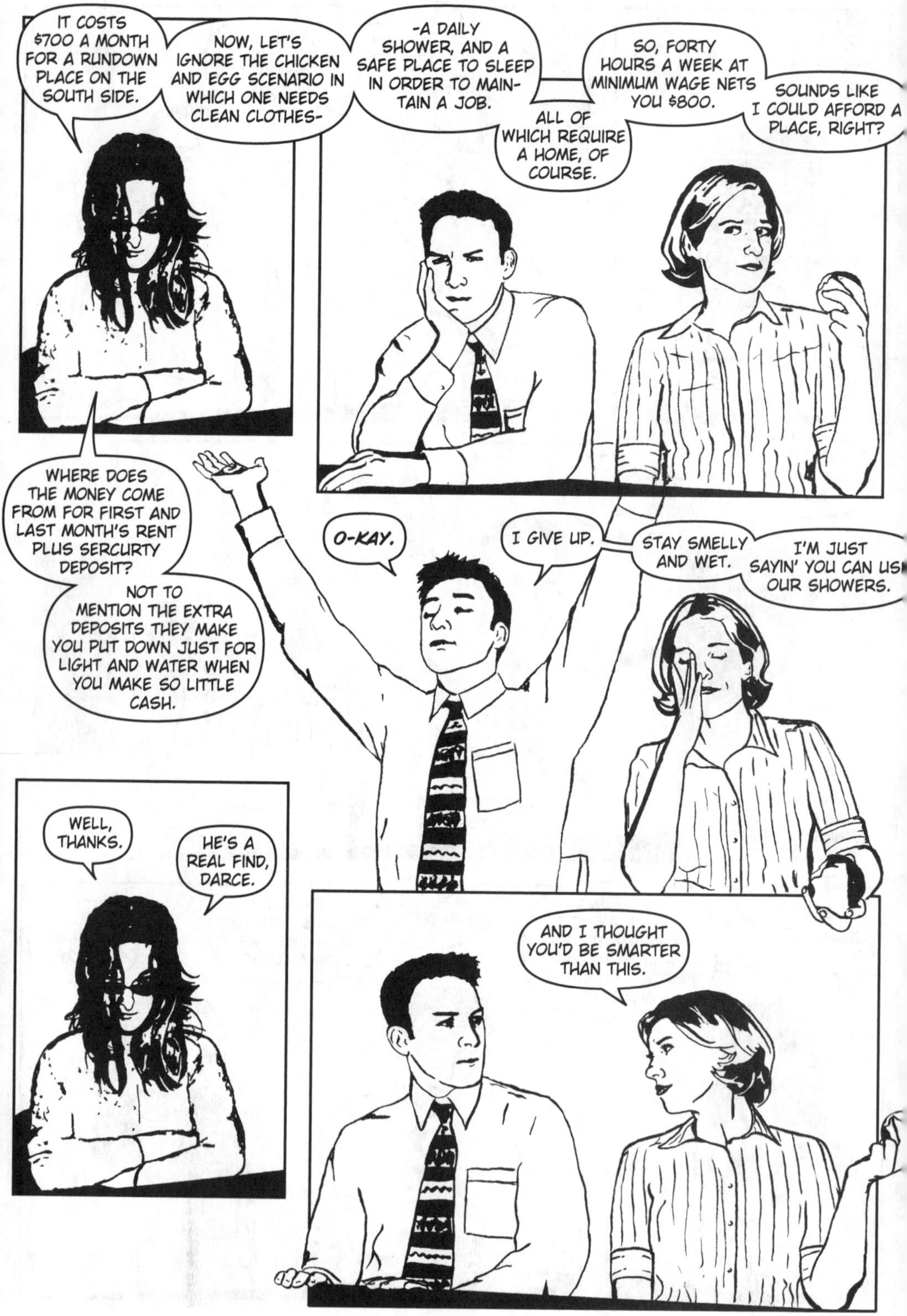
IT COSTS $700 A MONTH FOR A RUNDOWN PLACE ON THE SOUTH SIDE.
NOW, LET'S IGNORE THE CHICKEN AND EGG SCENARIO IN WHICH ONE NEEDS CLEAN CLOTHES-
-A DAILY SHOWER, AND A SAFE PLACE TO SLEEP IN ORDER TO MAIN-TAIN A JOB.
ALL OF WHICH REQUIRE A HOME, OF COURSE.
SO, FORTY HOURS A WEEK AT MINIMUM WAGE NETS YOU $800.
SOUNDS LIKE I COULD AFFORD A PLACE, RIGHT?
WHERE DOES THE MONEY COME FROM FOR FIRST AND LAST MONTH'S RENT PLUS SERCURTY DEPOSIT?
NOT TO MENTION THE EXTRA DEPOSITS THEY MAKE YOU PUT DOWN JUST FOR LIGHT AND WATER WHEN YOU MAKE SO LITTLE CASH.
O-KAY.
I GIVE UP.
STAY SMELLY AND WET.
I'M JUST SAYIN' YOU CAN US OUR SHOWERS.
WELL, THANKS.
HE'S A REAL FIND, DARCE.
AND I THOUGHT YOU'D BE SMARTER THAN THIS.

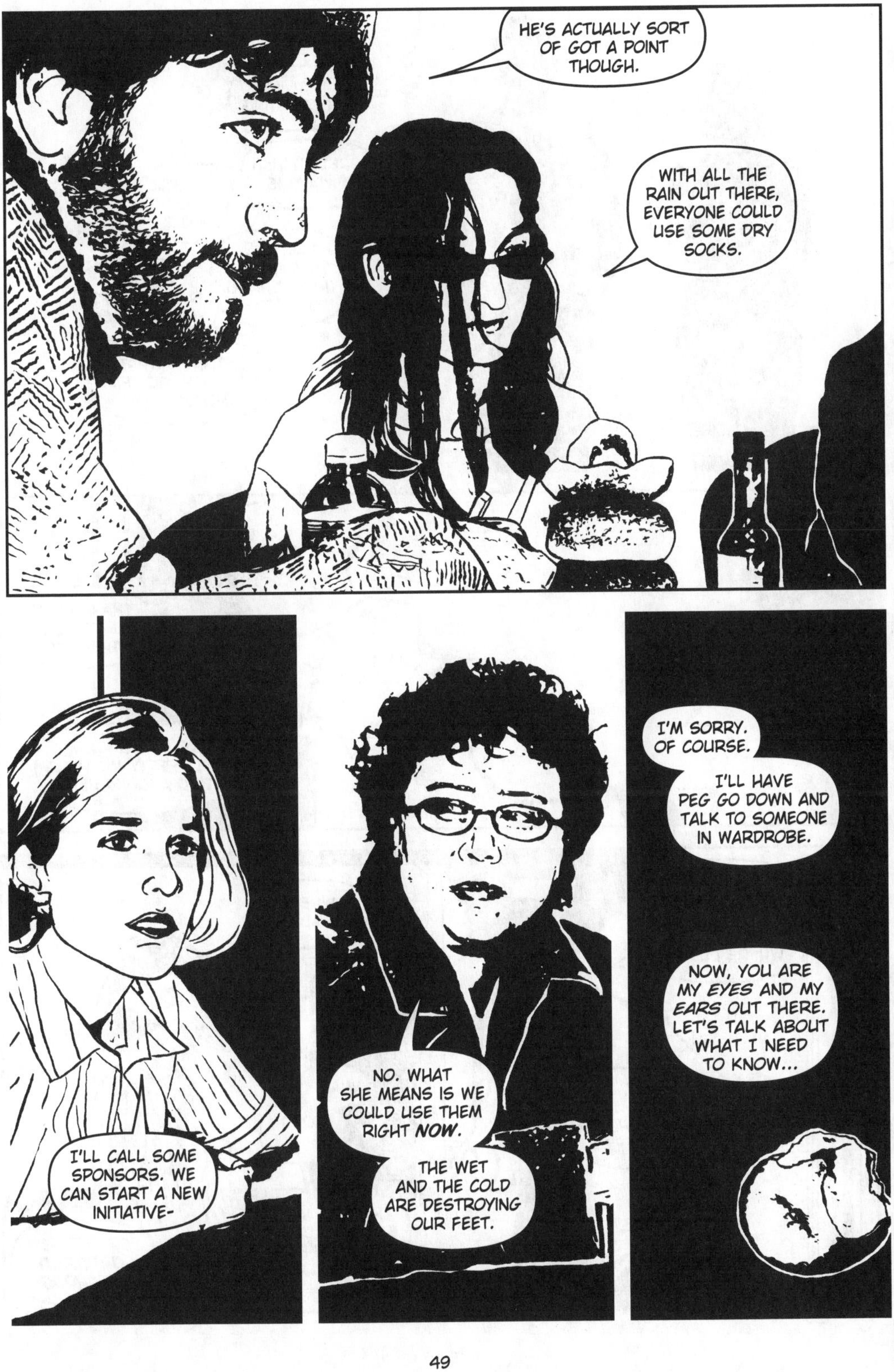
HE'S ACTUALLY SORT OF GOT A POINT THOUGH.
WITH ALL THE RAIN OUT THERE, EVERYONE COULD USE SOME DRY SOCKS.
I'LL CALL SOME SPONSORS. WE CAN START A NEW INITIATIVE-
NO. WHAT SHE MEANS IS WE COULD USE THEM RIGHT *NOW*.
THE WET AND THE COLD ARE DESTROYING OUR FEET.
I'M SORRY. OF COURSE.
I'LL HAVE PEG GO DOWN AND TALK TO SOMEONE IN WARDROBE.
NOW, YOU ARE MY *EYES* AND MY *EARS* OUT THERE. LET'S TALK ABOUT WHAT I NEED TO KNOW...

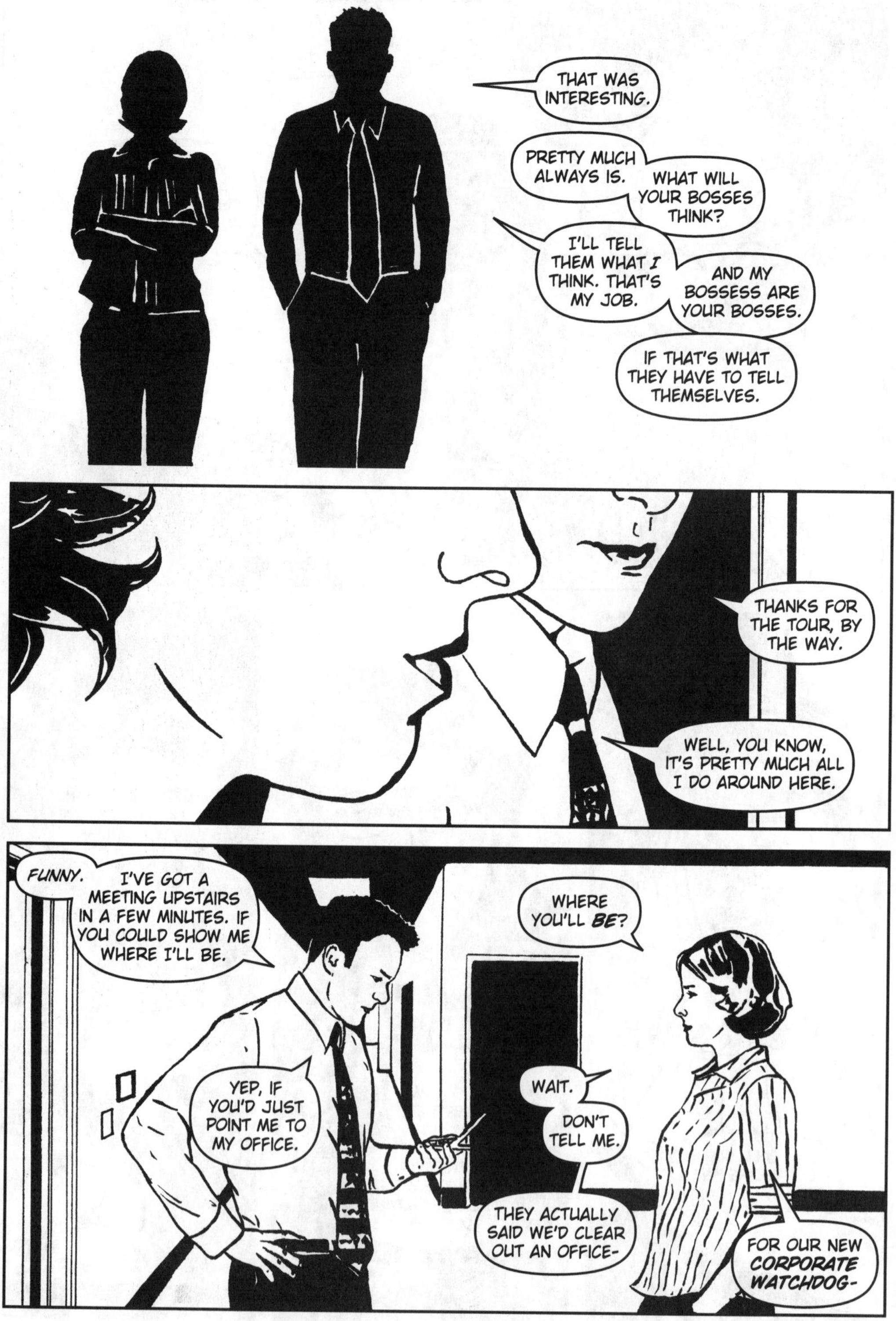
THAT WAS INTERESTING.
PRETTY MUCH ALWAYS IS.
WHAT WILL YOUR BOSSES THINK?
I'LL TELL THEM WHAT *I* THINK. THAT'S MY JOB.
AND MY BOSSESS ARE YOUR BOSSES.
IF THAT'S WHAT THEY HAVE TO TELL THEMSELVES.
THANKS FOR THE TOUR, BY THE WAY.
WELL, YOU KNOW, IT'S PRETTY MUCH ALL I DO AROUND HERE.
FUNNY.
I'VE GOT A MEETING UPSTAIRS IN A FEW MINUTES. IF YOU COULD SHOW ME WHERE I'LL BE.
WHERE YOU'LL ***BE***?
YEP, IF YOU'D JUST POINT ME TO MY OFFICE.
WAIT.
DON'T TELL ME.
THEY ACTUALLY SAID WE'D CLEAR OUT AN OFFICE-
FOR OUR NEW ***CORPORATE WATCHDOG-***

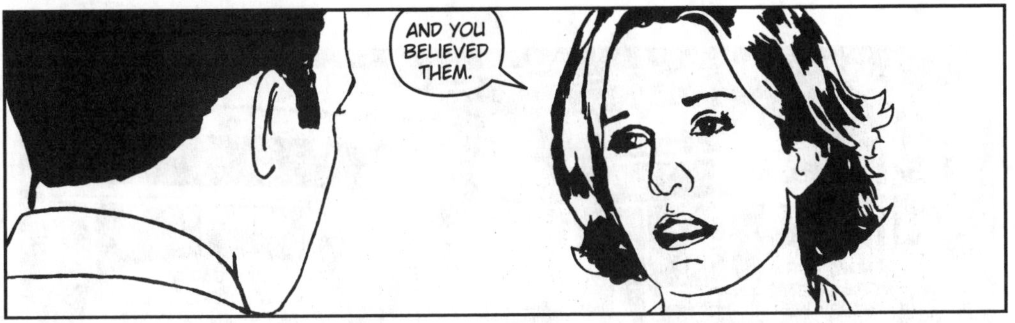
AND YOU BELIEVED THEM.

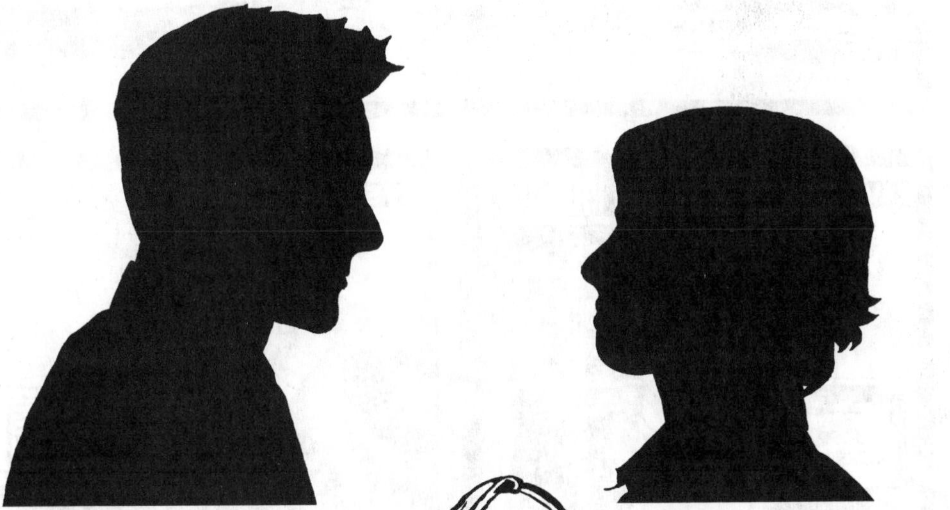

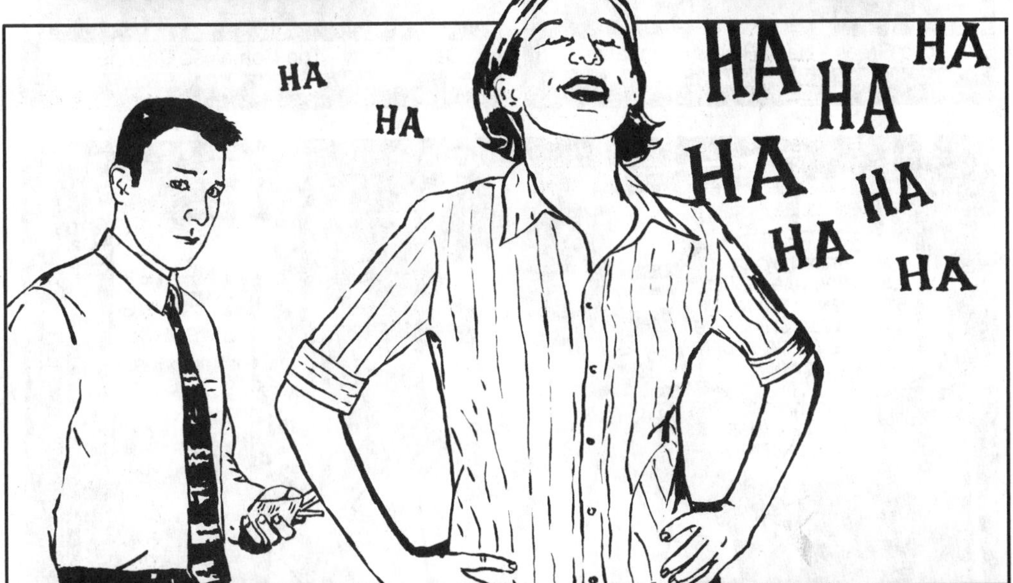
HA
HA
HA
HA
HA
HA
HA
HA
HA

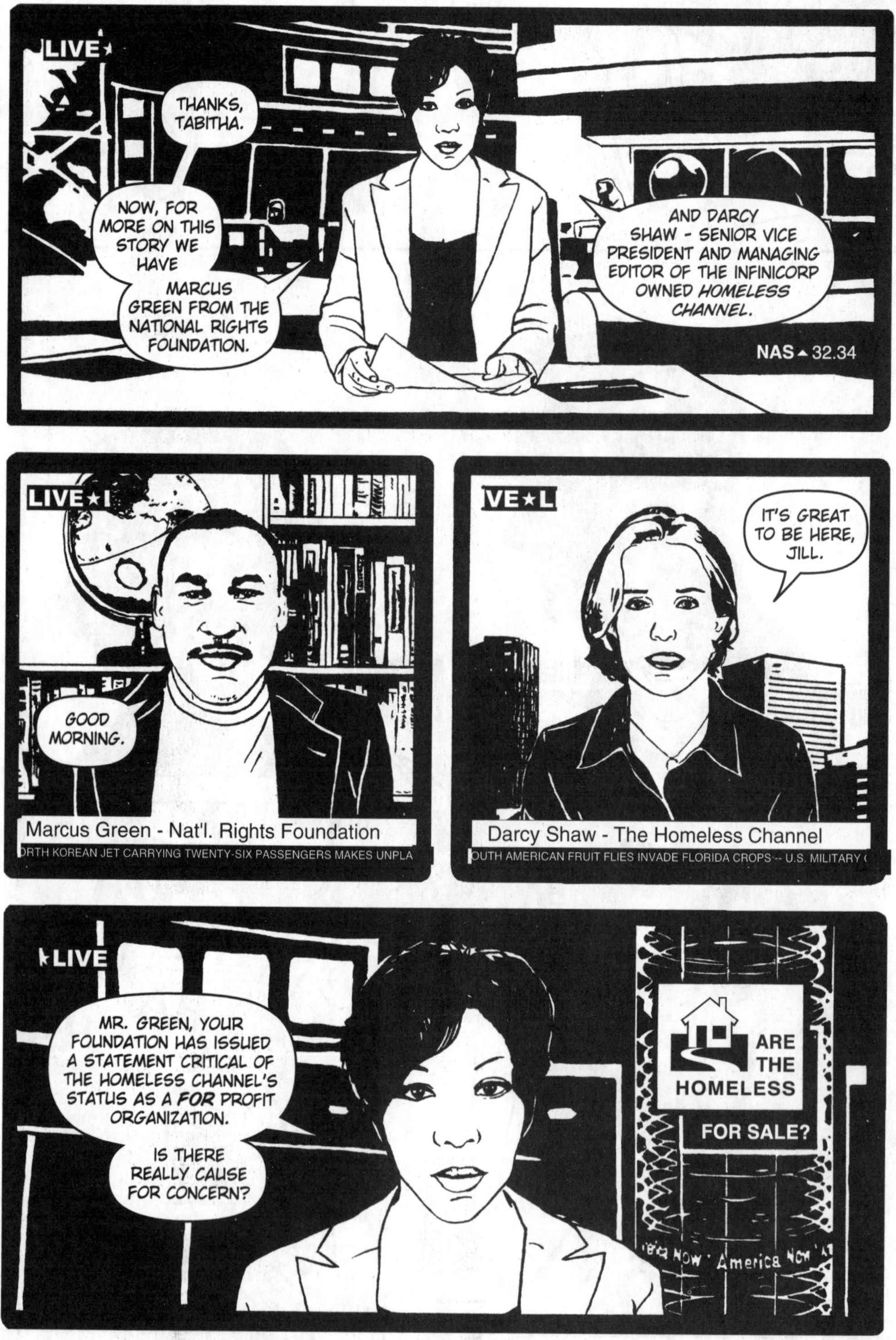

LIVE
THANKS, TABITHA.
NOW, FOR MORE ON THIS STORY WE HAVE
MARCUS GREEN FROM THE NATIONAL RIGHTS FOUNDATION.
AND DARCY SHAW - SENIOR VICE PRESIDENT AND MANAGING EDITOR OF THE INFINICORP OWNED *HOMELESS CHANNEL*.
NAS ▲ 32.34
LIVE★
GOOD MORNING.
Marcus Green - Nat'l. Rights Foundation
DRTH KOREAN JET CARRYING TWENTY-SIX PASSENGERS MAKES UNPLA
VE★L
IT'S GREAT TO BE HERE, JILL.
Darcy Shaw - The Homeless Channel
OUTH AMERICAN FRUIT FLIES INVADE FLORIDA CROPS -- U.S. MILITARY
★LIVE
MR. GREEN, YOUR FOUNDATION HAS ISSUED A STATEMENT CRITICAL OF THE HOMELESS CHANNEL'S STATUS AS A ***FOR*** PROFIT ORGANIZATION.
IS THERE REALLY CAUSE FOR CONCERN?
ARE THE HOMELESS
FOR SALE?
America NOW · America NOW

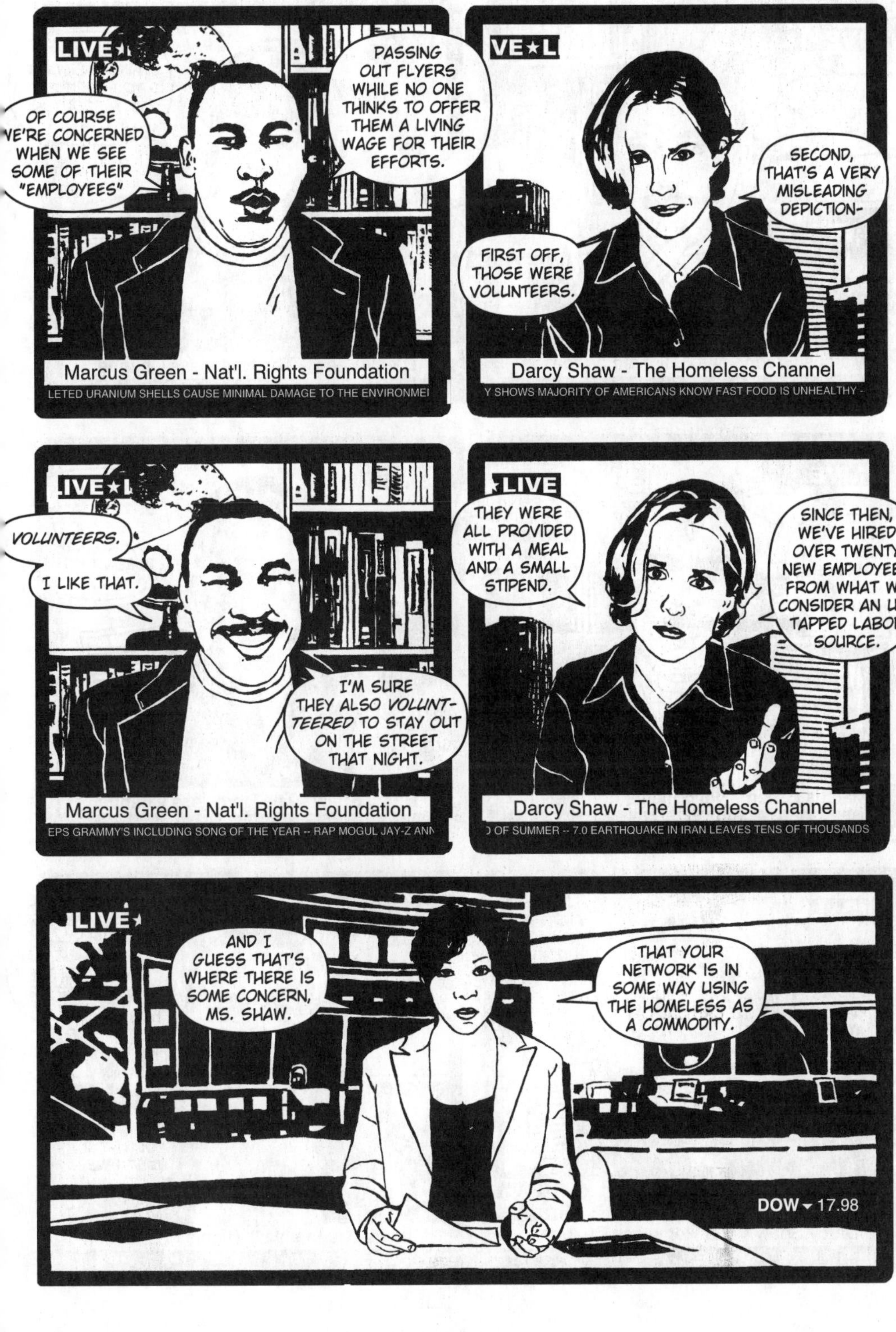
LIVE★
OF COURSE WE'RE CONCERNED WHEN WE SEE SOME OF THEIR "EMPLOYEES"
PASSING OUT FLYERS WHILE NO ONE THINKS TO OFFER THEM A LIVING WAGE FOR THEIR EFFORTS.
Marcus Green - Nat'l. Rights Foundation
LETED URANIUM SHELLS CAUSE MINIMAL DAMAGE TO THE ENVIRONME
VE★L
FIRST OFF, THOSE WERE VOLUNTEERS.
SECOND, THAT'S A VERY MISLEADING DEPICTION-
Darcy Shaw - The Homeless Channel
Y SHOWS MAJORITY OF AMERICANS KNOW FAST FOOD IS UNHEALTHY -
LIVE★L
VOLUNTEERS.
I LIKE THAT.
I'M SURE THEY ALSO VOLUNTEERED TO STAY OUT ON THE STREET THAT NIGHT.
Marcus Green - Nat'l. Rights Foundation
EPS GRAMMY'S INCLUDING SONG OF THE YEAR -- RAP MOGUL JAY-Z ANN
★LIVE
THEY WERE ALL PROVIDED WITH A MEAL AND A SMALL STIPEND.
SINCE THEN, WE'VE HIRED OVER TWENTY NEW EMPLOYEES FROM WHAT WE CONSIDER AN UNTAPPED LABOR SOURCE.
Darcy Shaw - The Homeless Channel
OF SUMMER -- 7.0 EARTHQUAKE IN IRAN LEAVES TENS OF THOUSANDS
LIVE★
AND I GUESS THAT'S WHERE THERE IS SOME CONCERN, MS. SHAW.
THAT YOUR NETWORK IS IN SOME WAY USING THE HOMELESS AS A COMMODITY.
DOW ▾ 17.98

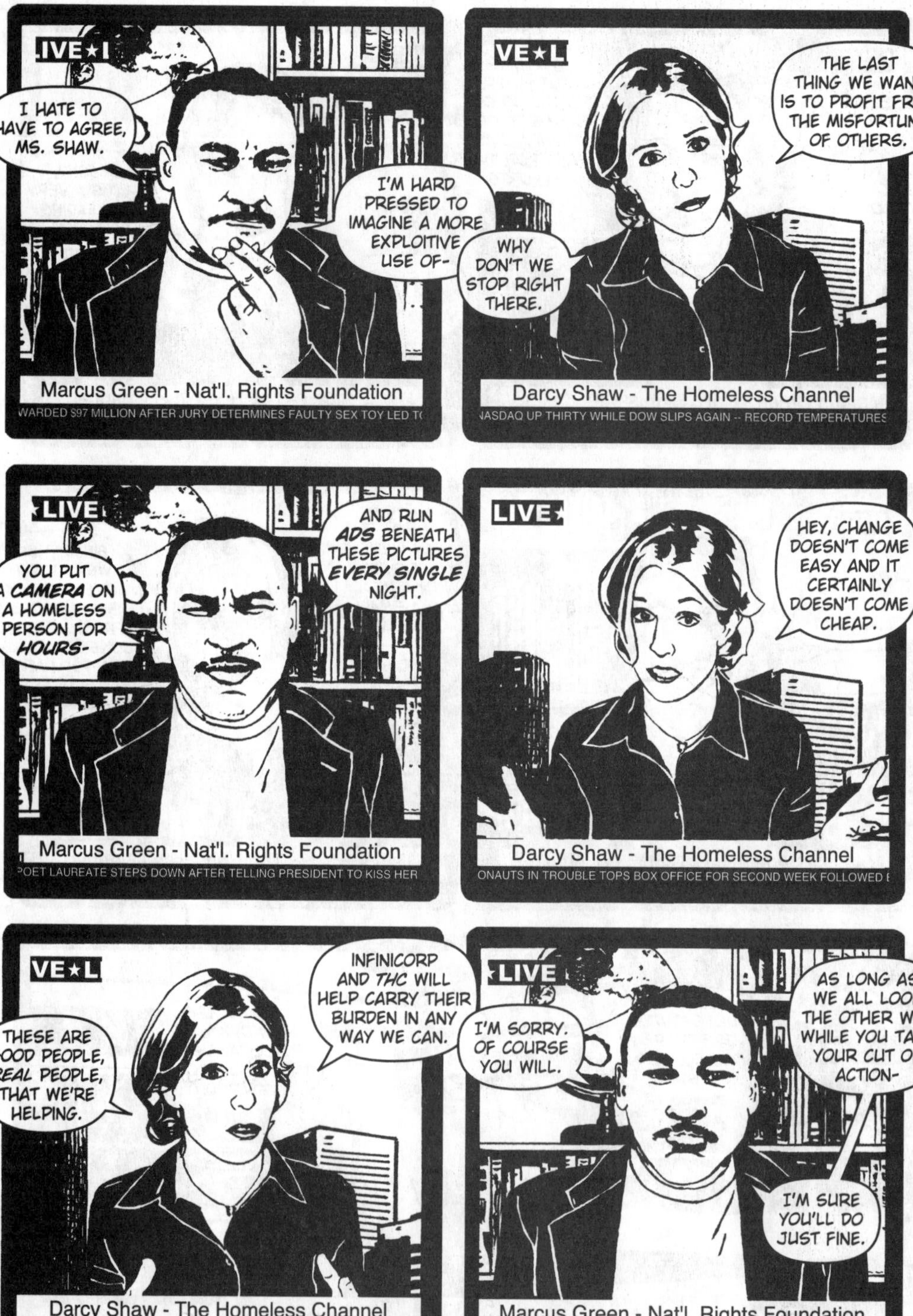
I HATE TO HAVE TO AGREE, MS. SHAW.
I'M HARD PRESSED TO IMAGINE A MORE EXPLOITIVE USE OF-
Marcus Green - Nat'l. Rights Foundation
WARDED $97 MILLION AFTER JURY DETERMINES FAULTY SEX TOY LED T
THE LAST THING WE WANT IS TO PROFIT FROM THE MISFORTUNE OF OTHERS.
WHY DON'T WE STOP RIGHT THERE.
Darcy Shaw - The Homeless Channel
NASDAQ UP THIRTY WHILE DOW SLIPS AGAIN -- RECORD TEMPERATURES
YOU PUT A CAMERA ON A HOMELESS PERSON FOR HOURS-
AND RUN ADS BENEATH THESE PICTURES EVERY SINGLE NIGHT.
Marcus Green - Nat'l. Rights Foundation
POET LAUREATE STEPS DOWN AFTER TELLING PRESIDENT TO KISS HER
HEY, CHANGE DOESN'T COME EASY AND IT CERTAINLY DOESN'T COME CHEAP.
Darcy Shaw - The Homeless Channel
ONAUTS IN TROUBLE TOPS BOX OFFICE FOR SECOND WEEK FOLLOWED
THESE ARE GOOD PEOPLE, REAL PEOPLE, THAT WE'RE HELPING.
INFINICORP AND THC WILL HELP CARRY THEIR BURDEN IN ANY WAY WE CAN.
Darcy Shaw - The Homeless Channel
EW JERSEY UNDERCOVER OFFICER KILLED BY FRIENDLY FIRE HONORED
I'M SORRY. OF COURSE YOU WILL.
AS LONG AS WE ALL LOOK THE OTHER WAY WHILE YOU TAKE YOUR CUT OF ACTION-
I'M SURE YOU'LL DO JUST FINE.
Marcus Green - Nat'l. Rights Foundation
PE BLESSES GRAFFITI ARTISTS DURING STAGED "TAGGING" DEMONSTRA

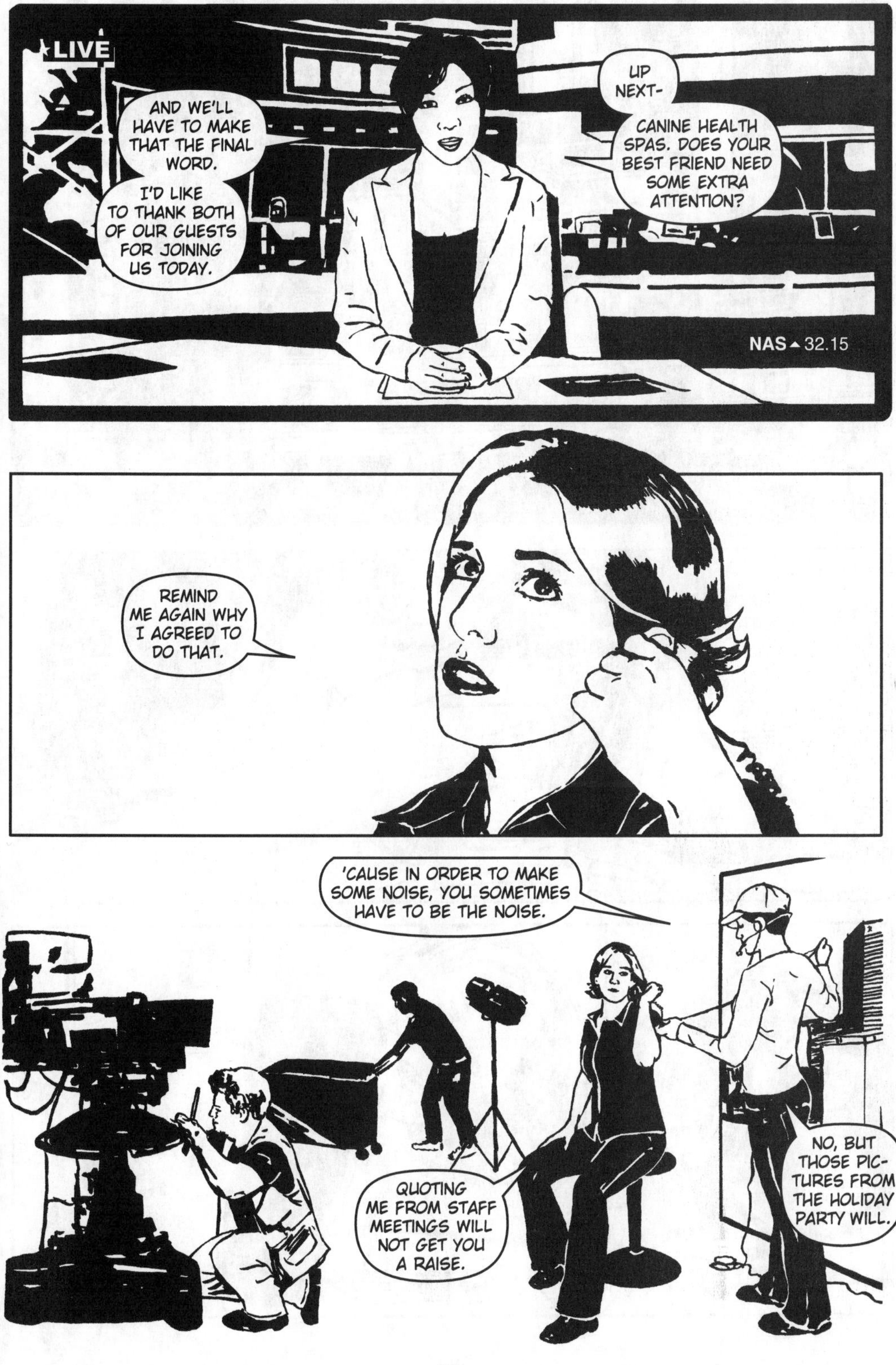
LIVE
AND WE'LL HAVE TO MAKE THAT THE FINAL WORD.
I'D LIKE TO THANK BOTH OF OUR GUESTS FOR JOINING US TODAY.
UP NEXT-
CANINE HEALTH SPAS. DOES YOUR BEST FRIEND NEED SOME EXTRA ATTENTION?
NAS ▲ 32.15
REMIND ME AGAIN WHY I AGREED TO DO THAT.
'CAUSE IN ORDER TO MAKE SOME NOISE, YOU SOMETIMES HAVE TO BE THE NOISE.
QUOTING ME FROM STAFF MEETINGS WILL NOT GET YOU A RAISE.
NO, BUT THOSE PICTURES FROM THE HOLIDAY PARTY WILL.

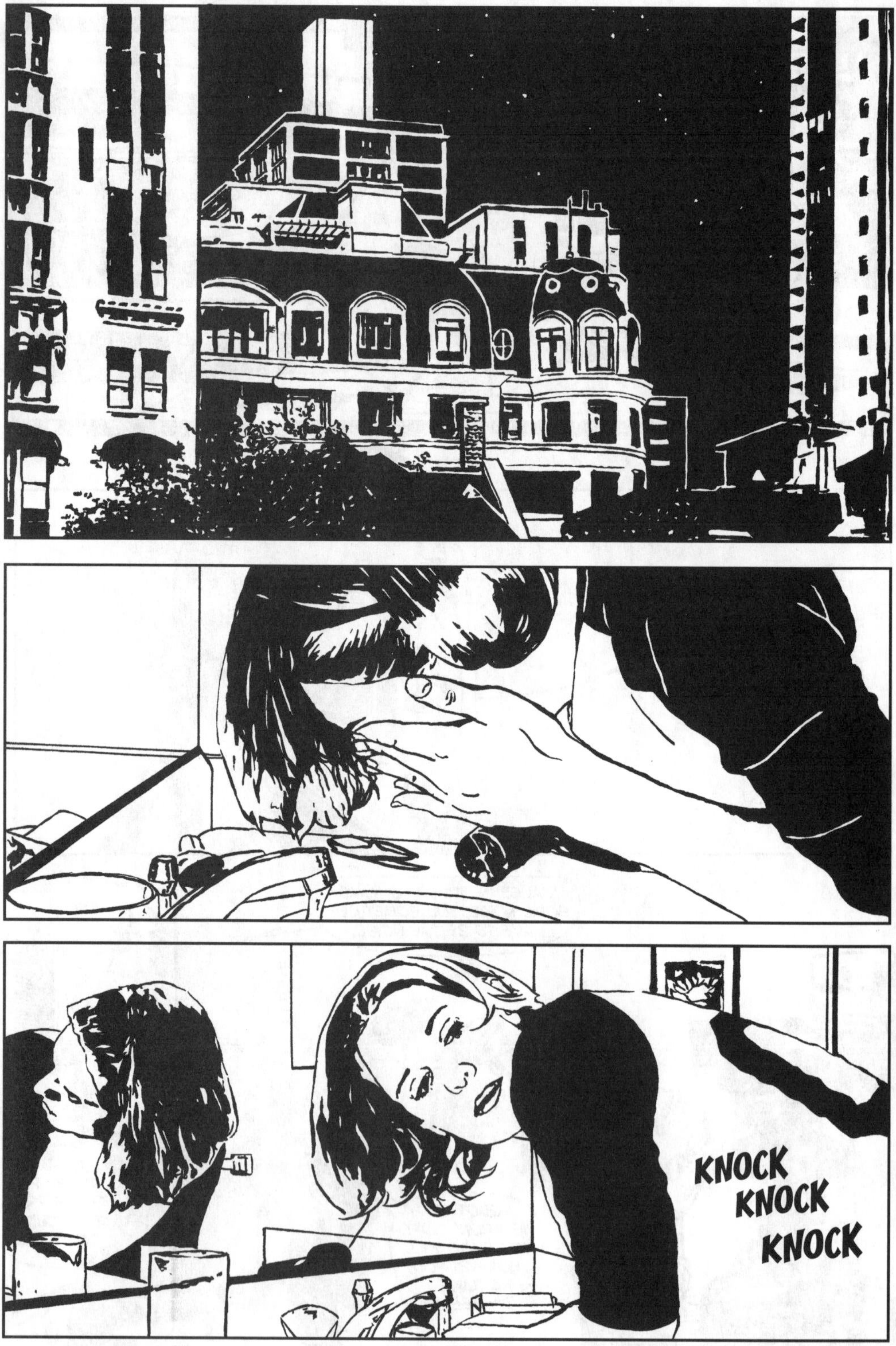
KNOCK
KNOCK
KNOCK

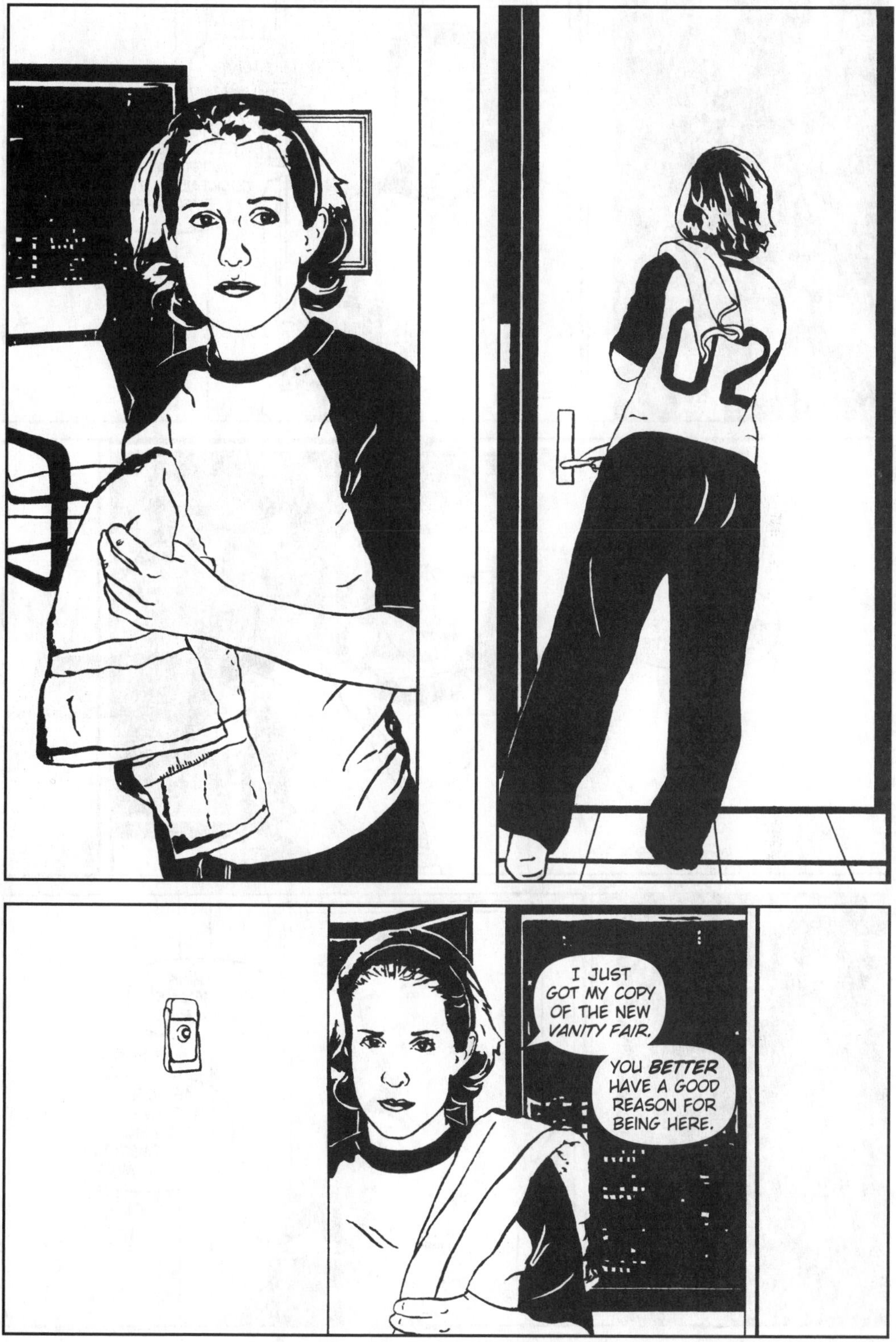

I JUST GOT MY COPY OF THE NEW VANITY FAIR.
YOU BETTER HAVE A GOOD REASON FOR BEING HERE.

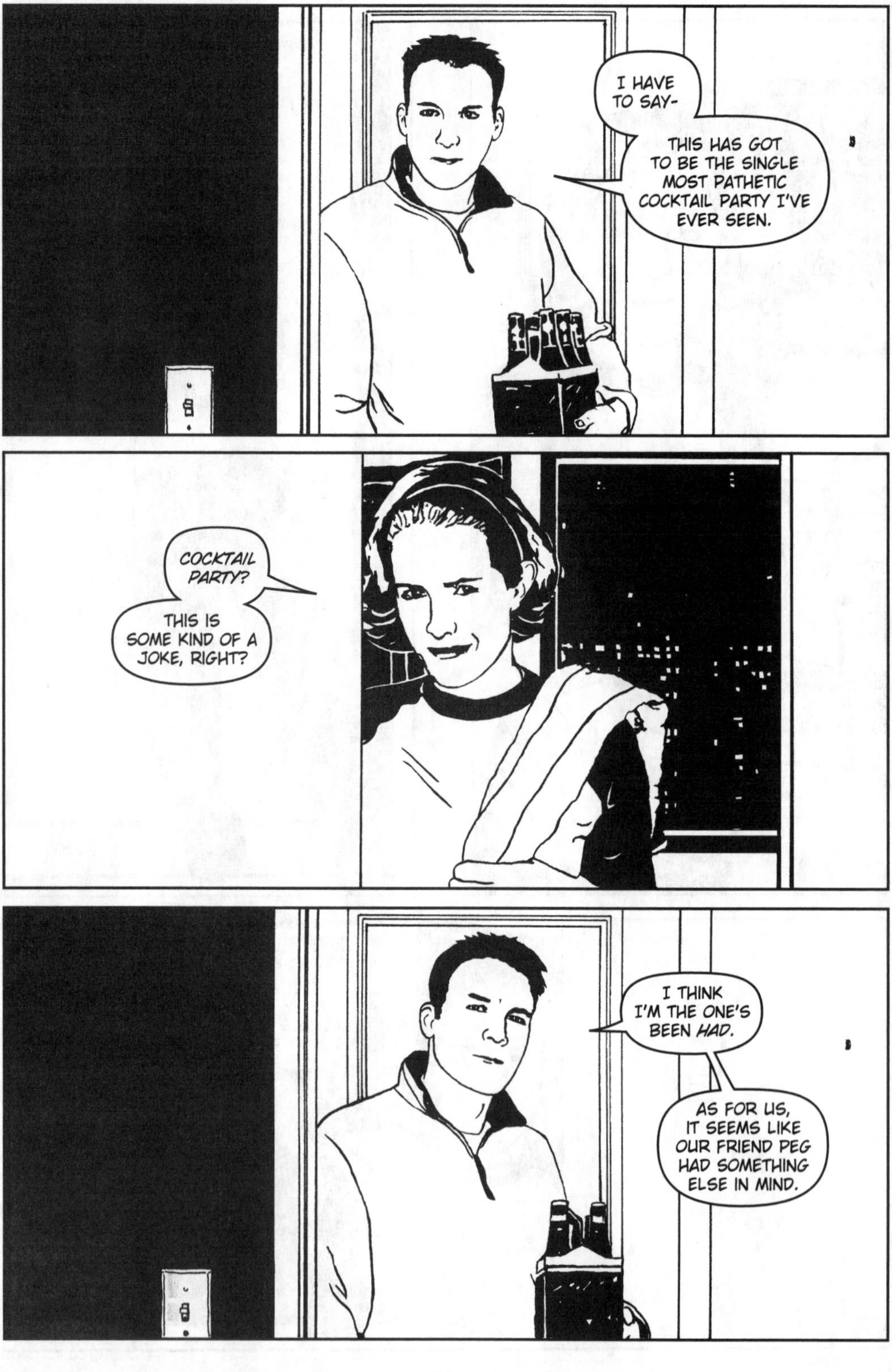
I HAVE TO SAY-
THIS HAS GOT TO BE THE SINGLE MOST PATHETIC COCKTAIL PARTY I'VE EVER SEEN.
COCKTAIL PARTY?
THIS IS SOME KIND OF A JOKE, RIGHT?
I THINK I'M THE ONE'S BEEN *HAD*.
AS FOR US, IT SEEMS LIKE OUR FRIEND PEG HAD SOMETHING ELSE IN MIND.

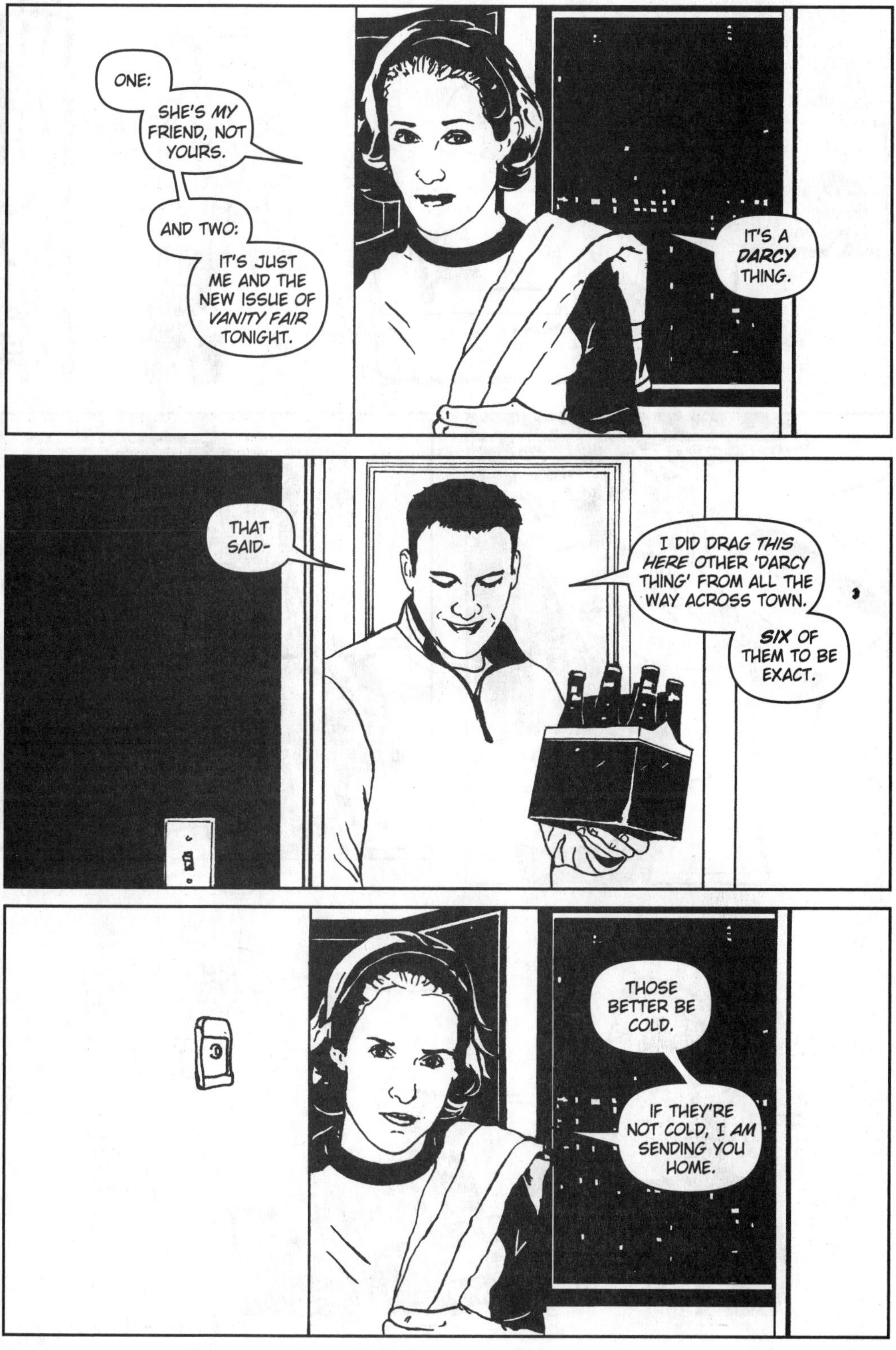
ONE:
SHE'S *MY* FRIEND, NOT YOURS.
AND TWO:
IT'S JUST ME AND THE NEW ISSUE OF *VANITY FAIR* TONIGHT.
IT'S A ***DARCY*** THING.
THAT SAID-
I DID DRAG *THIS HERE* OTHER 'DARCY THING' FROM ALL THE WAY ACROSS TOWN.
SIX OF THEM TO BE EXACT.
THOSE BETTER BE COLD.
IF THEY'RE NOT COLD, I *AM* SENDING YOU HOME.

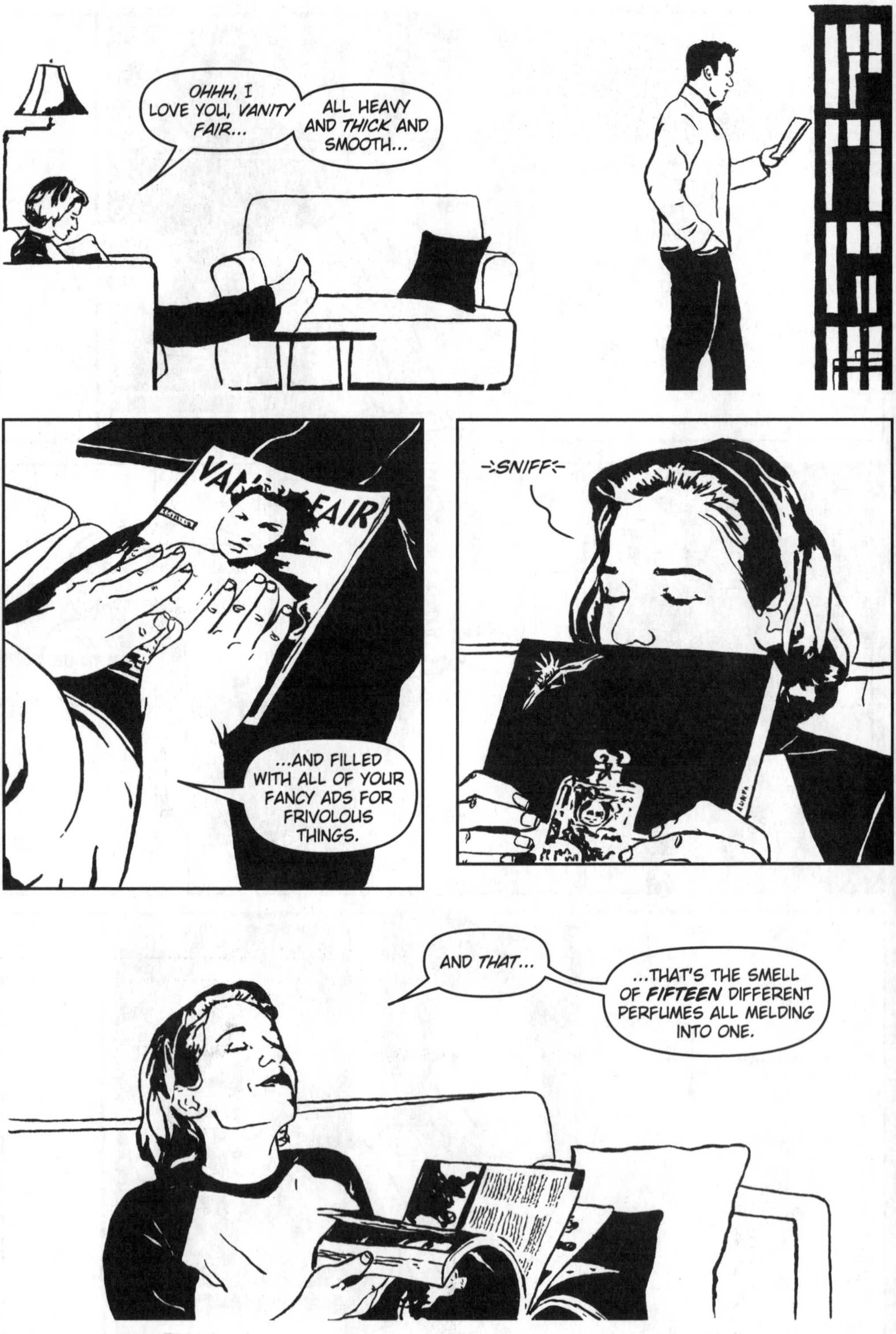
OHHH, I LOVE YOU, *VANITY FAIR*...
ALL HEAVY AND *THICK* AND SMOOTH...
...AND FILLED WITH ALL OF YOUR FANCY ADS FOR FRIVOLOUS THINGS.
-SNIFF-
AND *THAT*...
...THAT'S THE SMELL OF ***FIFTEEN*** DIFFERENT PERFUMES ALL MELDING INTO ONE.

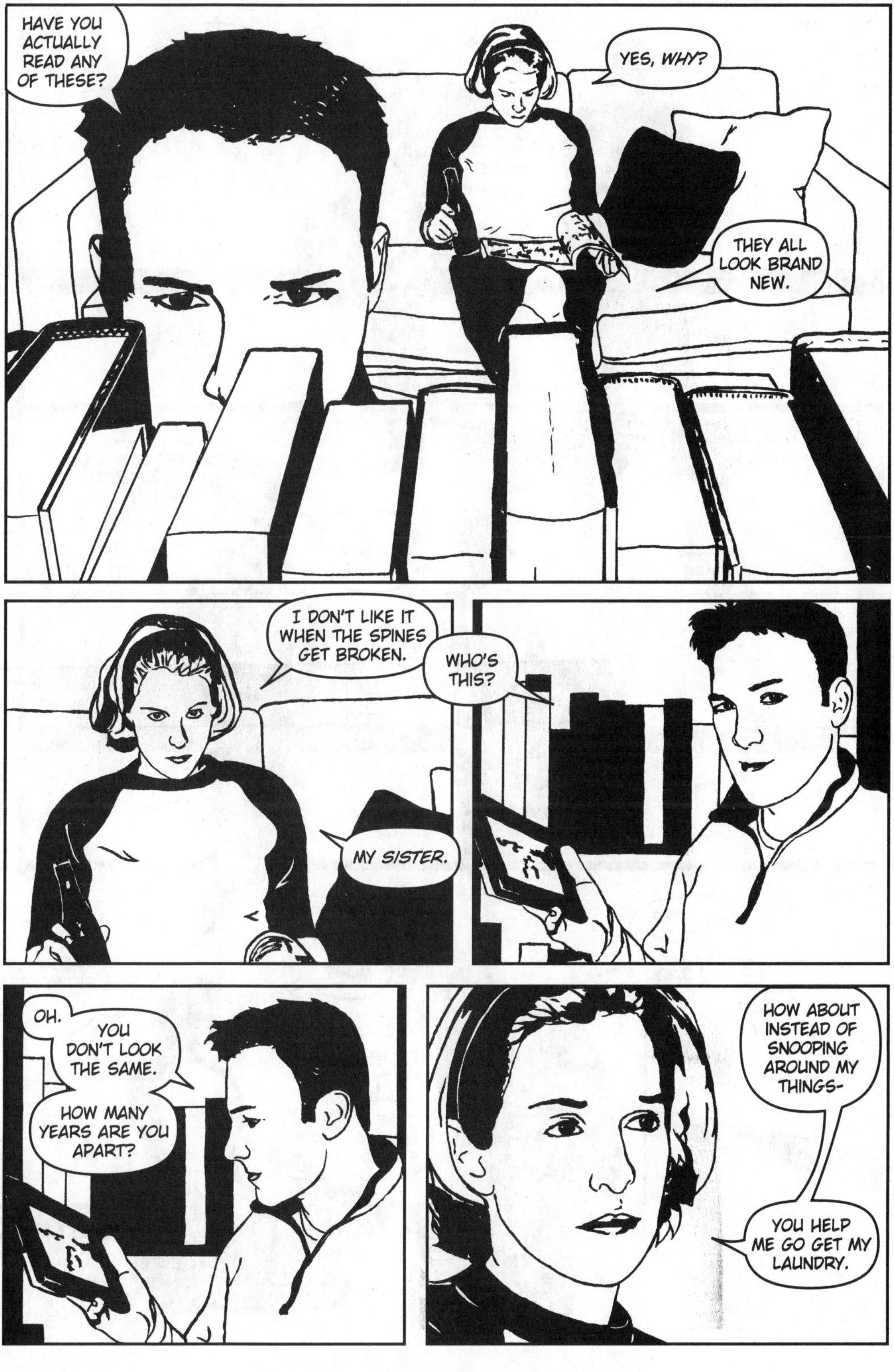
HAVE YOU ACTUALLY READ ANY OF THESE?
YES, WHY?
THEY ALL LOOK BRAND NEW.
I DON'T LIKE IT WHEN THE SPINES GET BROKEN.
WHO'S THIS?
MY SISTER.
OH.
YOU DON'T LOOK THE SAME.
HOW MANY YEARS ARE YOU APART?
HOW ABOUT INSTEAD OF SNOOPING AROUND MY THINGS-
YOU HELP ME GO GET MY LAUNDRY.

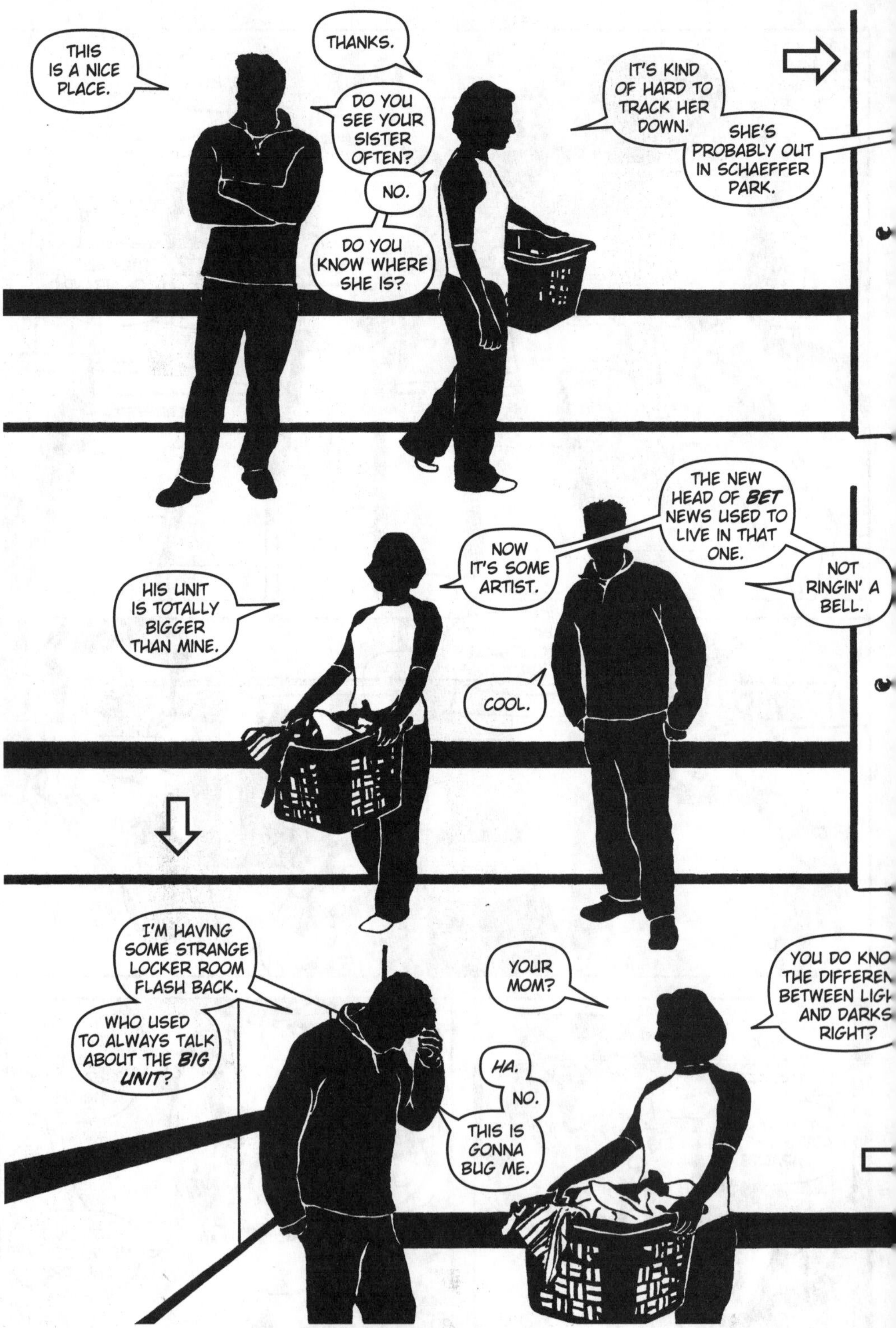
THIS IS A NICE PLACE.
THANKS.
DO YOU SEE YOUR SISTER OFTEN?
NO.
DO YOU KNOW WHERE SHE IS?
IT'S KIND OF HARD TO TRACK HER DOWN.
SHE'S PROBABLY OUT IN SCHAEFFER PARK.
THE NEW HEAD OF *BET* NEWS USED TO LIVE IN THAT ONE.
NOW IT'S SOME ARTIST.
NOT RINGIN' A BELL.
HIS UNIT IS TOTALLY BIGGER THAN MINE.
COOL.
I'M HAVING SOME STRANGE LOCKER ROOM FLASH BACK.
WHO USED TO ALWAYS TALK ABOUT THE *BIG UNIT*?
YOUR MOM?
HA.
NO.
THIS IS GONNA BUG ME.

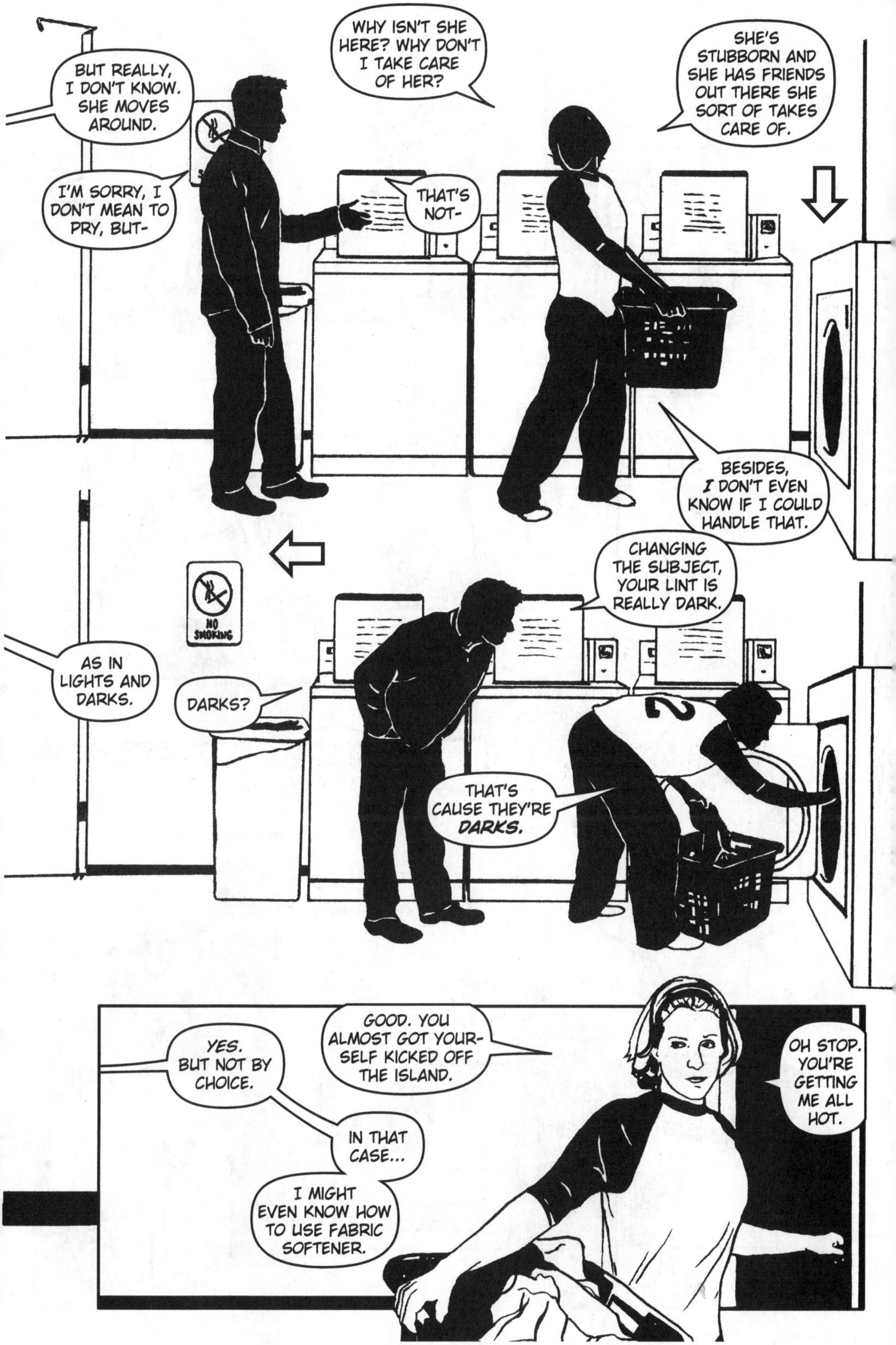

BUT REALLY, I DON'T KNOW. SHE MOVES AROUND.
WHY ISN'T SHE HERE? WHY DON'T I TAKE CARE OF HER?
SHE'S STUBBORN AND SHE HAS FRIENDS OUT THERE SHE SORT OF TAKES CARE OF.
I'M SORRY, I DON'T MEAN TO PRY, BUT-
THAT'S NOT-
BESIDES, *I* DON'T EVEN KNOW IF I COULD HANDLE THAT.
CHANGING THE SUBJECT, YOUR LINT IS REALLY DARK.
NO SMOKING
DARKS?
AS IN LIGHTS AND DARKS.
THAT'S CAUSE THEY'RE ***DARKS.***
2
GOOD. YOU ALMOST GOT YOURSELF KICKED OFF THE ISLAND.
YES. BUT NOT BY CHOICE.
OH STOP. YOU'RE GETTING ME ALL HOT.
IN THAT CASE...
I MIGHT EVEN KNOW HOW TO USE FABRIC SOFTENER.

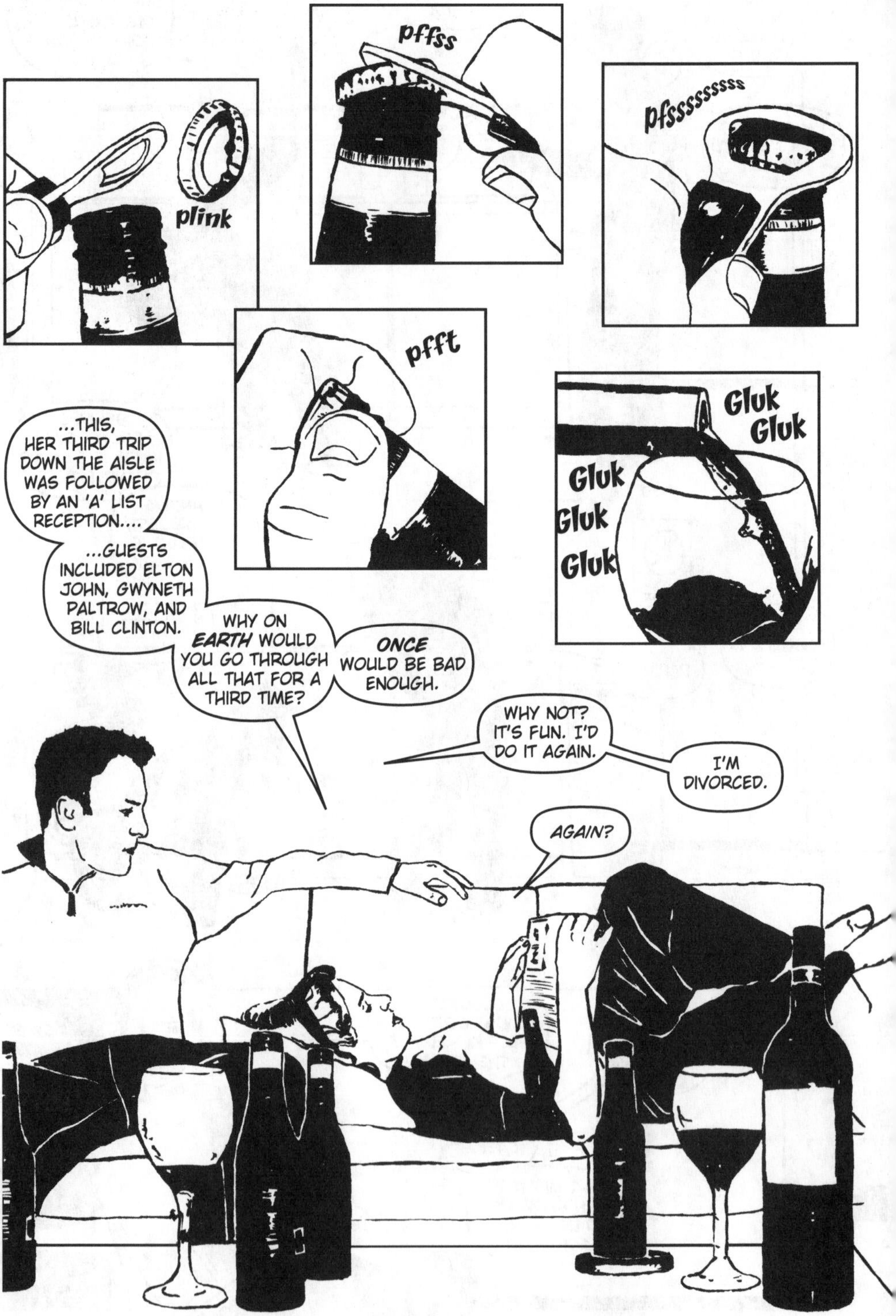
plink
pffss
pfssssssss
pfft
Gluk Gluk
Gluk Gluk Gluk
...THIS, HER THIRD TRIP DOWN THE AISLE WAS FOLLOWED BY AN 'A' LIST RECEPTION....
...GUESTS INCLUDED ELTON JOHN, GWYNETH PALTROW, AND BILL CLINTON.
WHY ON *EARTH* WOULD YOU GO THROUGH ALL THAT FOR A THIRD TIME?
ONCE WOULD BE BAD ENOUGH.
WHY NOT? IT'S FUN. I'D DO IT AGAIN.
I'M DIVORCED.
AGAIN?

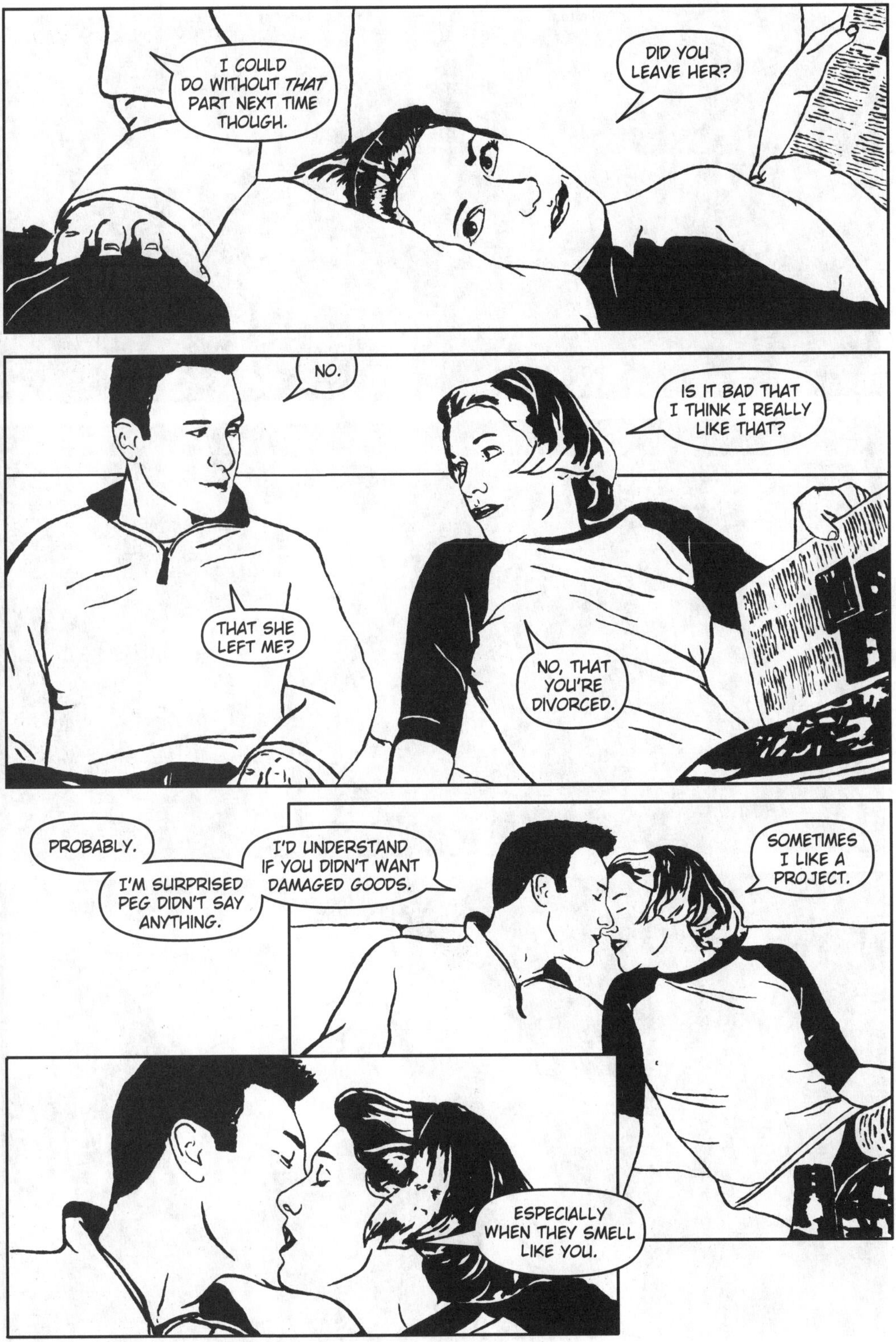
I COULD DO WITHOUT *THAT* PART NEXT TIME THOUGH.
DID YOU LEAVE HER?
NO.
IS IT BAD THAT I THINK I REALLY LIKE THAT?
THAT SHE LEFT ME?
NO, THAT YOU'RE DIVORCED.
PROBABLY.
I'M SURPRISED PEG DIDN'T SAY ANYTHING.
I'D UNDERSTAND IF YOU DIDN'T WANT DAMAGED GOODS.
SOMETIMES I LIKE A PROJECT.
ESPECIALLY WHEN THEY SMELL LIKE YOU.

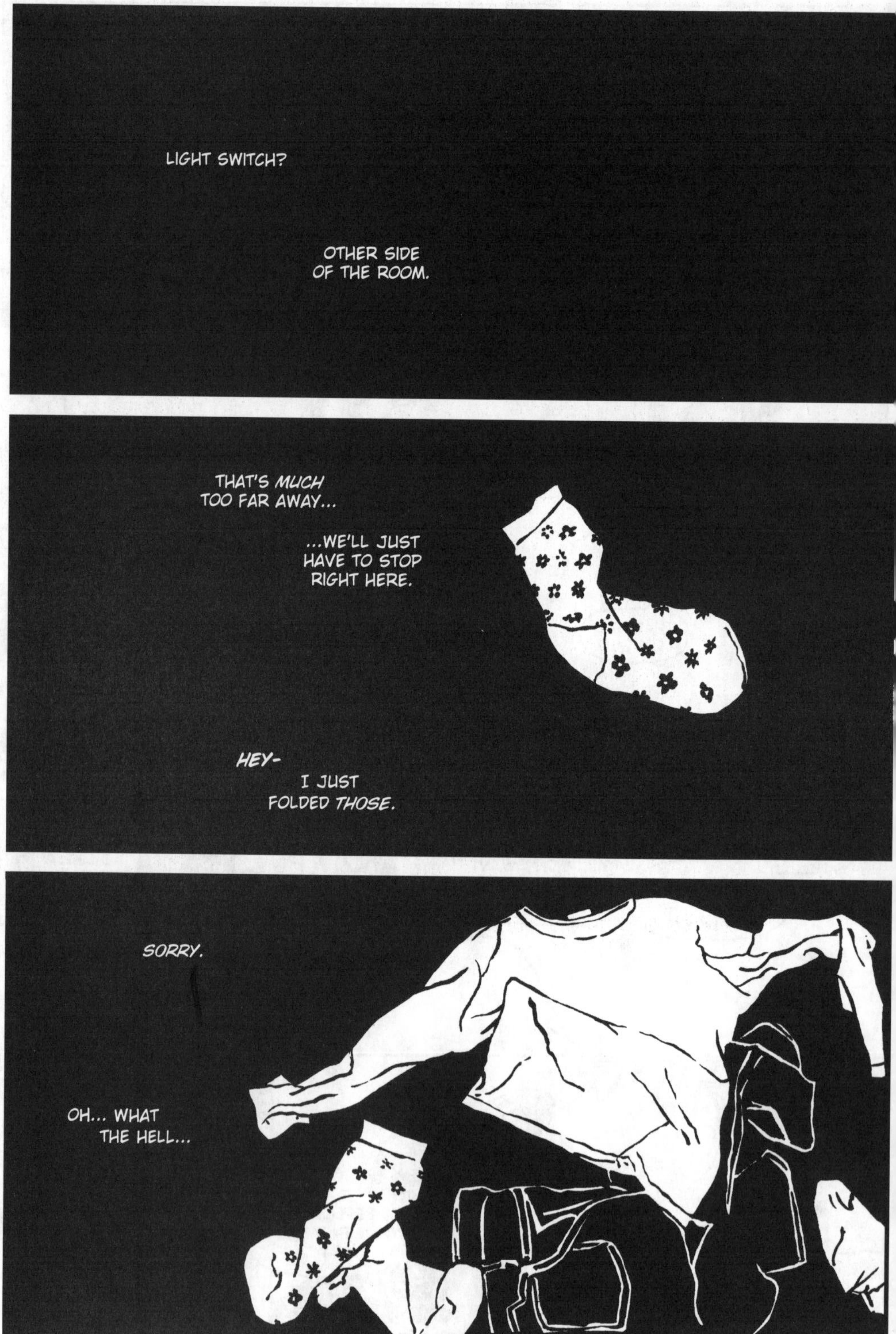
LIGHT SWITCH?
OTHER SIDE OF THE ROOM.
THAT'S *MUCH* TOO FAR AWAY...
...WE'LL JUST HAVE TO STOP RIGHT HERE.
HEY- I JUST FOLDED *THOSE.*
SORRY.
OH... WHAT THE HELL...

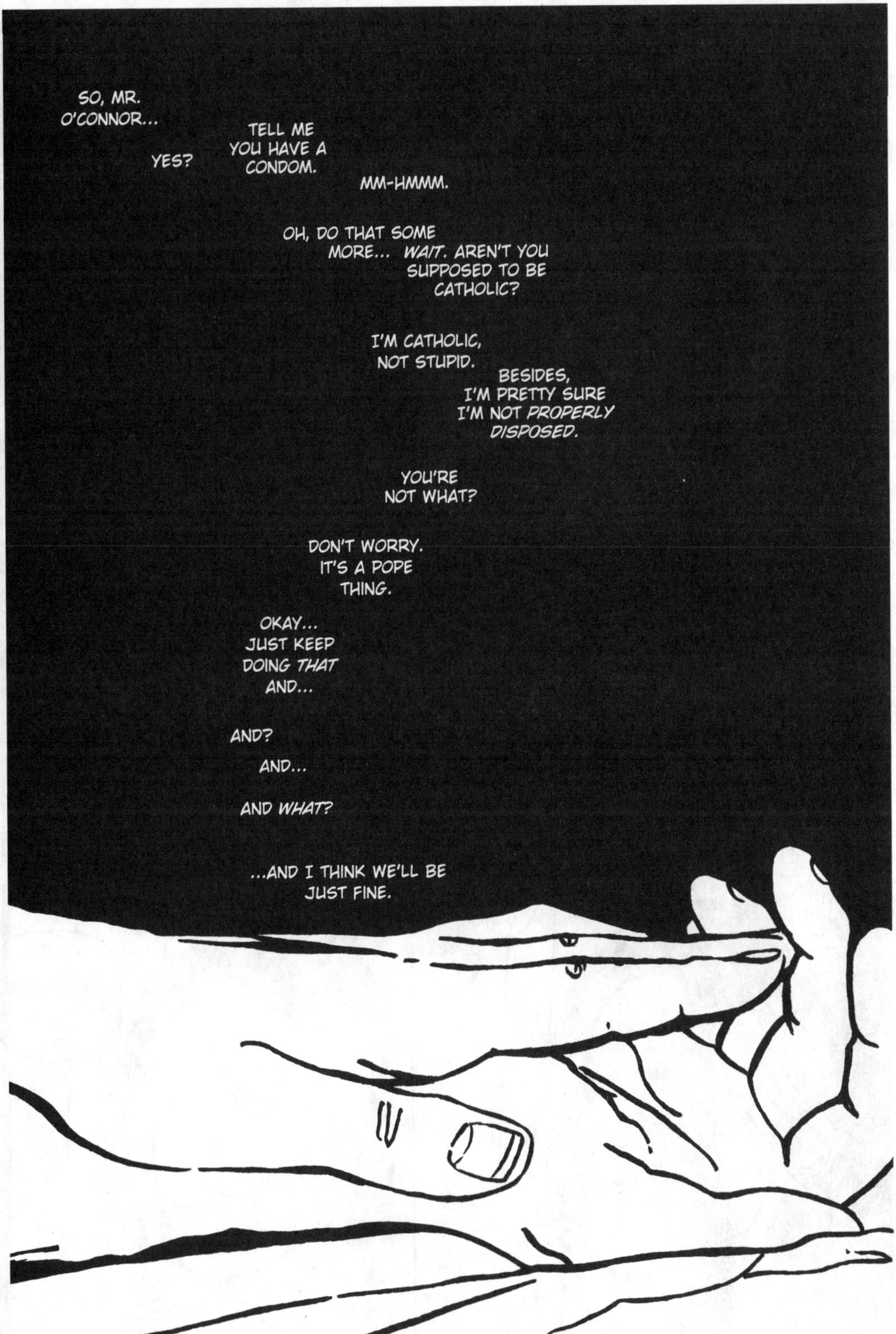

SO, MR. O'CONNOR...
YES?
TELL ME YOU HAVE A CONDOM.
MM-HMMM.
OH, DO THAT SOME MORE... *WAIT*. AREN'T YOU SUPPOSED TO BE CATHOLIC?
I'M CATHOLIC, NOT STUPID.
BESIDES, I'M PRETTY SURE I'M NOT *PROPERLY DISPOSED*.
YOU'RE NOT WHAT?
DON'T WORRY. IT'S A POPE THING.
OKAY... JUST KEEP DOING *THAT* AND...
AND?
AND...
AND *WHAT?*
...AND I THINK WE'LL BE JUST FINE.

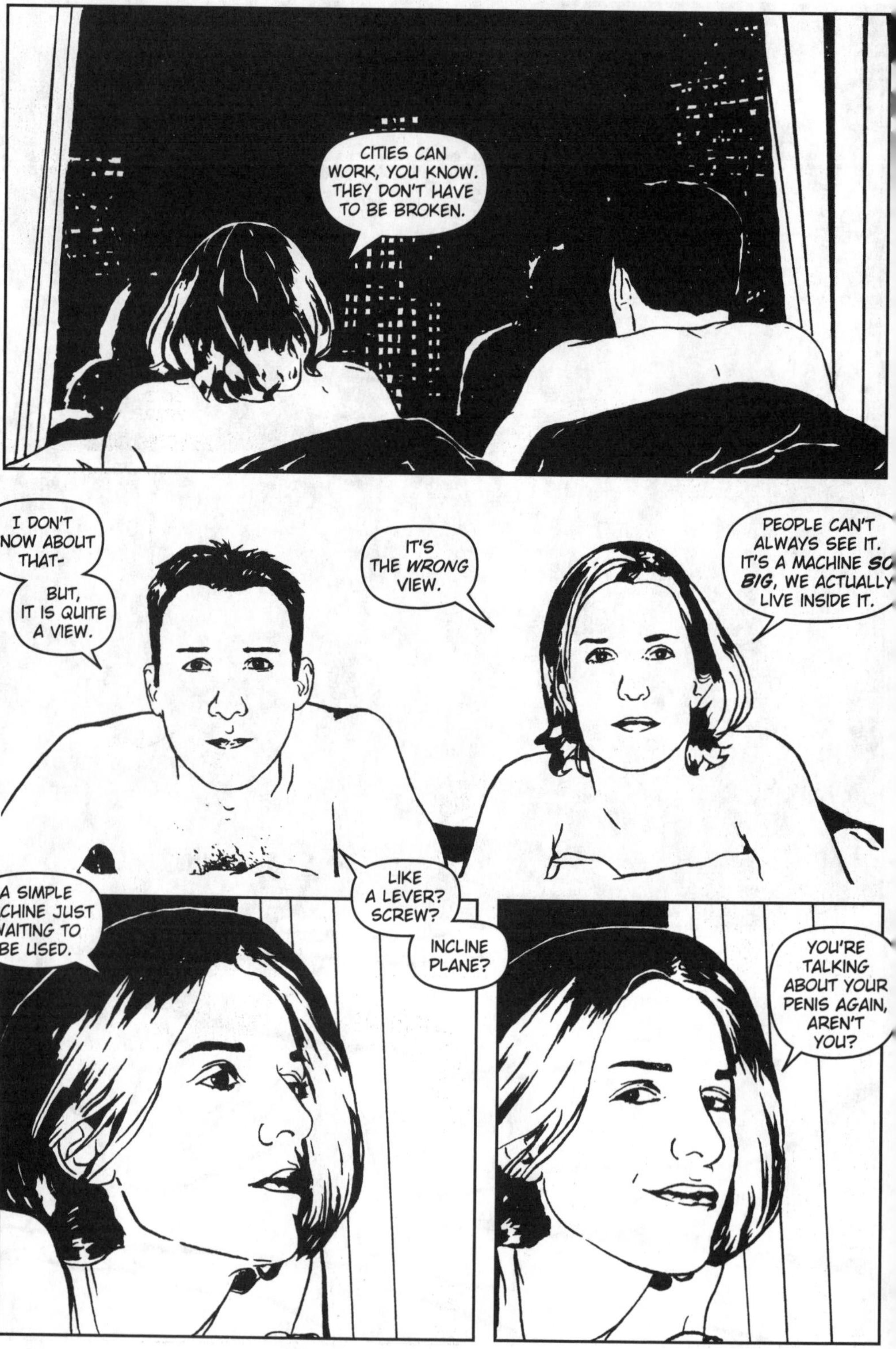
CITIES CAN WORK, YOU KNOW. THEY DON'T HAVE TO BE BROKEN.
I DON'T KNOW ABOUT THAT-
BUT, IT IS QUITE A VIEW.
IT'S THE *WRONG* VIEW.
PEOPLE CAN'T ALWAYS SEE IT. IT'S A MACHINE ***SO BIG***, WE ACTUALLY LIVE INSIDE IT.
A SIMPLE MACHINE JUST WAITING TO BE USED.
LIKE A LEVER? SCREW?
INCLINE PLANE?
YOU'RE TALKING ABOUT YOUR PENIS AGAIN, AREN'T YOU?

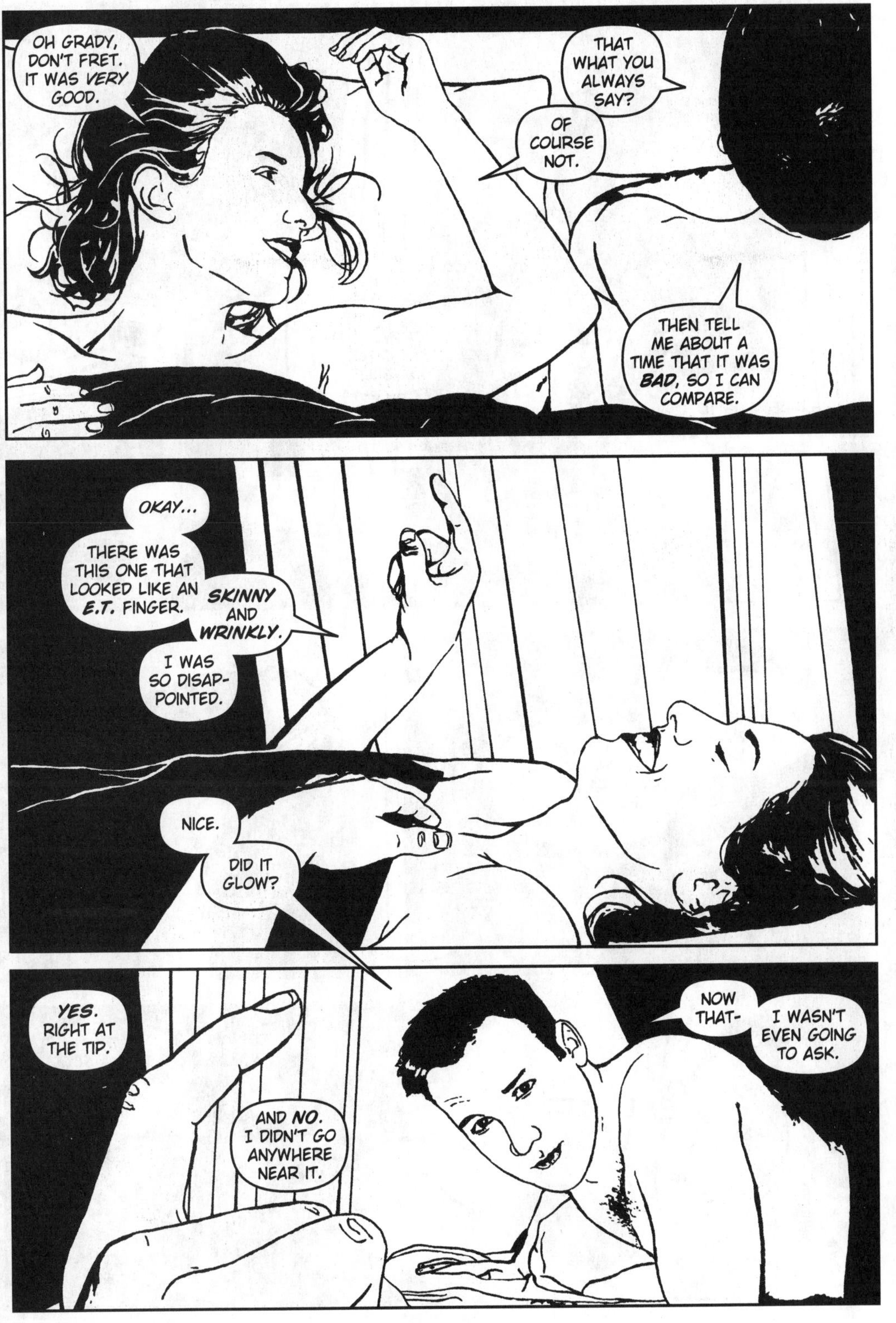
OH GRADY, DON'T FRET. IT WAS VERY GOOD.
THAT WHAT YOU ALWAYS SAY?
OF COURSE NOT.
THEN TELL ME ABOUT A TIME THAT IT WAS BAD, SO I CAN COMPARE.
OKAY...
THERE WAS THIS ONE THAT LOOKED LIKE AN E.T. FINGER.
SKINNY AND WRINKLY.
I WAS SO DISAP-POINTED.
NICE.
DID IT GLOW?
YES. RIGHT AT THE TIP.
AND NO. I DIDN'T GO ANYWHERE NEAR IT.
NOW THAT-
I WASN'T EVEN GOING TO ASK.

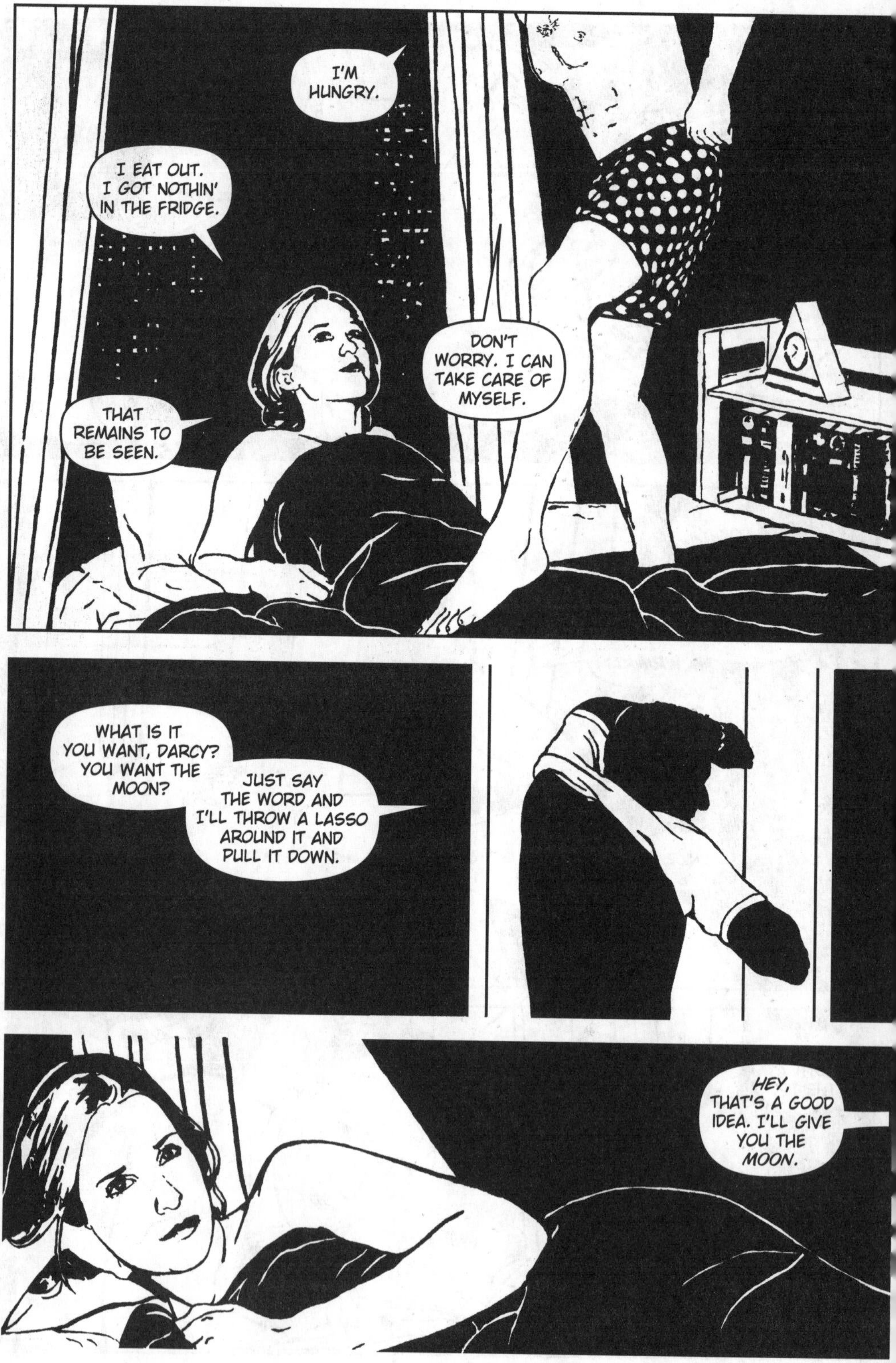
I'M HUNGRY.
I EAT OUT. I GOT NOTHIN' IN THE FRIDGE.
DON'T WORRY. I CAN TAKE CARE OF MYSELF.
THAT REMAINS TO BE SEEN.
WHAT IS IT YOU WANT, DARCY? YOU WANT THE MOON?
JUST SAY THE WORD AND I'LL THROW A LASSO AROUND IT AND PULL IT DOWN.
HEY, THAT'S A GOOD IDEA. I'LL GIVE YOU THE *MOON.*

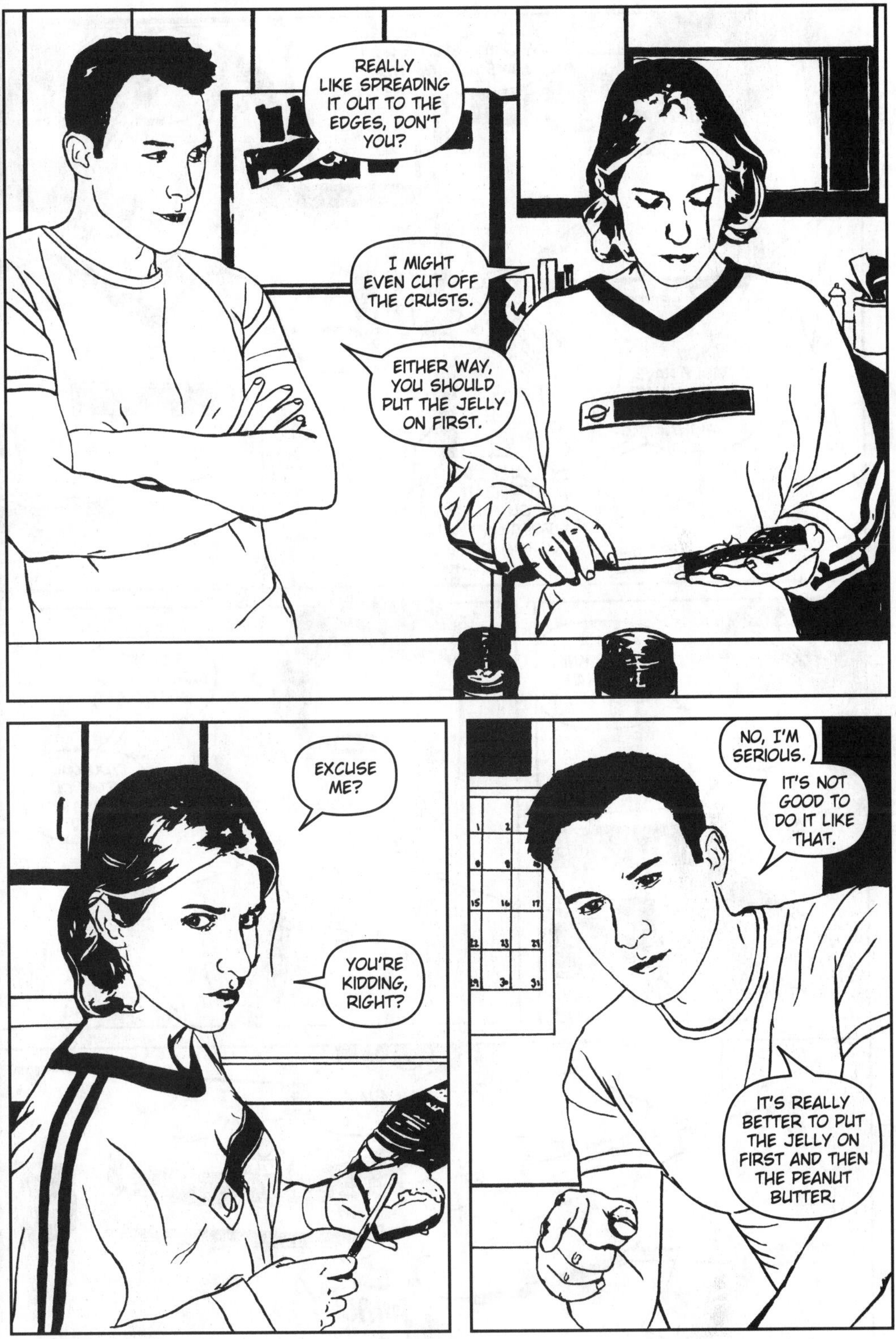
REALLY LIKE SPREADING IT OUT TO THE EDGES, DON'T YOU?
I MIGHT EVEN CUT OFF THE CRUSTS.
EITHER WAY, YOU SHOULD PUT THE JELLY ON FIRST.
EXCUSE ME?
YOU'RE KIDDING, RIGHT?
NO, I'M SERIOUS.
IT'S NOT GOOD TO DO IT LIKE THAT.
IT'S REALLY BETTER TO PUT THE JELLY ON FIRST AND THEN THE PEANUT BUTTER.

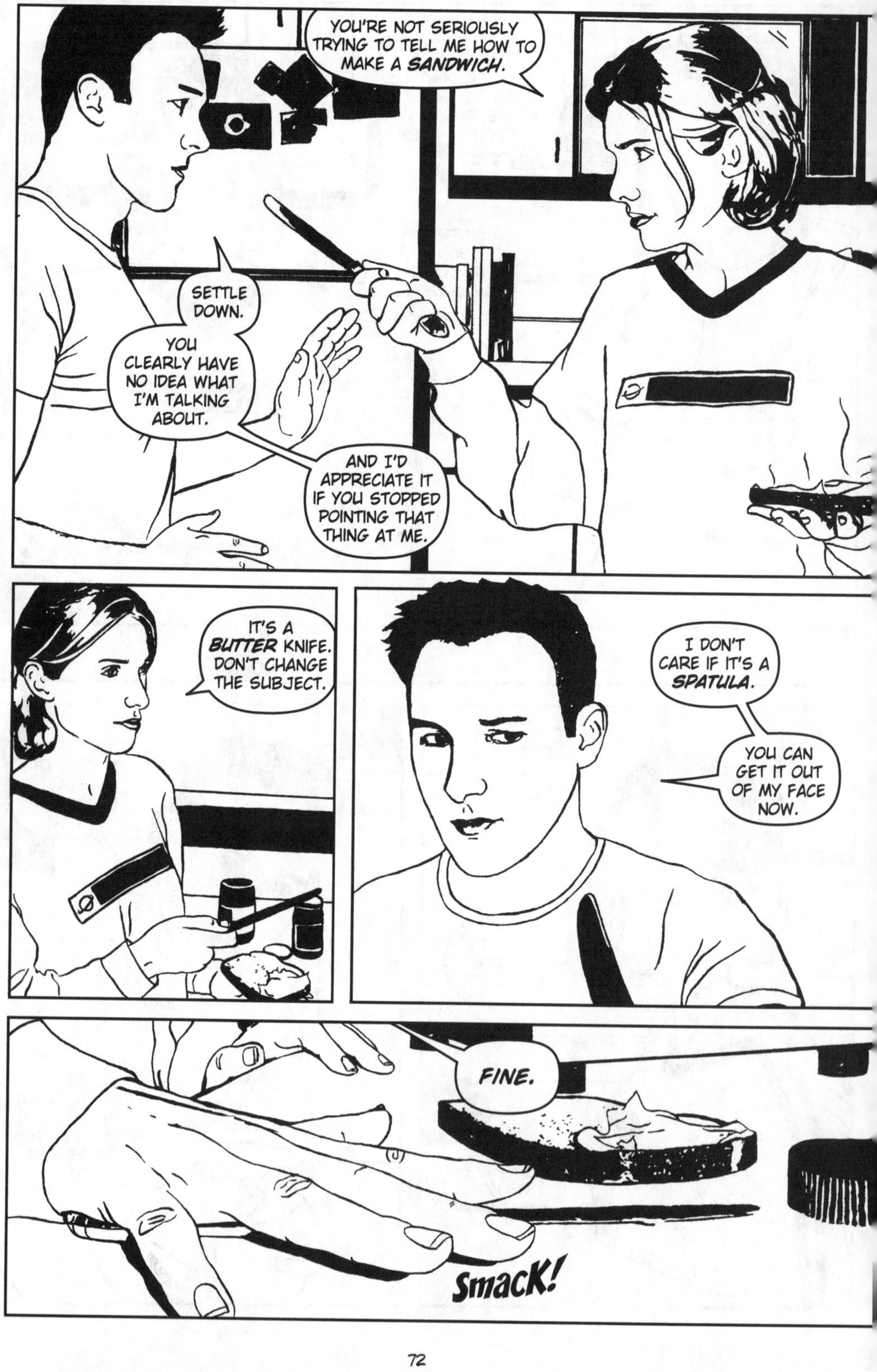
YOU'RE NOT SERIOUSLY TRYING TO TELL ME HOW TO MAKE A SANDWICH.
SETTLE DOWN.
YOU CLEARLY HAVE NO IDEA WHAT I'M TALKING ABOUT.
AND I'D APPRECIATE IT IF YOU STOPPED POINTING THAT THING AT ME.
IT'S A BUTTER KNIFE. DON'T CHANGE THE SUBJECT.
I DON'T CARE IF IT'S A SPATULA.
YOU CAN GET IT OUT OF MY FACE NOW.
FINE.
SMACK!

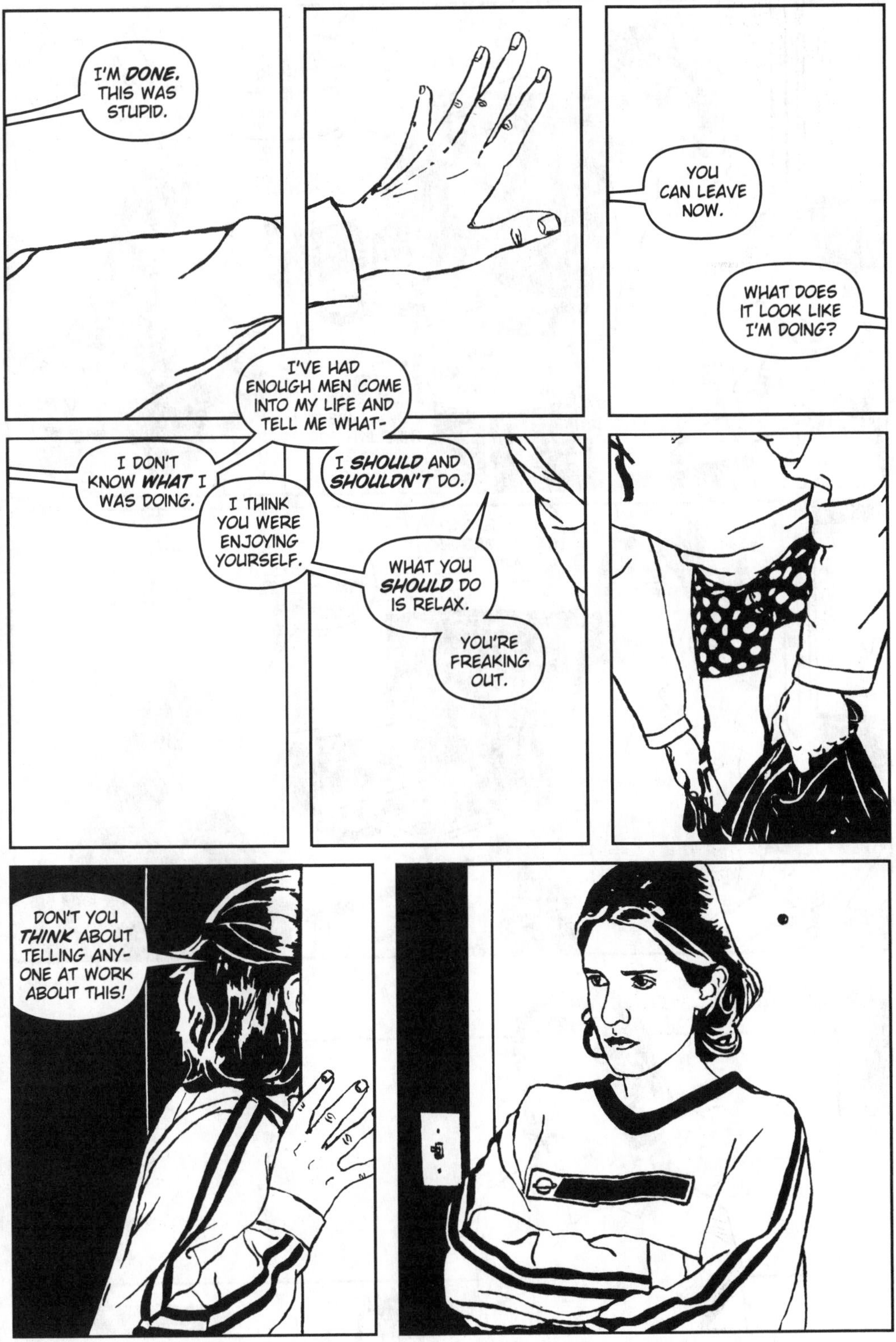
I'M DONE. THIS WAS STUPID.
YOU CAN LEAVE NOW.
WHAT DOES IT LOOK LIKE I'M DOING?
I DON'T KNOW WHAT I WAS DOING.
I THINK YOU WERE ENJOYING YOURSELF.
I'VE HAD ENOUGH MEN COME INTO MY LIFE AND TELL ME WHAT-
I SHOULD AND SHOULDN'T DO.
WHAT YOU SHOULD DO IS RELAX.
YOU'RE FREAKING OUT.
DON'T YOU THINK ABOUT TELLING ANY-ONE AT WORK ABOUT THIS!

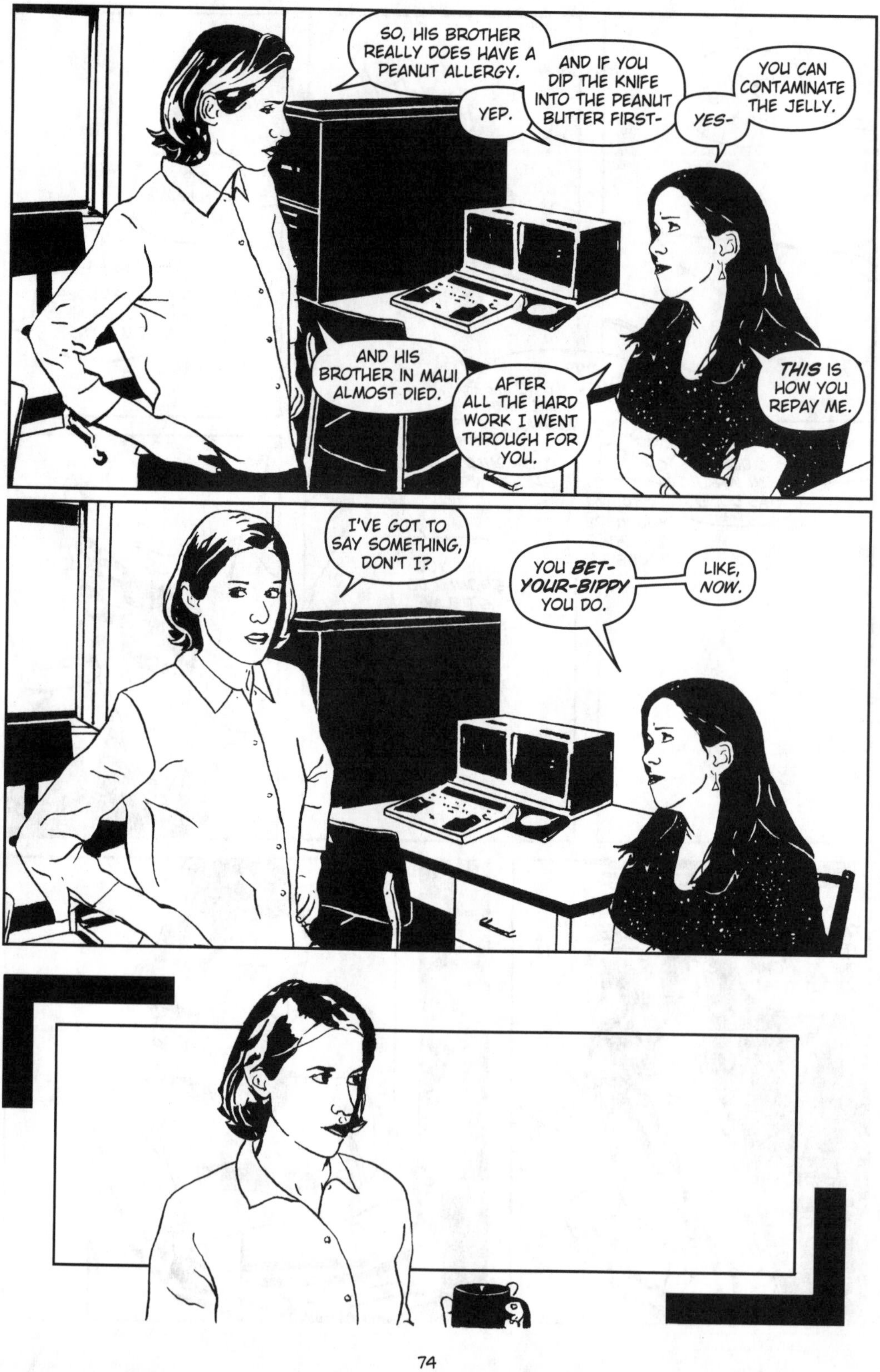

SO, HIS BROTHER REALLY DOES HAVE A PEANUT ALLERGY.
YEP.
AND IF YOU DIP THE KNIFE INTO THE PEANUT BUTTER FIRST-
YES-
YOU CAN CONTAMINATE THE JELLY.
AND HIS BROTHER IN MAUI ALMOST DIED.
AFTER ALL THE HARD WORK I WENT THROUGH FOR YOU.
THIS IS HOW YOU REPAY ME.
I'VE GOT TO SAY SOMETHING, DON'T I?
YOU BET-YOUR-BIPPY YOU DO.
LIKE, NOW.

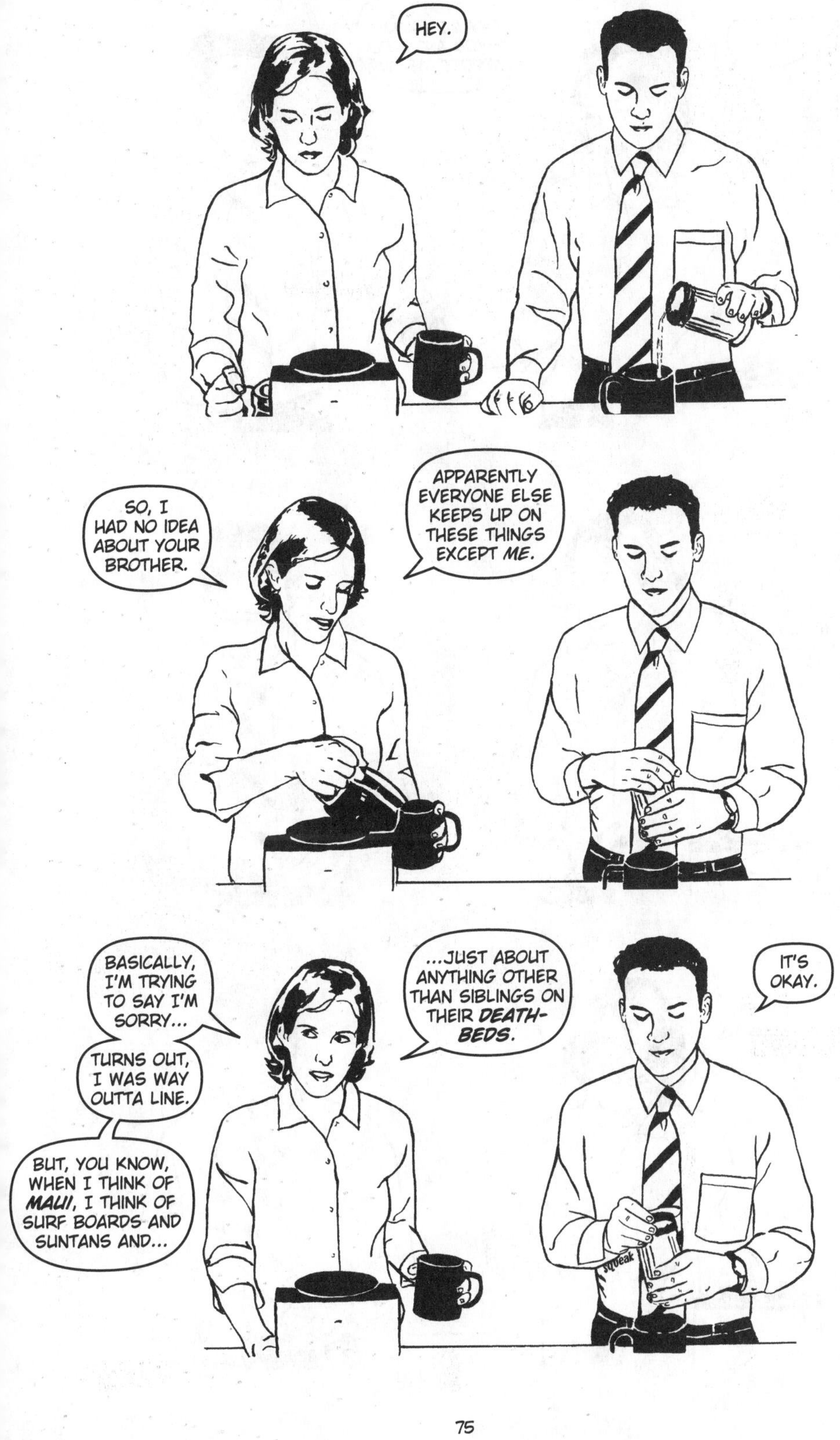
HEY.
SO, I HAD NO IDEA ABOUT YOUR BROTHER.
APPARENTLY EVERYONE ELSE KEEPS UP ON THESE THINGS EXCEPT *ME*.
BASICALLY, I'M TRYING TO SAY I'M SORRY...
TURNS OUT, I WAS WAY OUTTA LINE.
BUT, YOU KNOW, WHEN I THINK OF ***MAUI***, I THINK OF SURF BOARDS AND SUNTANS AND...
...JUST ABOUT ANYTHING OTHER THAN SIBLINGS ON THEIR ***DEATH-BEDS***.
IT'S OKAY.
squeak

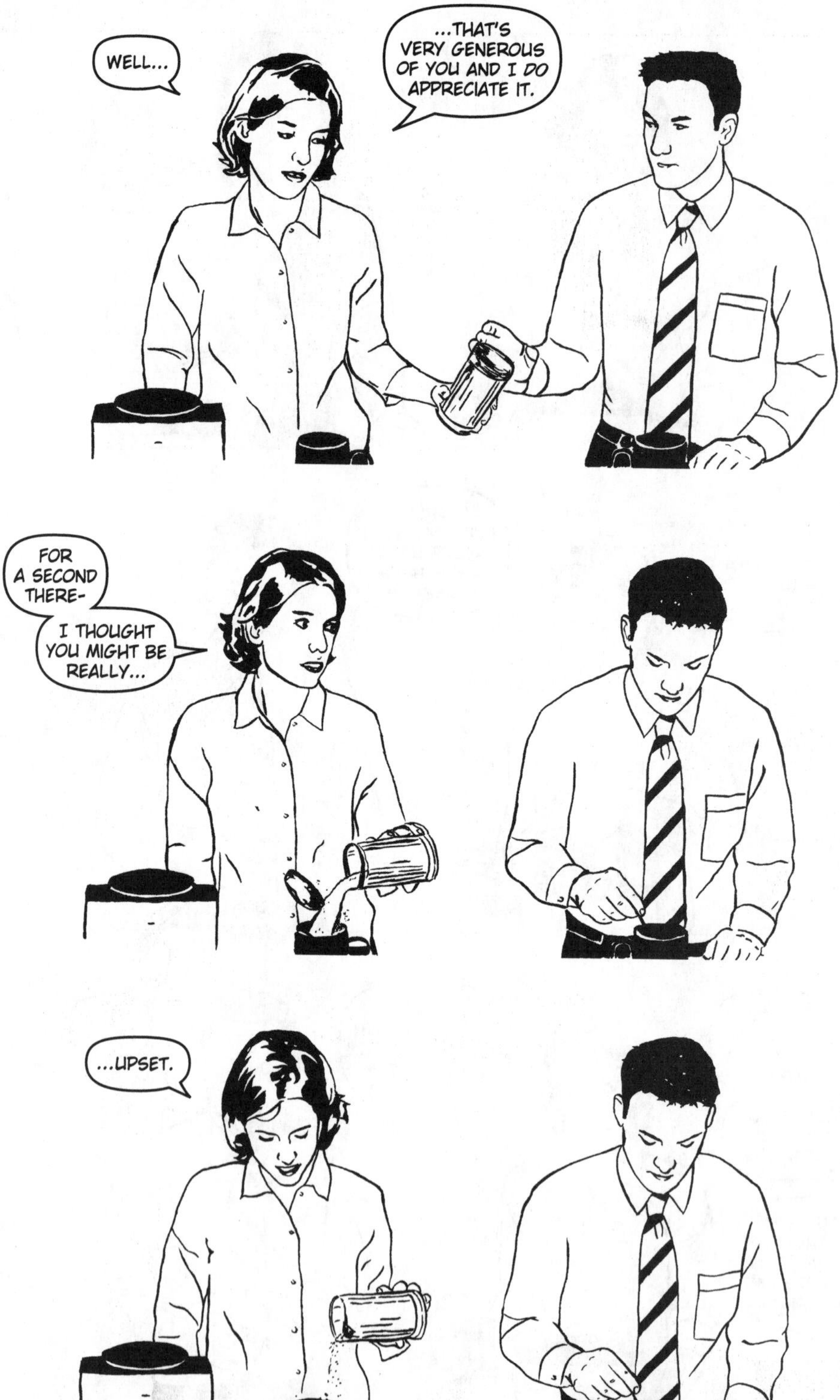
WELL...
...THAT'S VERY GENEROUS OF YOU AND I DO APPRECIATE IT.
FOR A SECOND THERE-
I THOUGHT YOU MIGHT BE REALLY...
...UPSET.

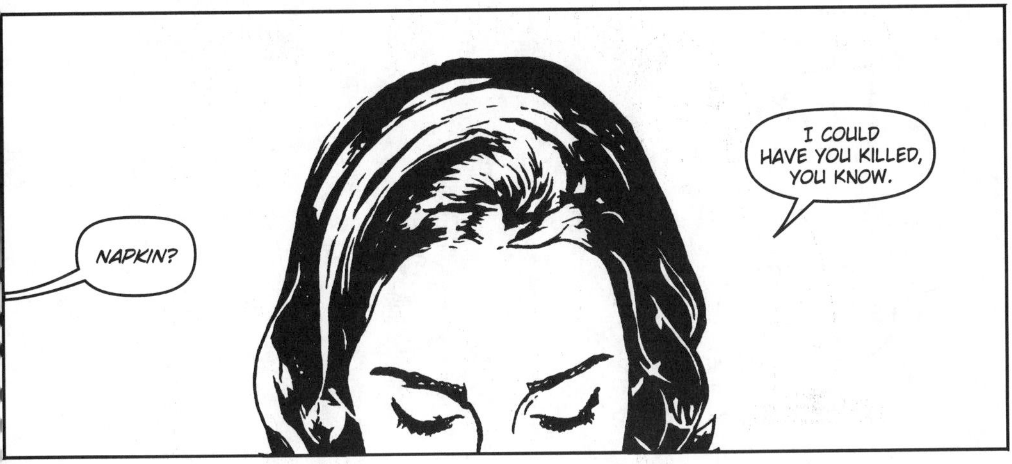
NAPKIN?
I COULD HAVE YOU KILLED, YOU KNOW.

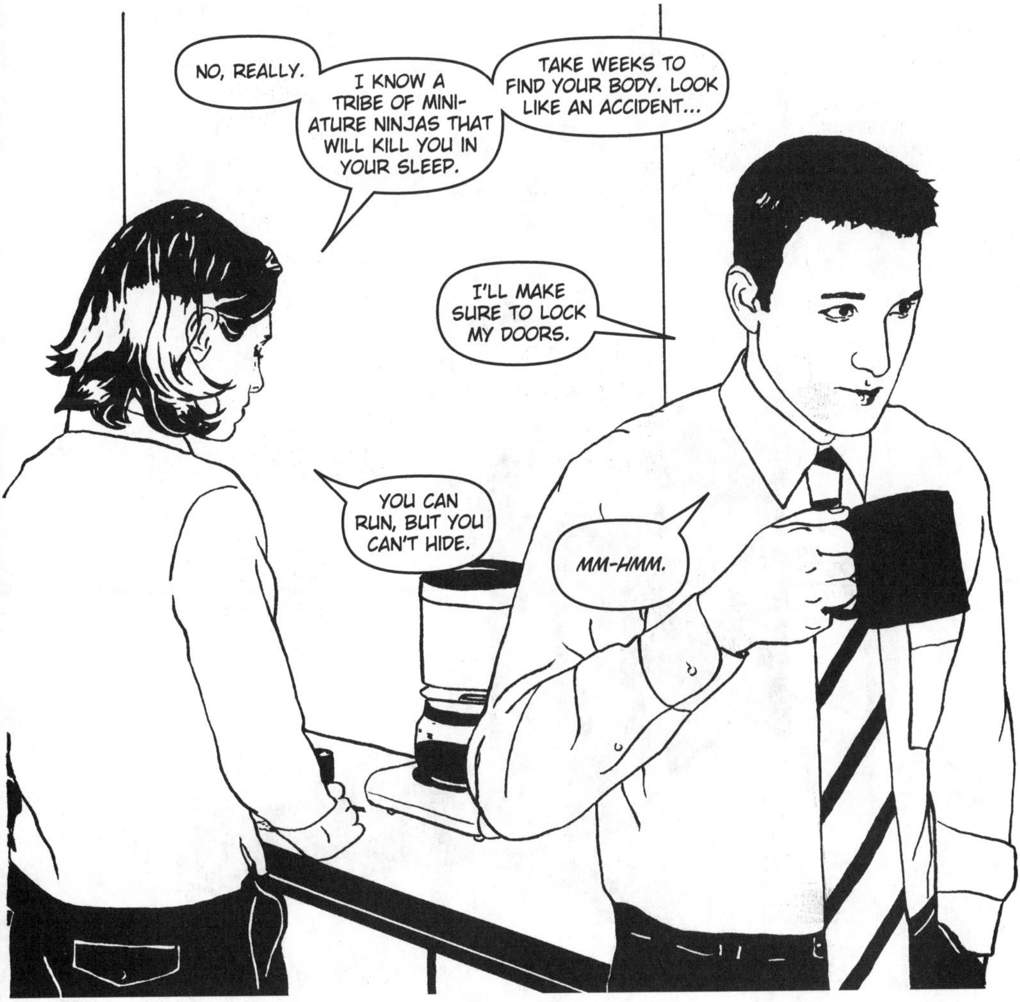
NO, REALLY.
I KNOW A TRIBE OF MINI-ATURE NINJAS THAT WILL KILL YOU IN YOUR SLEEP.
TAKE WEEKS TO FIND YOUR BODY. LOOK LIKE AN ACCIDENT...
I'LL MAKE SURE TO LOCK MY DOORS.
YOU CAN RUN, BUT YOU CAN'T HIDE.
MM-HMM.

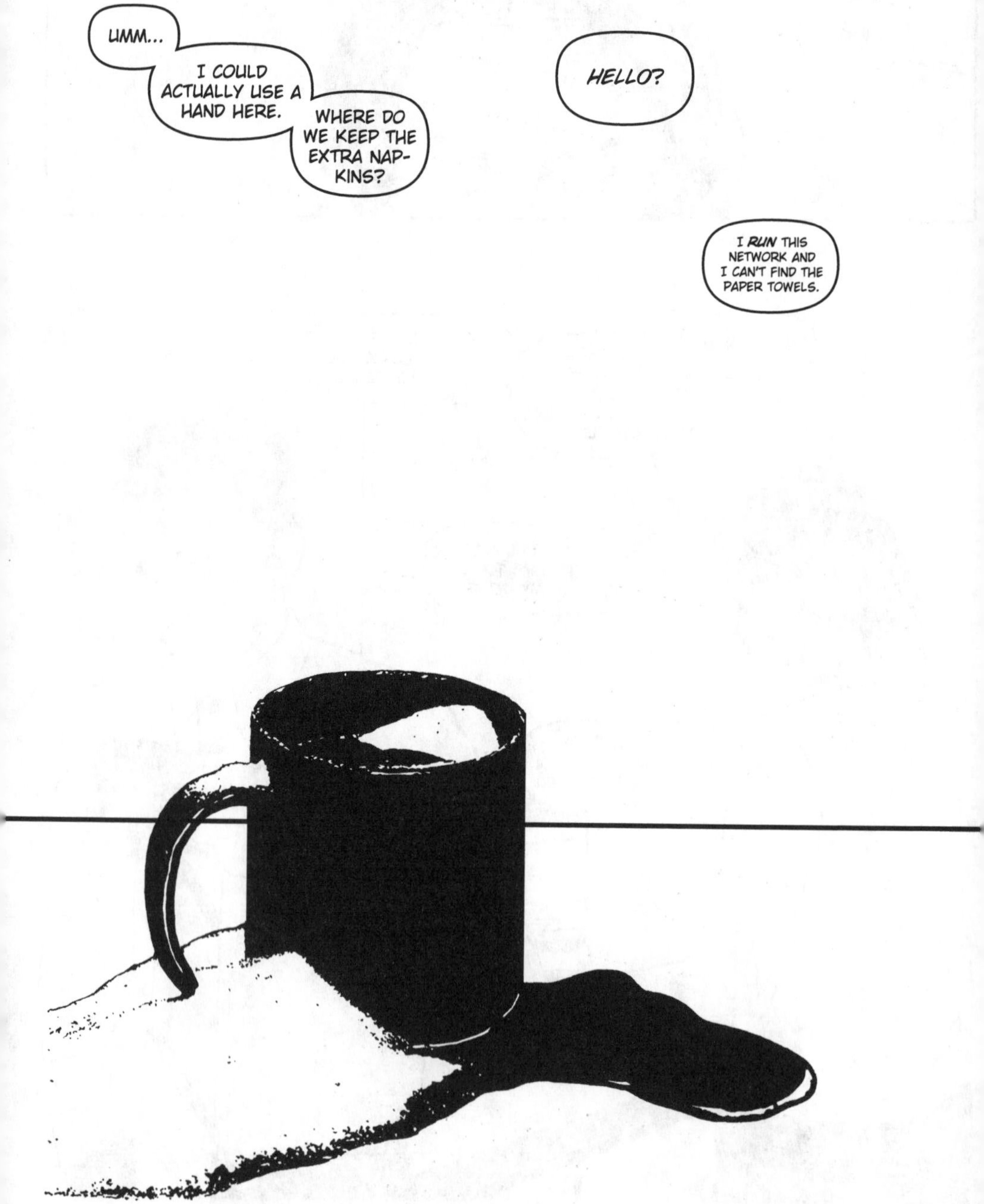
UMM...
I COULD ACTUALLY USE A HAND HERE.
WHERE DO WE KEEP THE EXTRA NAP-KINS?
HELLO?
I RUN THIS NETWORK AND I CAN'T FIND THE PAPER TOWELS.

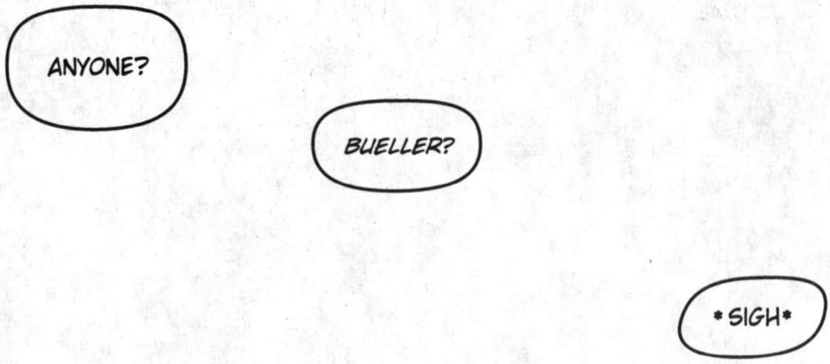
ANYONE?
BUELLER?
SIGH

3

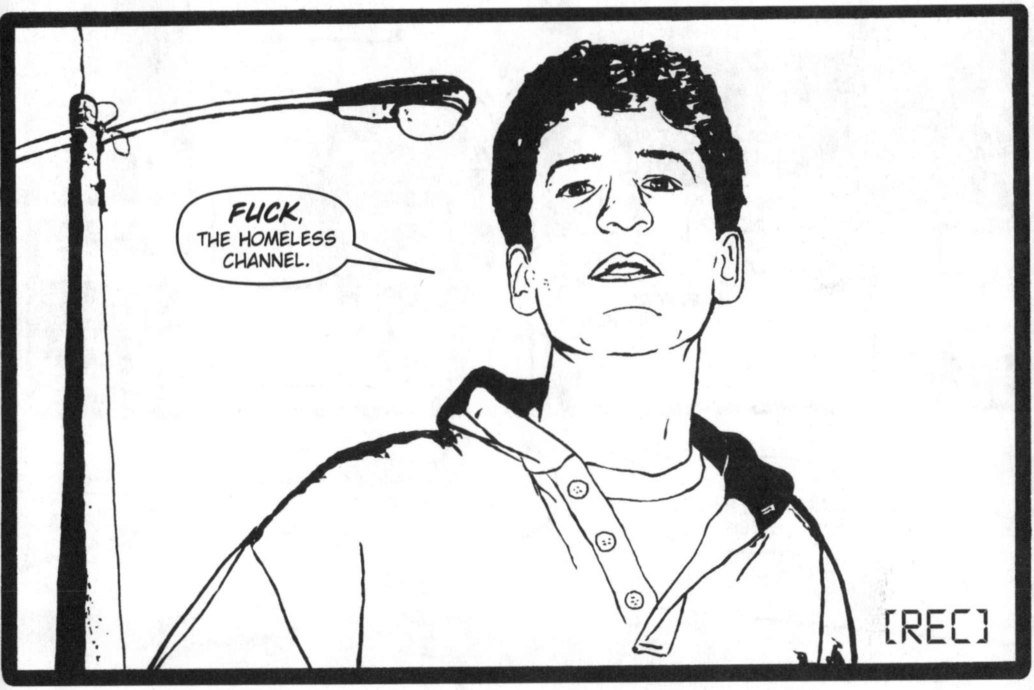
FUCK, THE HOMELESS CHANNEL.
[REC]

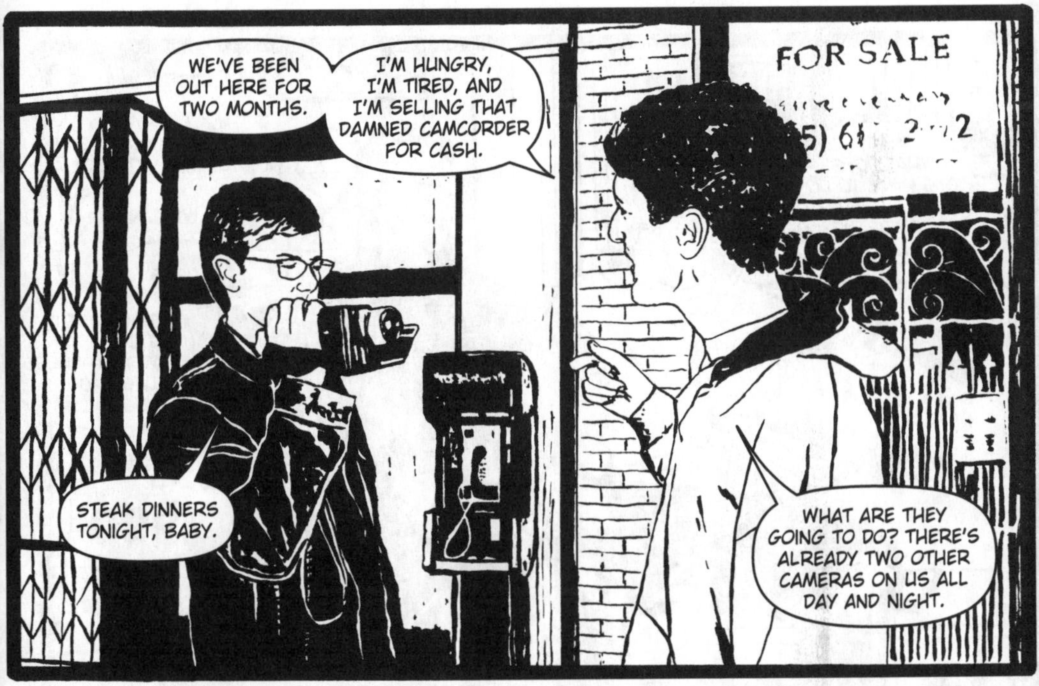
WE'VE BEEN OUT HERE FOR TWO MONTHS.
I'M HUNGRY, I'M TIRED, AND I'M SELLING THAT DAMNED CAMCORDER FOR CASH.
FOR SALE
STEAK DINNERS TONIGHT, BABY.
WHAT ARE THEY GOING TO DO? THERE'S ALREADY TWO OTHER CAMERAS ON US ALL DAY AND NIGHT.

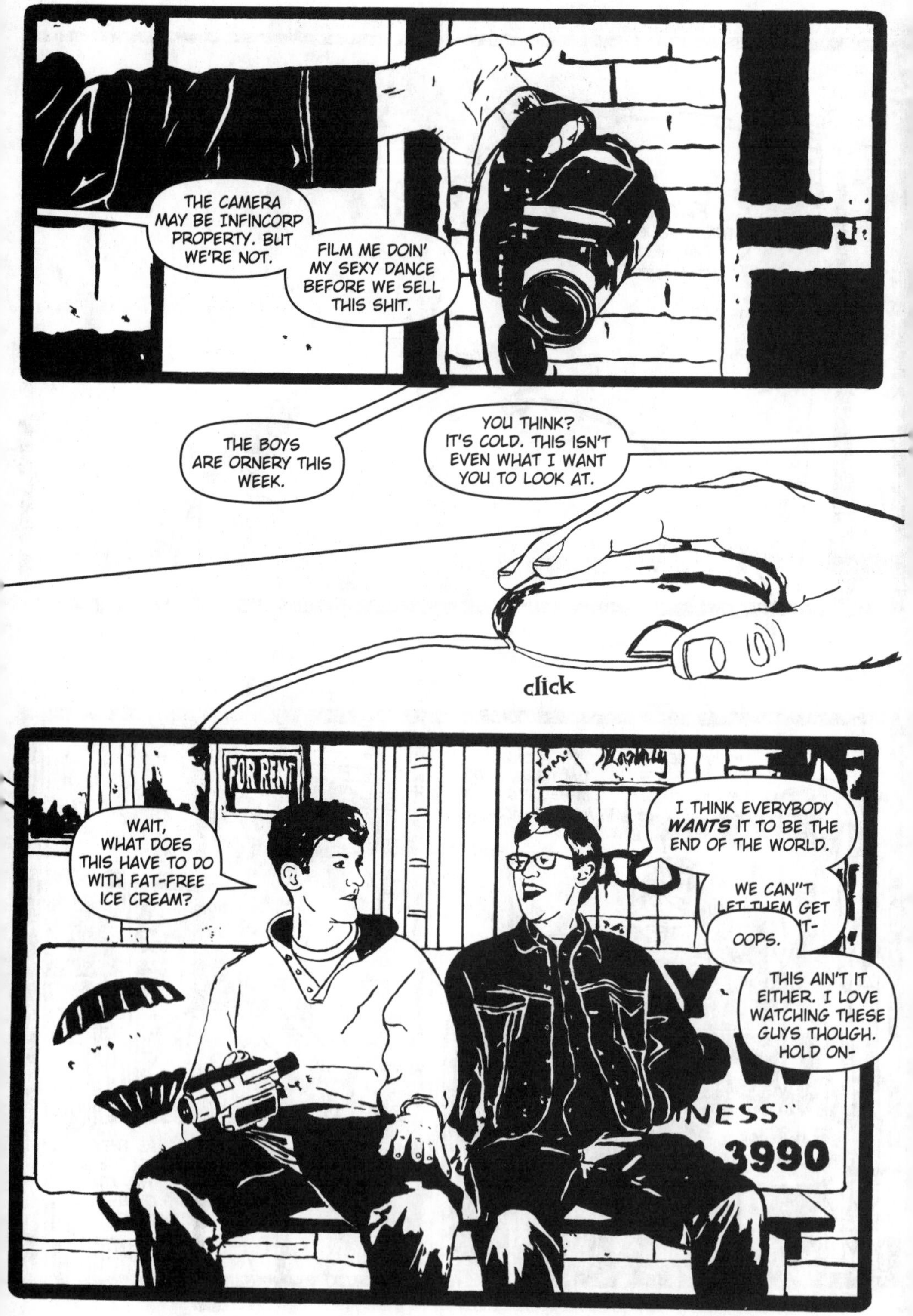
THE CAMERA MAY BE INFINCORP PROPERTY. BUT WE'RE NOT.
FILM ME DOIN' MY SEXY DANCE BEFORE WE SELL THIS SHIT.
THE BOYS ARE ORNERY THIS WEEK.
YOU THINK? IT'S COLD. THIS ISN'T EVEN WHAT I WANT YOU TO LOOK AT.
click
FOR RENT
WAIT, WHAT DOES THIS HAVE TO DO WITH FAT-FREE ICE CREAM?
I THINK EVERYBODY **WANTS** IT TO BE THE END OF THE WORLD.
WE CAN''T LET THEM GET
OOPS.
THIS AIN'T IT EITHER. I LOVE WATCHING THESE GUYS THOUGH. HOLD ON-
NESS
3990

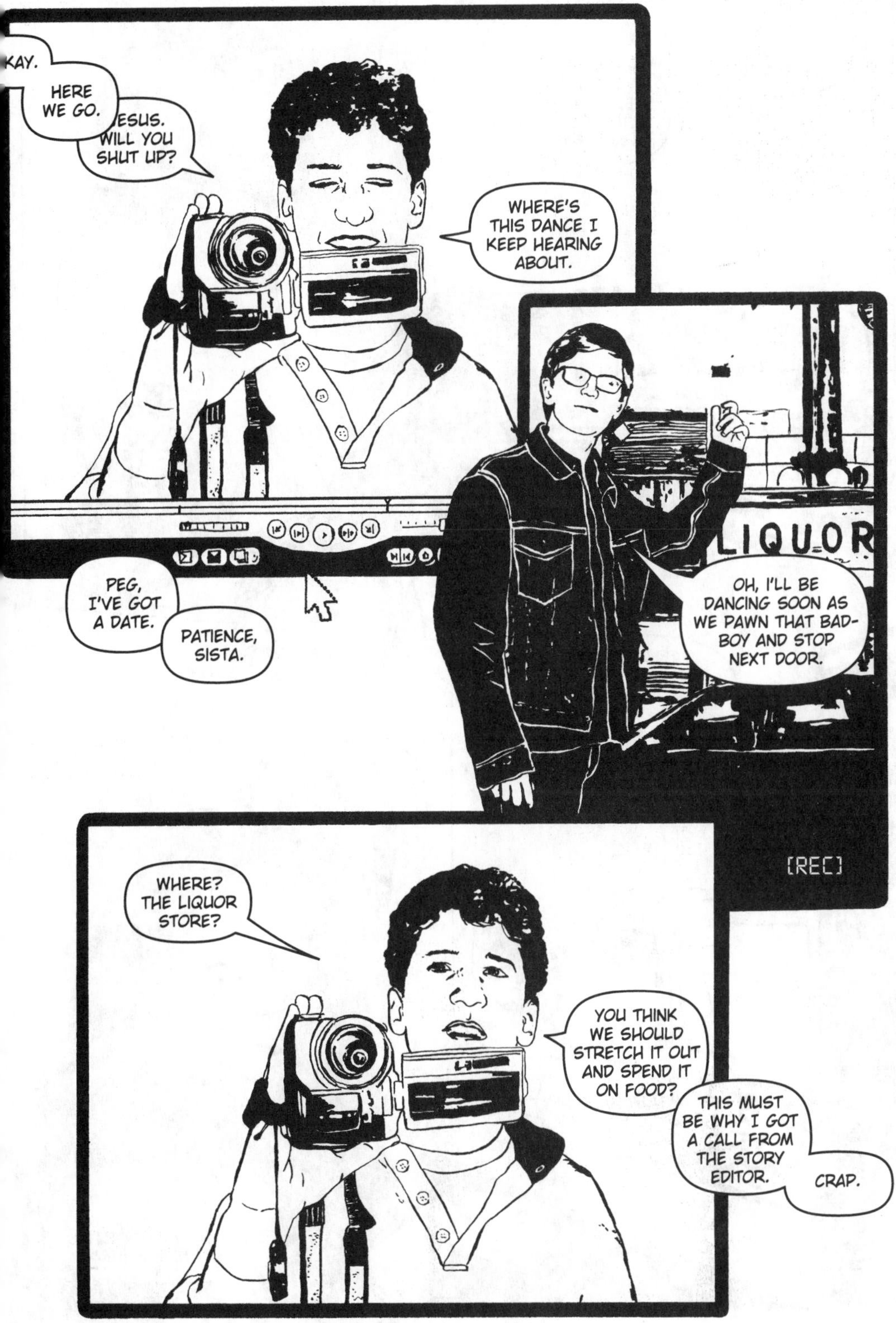
KAY.
HERE WE GO.
ESUS. WILL YOU SHUT UP?
WHERE'S THIS DANCE I KEEP HEARING ABOUT.
LIQUOR
OH, I'LL BE DANCING SOON AS WE PAWN THAT BAD-BOY AND STOP NEXT DOOR.
PEG, I'VE GOT A DATE.
PATIENCE, SISTA.
[REC]
WHERE? THE LIQUOR STORE?
YOU THINK WE SHOULD STRETCH IT OUT AND SPEND IT ON FOOD?
THIS MUST BE WHY I GOT A CALL FROM THE STORY EDITOR.
CRAP.

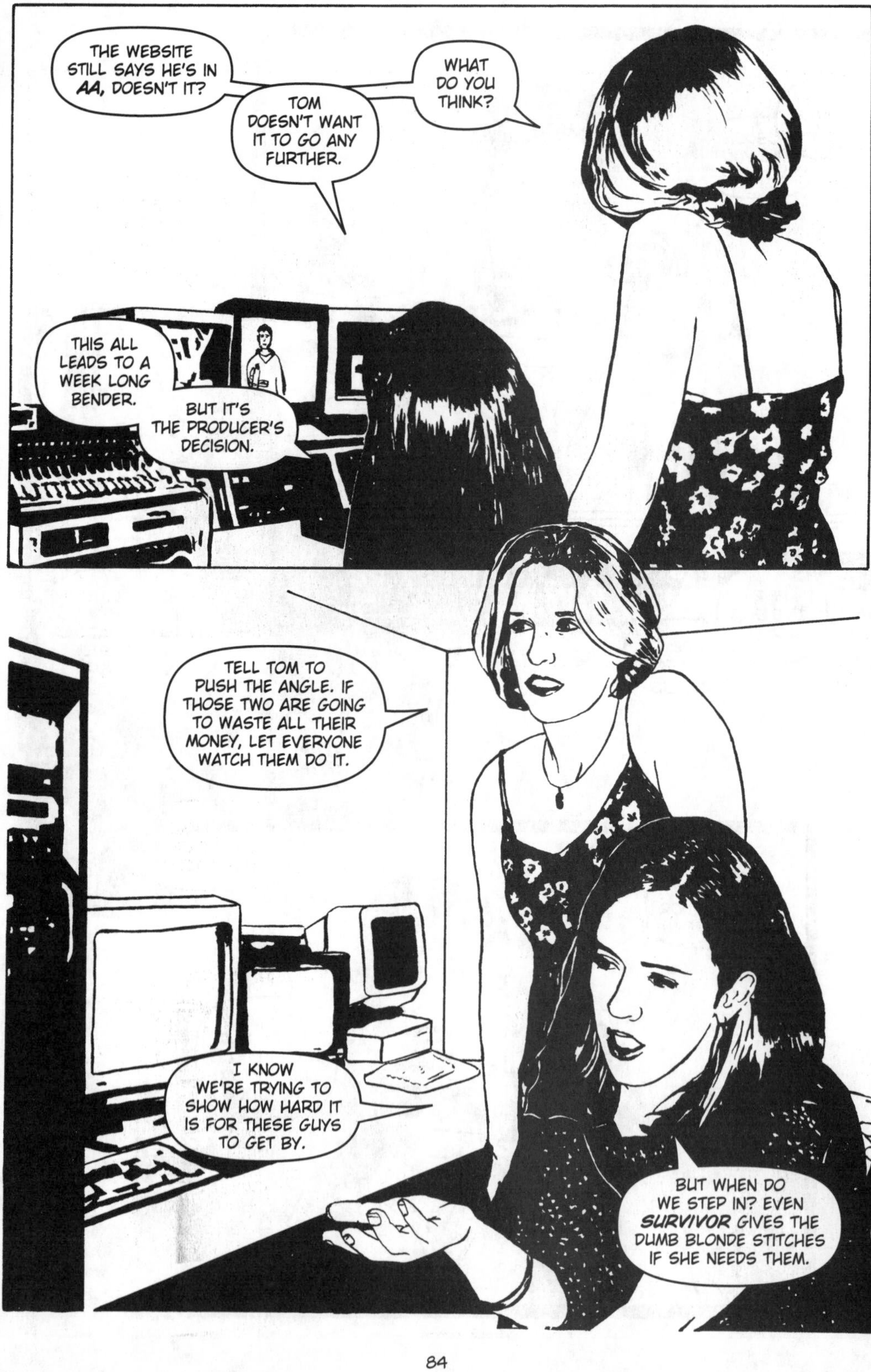
THE WEBSITE STILL SAYS HE'S IN *AA,* DOESN'T IT?
TOM DOESN'T WANT IT TO GO ANY FURTHER.
WHAT DO YOU THINK?
THIS ALL LEADS TO A WEEK LONG BENDER.
BUT IT'S THE PRODUCER'S DECISION.
TELL TOM TO PUSH THE ANGLE. IF THOSE TWO ARE GOING TO WASTE ALL THEIR MONEY, LET EVERYONE WATCH THEM DO IT.
I KNOW WE'RE TRYING TO SHOW HOW HARD IT IS FOR THESE GUYS TO GET BY.
BUT WHEN DO WE STEP IN? EVEN ***SURVIVOR*** GIVES THE DUMB BLONDE STITCHES IF SHE NEEDS THEM.

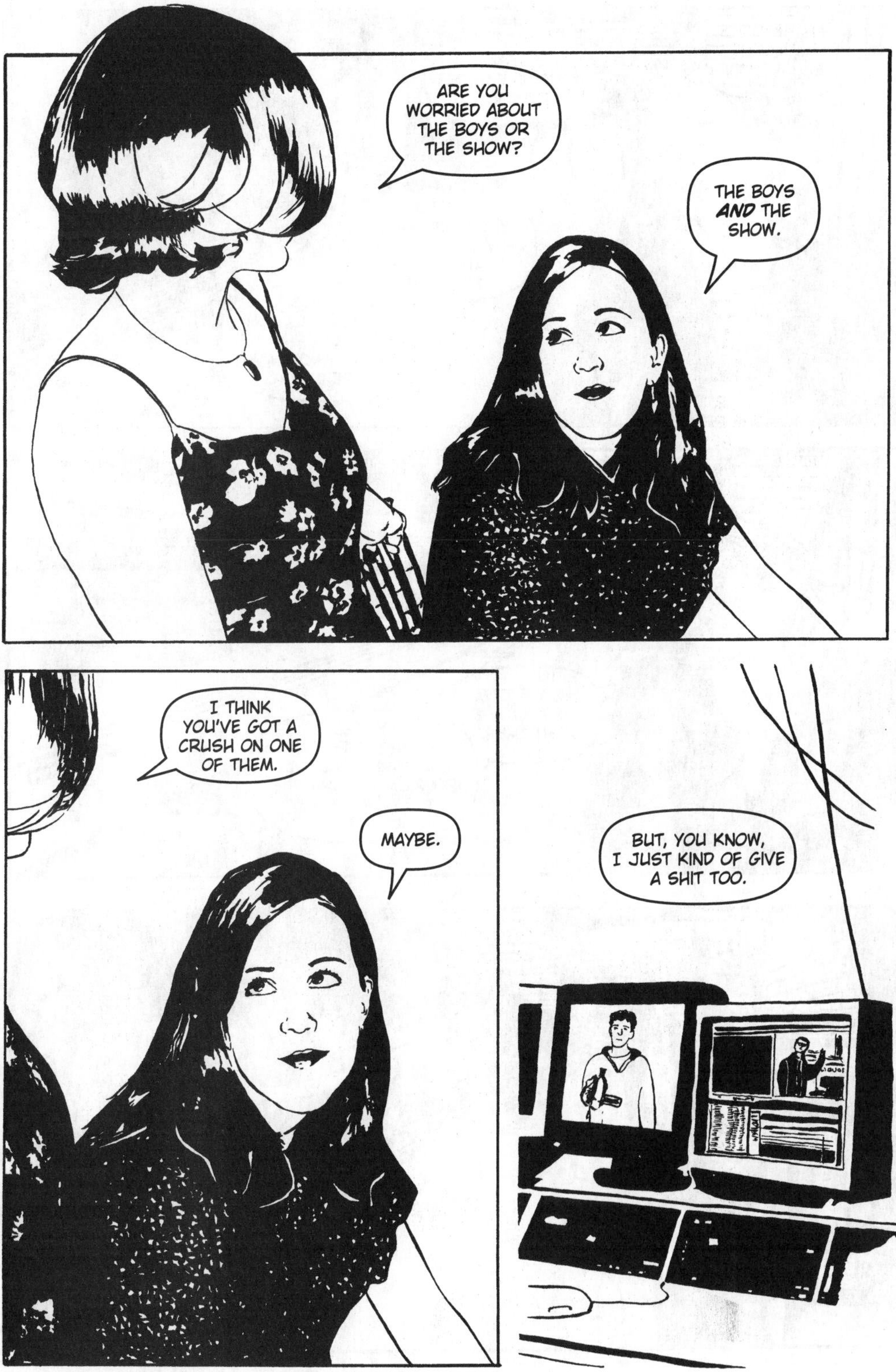
ARE YOU WORRIED ABOUT THE BOYS OR THE SHOW?
THE BOYS **AND** THE SHOW.
I THINK YOU'VE GOT A CRUSH ON ONE OF THEM.
MAYBE.
BUT, YOU KNOW, I JUST KIND OF GIVE A SHIT TOO.

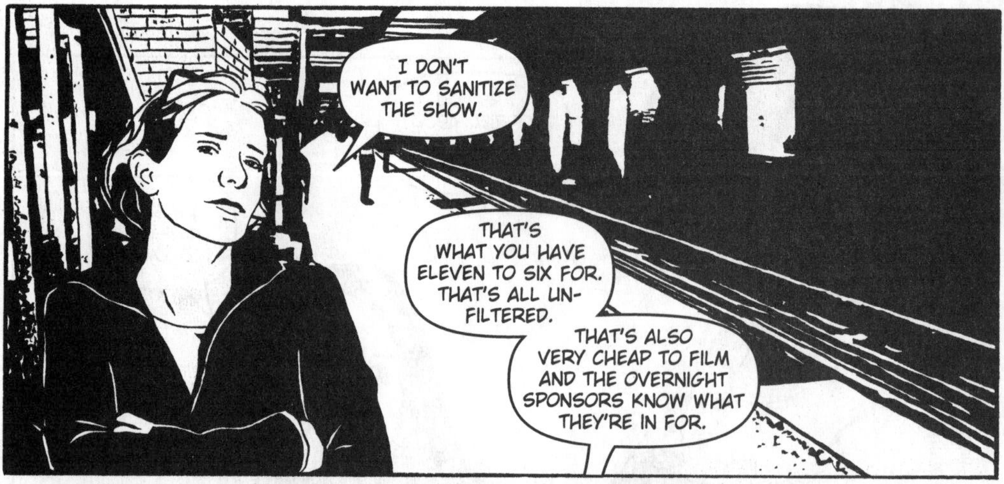
I DON'T WANT TO SANITIZE THE SHOW.
THAT'S WHAT YOU HAVE ELEVEN TO SIX FOR. THAT'S ALL UN-FILTERED.
THAT'S ALSO VERY CHEAP TO FILM AND THE OVERNIGHT SPONSORS KNOW WHAT THEY'RE IN FOR.

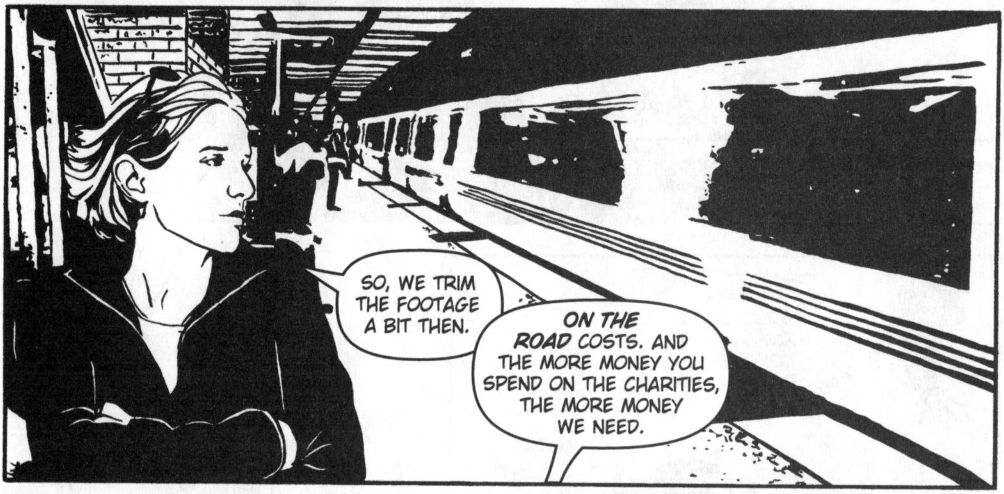
SO, WE TRIM THE FOOTAGE A BIT THEN.
ON THE ROAD COSTS. AND THE MORE MONEY YOU SPEND ON THE CHARITIES, THE MORE MONEY WE NEED.

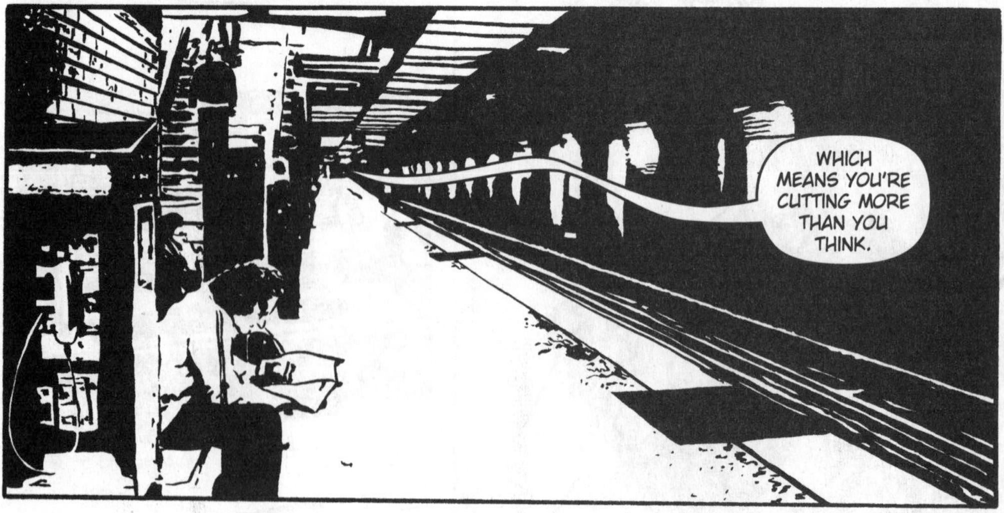
WHICH MEANS YOU'RE CUTTING MORE THAN YOU THINK.

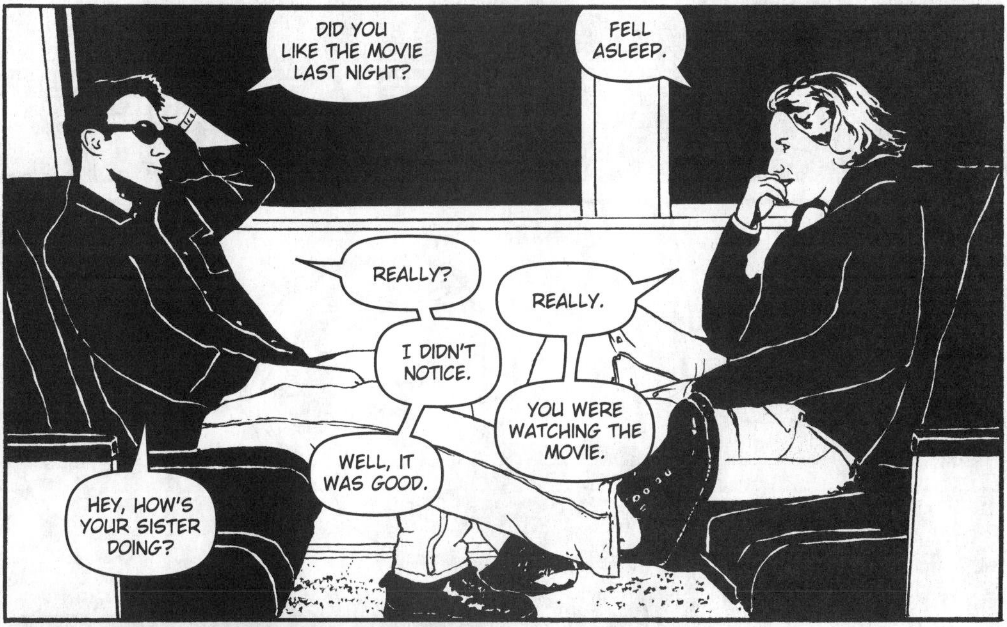
DID YOU LIKE THE MOVIE LAST NIGHT?
FELL ASLEEP.
REALLY?
REALLY.
I DIDN'T NOTICE.
YOU WERE WATCHING THE MOVIE.
WELL, IT WAS GOOD.
HEY, HOW'S YOUR SISTER DOING?

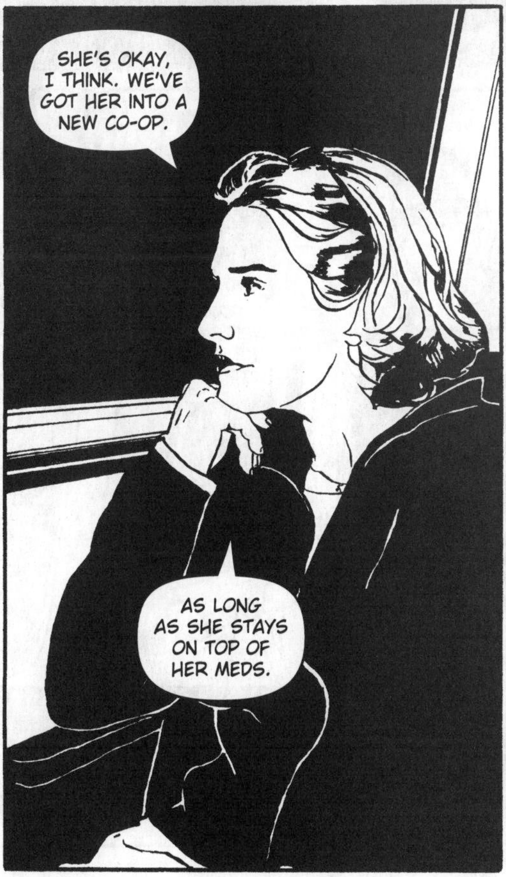
SHE'S OKAY, I THINK. WE'VE GOT HER INTO A NEW CO-OP.
AS LONG AS SHE STAYS ON TOP OF HER MEDS.

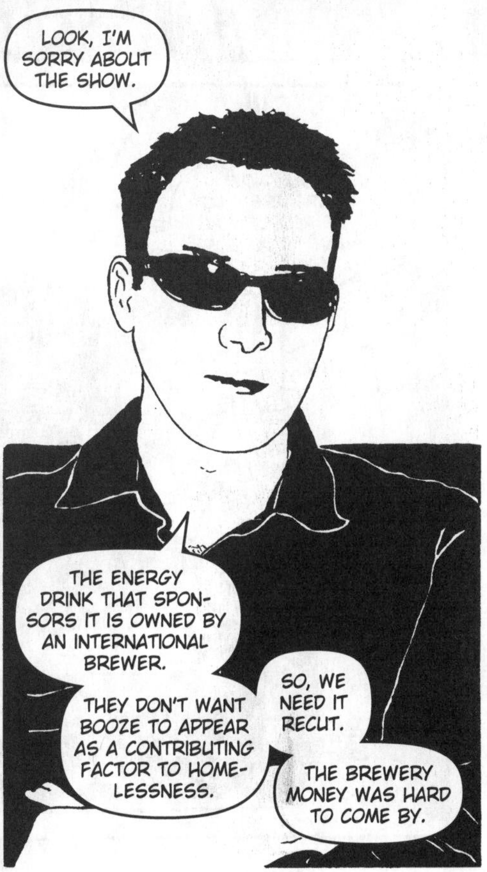
LOOK, I'M SORRY ABOUT THE SHOW.
THE ENERGY DRINK THAT SPON-SORS IT IS OWNED BY AN INTERNATIONAL BREWER.
THEY DON'T WANT BOOZE TO APPEAR AS A CONTRIBUTING FACTOR TO HOME-LESSNESS.
SO, WE NEED IT RECUT.
THE BREWERY MONEY WAS HARD TO COME BY.

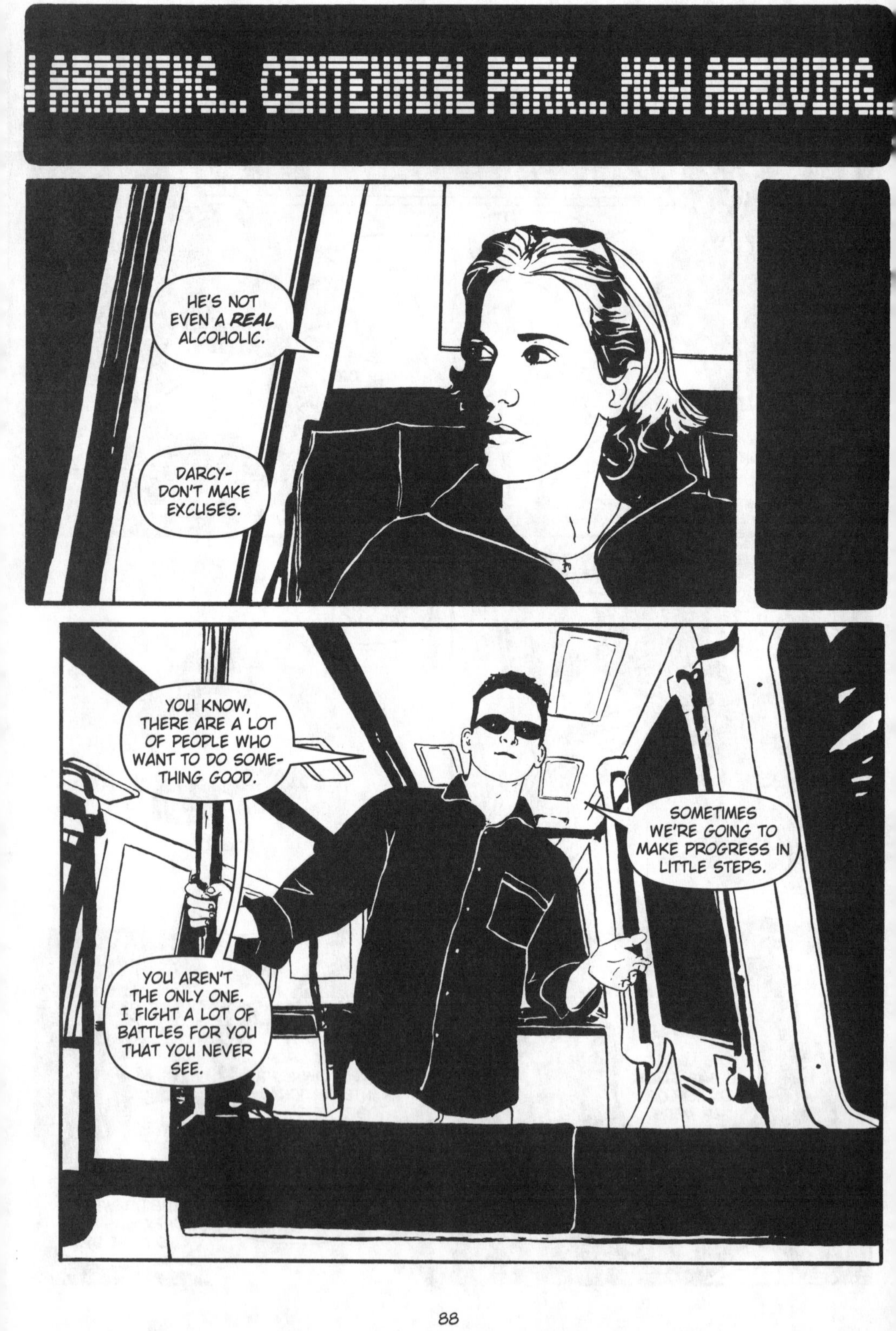

N ARRIVING... CENTENNIAL PARK... NOW ARRIVING...
HE'S NOT EVEN A *REAL* ALCOHOLIC.
DARCY- DON'T MAKE EXCUSES.
YOU KNOW, THERE ARE A LOT OF PEOPLE WHO WANT TO DO SOME-THING GOOD.
YOU AREN'T THE ONLY ONE. I FIGHT A LOT OF BATTLES FOR YOU THAT YOU NEVER SEE.
SOMETIMES WE'RE GOING TO MAKE PROGRESS IN LITTLE STEPS.

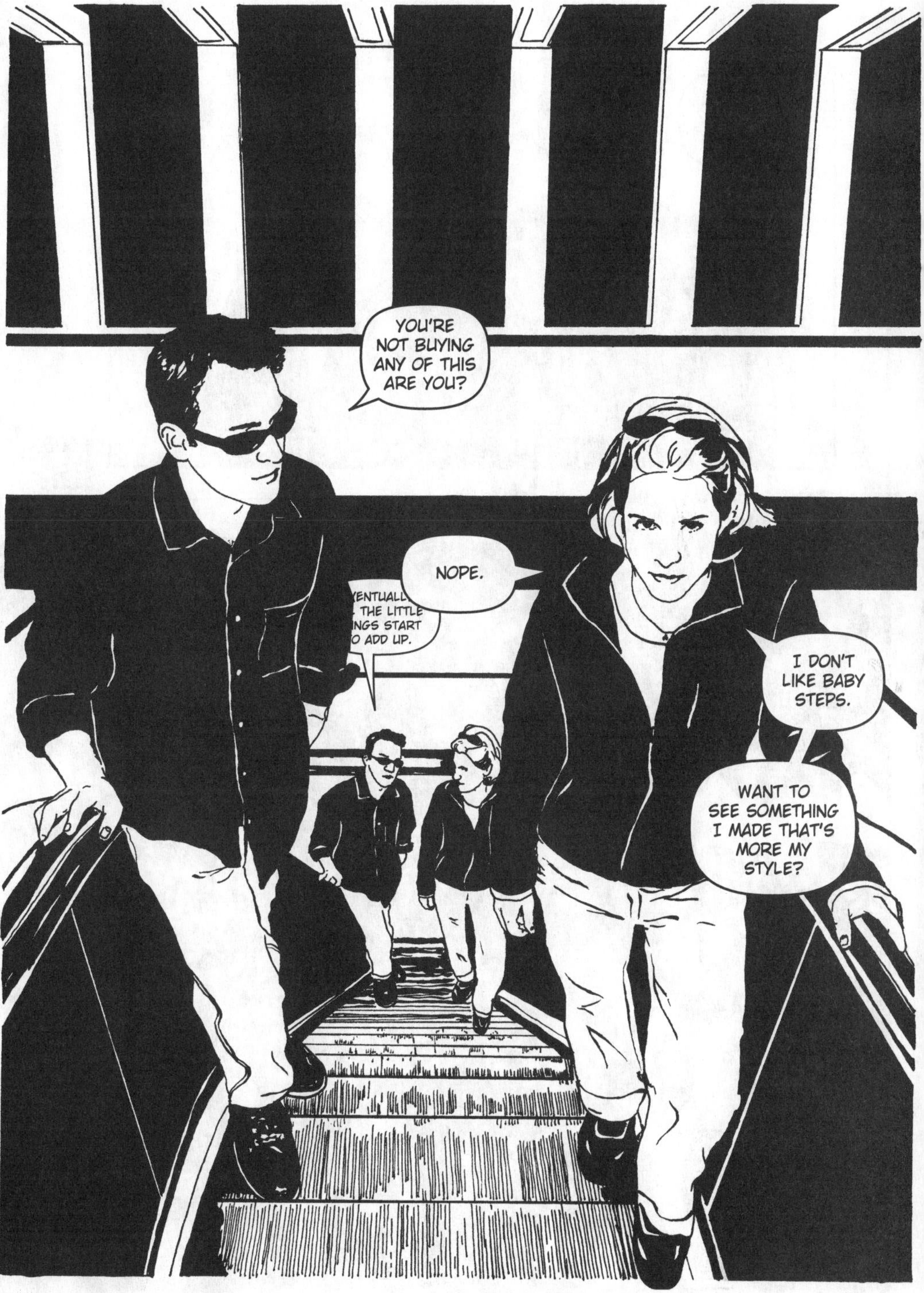
YOU'RE NOT BUYING ANY OF THIS ARE YOU?
ENTUALL
THE LITTLE
NGS START
O ADD UP.
NOPE.
I DON'T LIKE BABY STEPS.
WANT TO SEE SOMETHING I MADE THAT'S MORE MY STYLE?

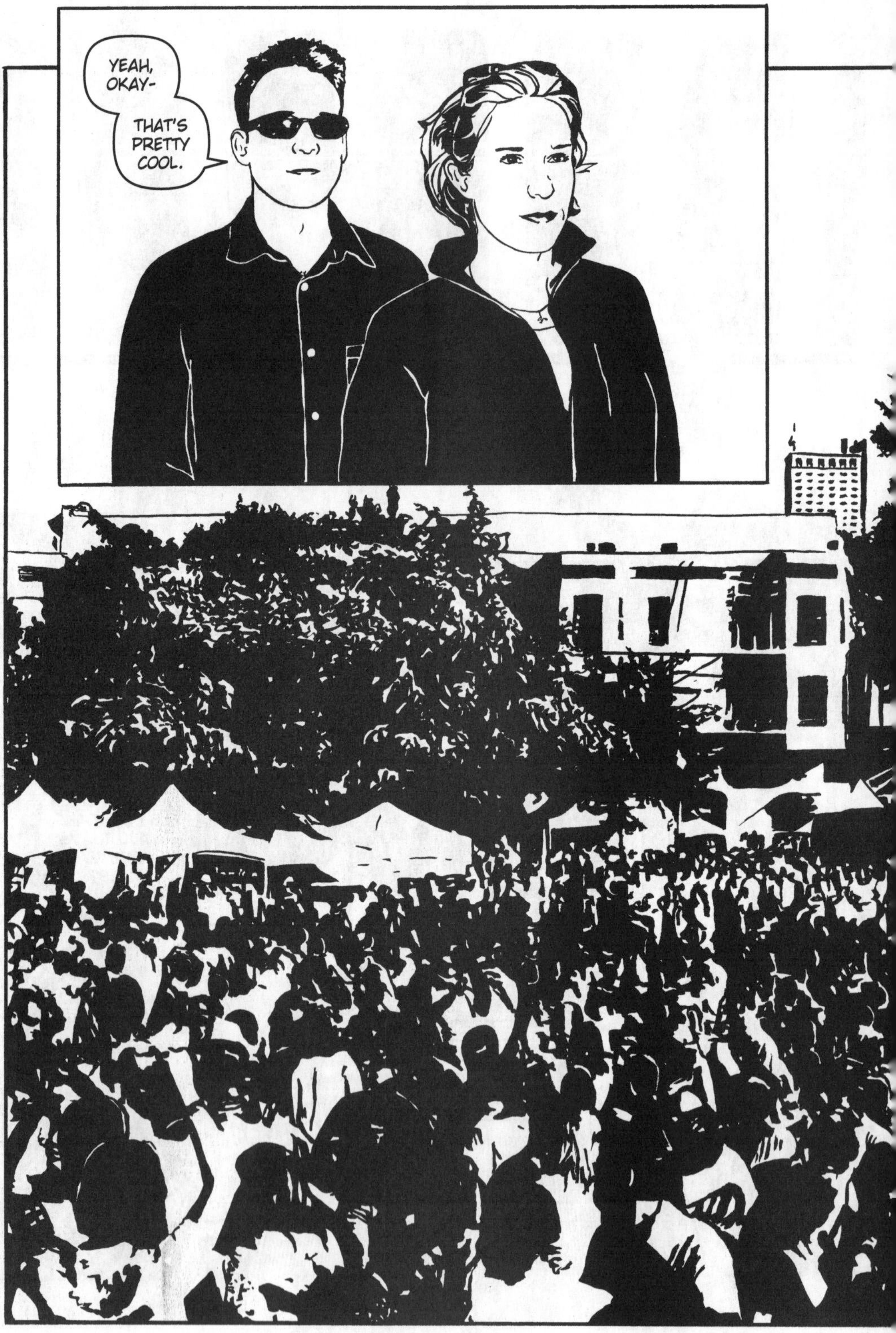
YEAH, OKAY-
THAT'S PRETTY COOL.

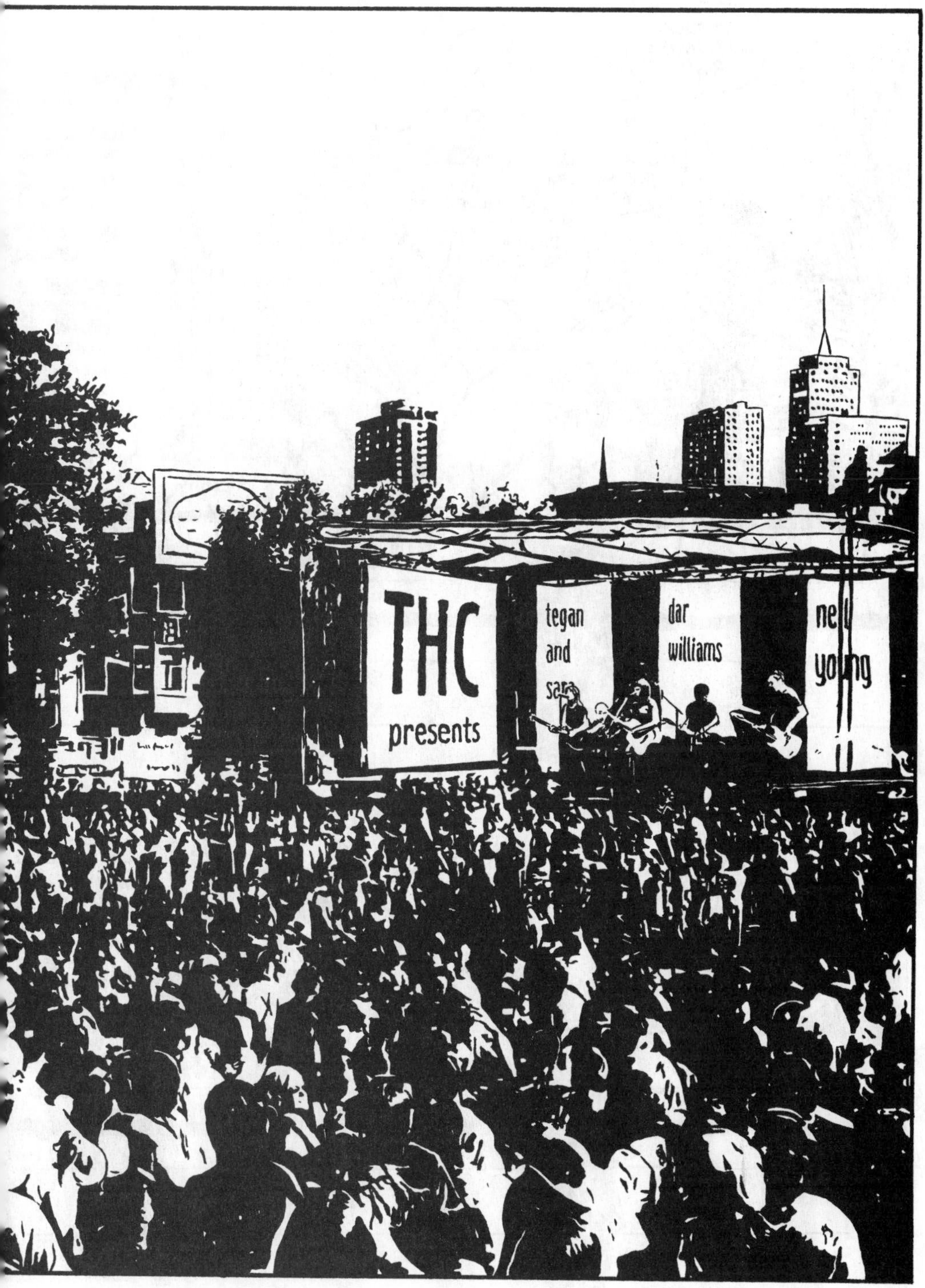
THC
presents
tegan
and
sara
dar
williams
neil
young

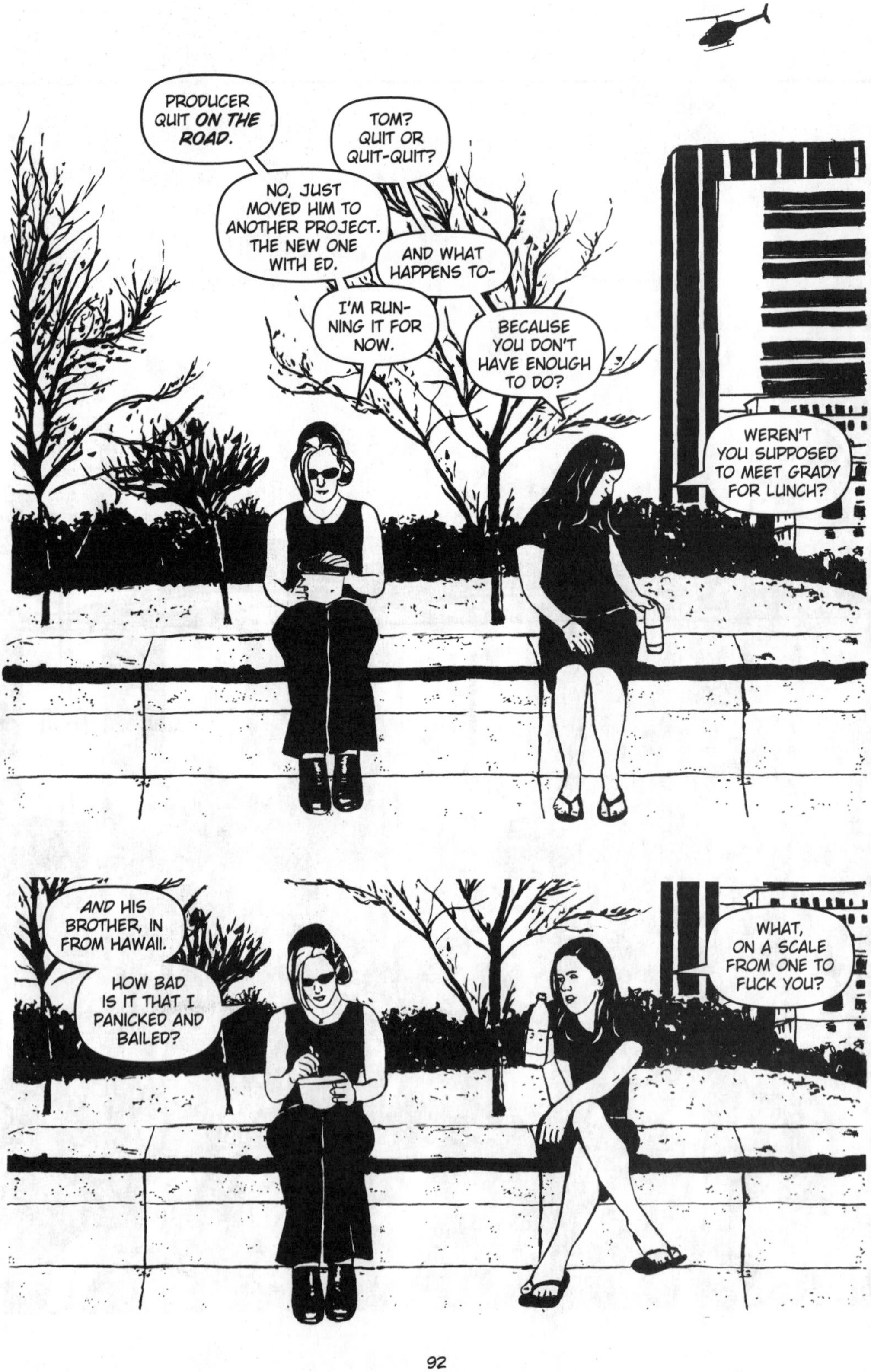
PRODUCER QUIT *ON THE ROAD.*
TOM? QUIT OR QUIT-QUIT?
NO, JUST MOVED HIM TO ANOTHER PROJECT. THE NEW ONE WITH ED.
AND WHAT HAPPENS TO-
I'M RUN-NING IT FOR NOW.
BECAUSE YOU DON'T HAVE ENOUGH TO DO?
WEREN'T YOU SUPPOSED TO MEET GRADY FOR LUNCH?
AND HIS BROTHER, IN FROM HAWAII.
HOW BAD IS IT THAT I PANICKED AND BAILED?
WHAT, ON A SCALE FROM ONE TO FUCK YOU?

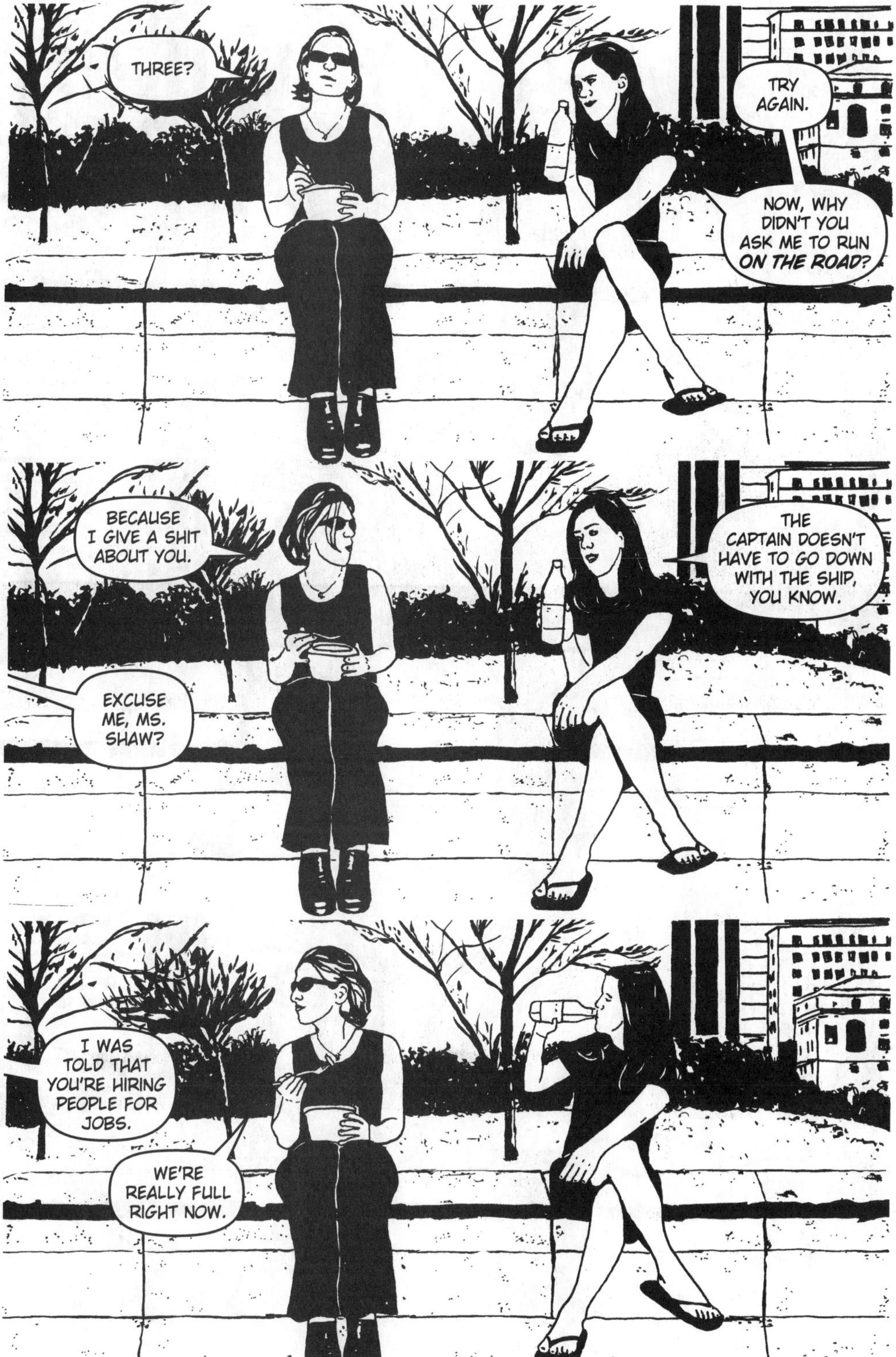
THREE?
TRY AGAIN.
NOW, WHY DIDN'T YOU ASK ME TO RUN ON THE ROAD?
BECAUSE I GIVE A SHIT ABOUT YOU.
THE CAPTAIN DOESN'T HAVE TO GO DOWN WITH THE SHIP, YOU KNOW.
EXCUSE ME, MS. SHAW?
I WAS TOLD THAT YOU'RE HIRING PEOPLE FOR JOBS.
WE'RE REALLY FULL RIGHT NOW.

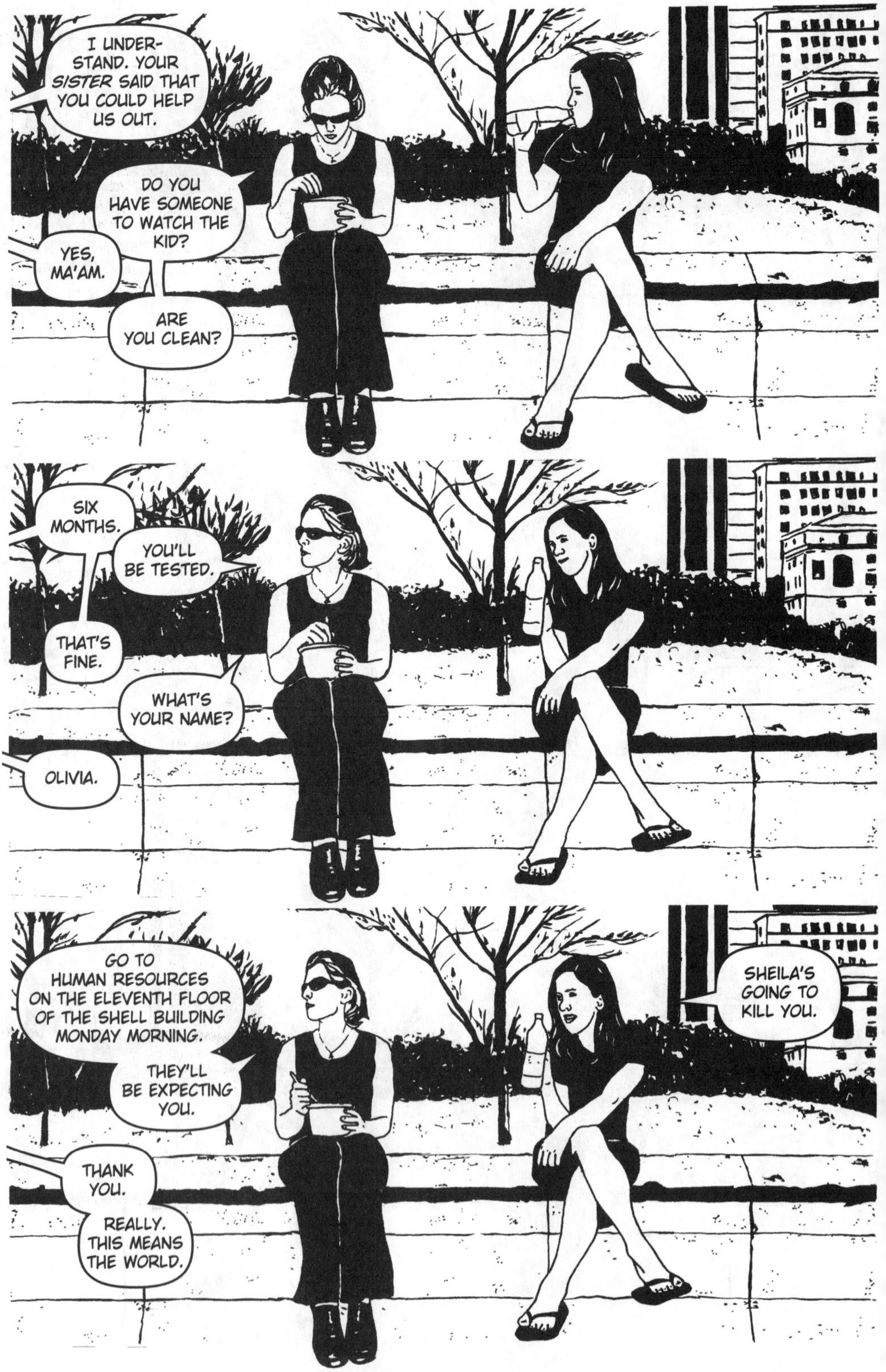

I UNDERSTAND. YOUR SISTER SAID THAT YOU COULD HELP US OUT.
DO YOU HAVE SOMEONE TO WATCH THE KID?
YES, MA'AM.
ARE YOU CLEAN?
SIX MONTHS.
YOU'LL BE TESTED.
THAT'S FINE.
WHAT'S YOUR NAME?
OLIVIA.
GO TO HUMAN RESOURCES ON THE ELEVENTH FLOOR OF THE SHELL BUILDING MONDAY MORNING.
THEY'LL BE EXPECTING YOU.
SHEILA'S GOING TO KILL YOU.
THANK YOU.
REALLY. THIS MEANS THE WORLD.

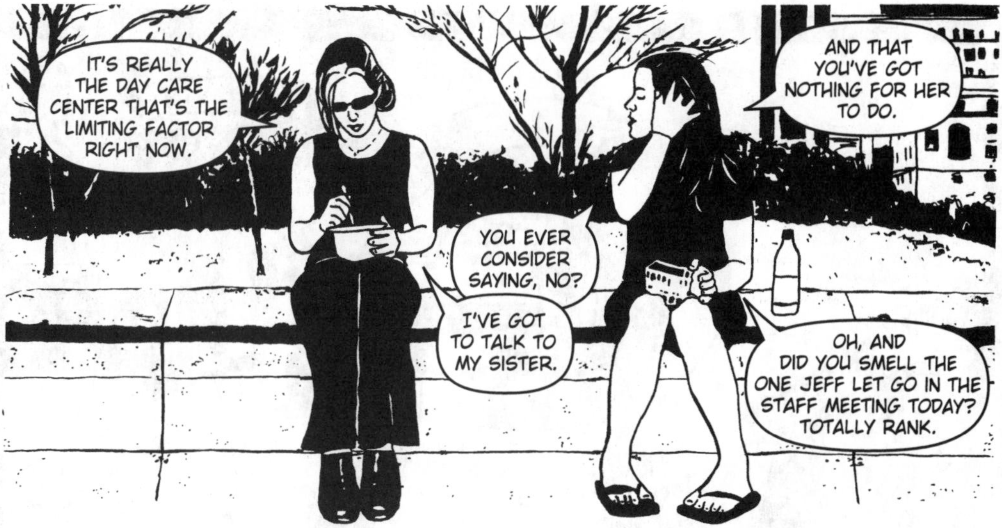
IT'S REALLY THE DAY CARE CENTER THAT'S THE LIMITING FACTOR RIGHT NOW.
AND THAT YOU'VE GOT NOTHING FOR HER TO DO.
YOU EVER CONSIDER SAYING, NO?
I'VE GOT TO TALK TO MY SISTER.
OH, AND DID YOU SMELL THE ONE JEFF LET GO IN THE STAFF MEETING TODAY? TOTALLY RANK.

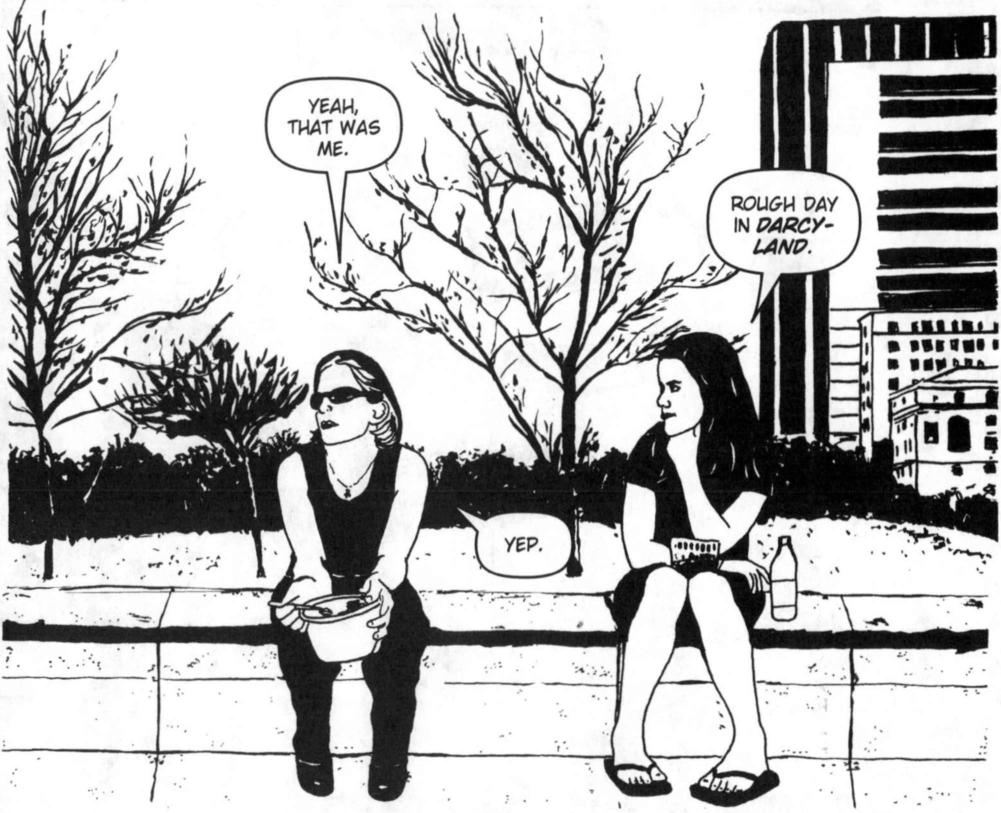
YEAH, THAT WAS ME.
ROUGH DAY IN *DARCY-LAND*.
YEP.

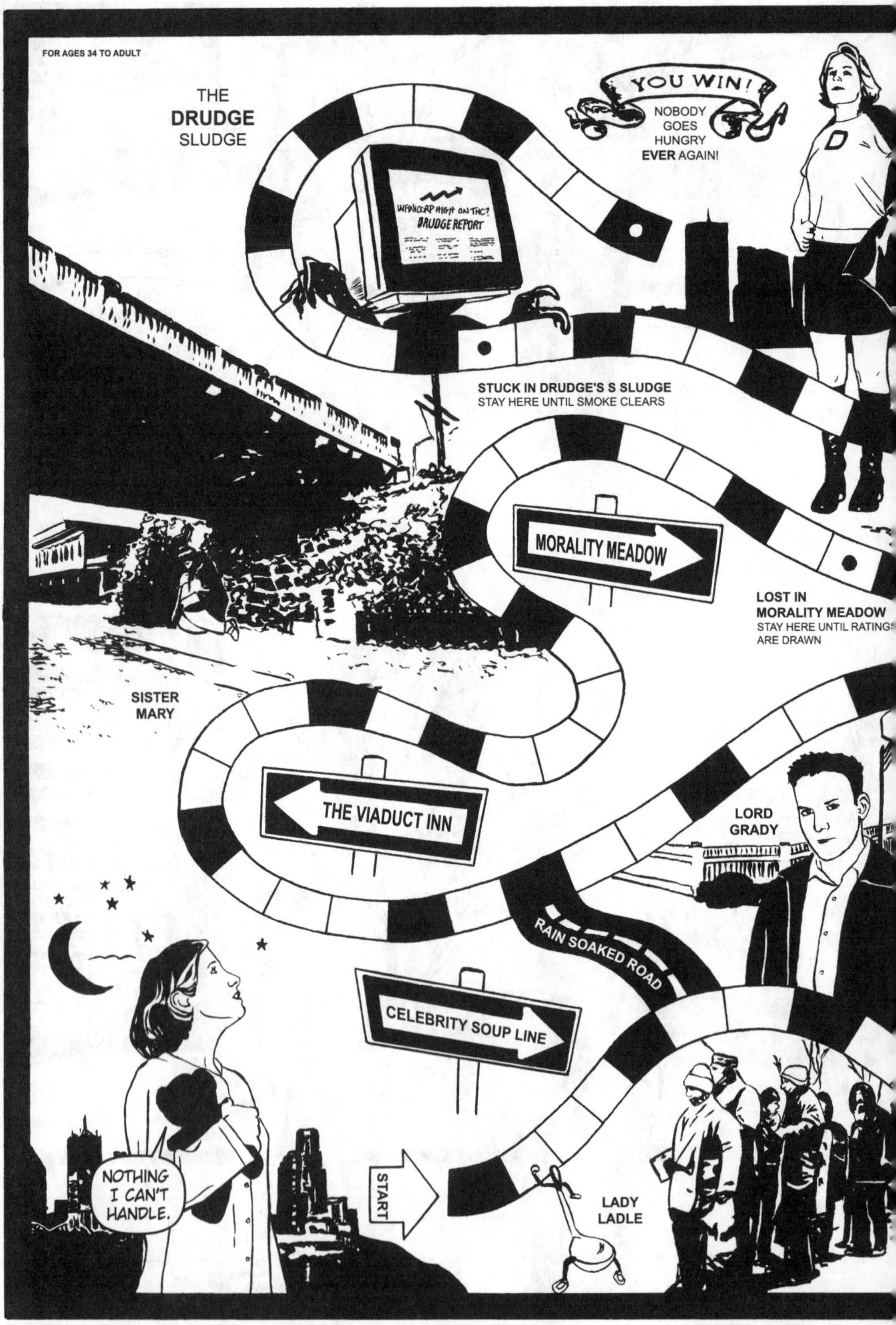

FOR AGES 34 TO ADULT
THE DRUDGE SLUDGE
YOU WIN!
NOBODY GOES HUNGRY EVER AGAIN!
INFAXCORP HIGH ON THC?
DRUDGE REPORT
STUCK IN DRUDGE'S S SLUDGE
STAY HERE UNTIL SMOKE CLEARS
MORALITY MEADOW
LOST IN MORALITY MEADOW
STAY HERE UNTIL RATINGS ARE DRAWN
SISTER MARY
THE VIADUCT INN
LORD GRADY
RAIN SOAKED ROAD
CELEBRITY SOUP LINE
NOTHING I CAN'T HANDLE.
START
LADY LADLE

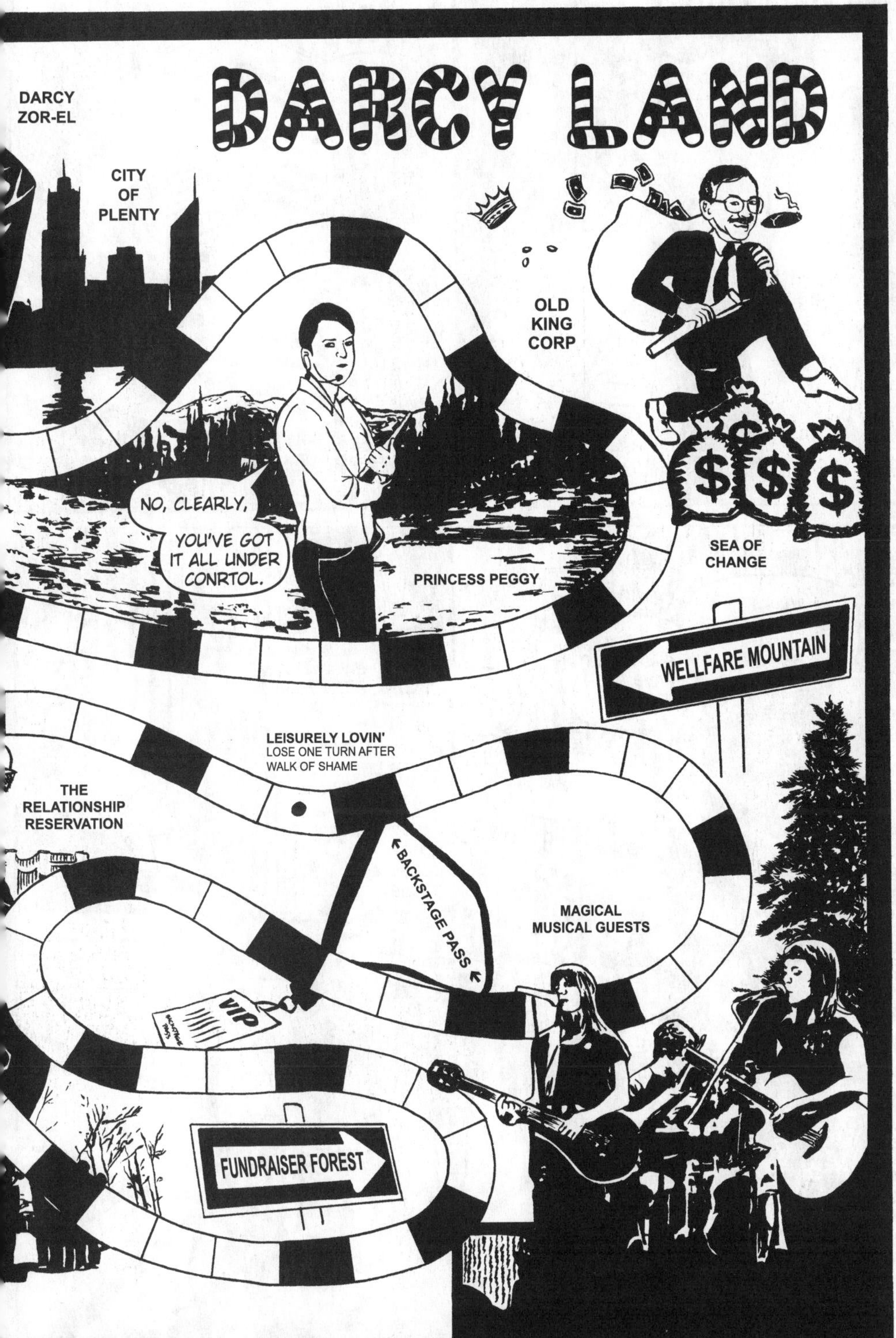
DARCY LAND
DARCY ZOR-EL
CITY OF PLENTY
OLD KING CORP
NO, CLEARLY, YOU'VE GOT IT ALL UNDER CONRTOL.
PRINCESS PEGGY
SEA OF CHANGE
WELLFARE MOUNTAIN
LEISURELY LOVIN'
LOSE ONE TURN AFTER WALK OF SHAME
THE RELATIONSHIP RESERVATION
BACKSTAGE PASS
MAGICAL MUSICAL GUESTS
VIP
FUNDRAISER FOREST

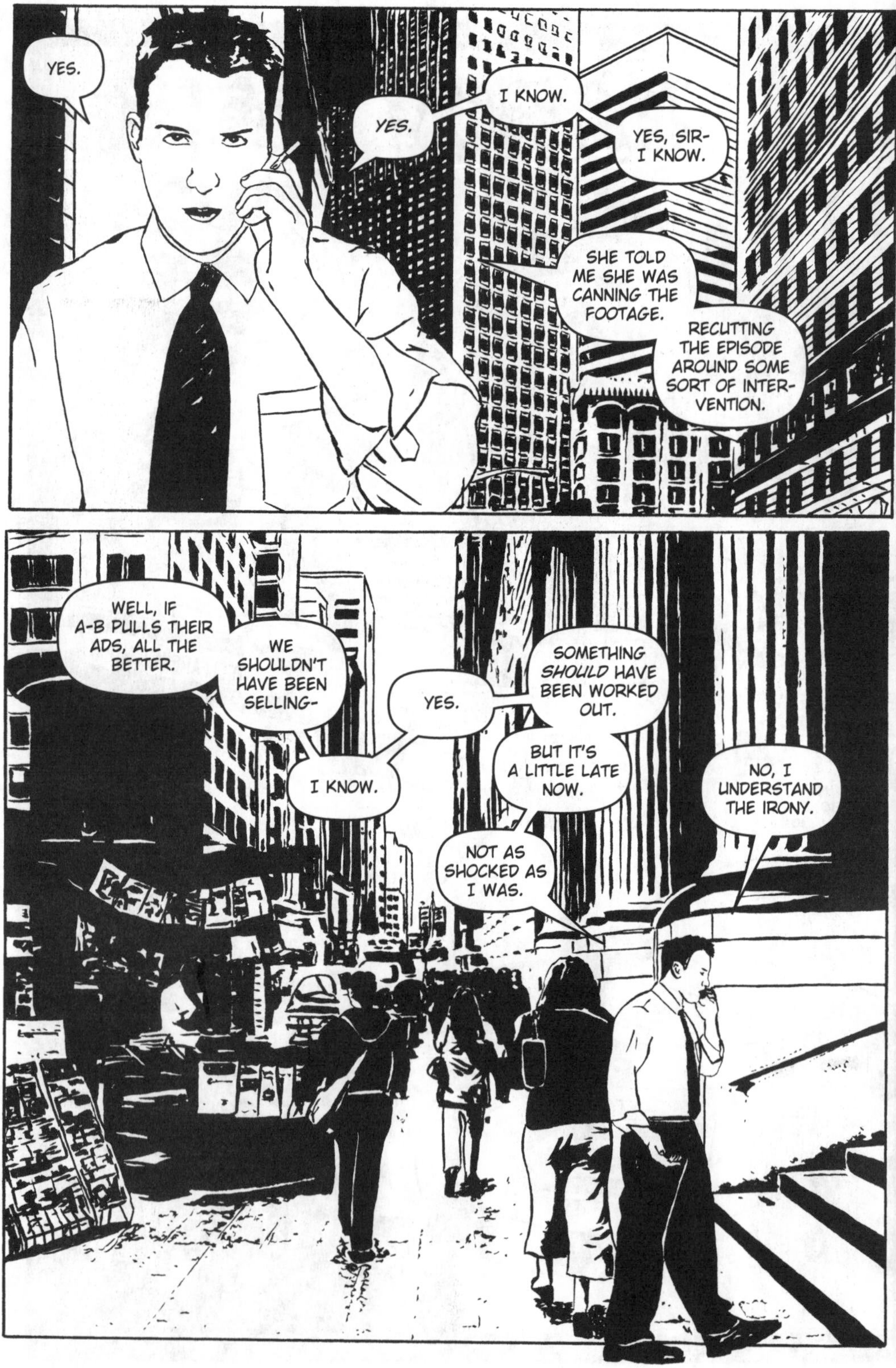
YES.
YES.
I KNOW.
YES, SIR-
I KNOW.
SHE TOLD ME SHE WAS CANNING THE FOOTAGE.
RECUTTING THE EPISODE AROUND SOME SORT OF INTER-VENTION.
WELL, IF A-B PULLS THEIR ADS, ALL THE BETTER.
WE SHOULDN'T HAVE BEEN SELLING-
I KNOW.
YES.
SOMETHING *SHOULD* HAVE BEEN WORKED OUT.
BUT IT'S A LITTLE LATE NOW.
NOT AS SHOCKED AS I WAS.
NO, I UNDERSTAND THE IRONY.

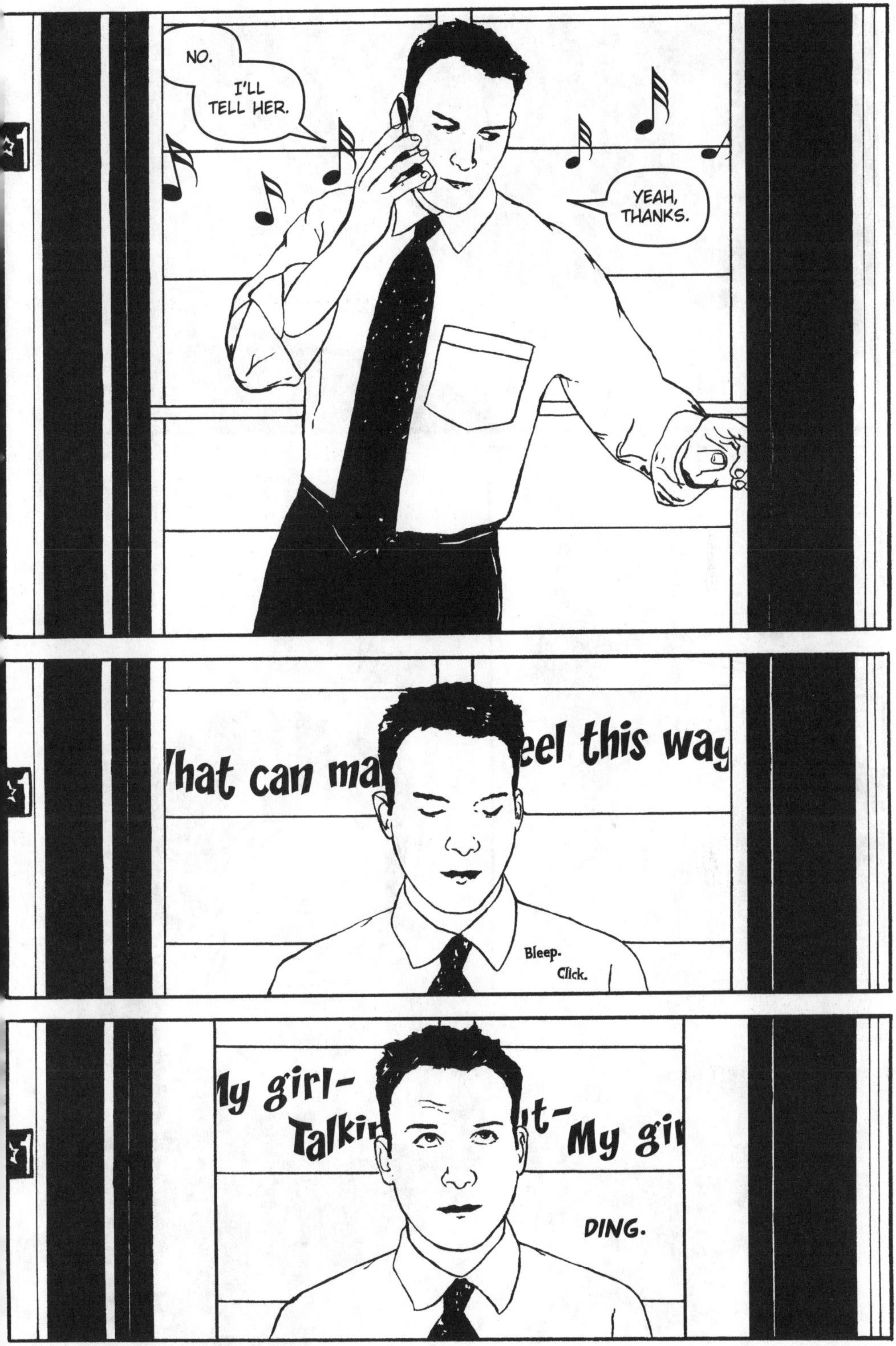
NO.
I'LL TELL HER.
YEAH, THANKS.
Bleep.
Click.
DING.

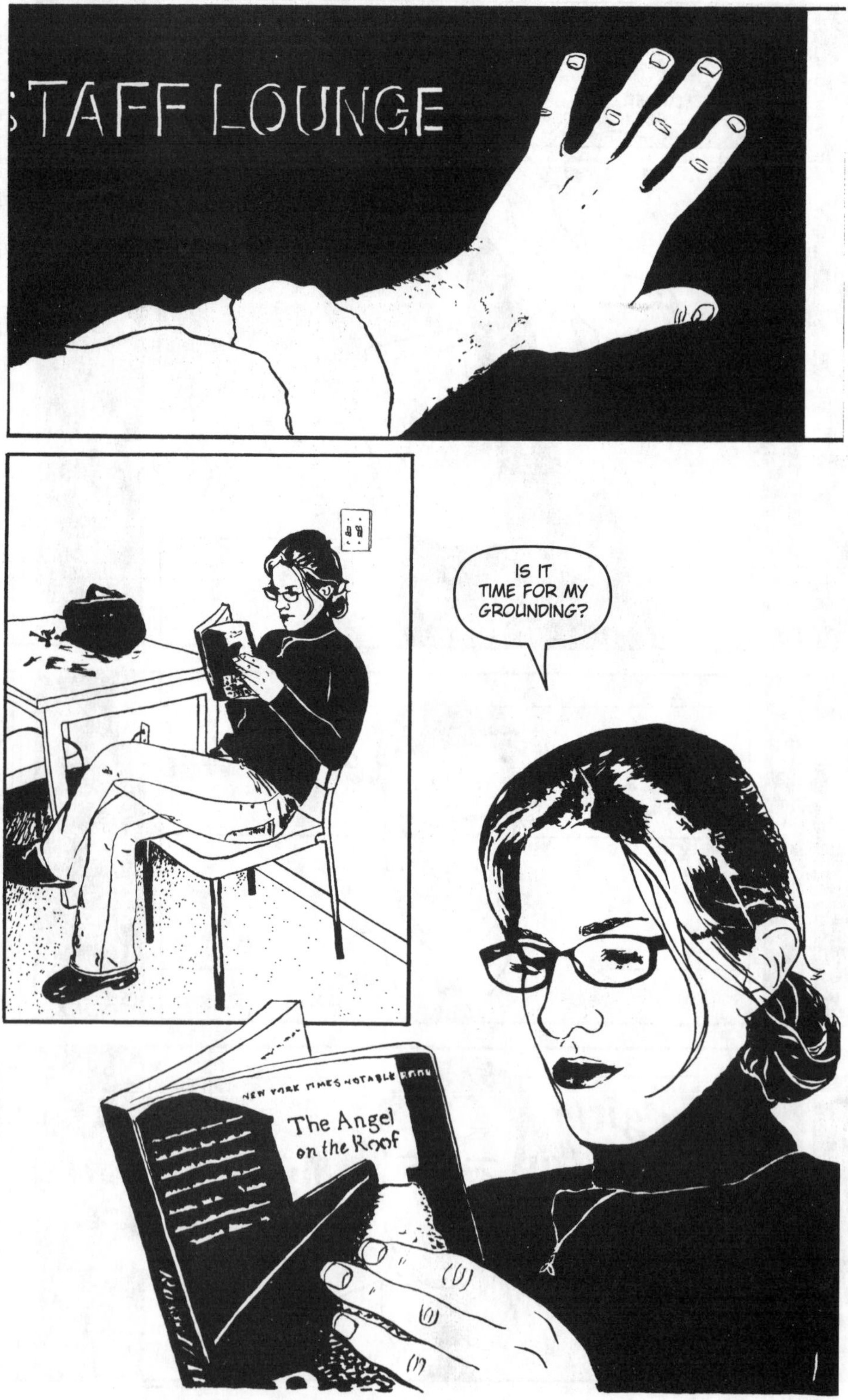
STAFF LOUNGE
IS IT TIME FOR MY GROUNDING?
NEW YORK TIMES NOTABLE
The Angel on the Roof

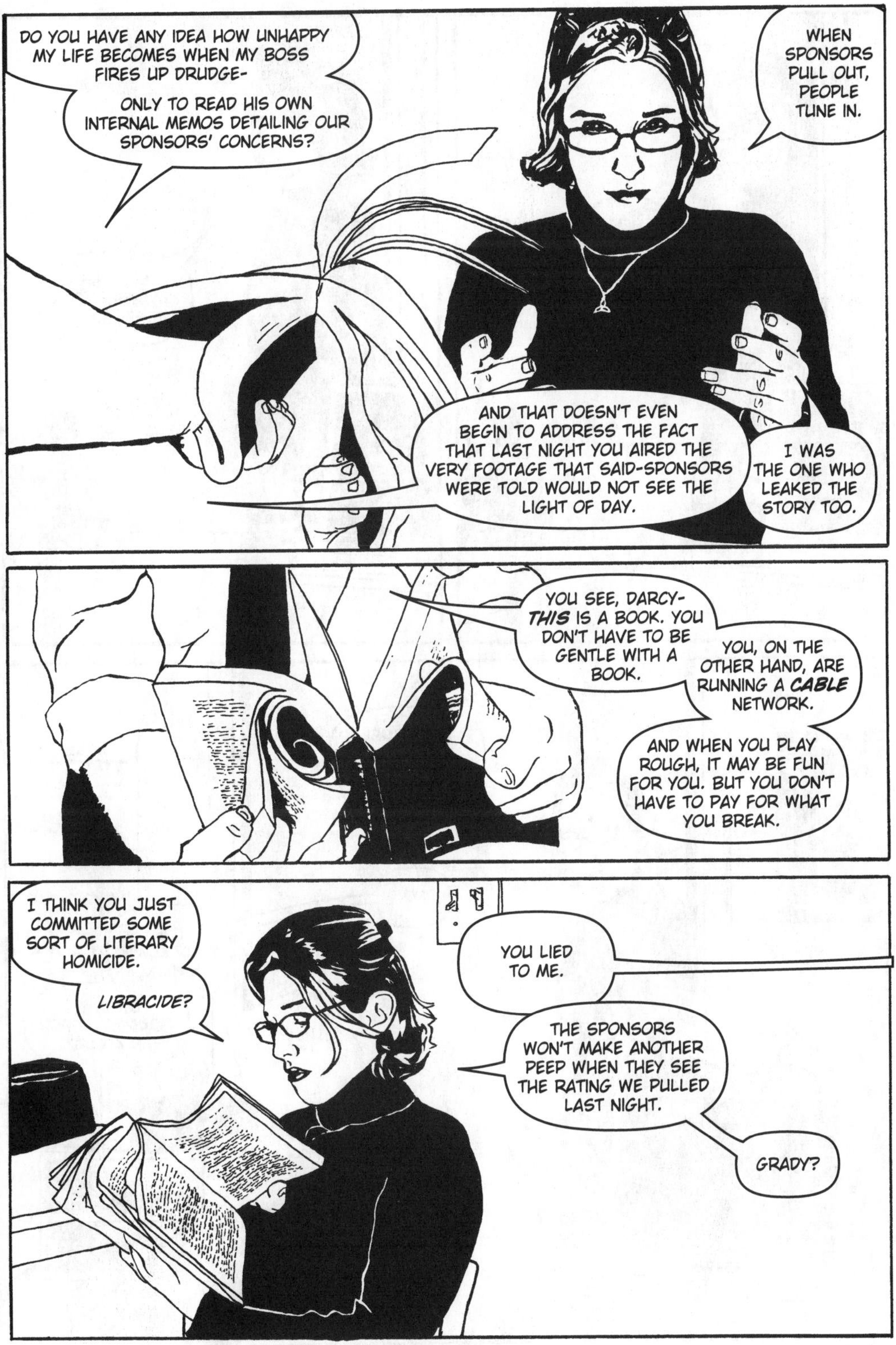
DO YOU HAVE ANY IDEA HOW UNHAPPY MY LIFE BECOMES WHEN MY BOSS FIRES UP DRUDGE-
ONLY TO READ HIS OWN INTERNAL MEMOS DETAILING OUR SPONSORS' CONCERNS?
WHEN SPONSORS PULL OUT, PEOPLE TUNE IN.
AND THAT DOESN'T EVEN BEGIN TO ADDRESS THE FACT THAT LAST NIGHT YOU AIRED THE VERY FOOTAGE THAT SAID-SPONSORS WERE TOLD WOULD NOT SEE THE LIGHT OF DAY.
I WAS THE ONE WHO LEAKED THE STORY TOO.
YOU SEE, DARCY- *THIS* IS A BOOK. YOU DON'T HAVE TO BE GENTLE WITH A BOOK.
YOU, ON THE OTHER HAND, ARE RUNNING A *CABLE* NETWORK.
AND WHEN YOU PLAY ROUGH, IT MAY BE FUN FOR YOU. BUT YOU DON'T HAVE TO PAY FOR WHAT YOU BREAK.
I THINK YOU JUST COMMITTED SOME SORT OF LITERARY HOMICIDE.
LIBRACIDE?
YOU LIED TO ME.
THE SPONSORS WON'T MAKE ANOTHER PEEP WHEN THEY SEE THE RATING WE PULLED LAST NIGHT.
GRADY?

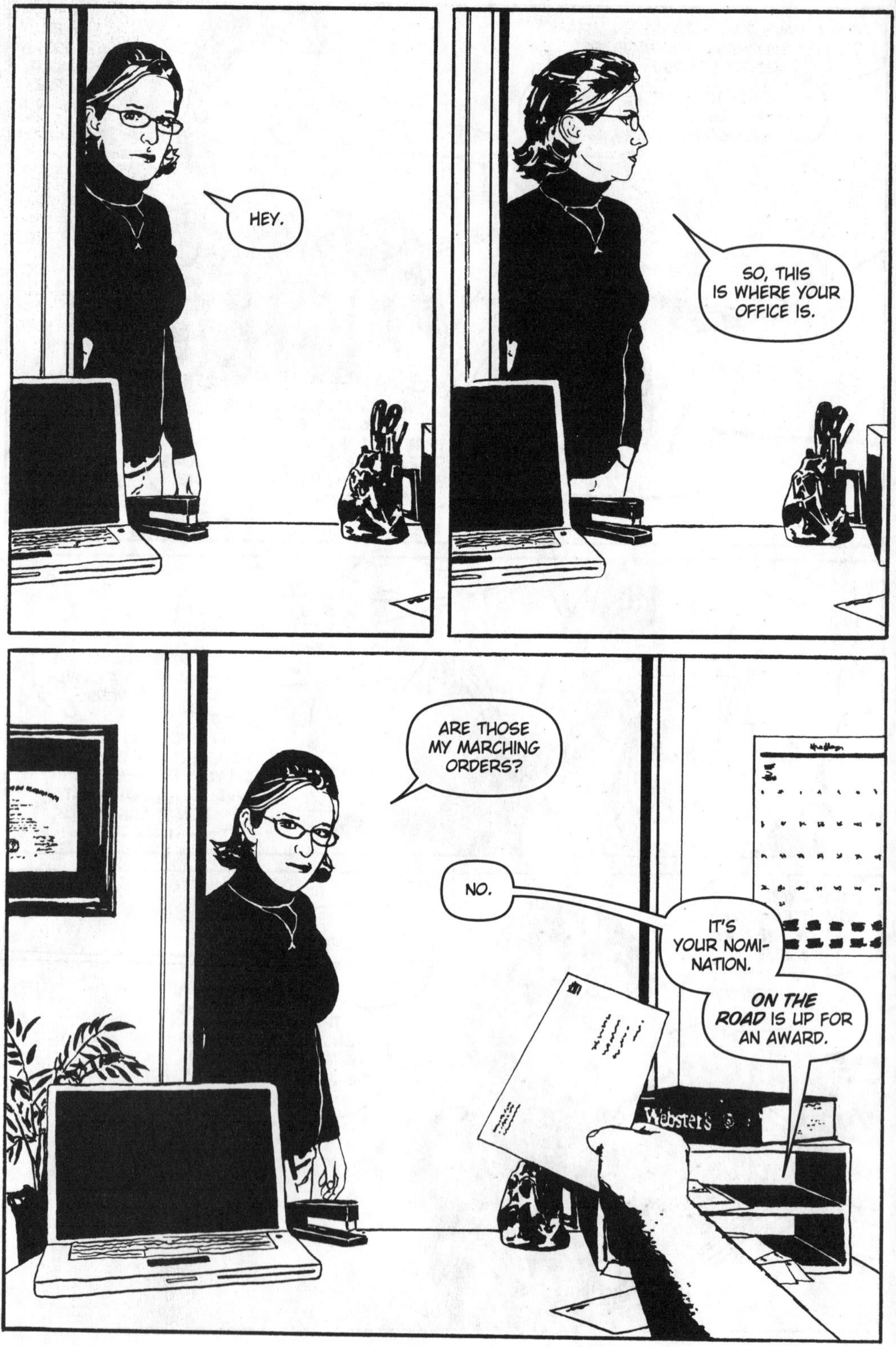
HEY.
SO, THIS IS WHERE YOUR OFFICE IS.
ARE THOSE MY MARCHING ORDERS?
NO.
IT'S YOUR NOMI-NATION.
ON THE ROAD IS UP FOR AN AWARD.
Webster's

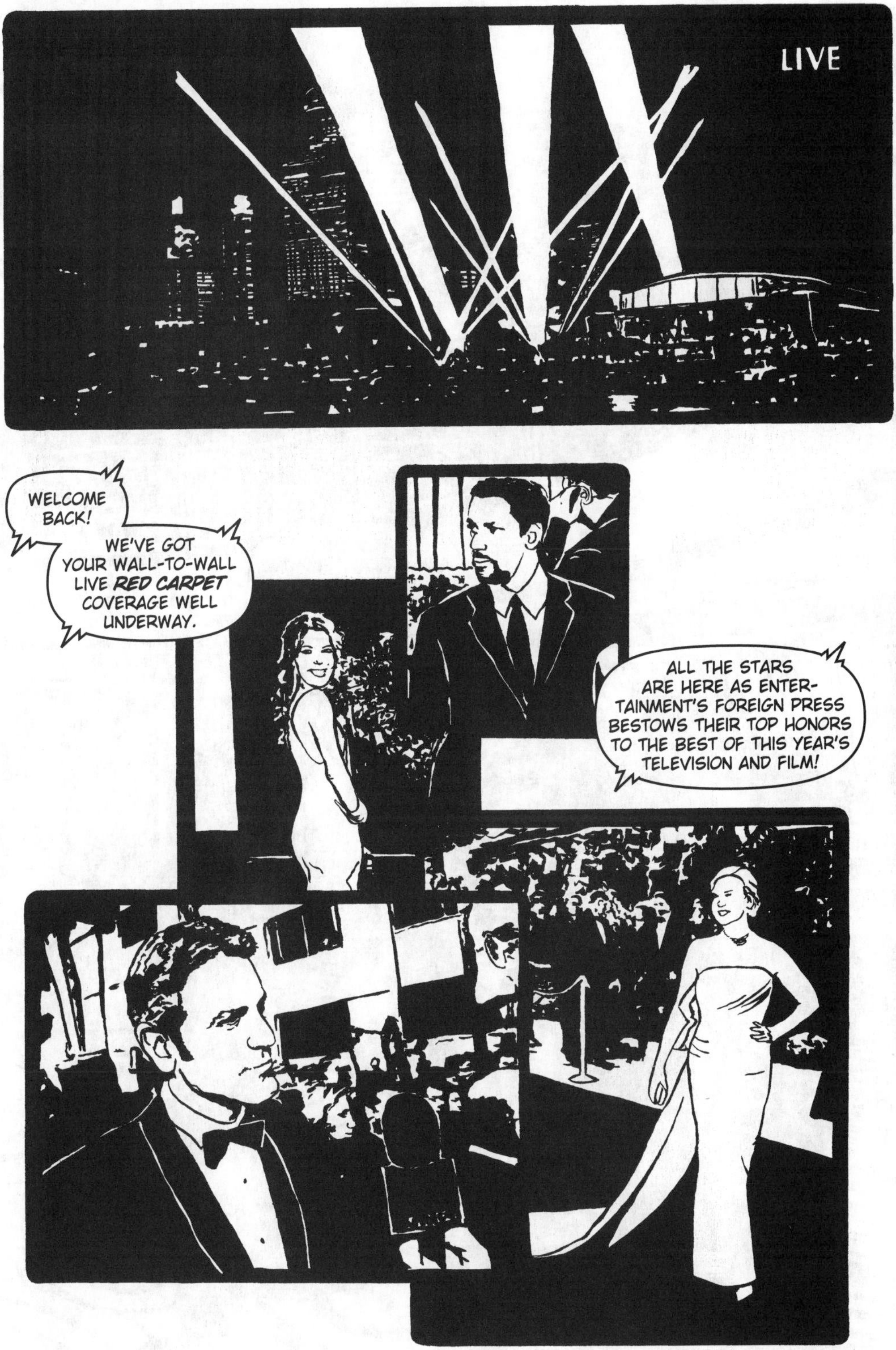
LIVE
WELCOME BACK!
WE'VE GOT YOUR WALL-TO-WALL LIVE RED CARPET COVERAGE WELL UNDERWAY.
ALL THE STARS ARE HERE AS ENTERTAINMENT'S FOREIGN PRESS BESTOWS THEIR TOP HONORS TO THE BEST OF THIS YEAR'S TELEVISION AND FILM!

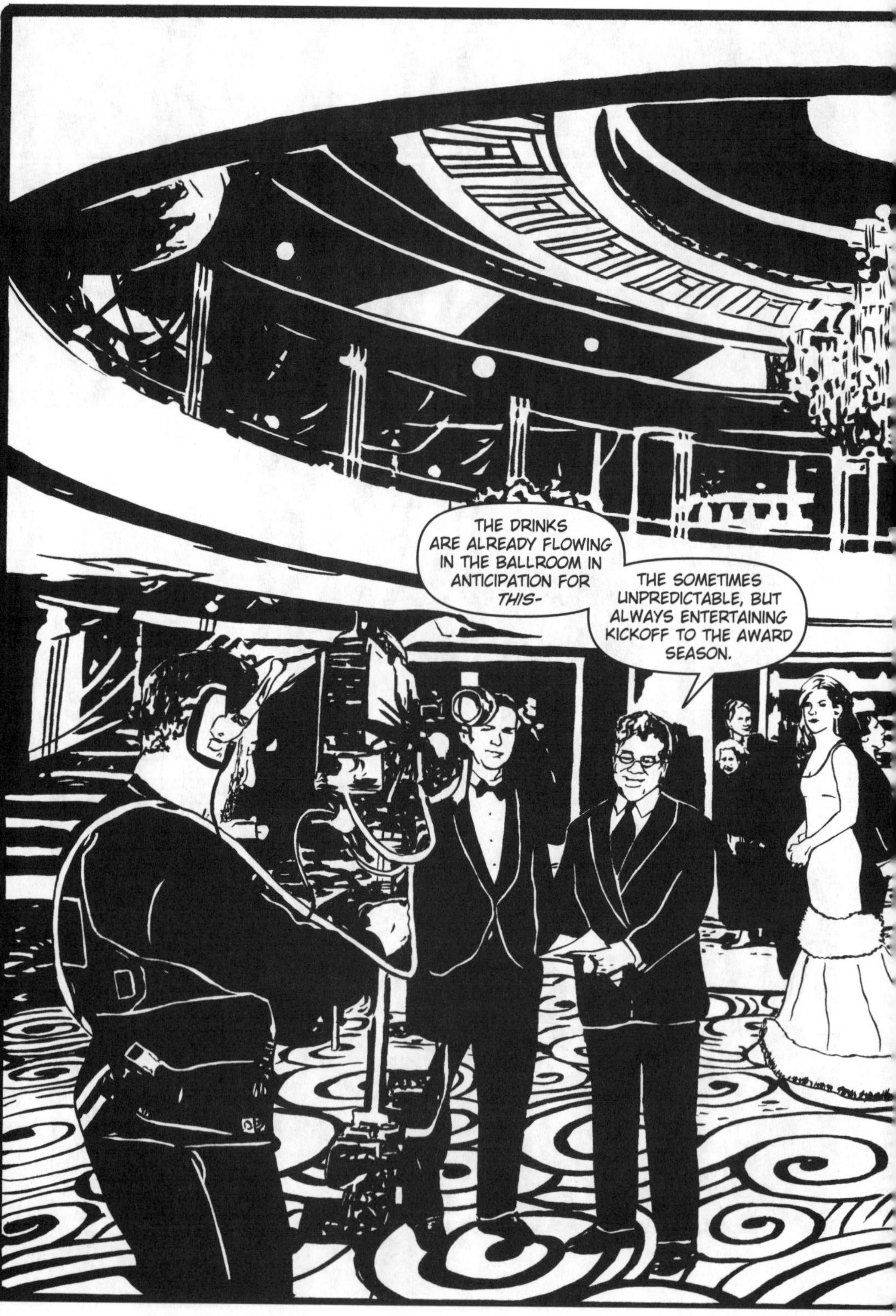
THE DRINKS ARE ALREADY FLOWING IN THE BALLROOM IN ANTICIPATION FOR *THIS*-
THE SOMETIMES UNPREDICTABLE, BUT ALWAYS ENTERTAINING KICKOFF TO THE AWARD SEASON.

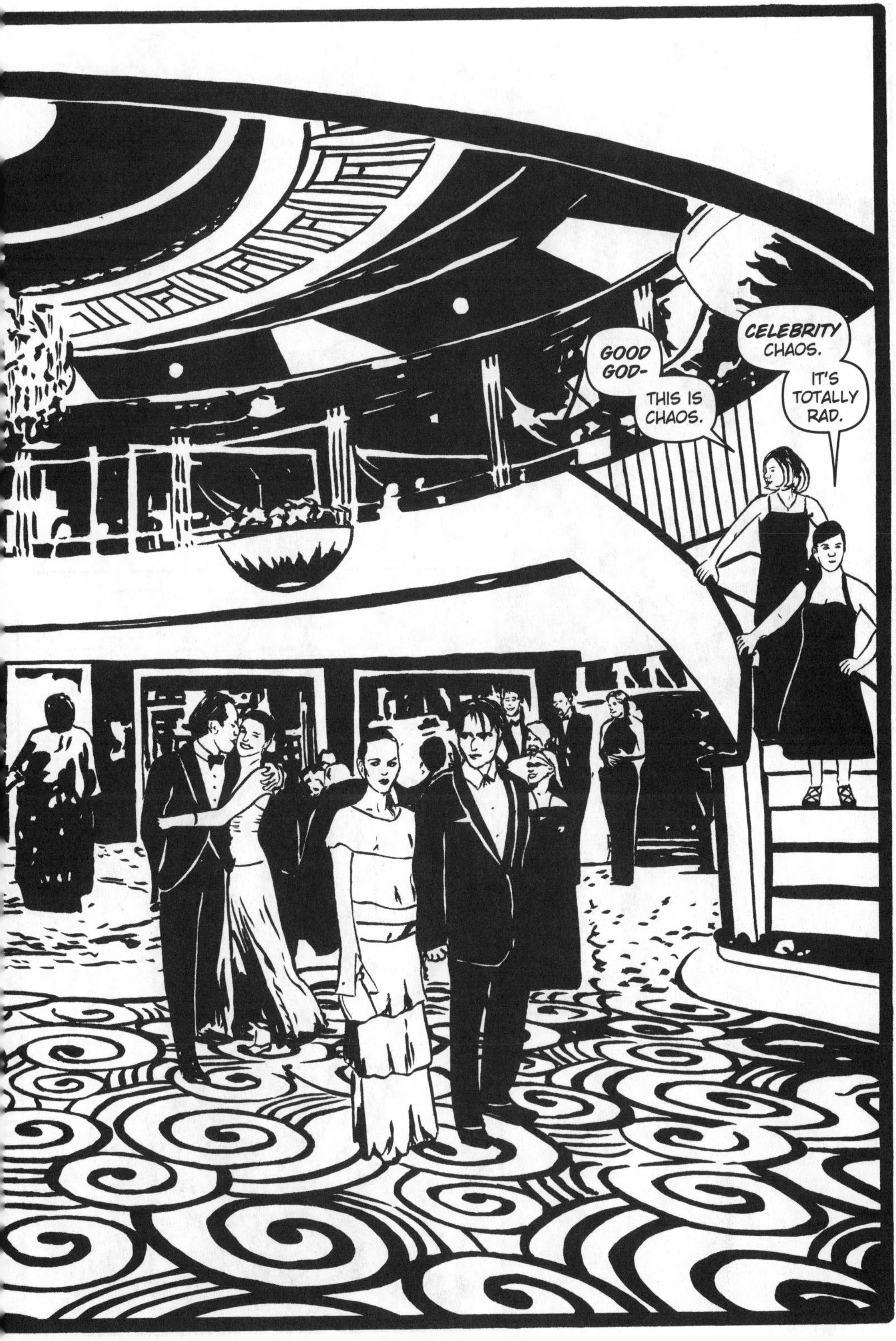
GOOD GOD-
THIS IS CHAOS.
CELEBRITY CHAOS.
IT'S TOTALLY RAD.

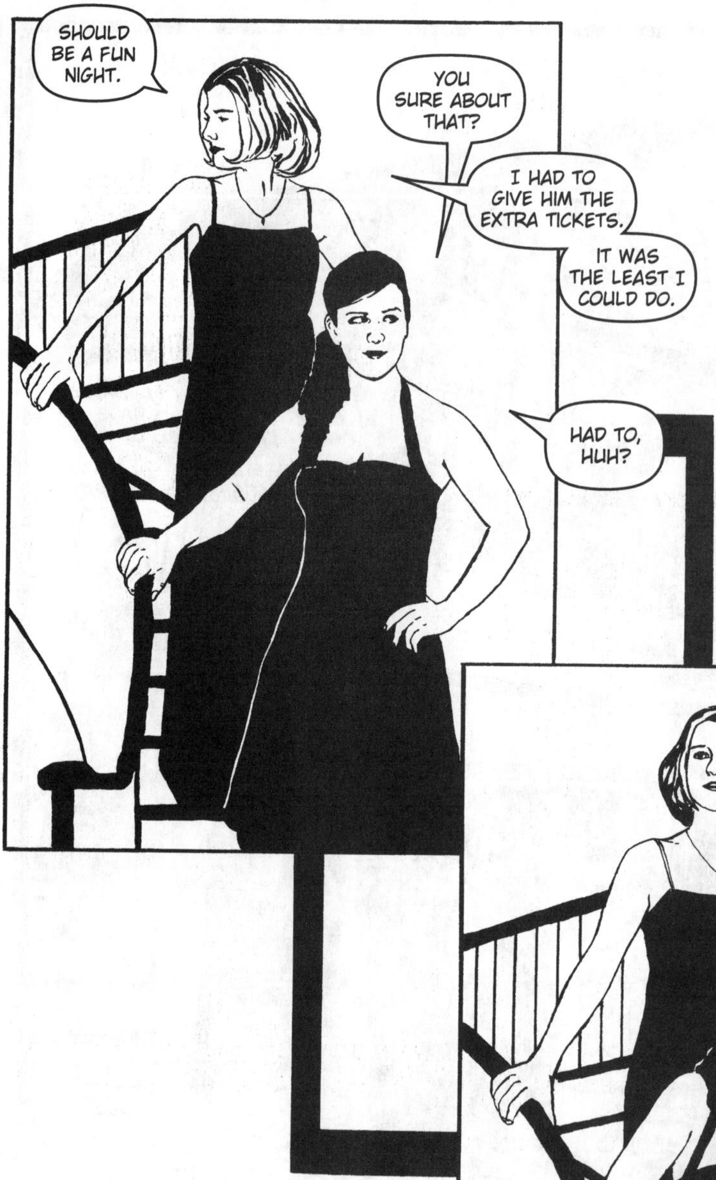
SHOULD BE A FUN NIGHT.
YOU SURE ABOUT THAT?
I HAD TO GIVE HIM THE EXTRA TICKETS.
IT WAS THE LEAST I COULD DO.
HAD TO, HUH?

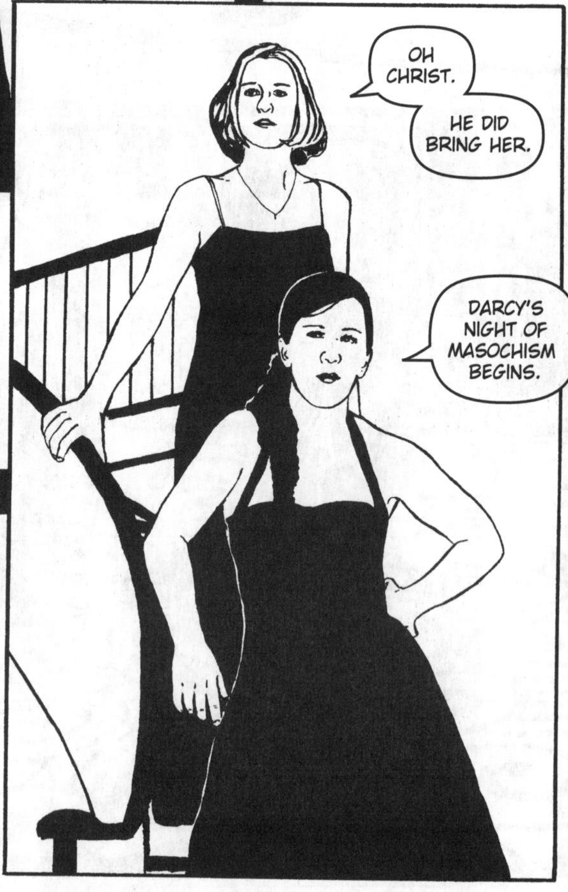
OH CHRIST.
HE DID BRING HER.
DARCY'S NIGHT OF MASOCHISM BEGINS.

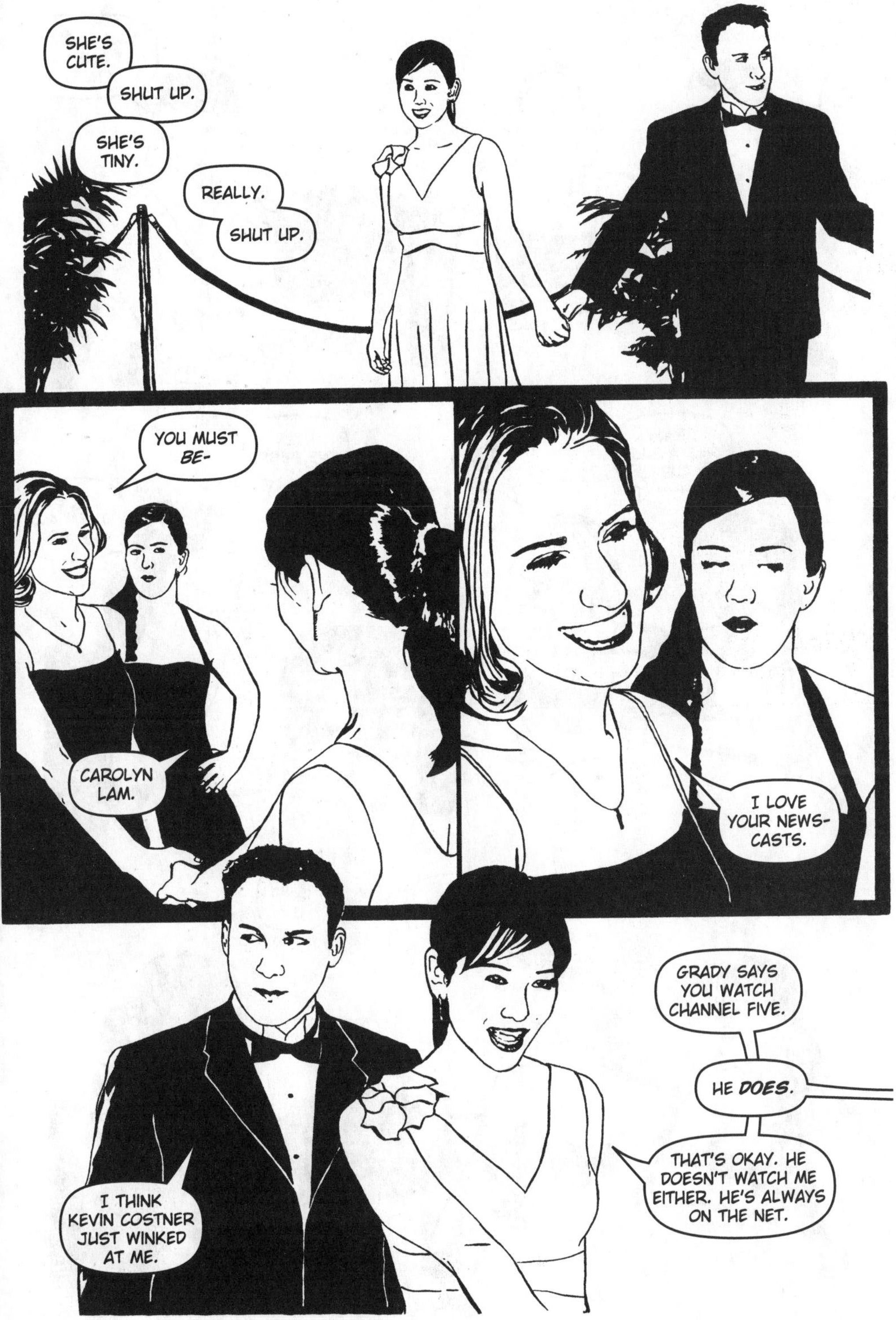
SHE'S CUTE.
SHUT UP.
SHE'S TINY.
REALLY.
SHUT UP.
YOU MUST BE-
CAROLYN LAM.
I LOVE YOUR NEWS-CASTS.
GRADY SAYS YOU WATCH CHANNEL FIVE.
HE *DOES*.
THAT'S OKAY. HE DOESN'T WATCH ME EITHER. HE'S ALWAYS ON THE NET.
I THINK KEVIN COSTNER JUST WINKED AT ME.

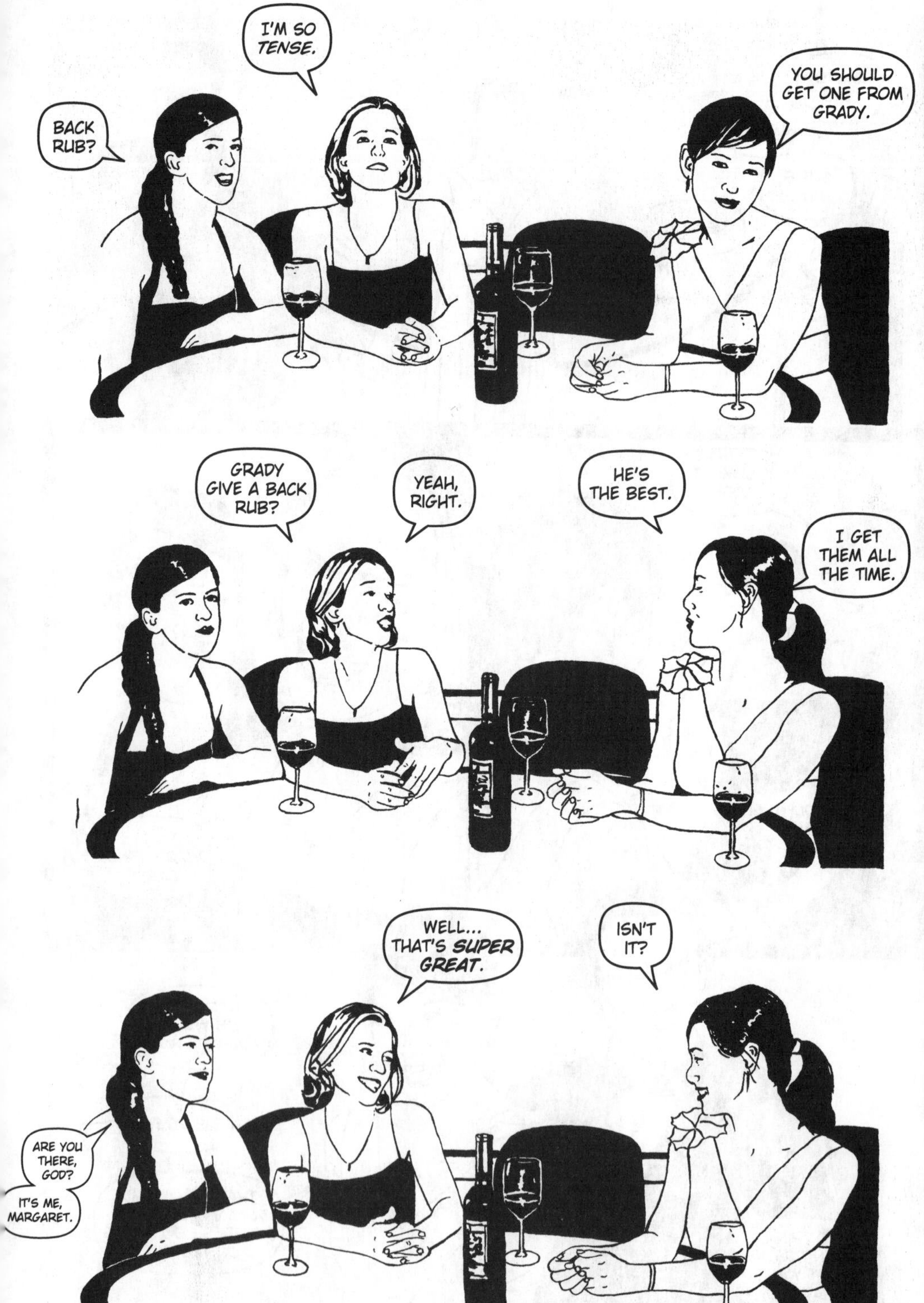
BACK RUB?
I'M SO *TENSE.*
YOU SHOULD GET ONE FROM GRADY.
GRADY GIVE A BACK RUB?
YEAH, RIGHT.
HE'S THE BEST.
I GET THEM ALL THE TIME.
WELL... THAT'S ***SUPER GREAT.***
ISN'T IT?
ARE YOU THERE, GOD?
IT'S ME, MARGARET.

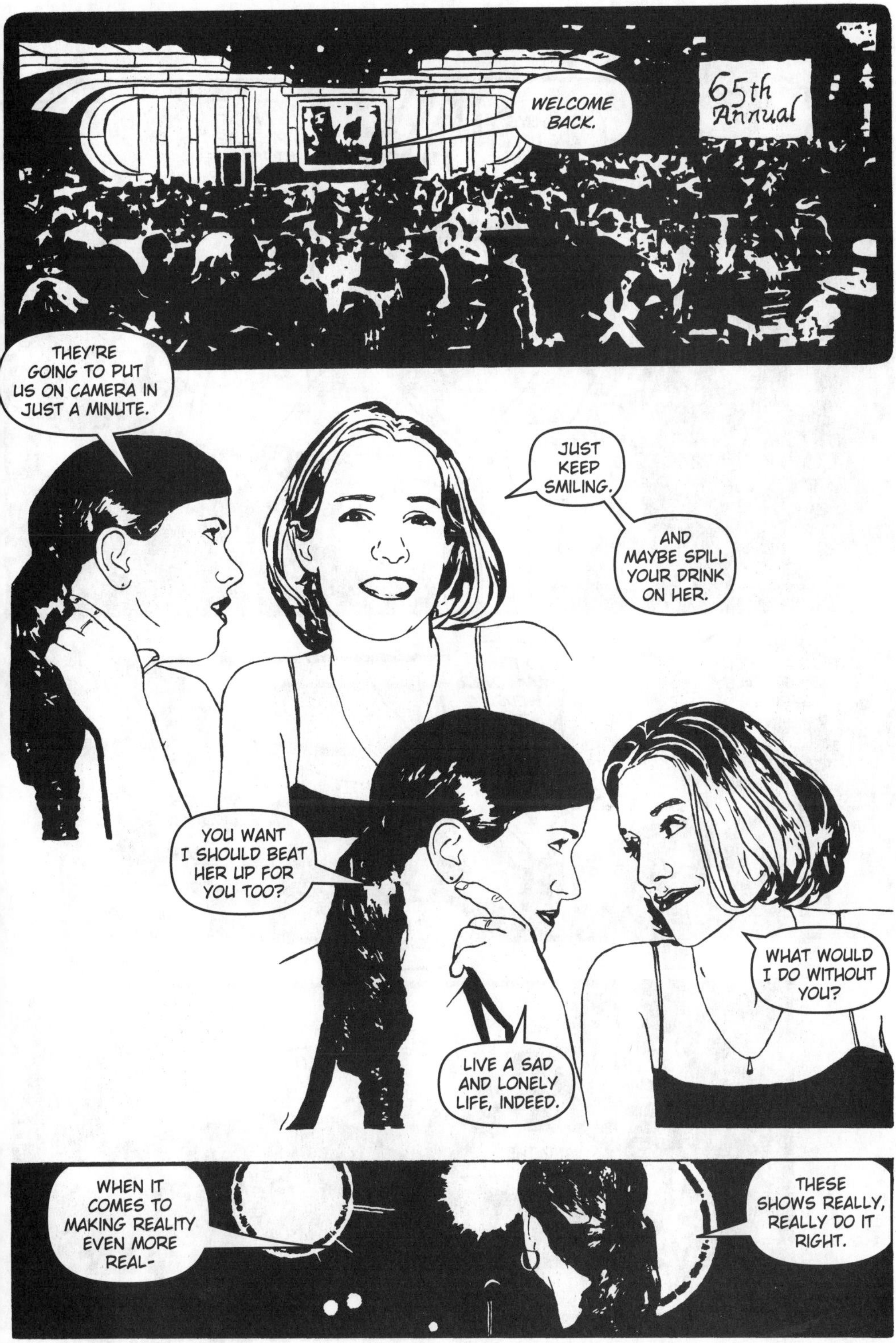
65th Annual
WELCOME BACK.
THEY'RE GOING TO PUT US ON CAMERA IN JUST A MINUTE.
JUST KEEP SMILING.
AND MAYBE SPILL YOUR DRINK ON HER.
YOU WANT I SHOULD BEAT HER UP FOR YOU TOO?
WHAT WOULD I DO WITHOUT YOU?
LIVE A SAD AND LONELY LIFE, INDEED.
WHEN IT COMES TO MAKING REALITY EVEN MORE REAL-
THESE SHOWS REALLY, REALLY DO IT RIGHT.

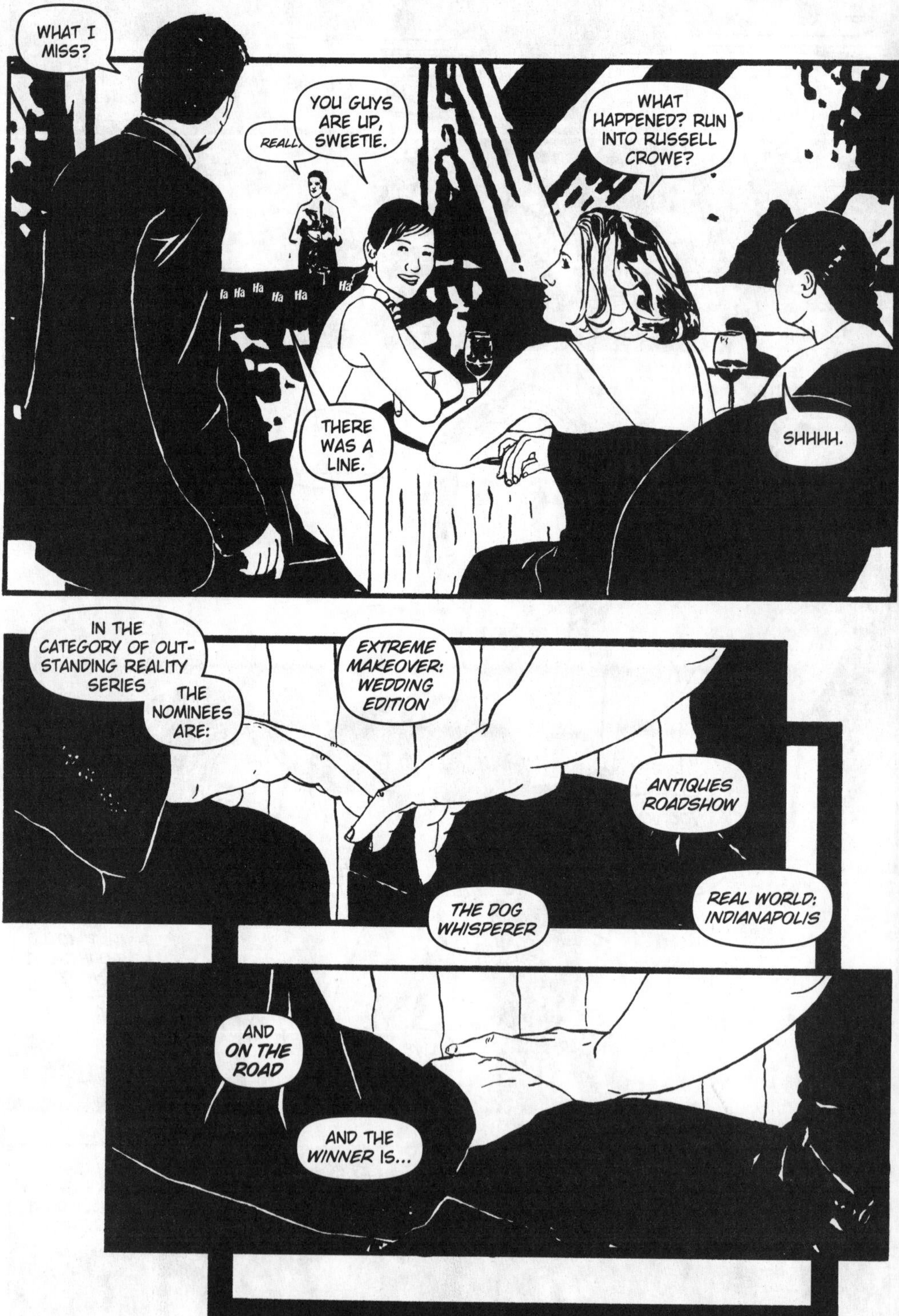
WHAT I MISS?
REALLY
YOU GUYS ARE UP, SWEETIE.
WHAT HAPPENED? RUN INTO RUSSELL CROWE?
Ha Ha Ha Ha Ha Ha
THERE WAS A LINE.
SHHHH.
IN THE CATEGORY OF OUT-STANDING REALITY SERIES
THE NOMINEES ARE:
EXTREME MAKEOVER: WEDDING EDITION
ANTIQUES ROADSHOW
THE DOG WHISPERER
REAL WORLD: INDIANAPOLIS
AND ON THE ROAD
AND THE WINNER IS...

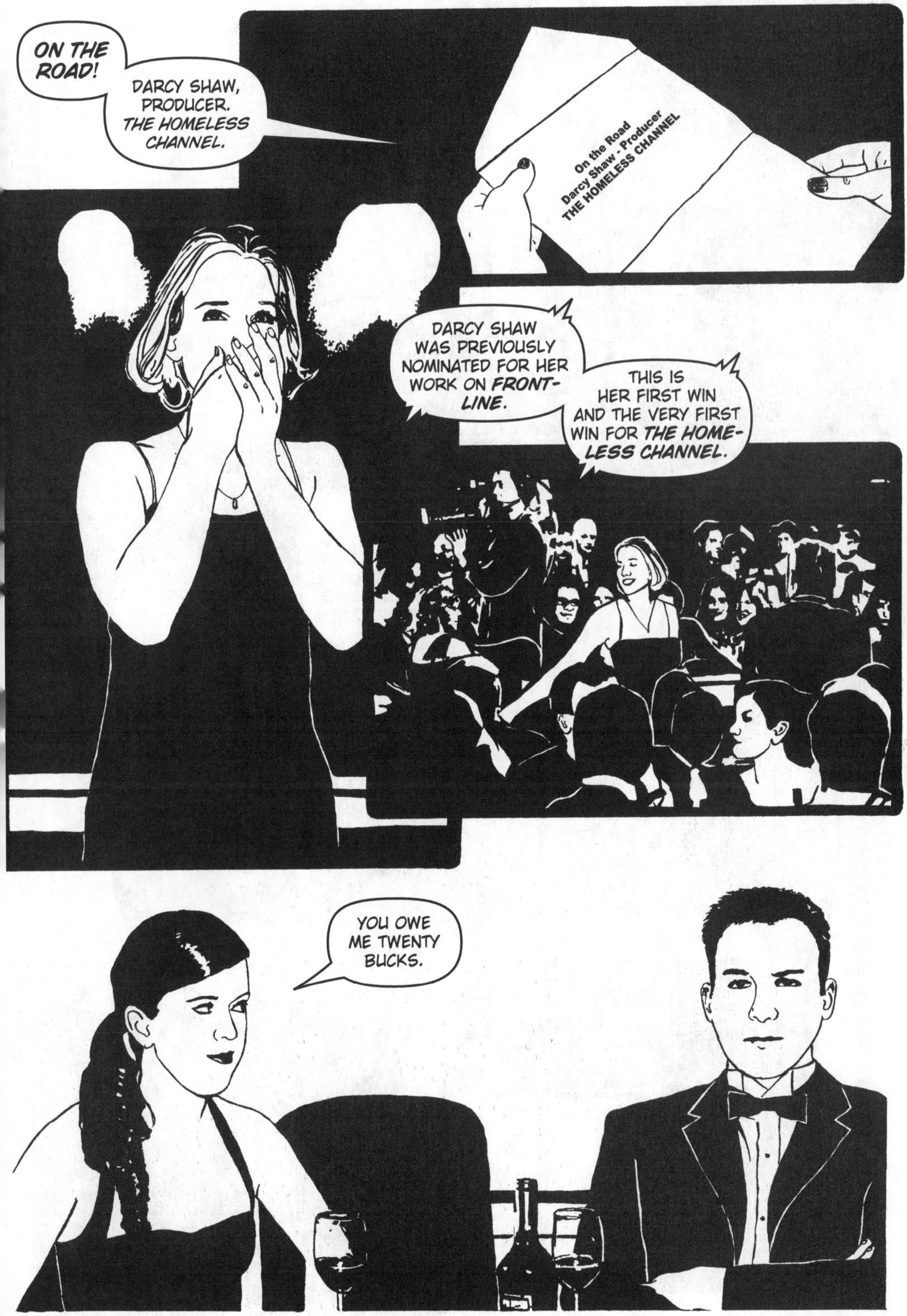
ON THE ROAD!
DARCY SHAW, PRODUCER. THE HOMELESS CHANNEL.
On the Road
Darcy Shaw - Producer
THE HOMELESS CHANNEL
DARCY SHAW WAS PREVIOUSLY NOMINATED FOR HER WORK ON FRONT-LINE.
THIS IS HER FIRST WIN AND THE VERY FIRST WIN FOR THE HOME-LESS CHANNEL.
YOU OWE ME TWENTY BUCKS.

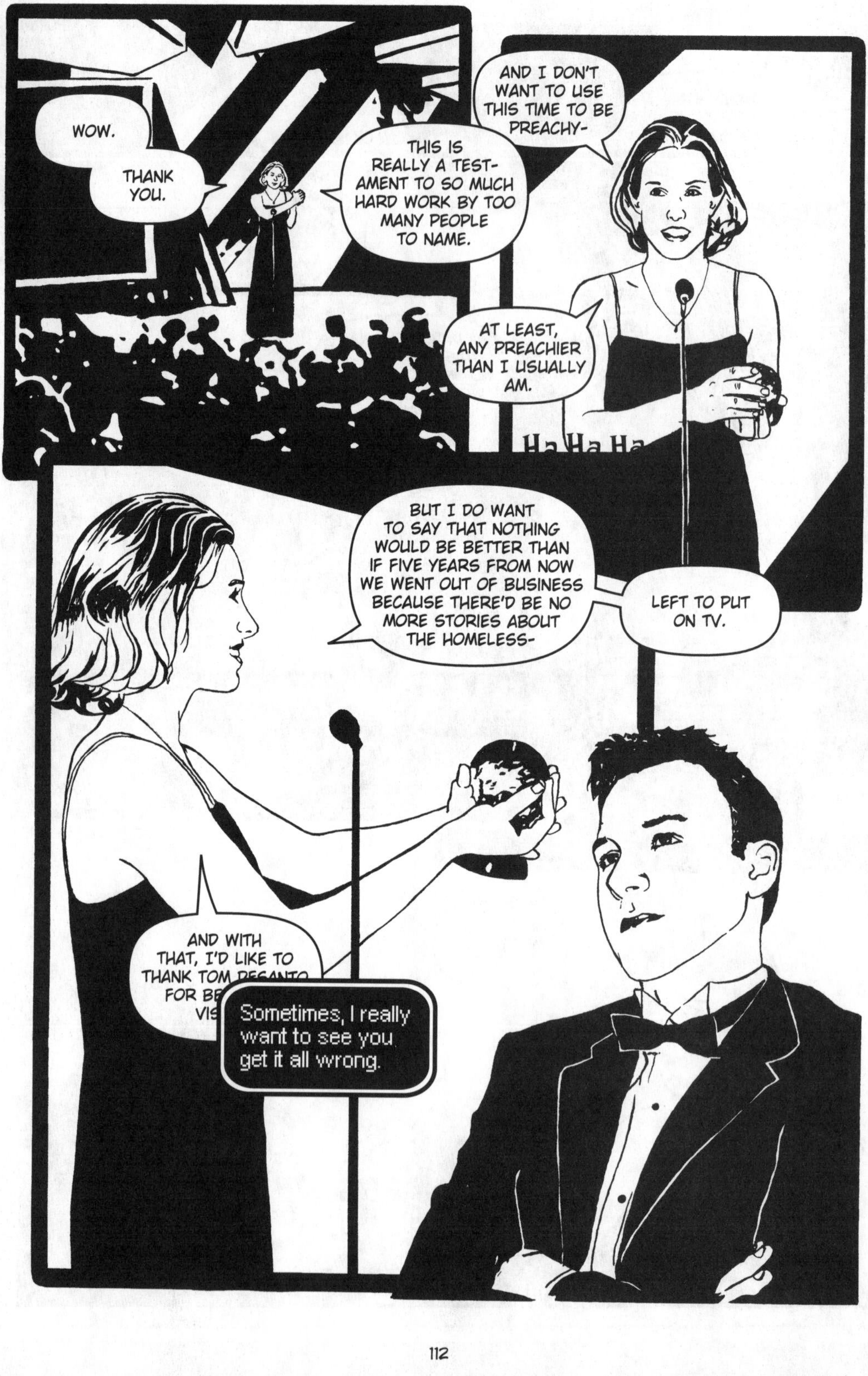
WOW.
THANK YOU.
THIS IS REALLY A TEST-AMENT TO SO MUCH HARD WORK BY TOO MANY PEOPLE TO NAME.
AND I DON'T WANT TO USE THIS TIME TO BE PREACHY-
AT LEAST, ANY PREACHIER THAN I USUALLY AM.
Ha Ha Ha
BUT I DO WANT TO SAY THAT NOTHING WOULD BE BETTER THAN IF FIVE YEARS FROM NOW WE WENT OUT OF BUSINESS BECAUSE THERE'D BE NO MORE STORIES ABOUT THE HOMELESS-
LEFT TO PUT ON TV.
AND WITH THAT, I'D LIKE TO THANK TOM
Sometimes, I really want to see you get it all wrong.

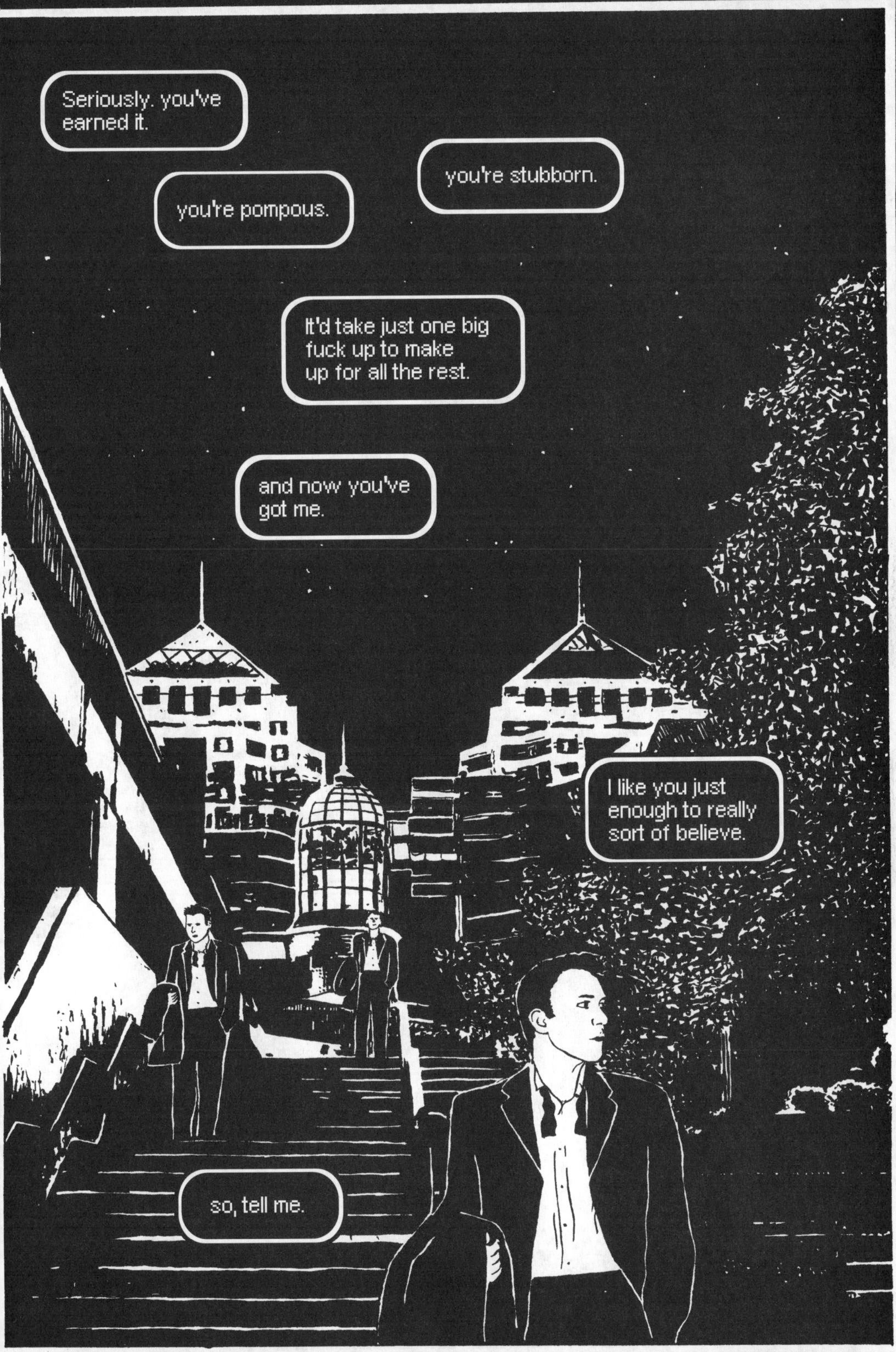
Seriously. you've earned it.
you're pompous.
you're stubborn.
It'd take just one big fuck up to make up for all the rest.
and now you've got me.
I like you just enough to really sort of believe.
so, tell me.

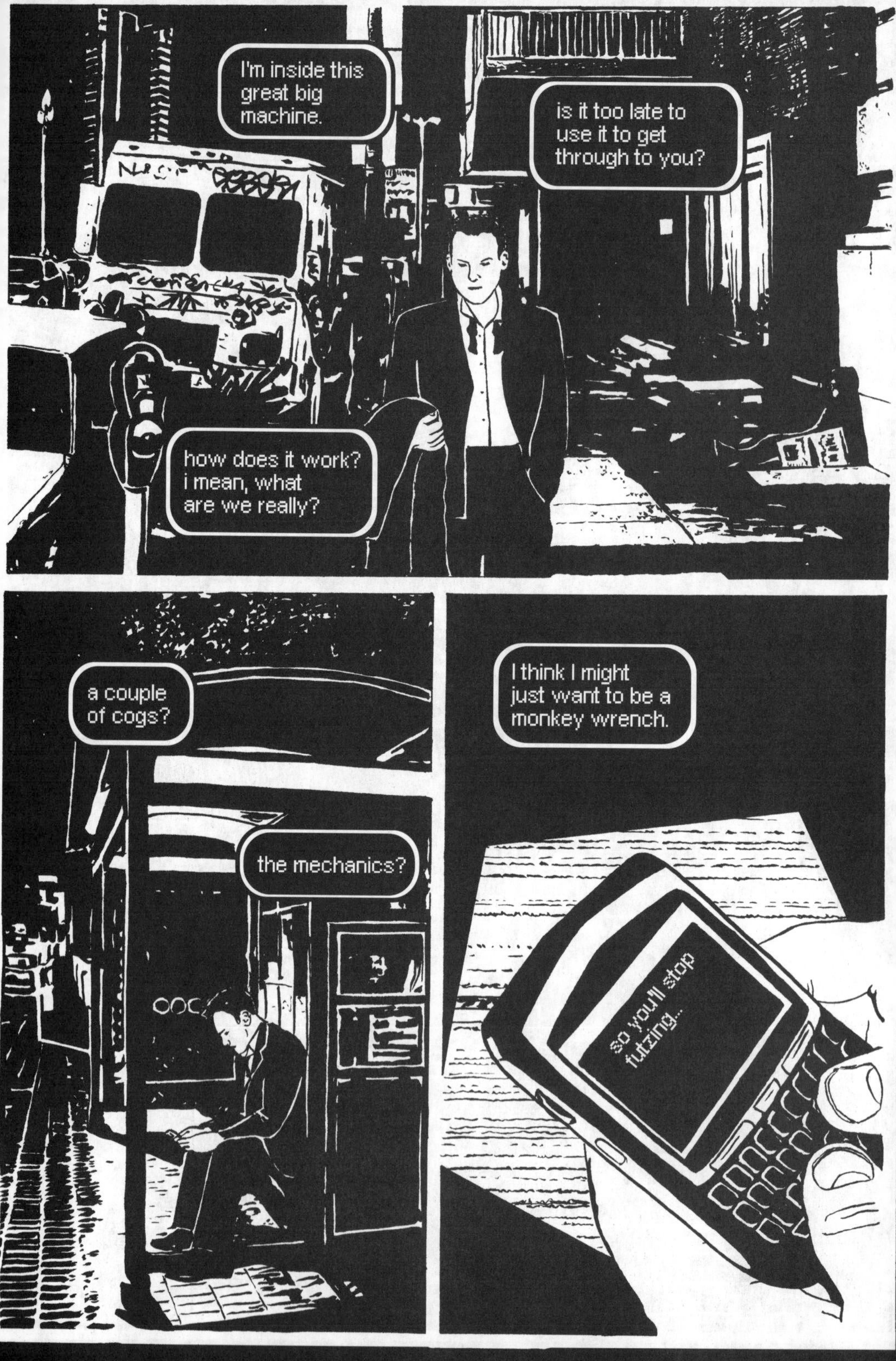
I'm inside this great big machine.
is it too late to use it to get through to you?
how does it work? i mean, what are we really?
a couple of cogs?
the mechanics?
I think I might just want to be a monkey wrench.
so you'll stop futzing...

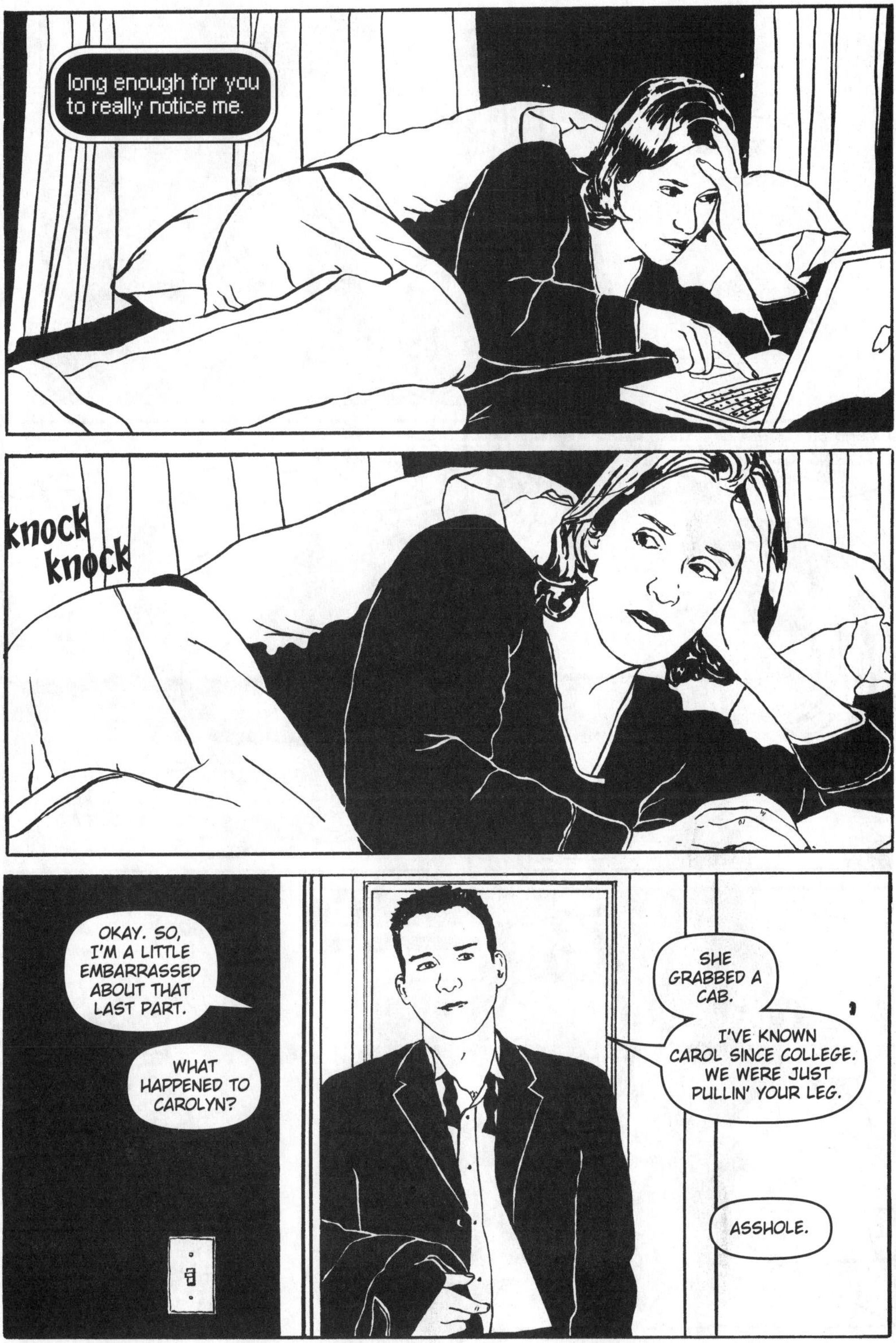
long enough for you to really notice me.
knock knock
OKAY. SO, I'M A LITTLE EMBARRASSED ABOUT THAT LAST PART.
WHAT HAPPENED TO CAROLYN?
SHE GRABBED A CAB.
I'VE KNOWN CAROL SINCE COLLEGE. WE WERE JUST PULLIN' YOUR LEG.
ASSHOLE.

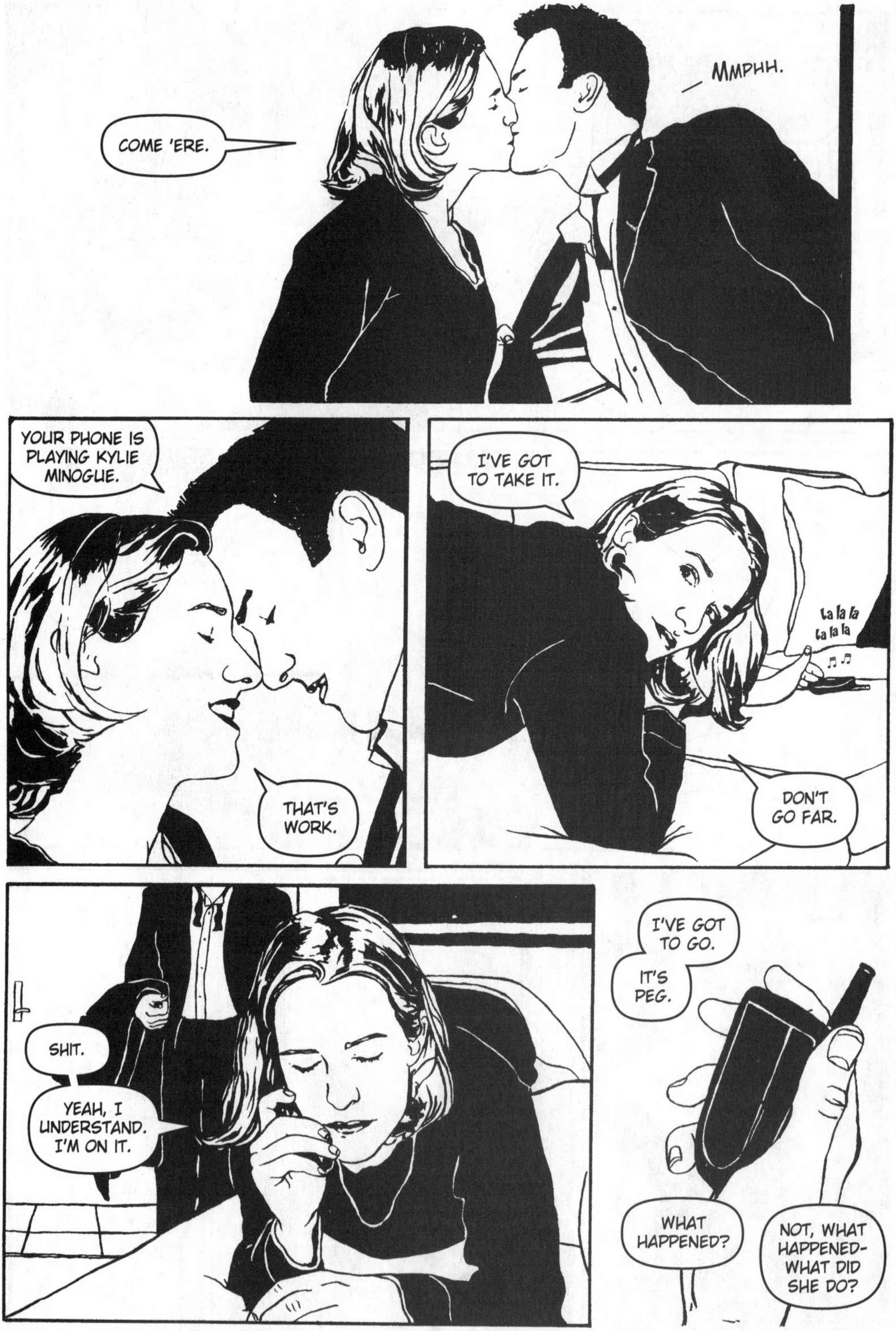
MMPHH.
COME 'ERE.
YOUR PHONE IS PLAYING KYLIE MINOGUE.
THAT'S WORK.
I'VE GOT TO TAKE IT.
La la la la la la
DON'T GO FAR.
SHIT.
YEAH, I UNDERSTAND. I'M ON IT.
I'VE GOT TO GO.
IT'S PEG.
WHAT HAPPENED?
NOT, WHAT HAPPENED- WHAT DID SHE DO?

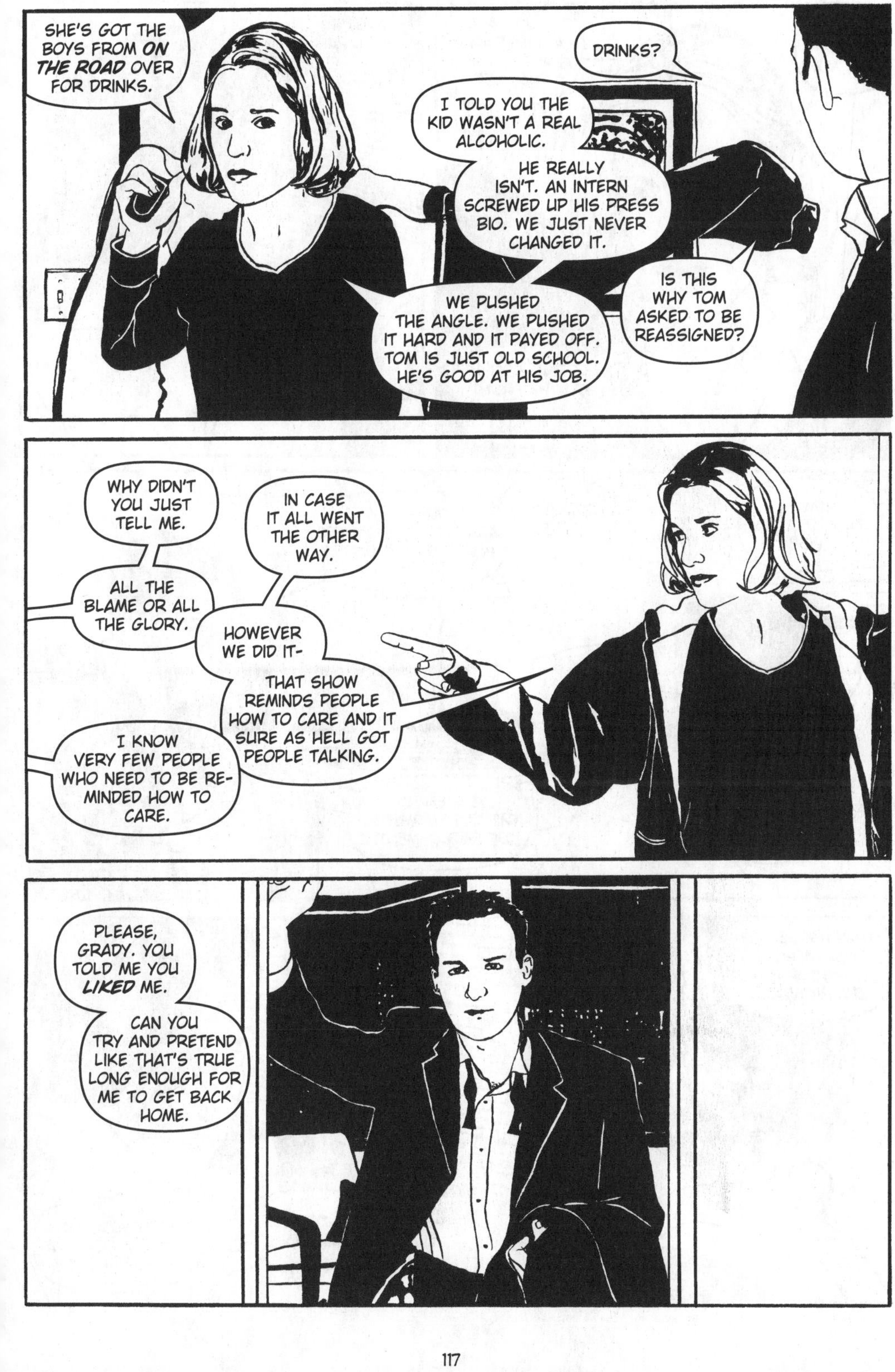
SHE'S GOT THE BOYS FROM ***ON THE ROAD*** OVER FOR DRINKS.
DRINKS?
I TOLD YOU THE KID WASN'T A REAL ALCOHOLIC.
HE REALLY ISN'T. AN INTERN SCREWED UP HIS PRESS BIO. WE JUST NEVER CHANGED IT.
WE PUSHED THE ANGLE. WE PUSHED IT HARD AND IT PAYED OFF. TOM IS JUST OLD SCHOOL. HE'S GOOD AT HIS JOB.
IS THIS WHY TOM ASKED TO BE REASSIGNED?
WHY DIDN'T YOU JUST TELL ME.
IN CASE IT ALL WENT THE OTHER WAY.
ALL THE BLAME OR ALL THE GLORY.
HOWEVER WE DID IT-
THAT SHOW REMINDS PEOPLE HOW TO CARE AND IT SURE AS HELL GOT PEOPLE TALKING.
I KNOW VERY FEW PEOPLE WHO NEED TO BE RE-MINDED HOW TO CARE.
PLEASE, GRADY. YOU TOLD ME YOU ***LIKED*** ME.
CAN YOU TRY AND PRETEND LIKE THAT'S TRUE LONG ENOUGH FOR ME TO GET BACK HOME.

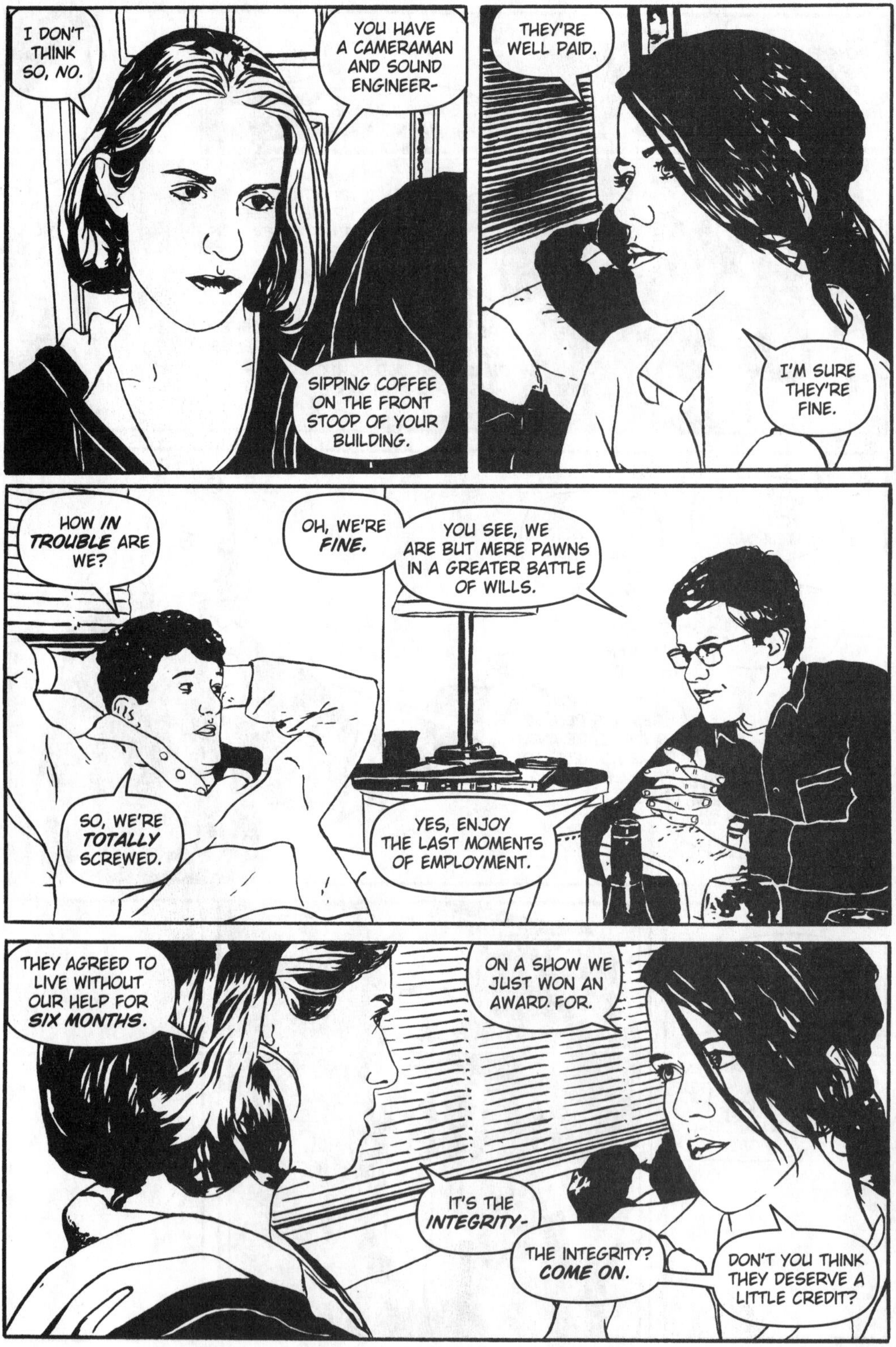
I DON'T THINK SO, *NO*.
YOU HAVE A CAMERAMAN AND SOUND ENGINEER-
SIPPING COFFEE ON THE FRONT STOOP OF YOUR BUILDING.
THEY'RE WELL PAID.
I'M SURE THEY'RE FINE.
HOW *IN TROUBLE* ARE WE?
OH, WE'RE *FINE.*
YOU SEE, WE ARE BUT MERE PAWNS IN A GREATER BATTLE OF WILLS.
SO, WE'RE *TOTALLY* SCREWED.
YES, ENJOY THE LAST MOMENTS OF EMPLOYMENT.
THEY AGREED TO LIVE WITHOUT OUR HELP FOR *SIX MONTHS*.
ON A SHOW WE JUST WON AN AWARD FOR.
IT'S THE *INTEGRITY*-
THE INTEGRITY? *COME ON*.
DON'T YOU THINK THEY DESERVE A LITTLE CREDIT?

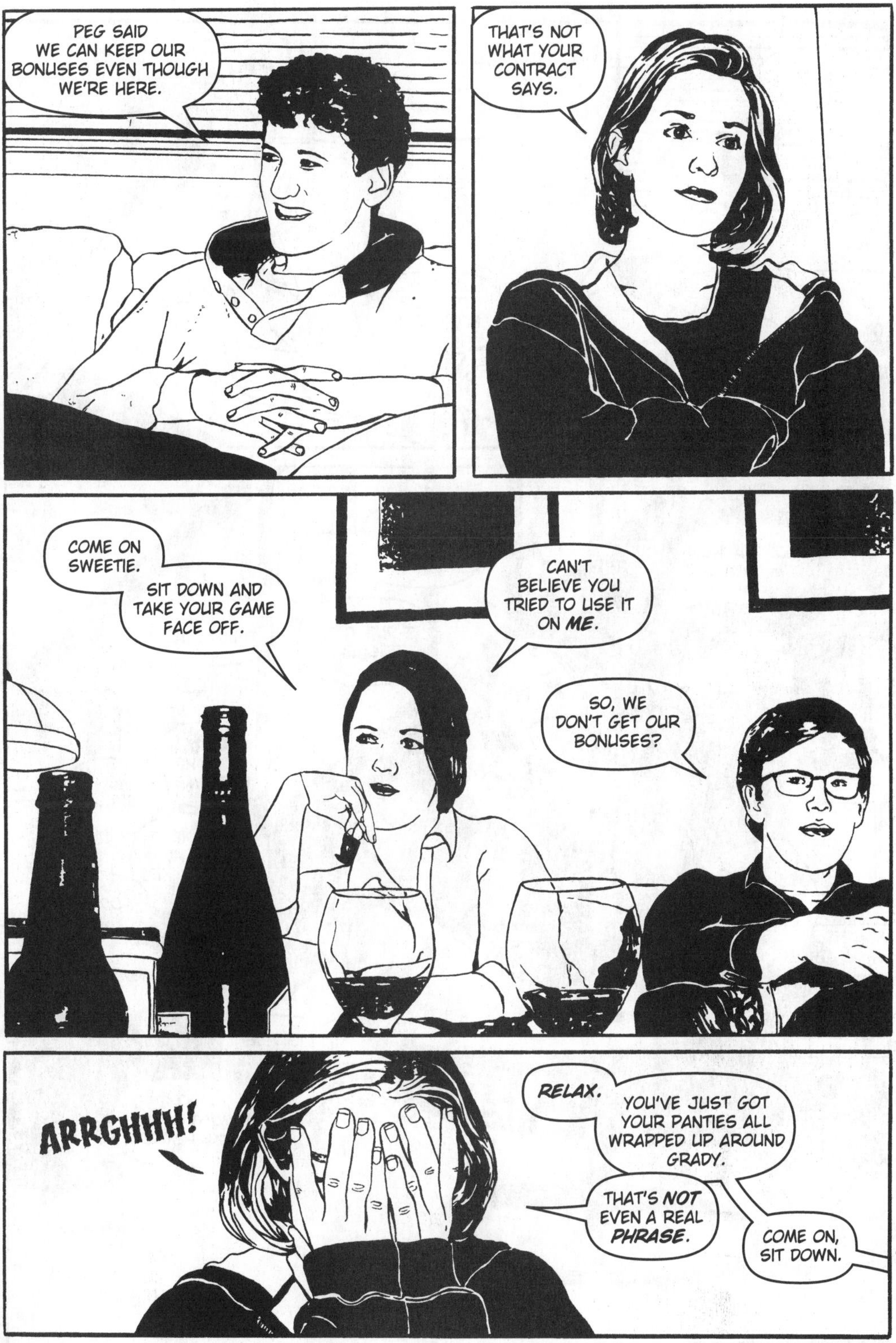
PEG SAID WE CAN KEEP OUR BONUSES EVEN THOUGH WE'RE HERE.
THAT'S NOT WHAT YOUR CONTRACT SAYS.
COME ON SWEETIE.
SIT DOWN AND TAKE YOUR GAME FACE OFF.
CAN'T BELIEVE YOU TRIED TO USE IT ON *ME*.
SO, WE DON'T GET OUR BONUSES?
ARRGHHH!
RELAX.
YOU'VE JUST GOT YOUR PANTIES ALL WRAPPED UP AROUND GRADY.
THAT'S *NOT* EVEN A REAL *PHRASE*.
COME ON, SIT DOWN.

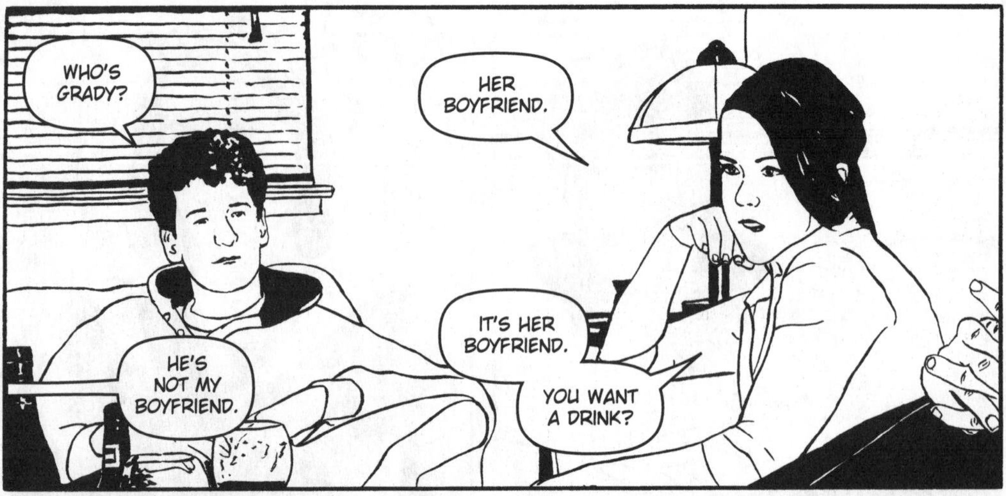
WHO'S GRADY?
HER BOYFRIEND.
HE'S NOT MY BOYFRIEND.
IT'S HER BOYFRIEND.
YOU WANT A DRINK?

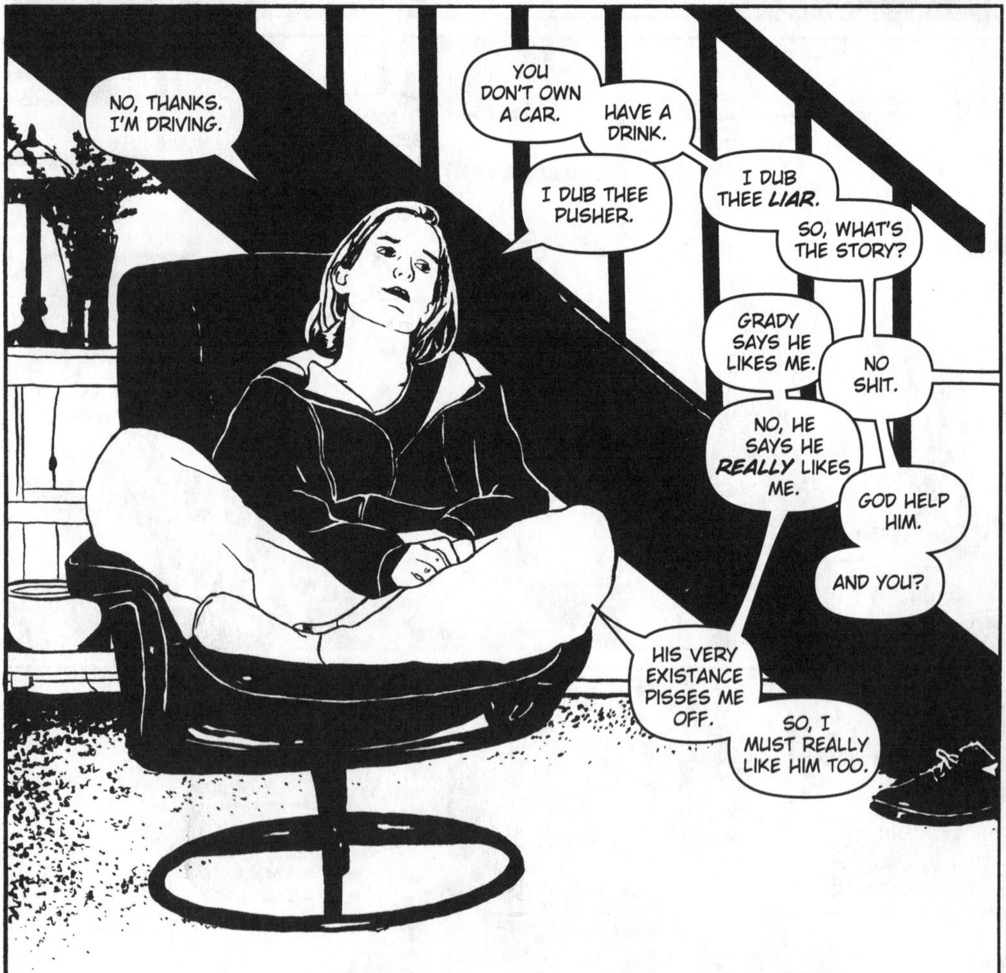
NO, THANKS. I'M DRIVING.
YOU DON'T OWN A CAR.
HAVE A DRINK.
I DUB THEE PUSHER.
I DUB THEE *LIAR*.
SO, WHAT'S THE STORY?
GRADY SAYS HE LIKES ME.
NO SHIT.
NO, HE SAYS HE *REALLY* LIKES ME.
GOD HELP HIM.
AND YOU?
HIS VERY EXISTANCE PISSES ME OFF.
SO, I MUST REALLY LIKE HIM TOO.

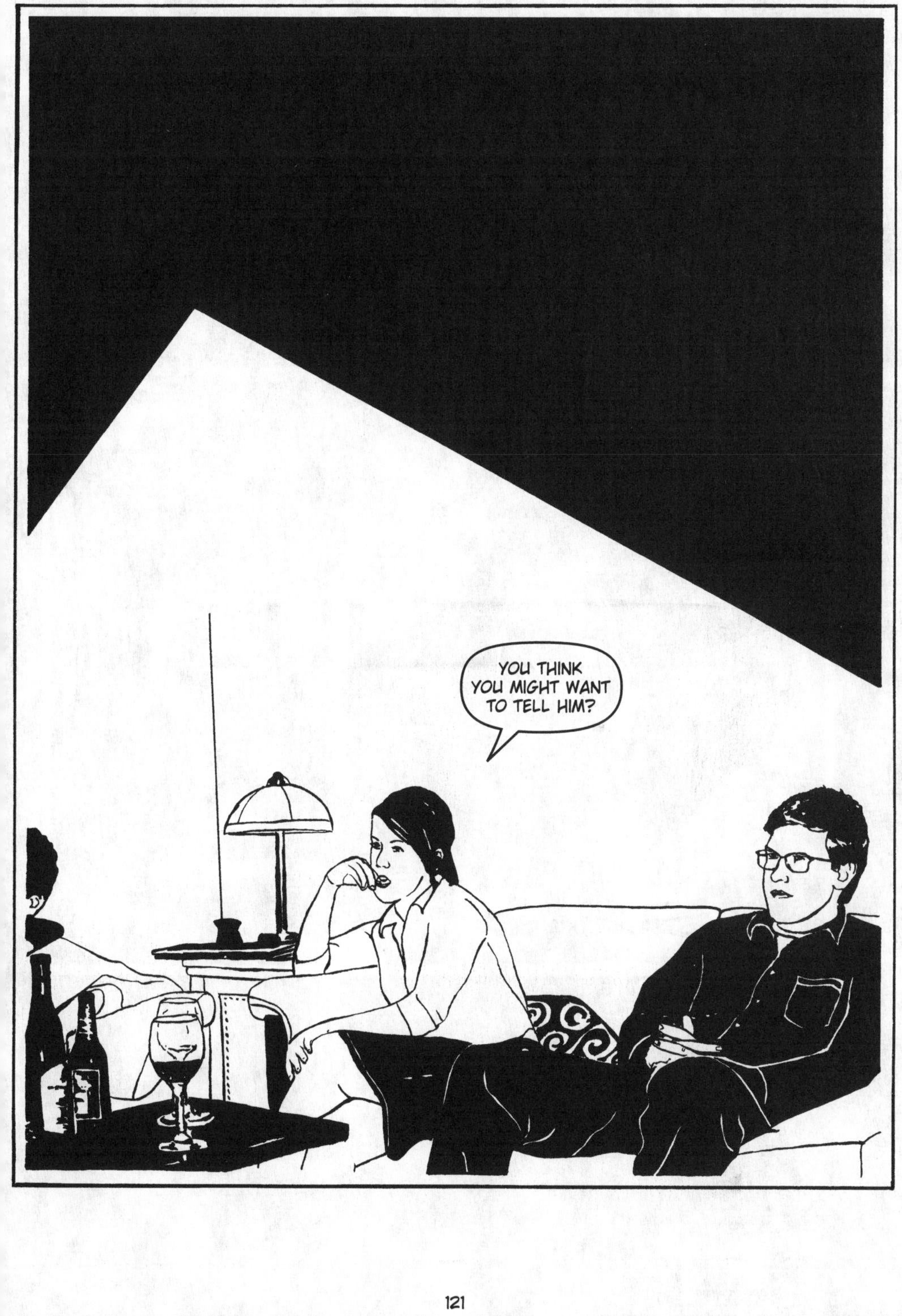
YOU THINK YOU MIGHT WANT TO TELL HIM?

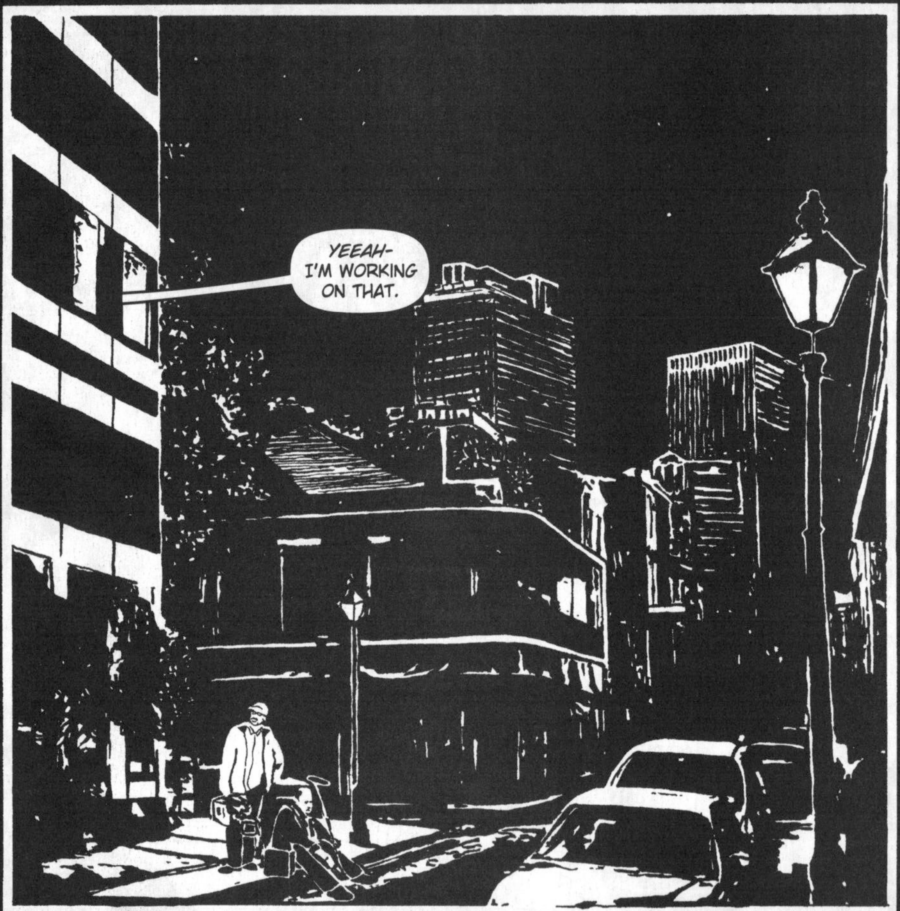
YEEAH-
I'M WORKING
ON THAT.

4

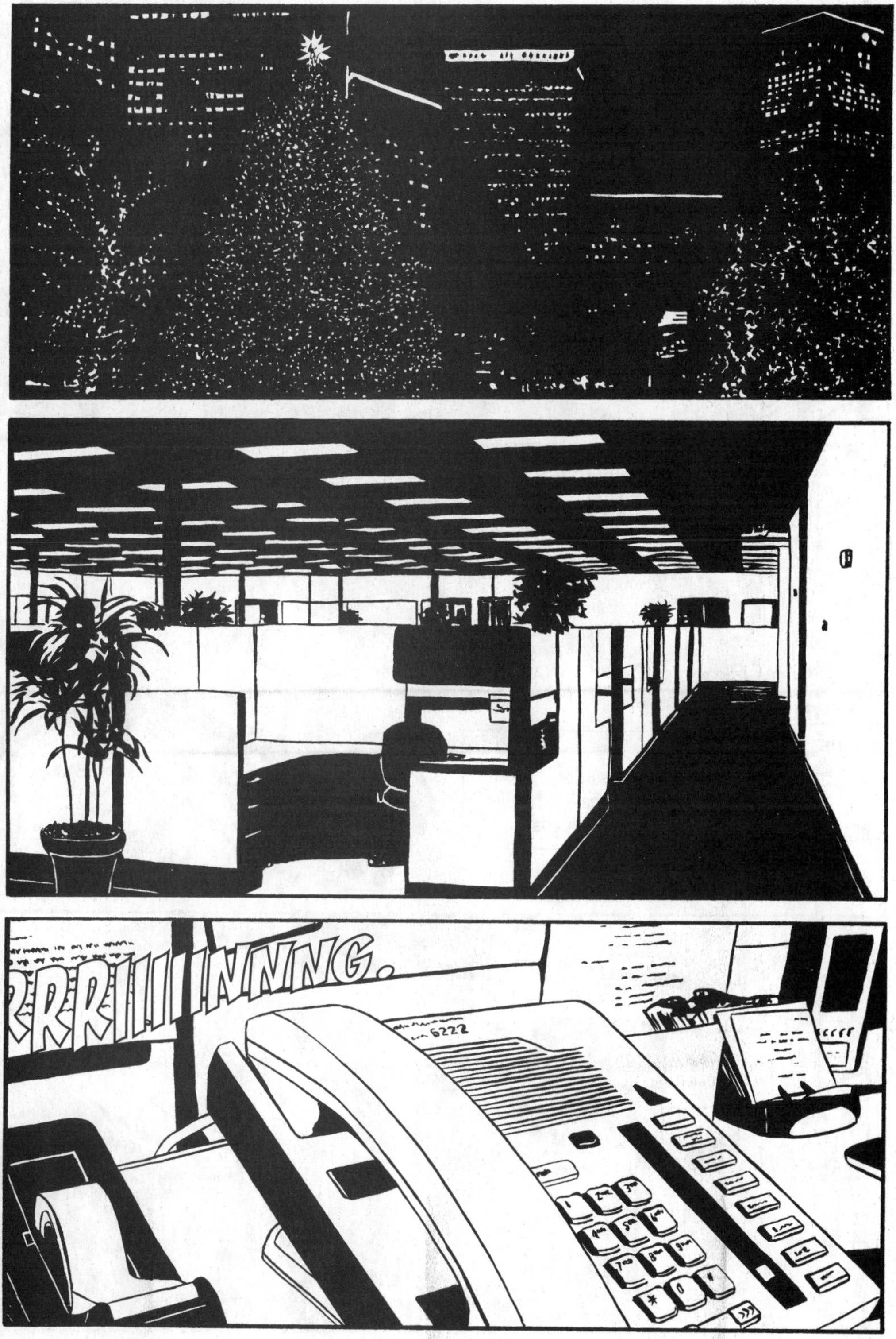
RRRIIIIINNNG.

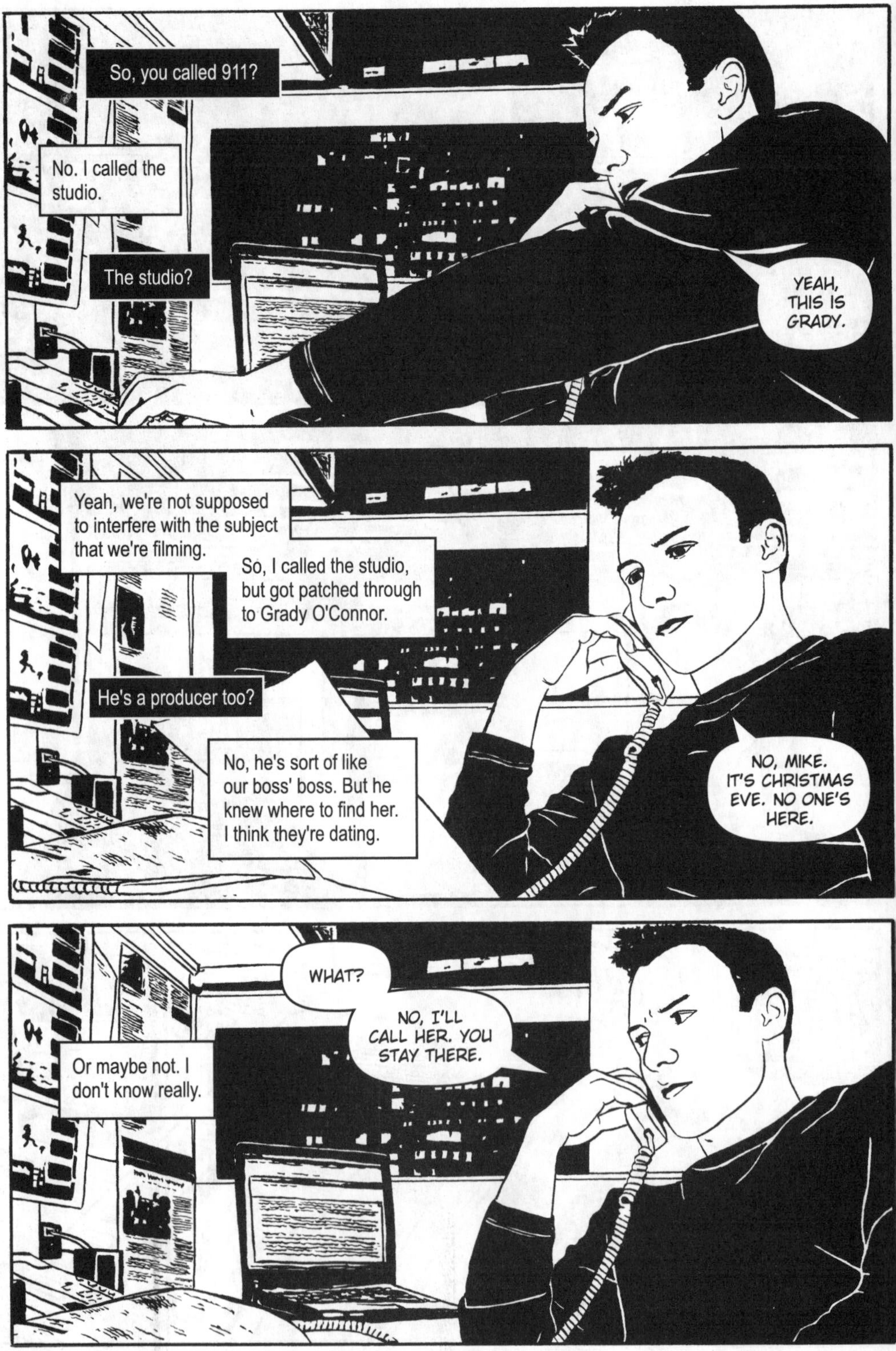

So, you called 911?
No. I called the studio.
The studio?
YEAH, THIS IS GRADY.
Yeah, we're not supposed to interfere with the subject that we're filming.
So, I called the studio, but got patched through to Grady O'Connor.
He's a producer too?
No, he's sort of like our boss' boss. But he knew where to find her. I think they're dating.
NO, MIKE. IT'S CHRISTMAS EVE. NO ONE'S HERE.
WHAT?
NO, I'LL CALL HER. YOU STAY THERE.
Or maybe not. I don't know really.

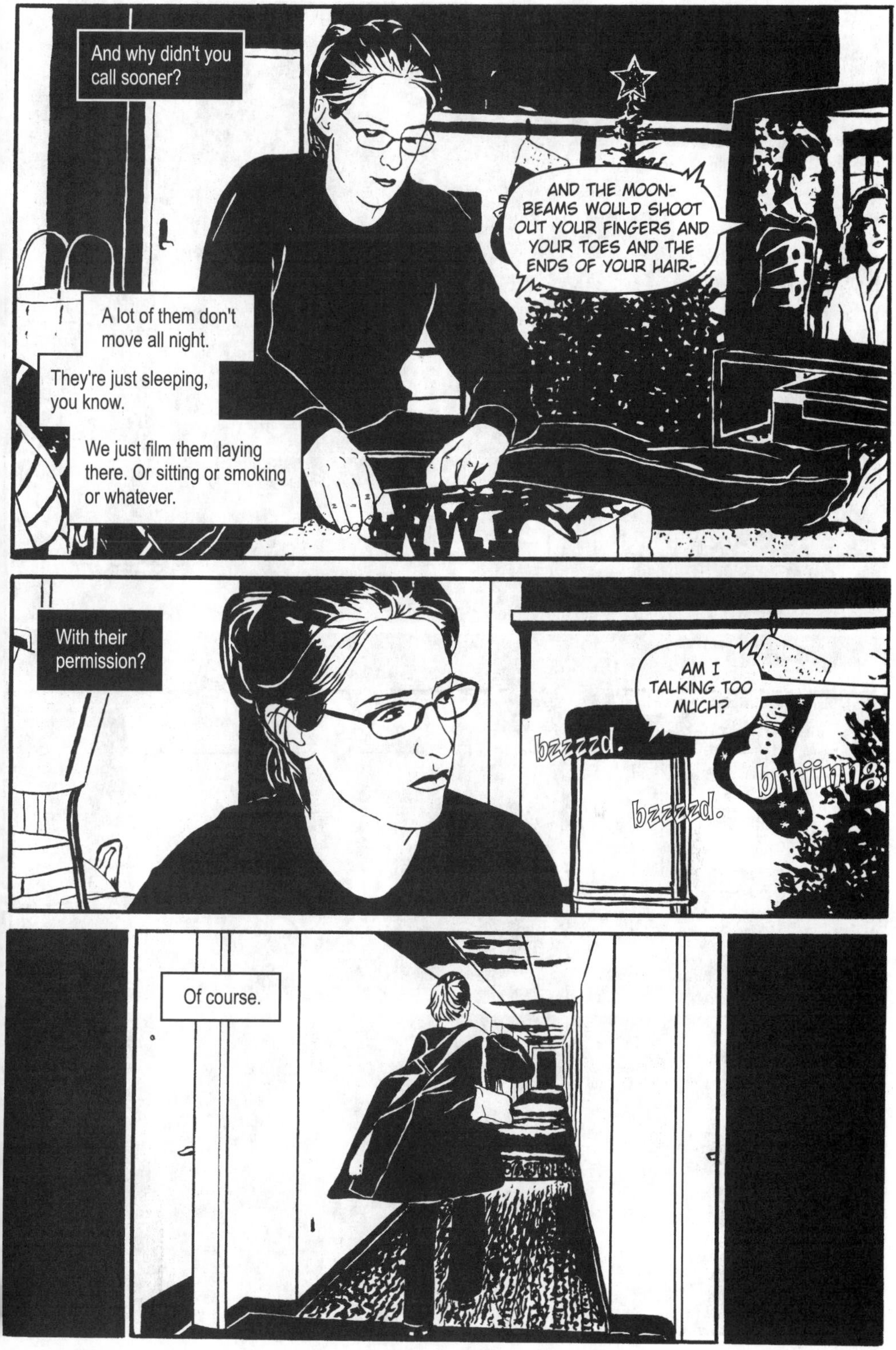

And why didn't you call sooner?
AND THE MOON-BEAMS WOULD SHOOT OUT YOUR FINGERS AND YOUR TOES AND THE ENDS OF YOUR HAIR-
A lot of them don't move all night.
They're just sleeping, you know.
We just film them laying there. Or sitting or smoking or whatever.
With their permission?
AM I TALKING TOO MUCH?
bzzzzd.
bzzzzd.
brriinng
Of course.

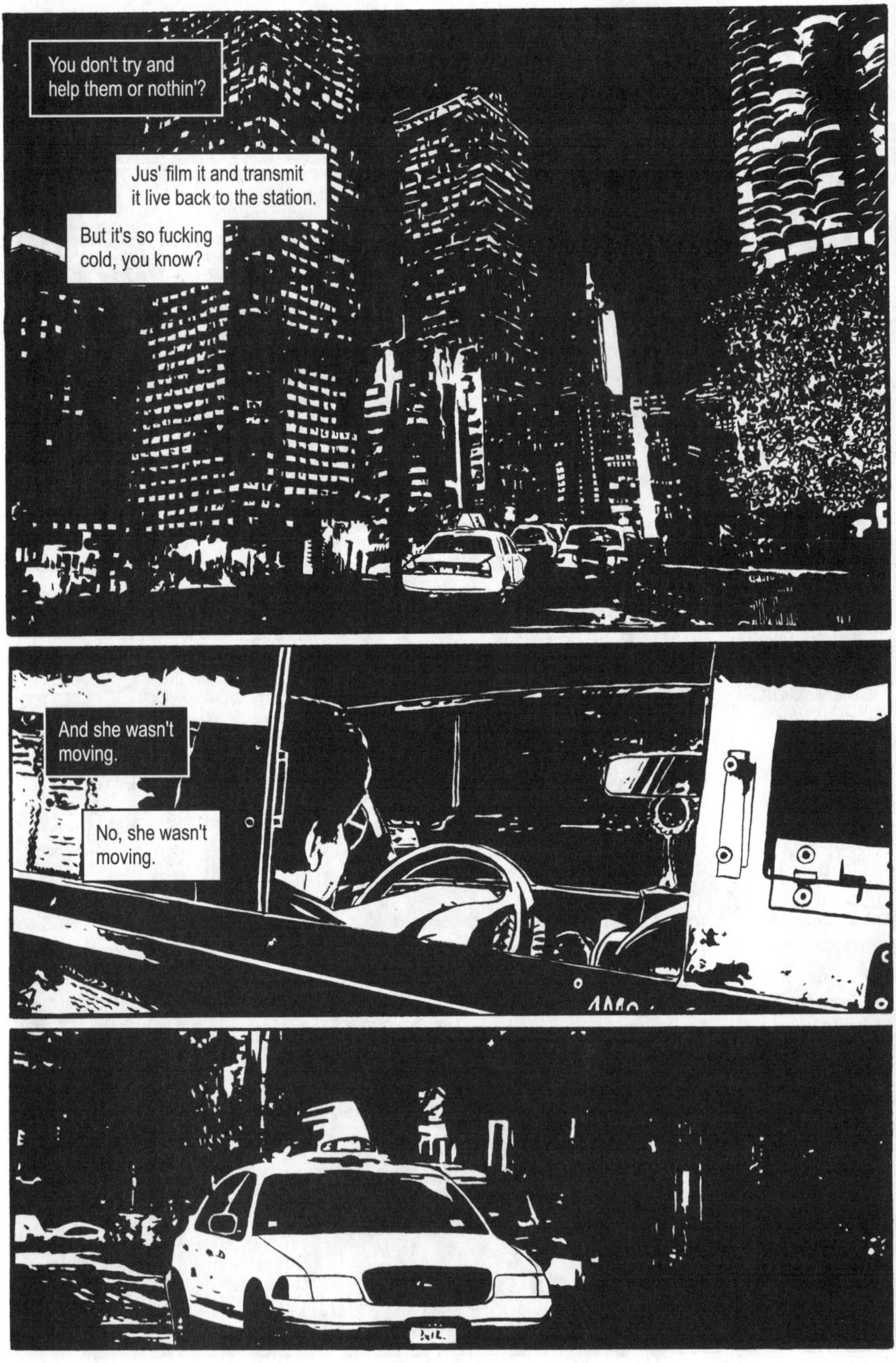
You don't try and help them or nothin'?
Jus' film it and transmit it live back to the station.
But it's so fucking cold, you know?
And she wasn't moving.
No, she wasn't moving.

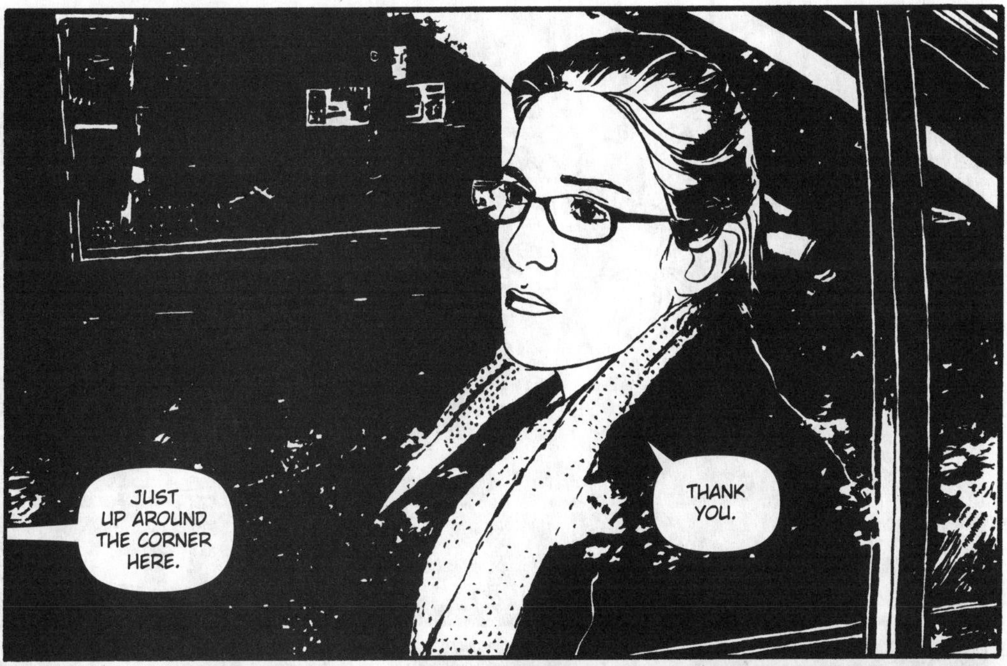
JUST UP AROUND THE CORNER HERE.
THANK YOU.

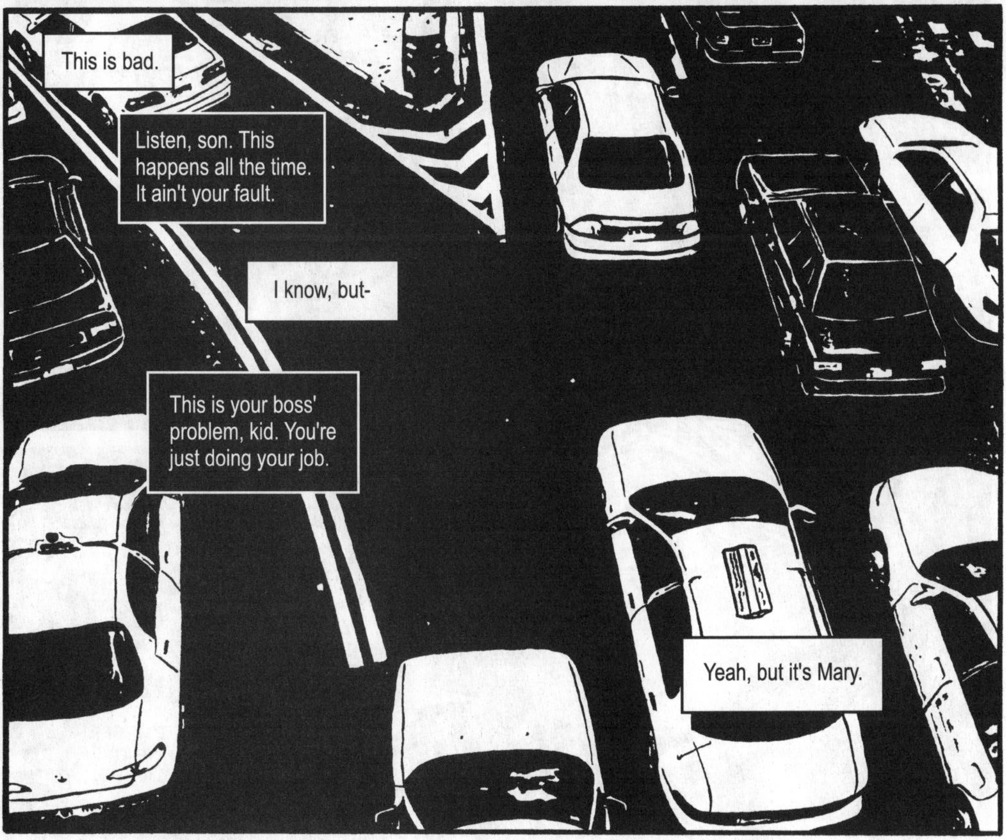
This is bad.
Listen, son. This happens all the time. It ain't your fault.
I know, but-
This is your boss' problem, kid. You're just doing your job.
Yeah, but it's Mary.

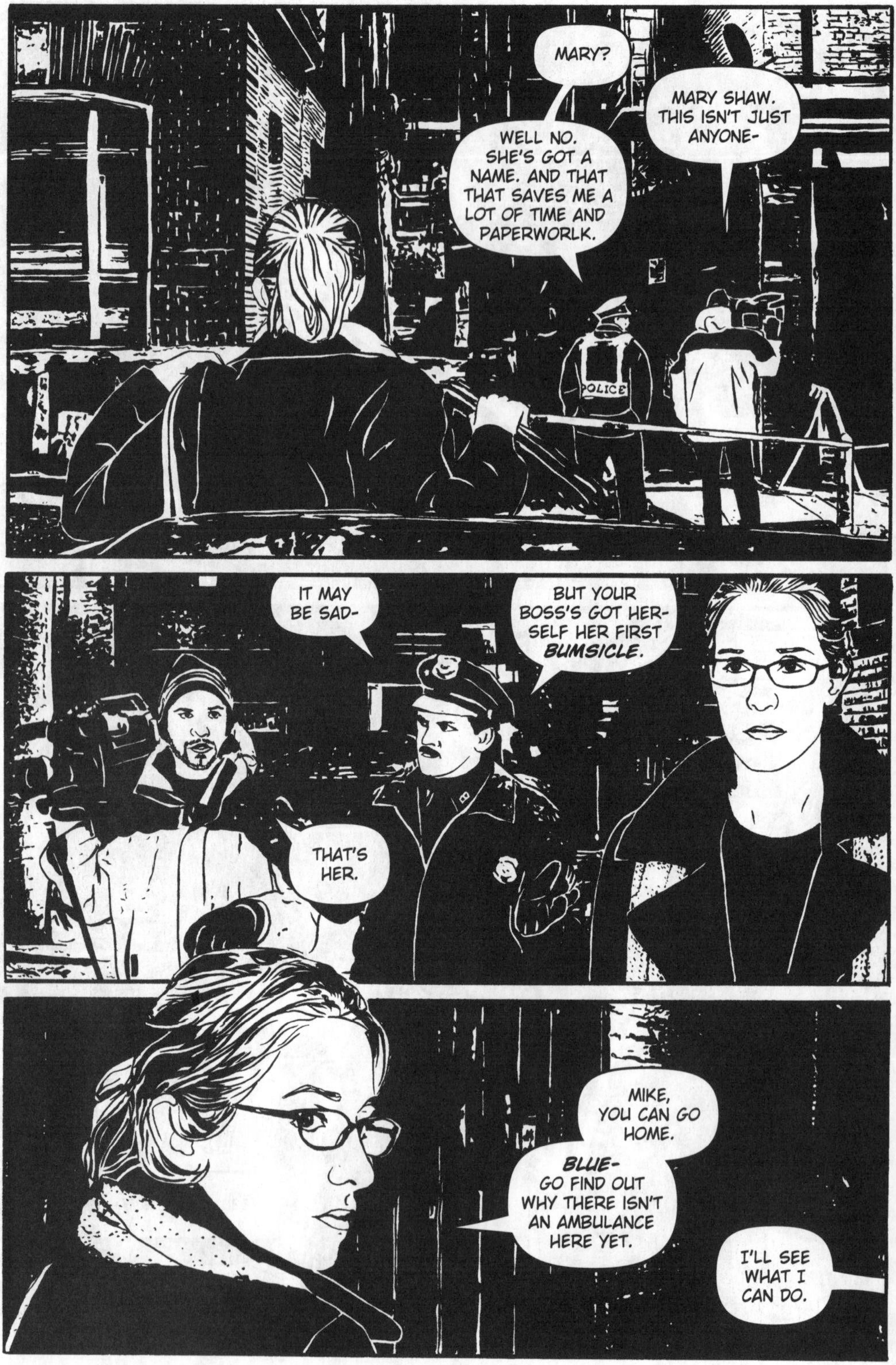
MARY?
WELL NO. SHE'S GOT A NAME. AND THAT THAT SAVES ME A LOT OF TIME AND PAPERWORLK.
MARY SHAW. THIS ISN'T JUST ANYONE-
POLICE
IT MAY BE SAD-
BUT YOUR BOSS'S GOT HER-SELF HER FIRST *BUMSICLE*.
THAT'S HER.
MIKE, YOU CAN GO HOME.
BLUE- GO FIND OUT WHY THERE ISN'T AN AMBULANCE HERE YET.
I'LL SEE WHAT I CAN DO.

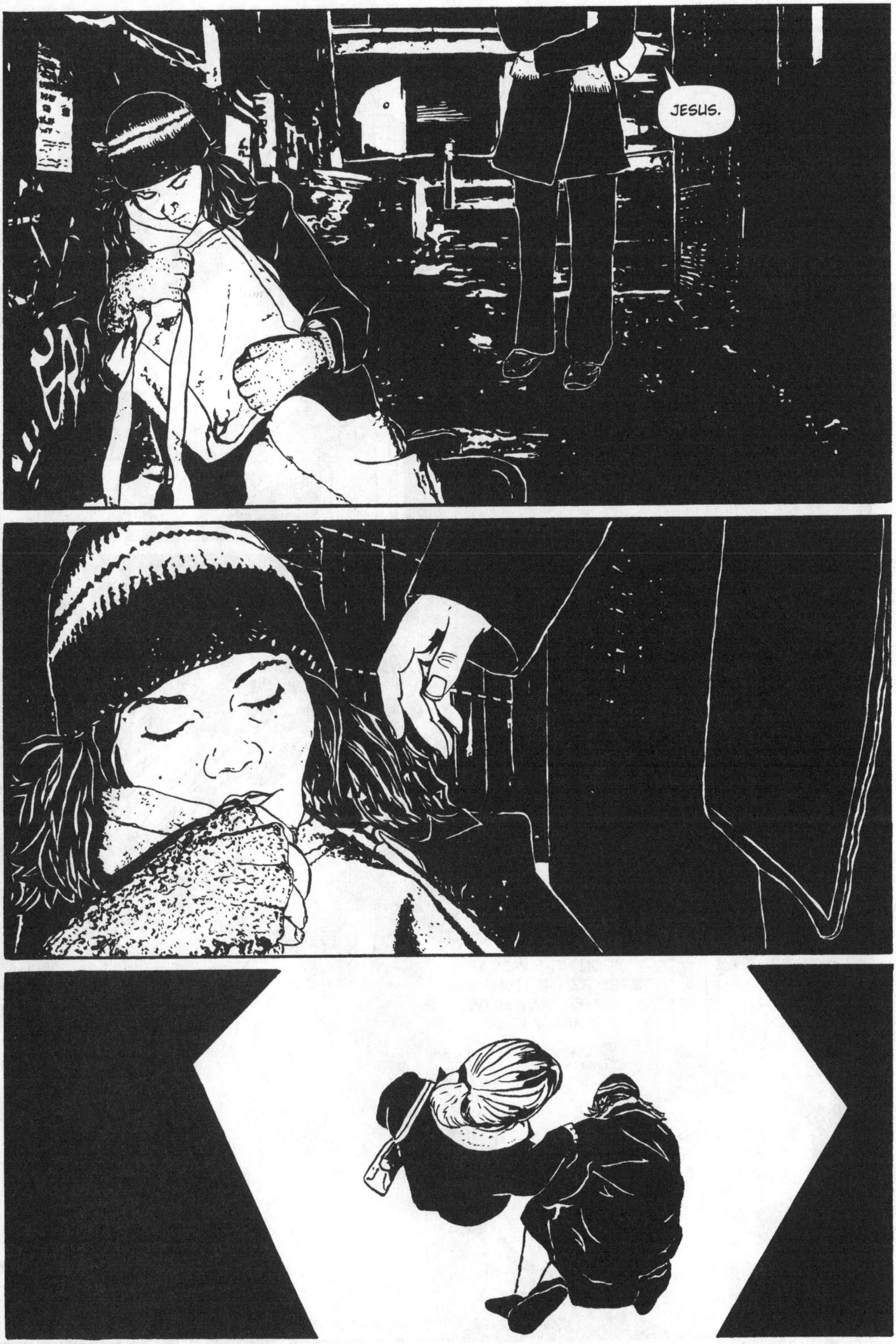
JESUS.

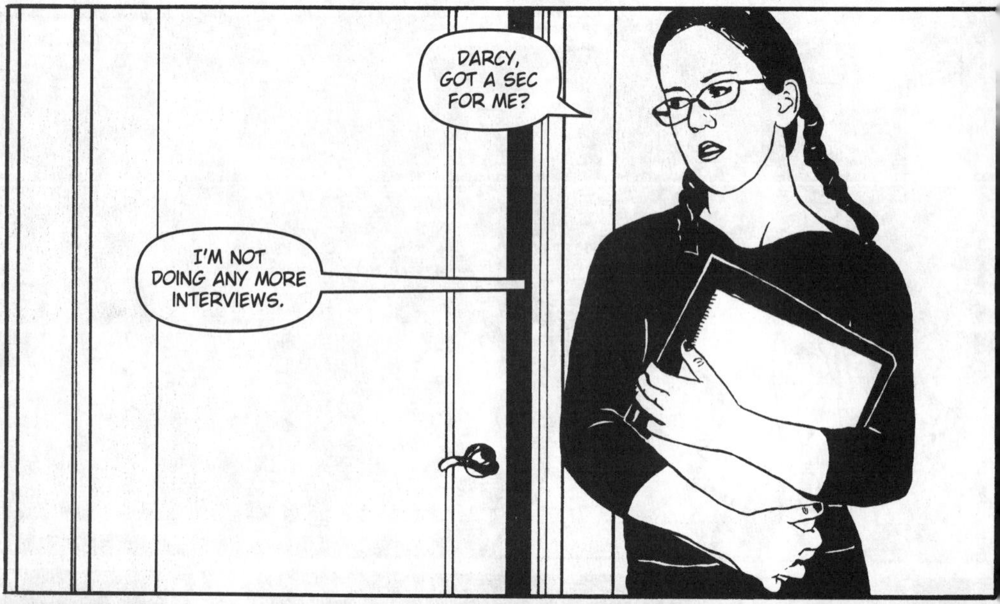
DARCY, GOT A SEC FOR ME?
I'M NOT DOING ANY MORE INTERVIEWS.

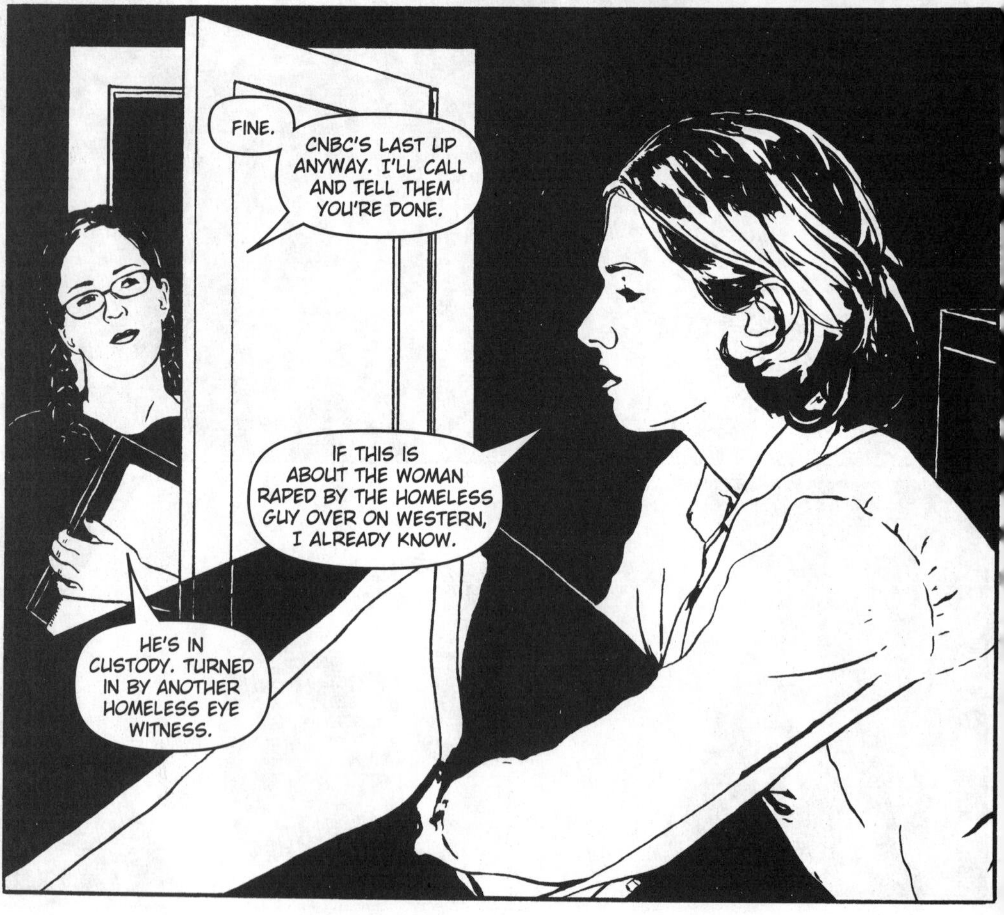
FINE.
CNBC'S LAST UP ANYWAY. I'LL CALL AND TELL THEM YOU'RE DONE.
IF THIS IS ABOUT THE WOMAN RAPED BY THE HOMELESS GUY OVER ON WESTERN, I ALREADY KNOW.
HE'S IN CUSTODY. TURNED IN BY ANOTHER HOMELESS EYE WITNESS.

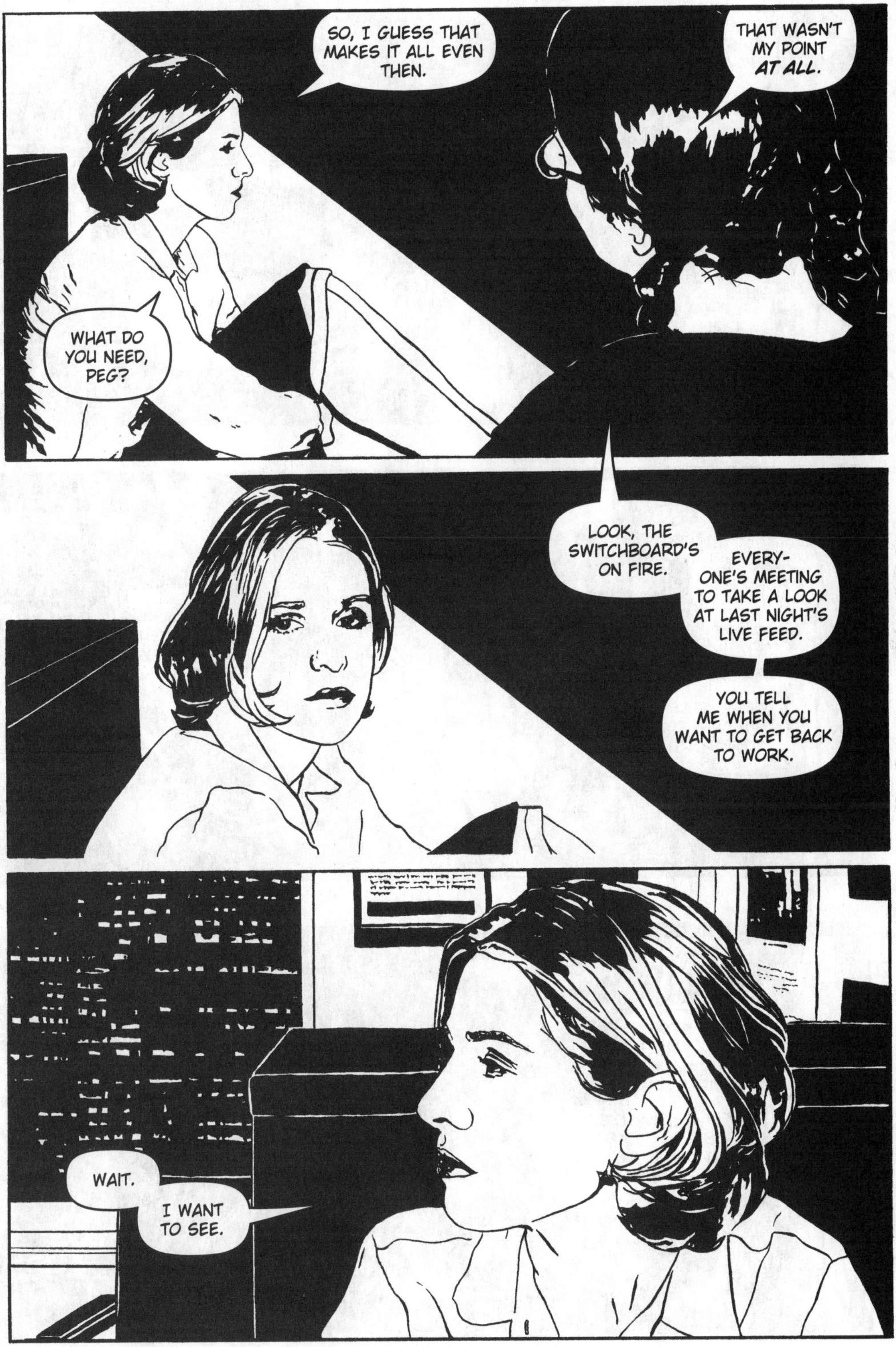
SO, I GUESS THAT MAKES IT ALL EVEN THEN.
THAT WASN'T MY POINT *AT ALL.*
WHAT DO YOU NEED, PEG?
LOOK, THE SWITCHBOARD'S ON FIRE.
EVERY-ONE'S MEETING TO TAKE A LOOK AT LAST NIGHT'S LIVE FEED.
YOU TELL ME WHEN YOU WANT TO GET BACK TO WORK.
WAIT.
I WANT TO SEE.

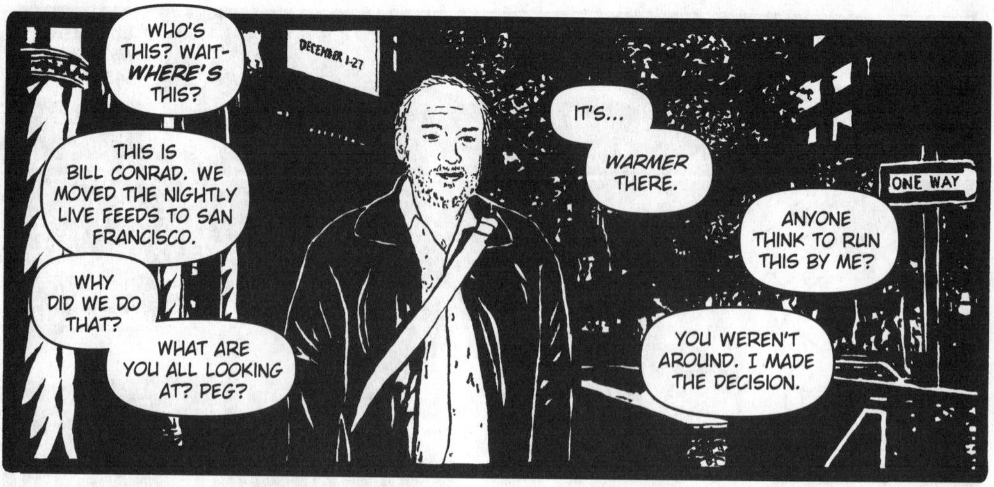
WHO'S THIS? WAIT- WHERE'S THIS?
DECEMBER 1-27
THIS IS BILL CONRAD. WE MOVED THE NIGHTLY LIVE FEEDS TO SAN FRANCISCO.
WHY DID WE DO THAT?
WHAT ARE YOU ALL LOOKING AT? PEG?
IT'S...
WARMER THERE.
ONE WAY
ANYONE THINK TO RUN THIS BY ME?
YOU WEREN'T AROUND. I MADE THE DECISION.

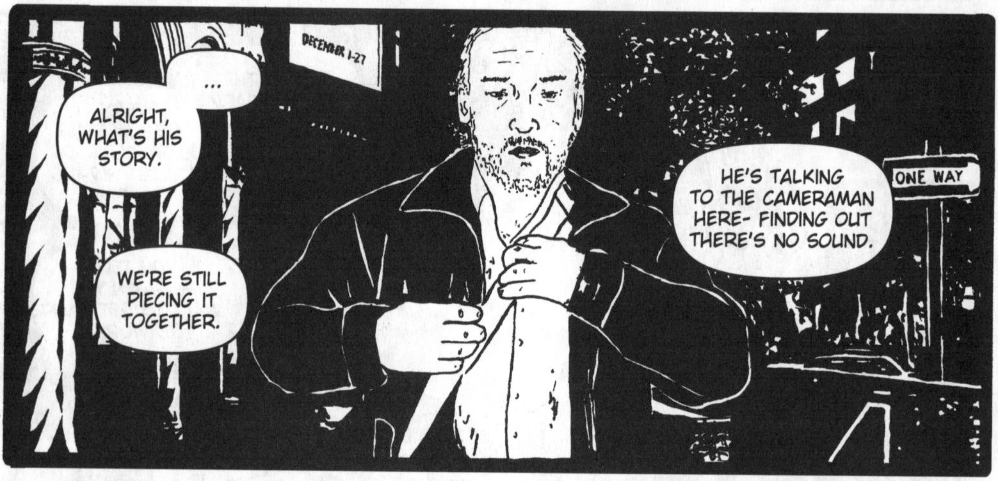
DECEMBER 1-27
...
ALRIGHT, WHAT'S HIS STORY.
ONE WAY
HE'S TALKING TO THE CAMERAMAN HERE- FINDING OUT THERE'S NO SOUND.
WE'RE STILL PIECING IT TOGETHER.

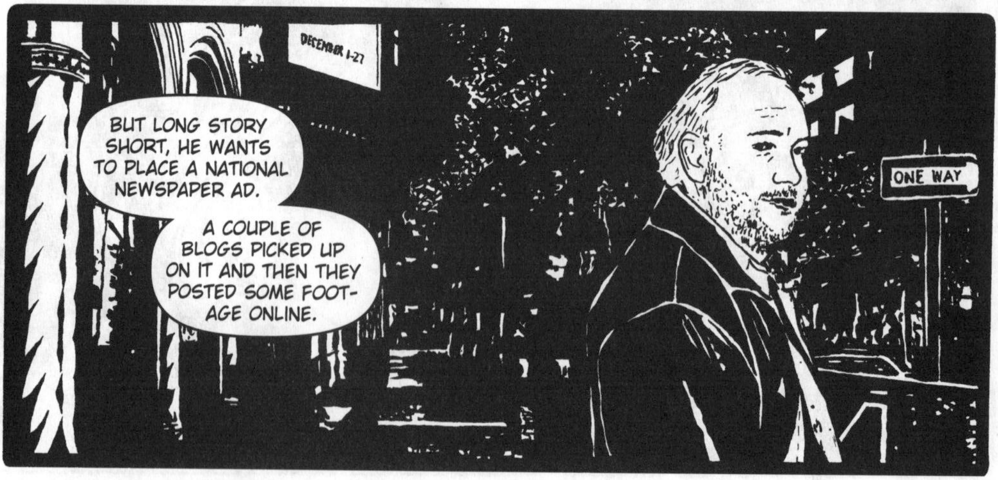
DECEMBER 1-27
BUT LONG STORY SHORT, HE WANTS TO PLACE A NATIONAL NEWSPAPER AD.
A COUPLE OF BLOGS PICKED UP ON IT AND THEN THEY POSTED SOME FOOT-AGE ONLINE.
ONE WAY

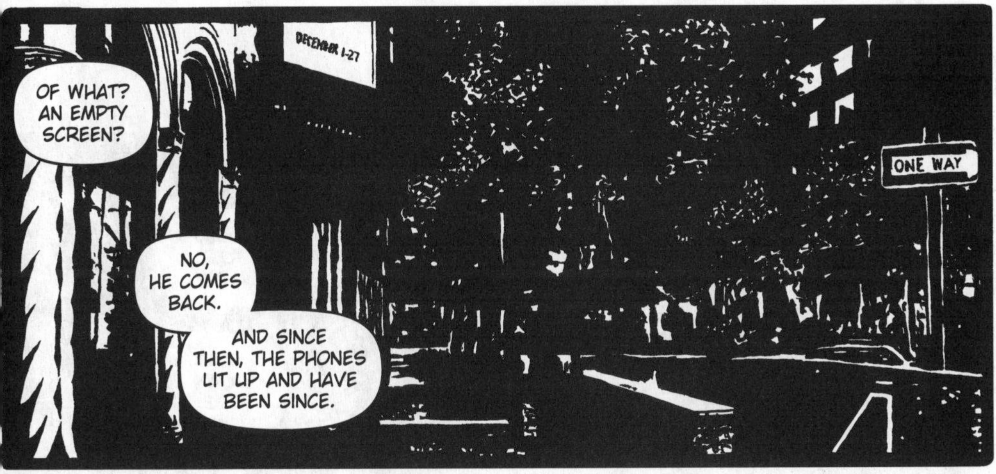
DECEMBER 1-27
OF WHAT? AN EMPTY SCREEN?
ONE WAY
NO, HE COMES BACK.
AND SINCE THEN, THE PHONES LIT UP AND HAVE BEEN SINCE.

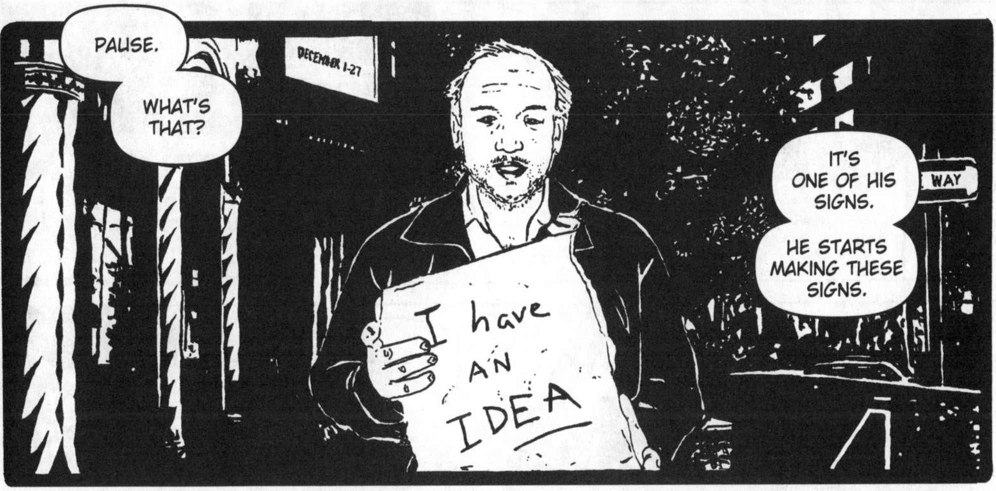
PAUSE.
WHAT'S THAT?
DECEMBER 1-27
IT'S ONE OF HIS SIGNS.
HE STARTS MAKING THESE SIGNS.
WAY
I have AN IDEA

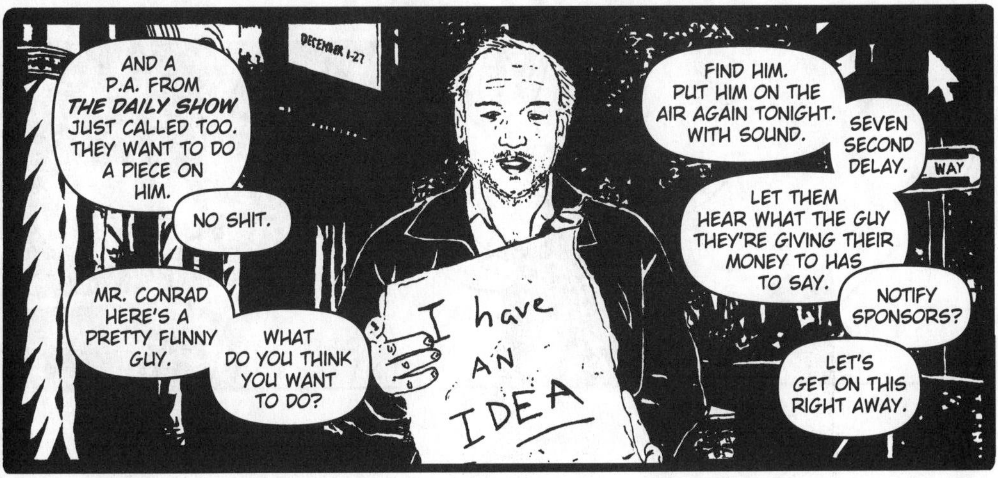
DECEMBER 1-27
AND A P.A. FROM *THE DAILY SHOW* JUST CALLED TOO. THEY WANT TO DO A PIECE ON HIM.
NO SHIT.
MR. CONRAD HERE'S A PRETTY FUNNY GUY.
WHAT DO YOU THINK YOU WANT TO DO?
FIND HIM. PUT HIM ON THE AIR AGAIN TONIGHT. WITH SOUND.
SEVEN SECOND DELAY.
WAY
LET THEM HEAR WHAT THE GUY THEY'RE GIVING THEIR MONEY TO HAS TO SAY.
NOTIFY SPONSORS?
LET'S GET ON THIS RIGHT AWAY.
I have AN IDEA

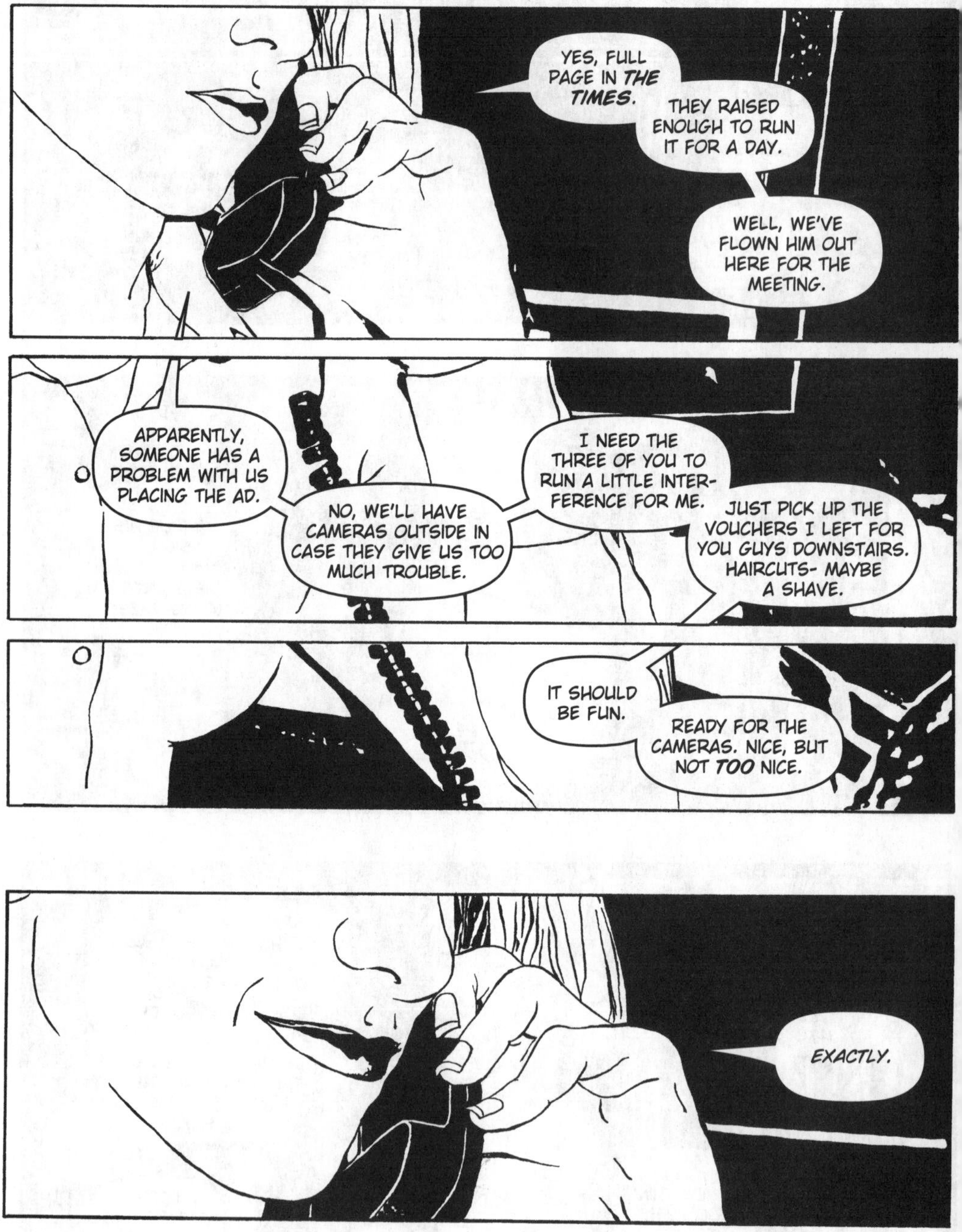
YES, FULL PAGE IN *THE TIMES*.
THEY RAISED ENOUGH TO RUN IT FOR A DAY.
WELL, WE'VE FLOWN HIM OUT HERE FOR THE MEETING.
APPARENTLY, SOMEONE HAS A PROBLEM WITH US PLACING THE AD.
NO, WE'LL HAVE CAMERAS OUTSIDE IN CASE THEY GIVE US TOO MUCH TROUBLE.
I NEED THE THREE OF YOU TO RUN A LITTLE INTER-FERENCE FOR ME.
JUST PICK UP THE VOUCHERS I LEFT FOR YOU GUYS DOWNSTAIRS. HAIRCUTS- MAYBE A SHAVE.
IT SHOULD BE FUN.
READY FOR THE CAMERAS. NICE, BUT NOT *TOO* NICE.
EXACTLY.

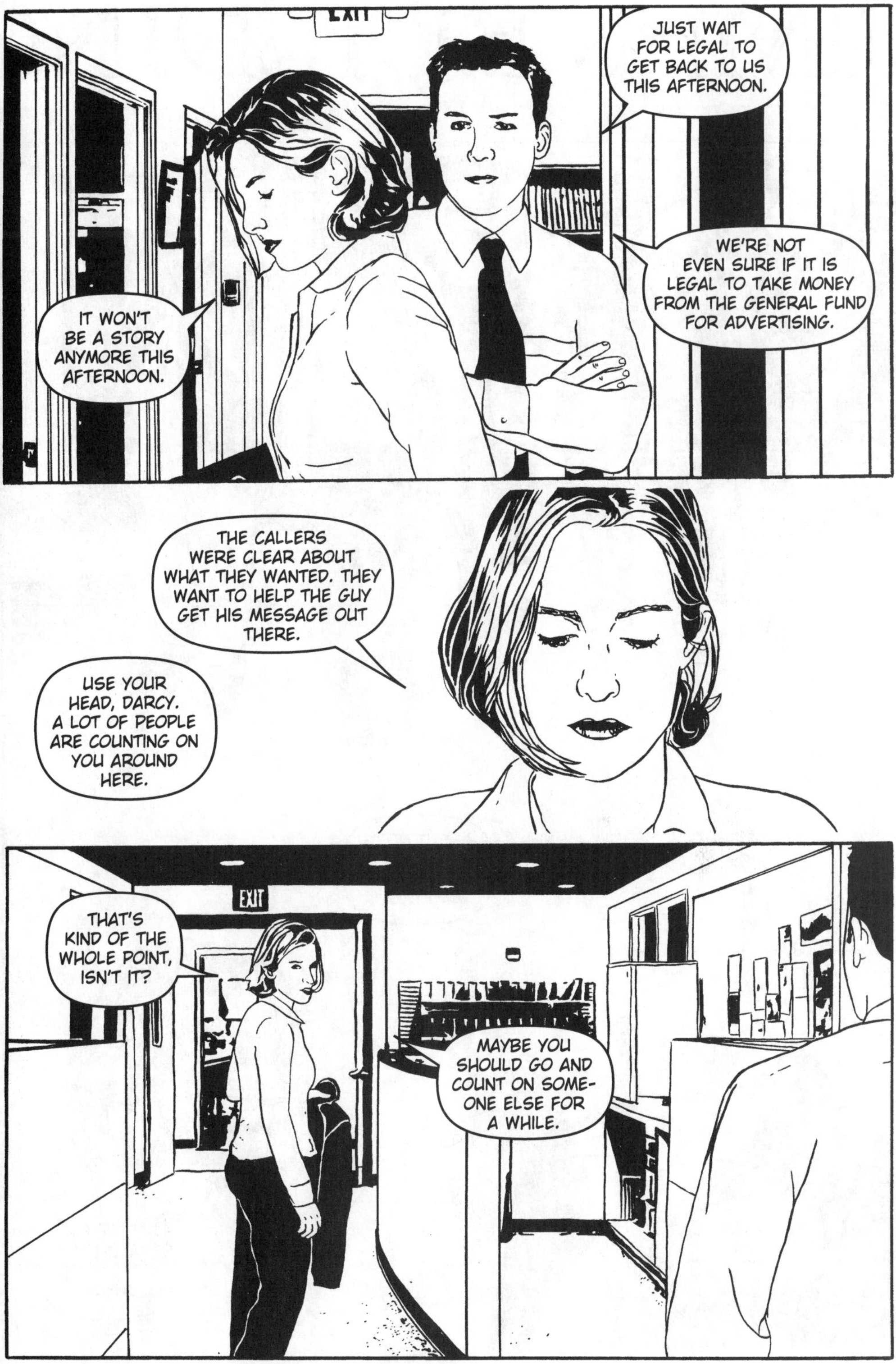
EXIT
JUST WAIT FOR LEGAL TO GET BACK TO US THIS AFTERNOON.
WE'RE NOT EVEN SURE IF IT IS LEGAL TO TAKE MONEY FROM THE GENERAL FUND FOR ADVERTISING.
IT WON'T BE A STORY ANYMORE THIS AFTERNOON.
THE CALLERS WERE CLEAR ABOUT WHAT THEY WANTED. THEY WANT TO HELP THE GUY GET HIS MESSAGE OUT THERE.
USE YOUR HEAD, DARCY. A LOT OF PEOPLE ARE COUNTING ON YOU AROUND HERE.
EXIT
THAT'S KIND OF THE WHOLE POINT, ISN'T IT?
MAYBE YOU SHOULD GO AND COUNT ON SOME-ONE ELSE FOR A WHILE.

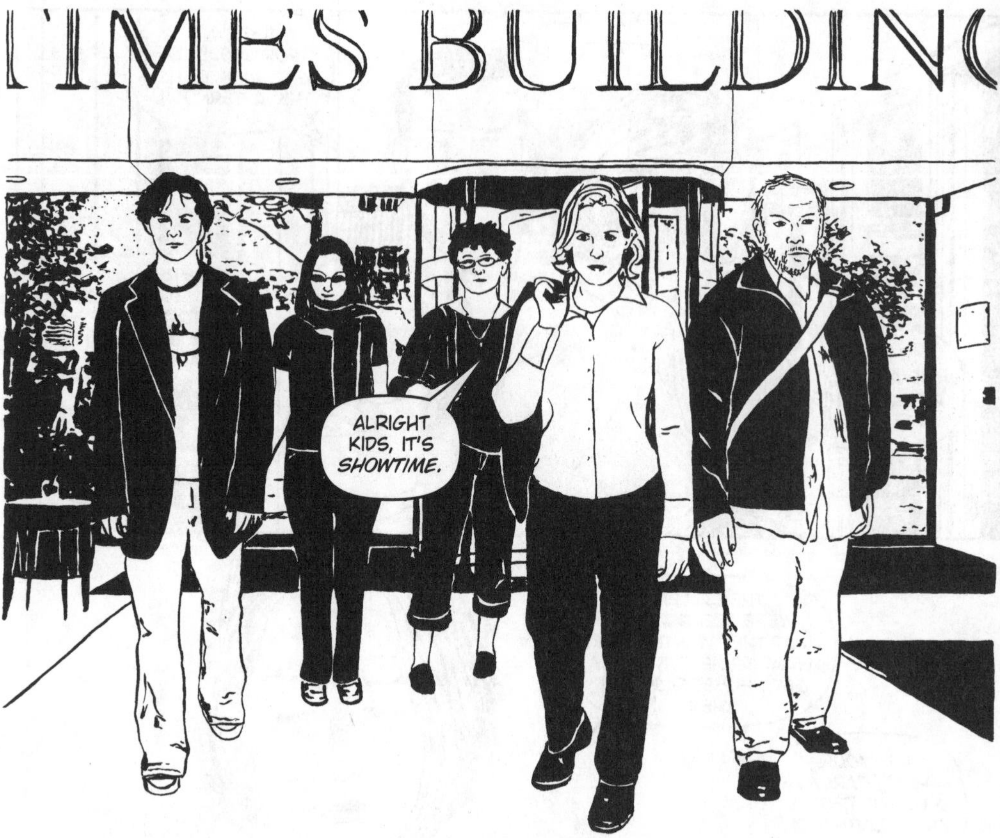
TIMES BUILDING
ALRIGHT KIDS, IT'S *SHOWTIME.*

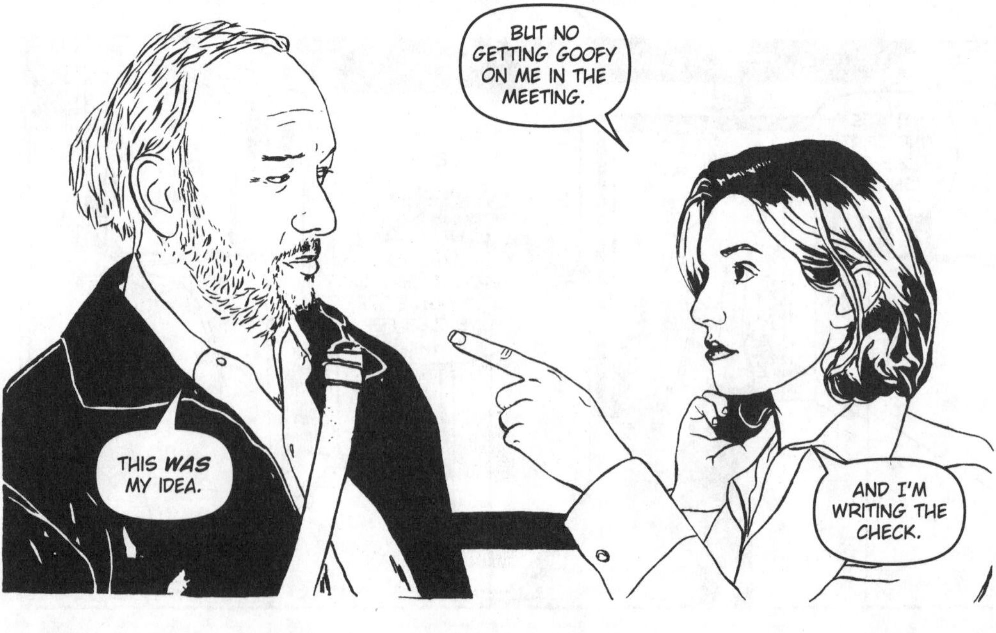
BUT NO GETTING GOOFY ON ME IN THE MEETING.
THIS ***WAS*** MY IDEA.
AND I'M WRITING THE CHECK.

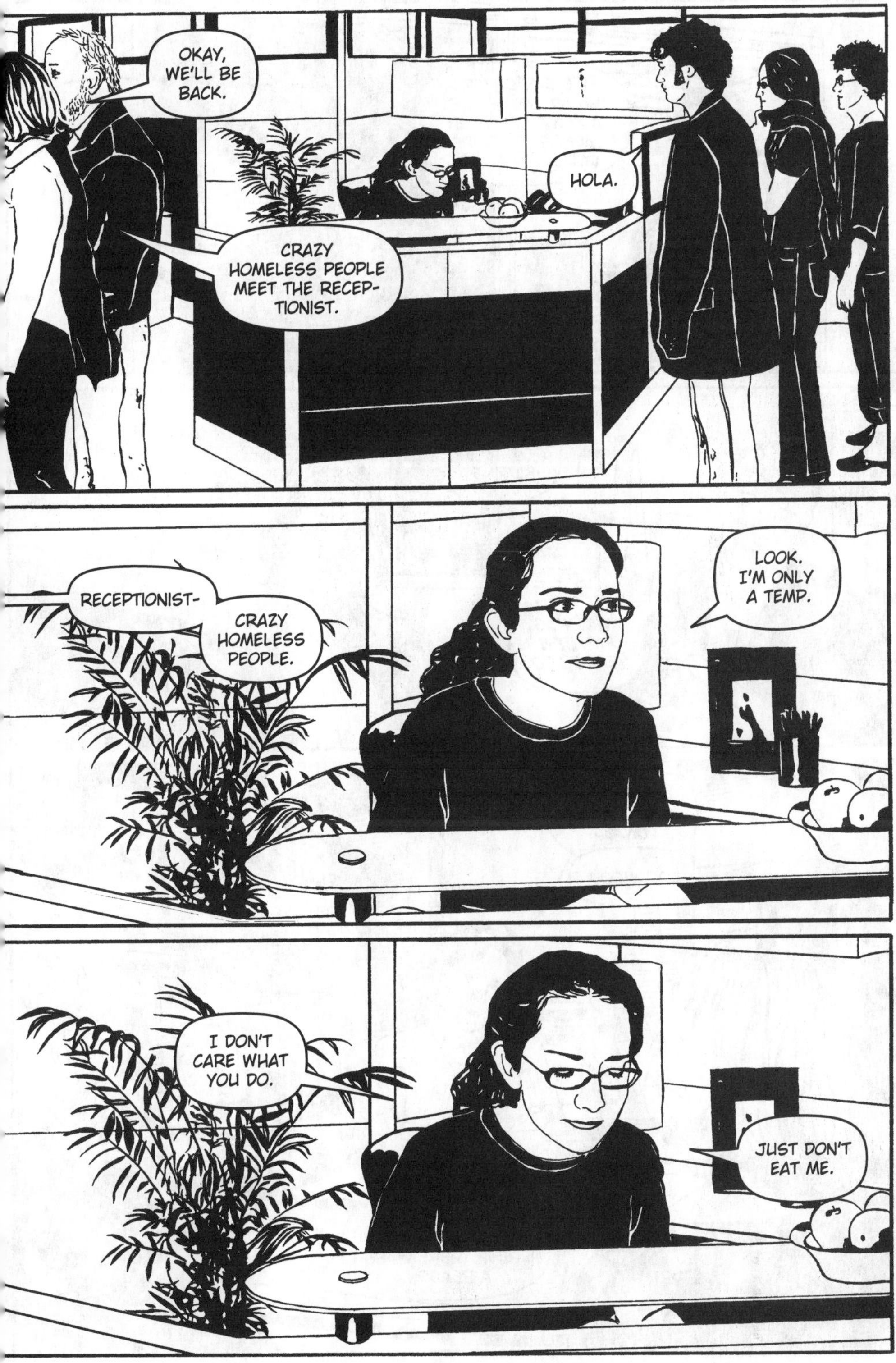
OKAY, WE'LL BE BACK.
HOLA.
CRAZY HOMELESS PEOPLE MEET THE RECEPTIONIST.
RECEPTIONIST-
CRAZY HOMELESS PEOPLE.
LOOK. I'M ONLY A TEMP.
I DON'T CARE WHAT YOU DO.
JUST DON'T EAT ME.

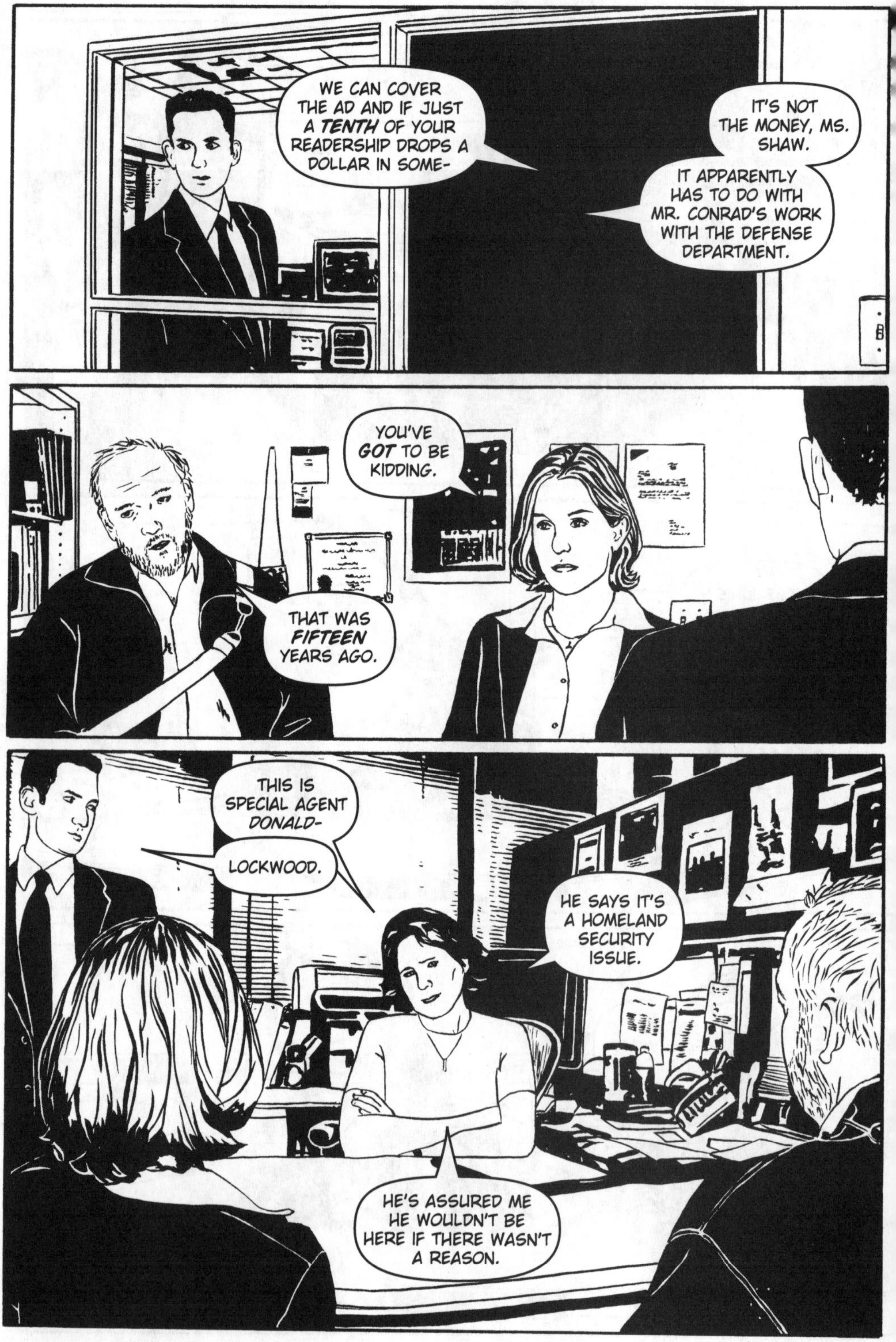
WE CAN COVER THE AD AND IF JUST A *TENTH* OF YOUR READERSHIP DROPS A DOLLAR IN SOME-
IT'S NOT THE MONEY, MS. SHAW.
IT APPARENTLY HAS TO DO WITH MR. CONRAD'S WORK WITH THE DEFENSE DEPARTMENT.
YOU'VE *GOT* TO BE KIDDING.
THAT WAS *FIFTEEN* YEARS AGO.
THIS IS SPECIAL AGENT *DONALD-*
LOCKWOOD.
HE SAYS IT'S A HOMELAND SECURITY ISSUE.
HE'S ASSURED ME HE WOULDN'T BE HERE IF THERE WASN'T A REASON.

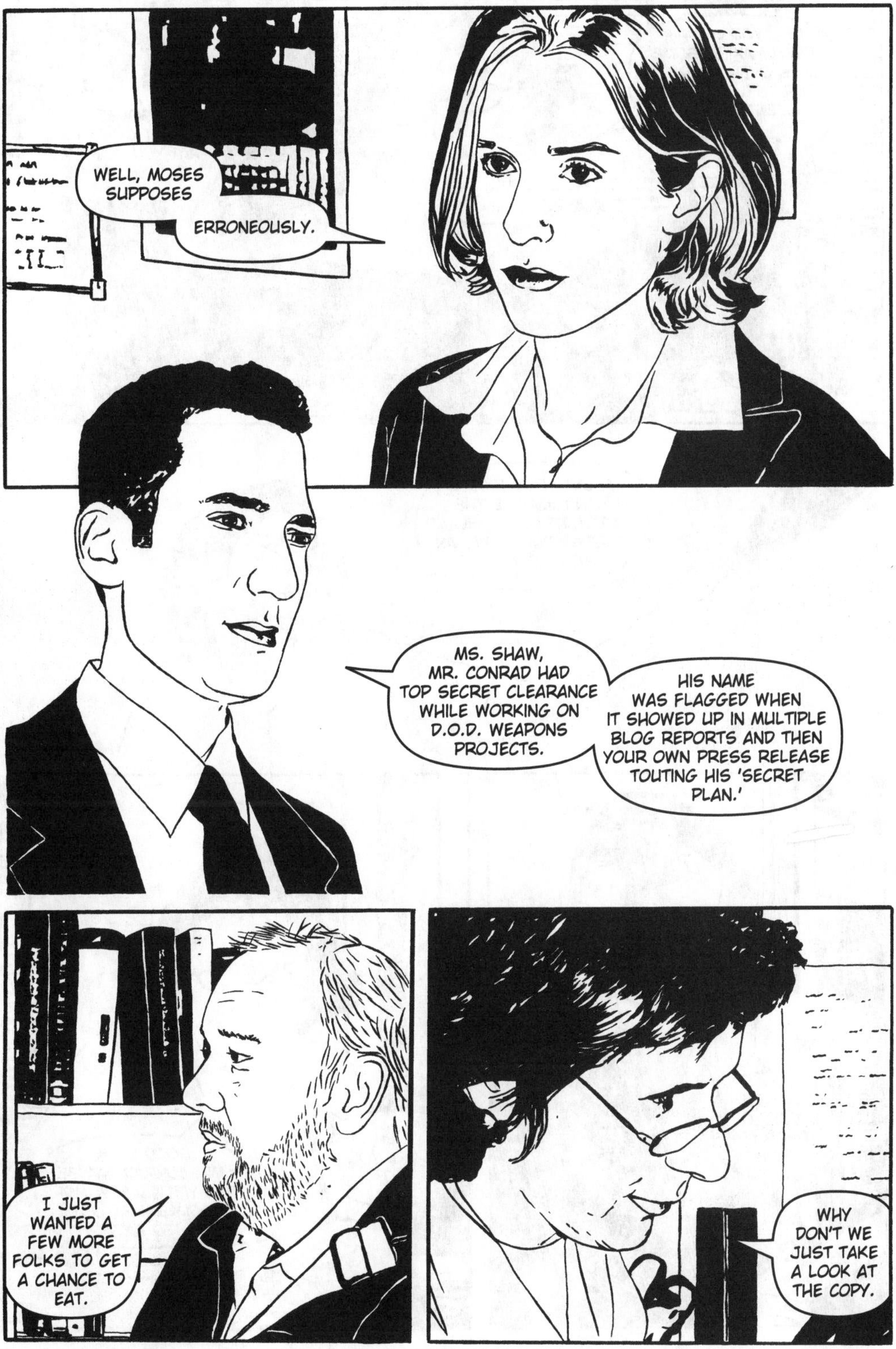
WELL, MOSES SUPPOSES
ERRONEOUSLY.
MS. SHAW, MR. CONRAD HAD TOP SECRET CLEARANCE WHILE WORKING ON D.O.D. WEAPONS PROJECTS.
HIS NAME WAS FLAGGED WHEN IT SHOWED UP IN MULTIPLE BLOG REPORTS AND THEN YOUR OWN PRESS RELEASE TOUTING HIS 'SECRET PLAN.'
I JUST WANTED A FEW MORE FOLKS TO GET A CHANCE TO EAT.
WHY DON'T WE JUST TAKE A LOOK AT THE COPY.

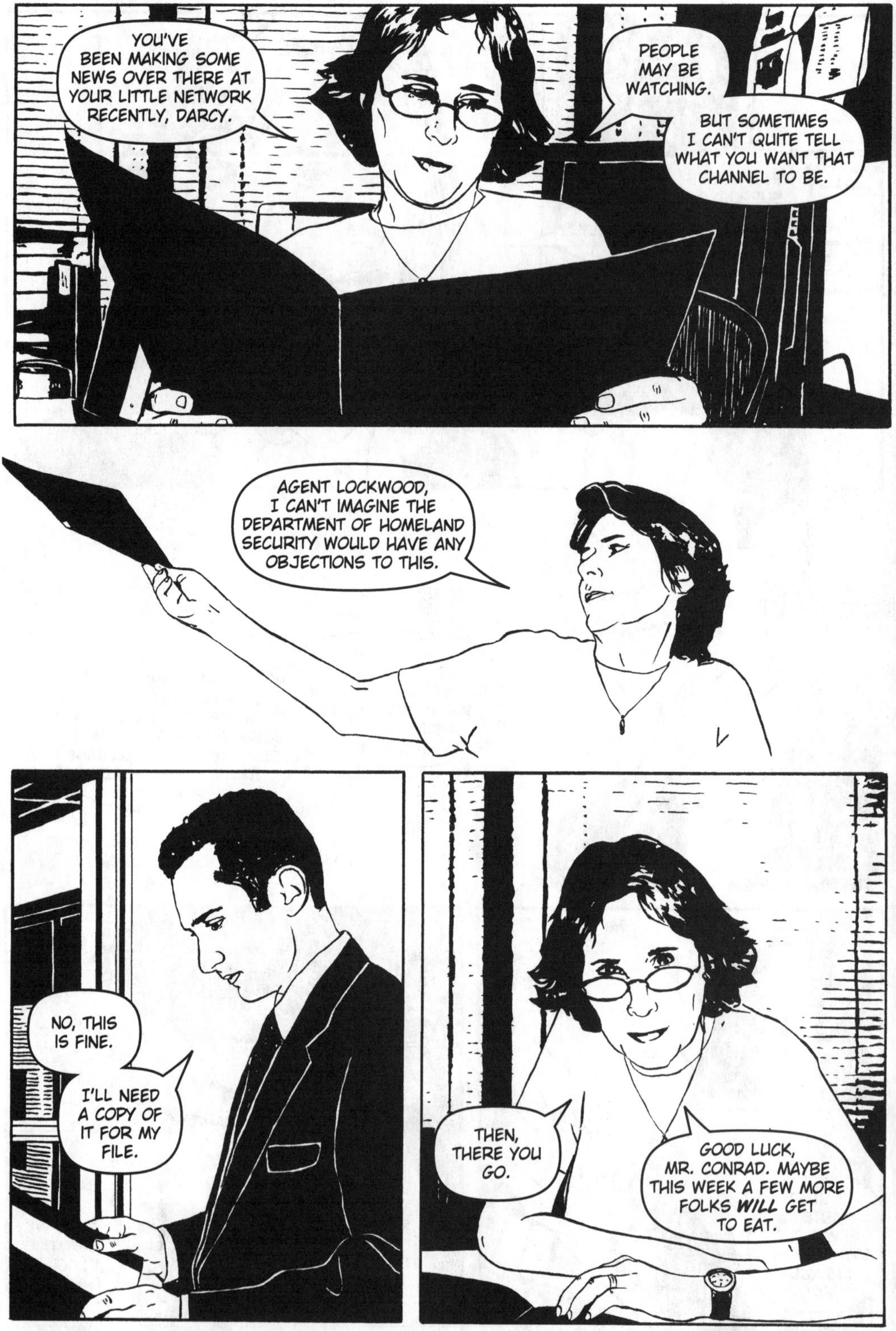
YOU'VE BEEN MAKING SOME NEWS OVER THERE AT YOUR LITTLE NETWORK RECENTLY, DARCY.
PEOPLE MAY BE WATCHING.
BUT SOMETIMES I CAN'T QUITE TELL WHAT YOU WANT THAT CHANNEL TO BE.
AGENT LOCKWOOD, I CAN'T IMAGINE THE DEPARTMENT OF HOMELAND SECURITY WOULD HAVE ANY OBJECTIONS TO THIS.
NO, THIS IS FINE.
I'LL NEED A COPY OF IT FOR MY FILE.
THEN, THERE YOU GO.
GOOD LUCK, MR. CONRAD. MAYBE THIS WEEK A FEW MORE FOLKS ***WILL*** GET TO EAT.

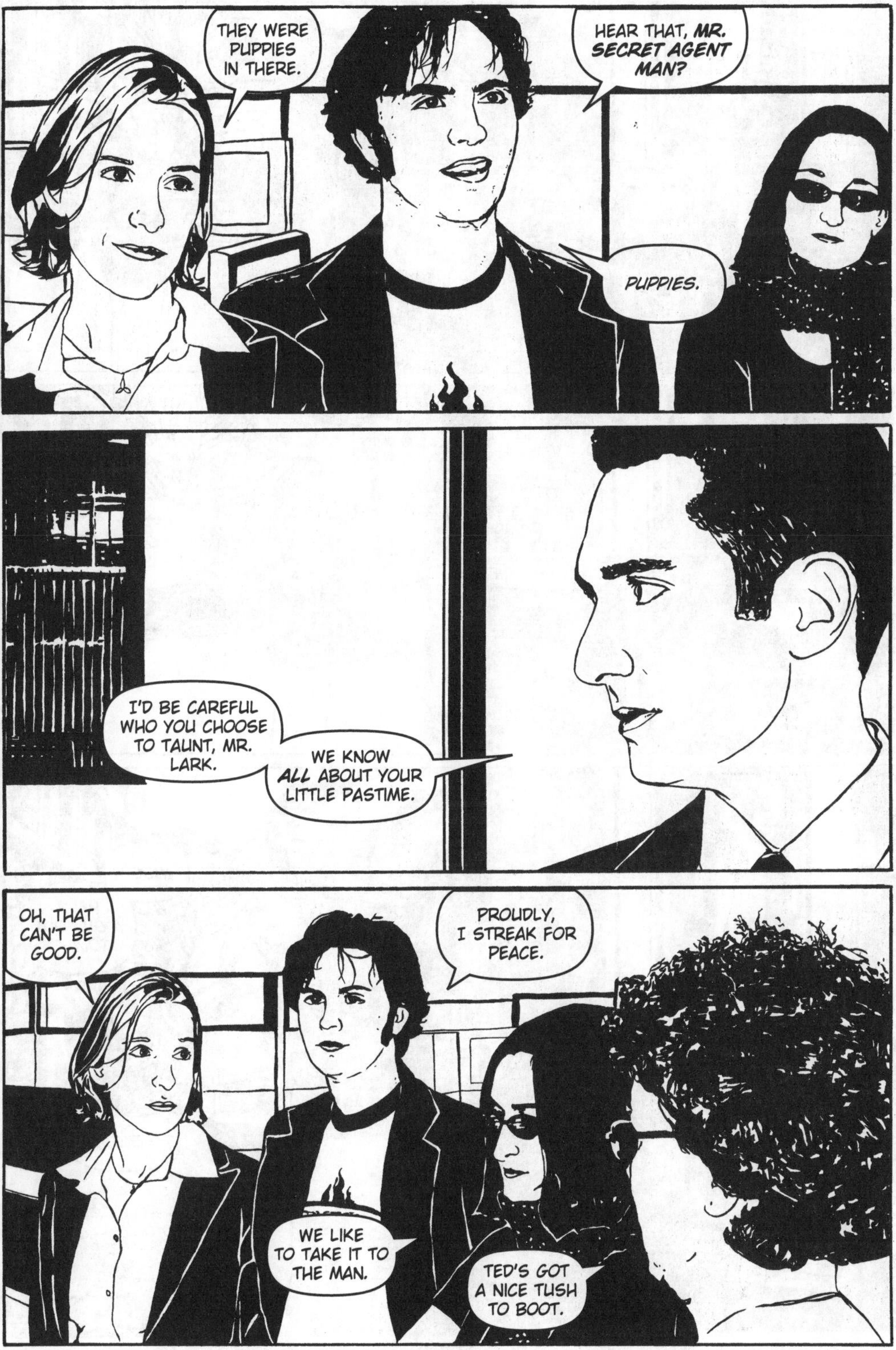
THEY WERE PUPPIES IN THERE.
HEAR THAT, MR. SECRET AGENT MAN?
PUPPIES.
I'D BE CAREFUL WHO YOU CHOOSE TO TAUNT, MR. LARK.
WE KNOW ALL ABOUT YOUR LITTLE PASTIME.
OH, THAT CAN'T BE GOOD.
PROUDLY, I STREAK FOR PEACE.
WE LIKE TO TAKE IT TO THE MAN.
TED'S GOT A NICE TUSH TO BOOT.

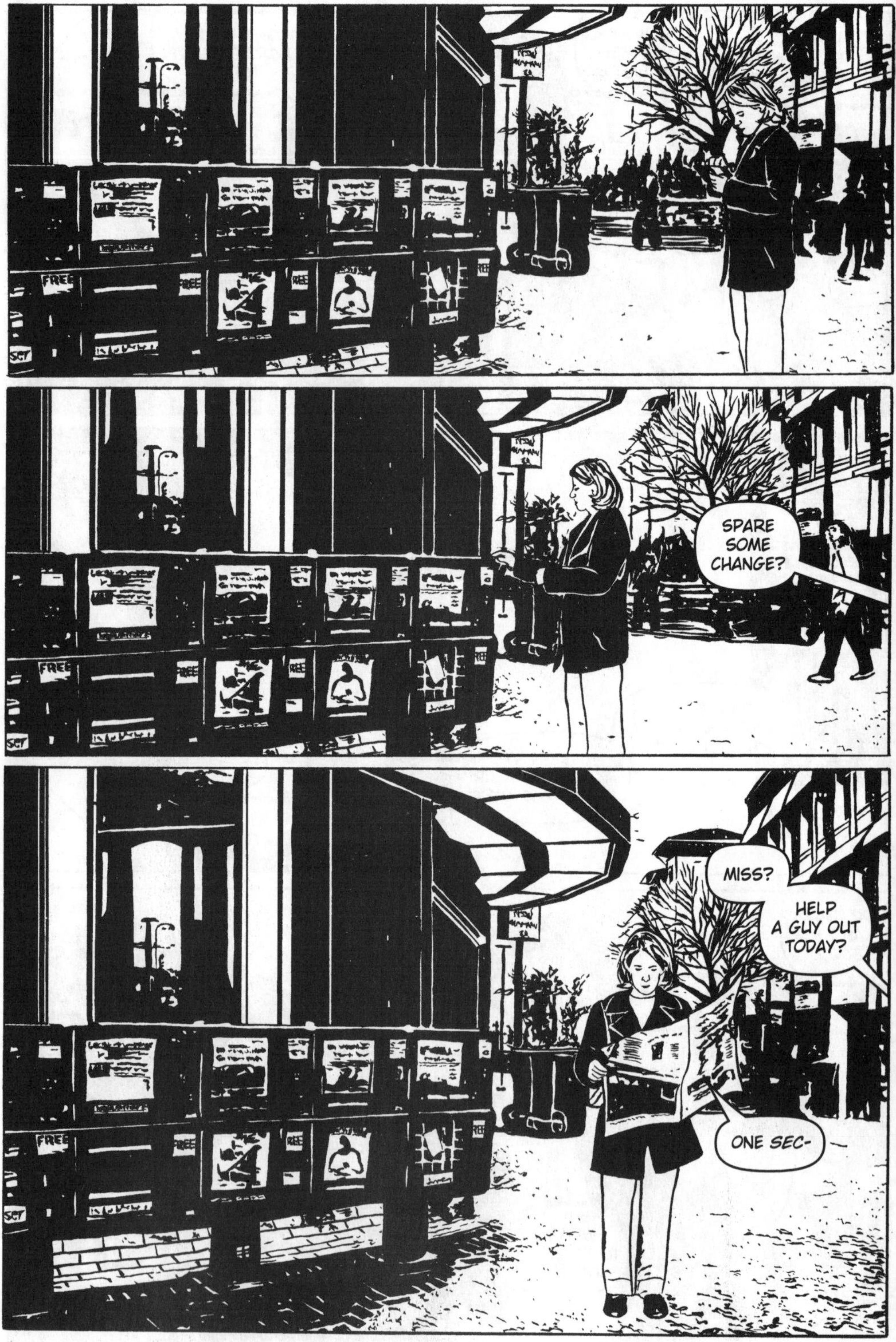
SPARE SOME CHANGE?
MISS?
HELP A GUY OUT TODAY?
ONE SEC-

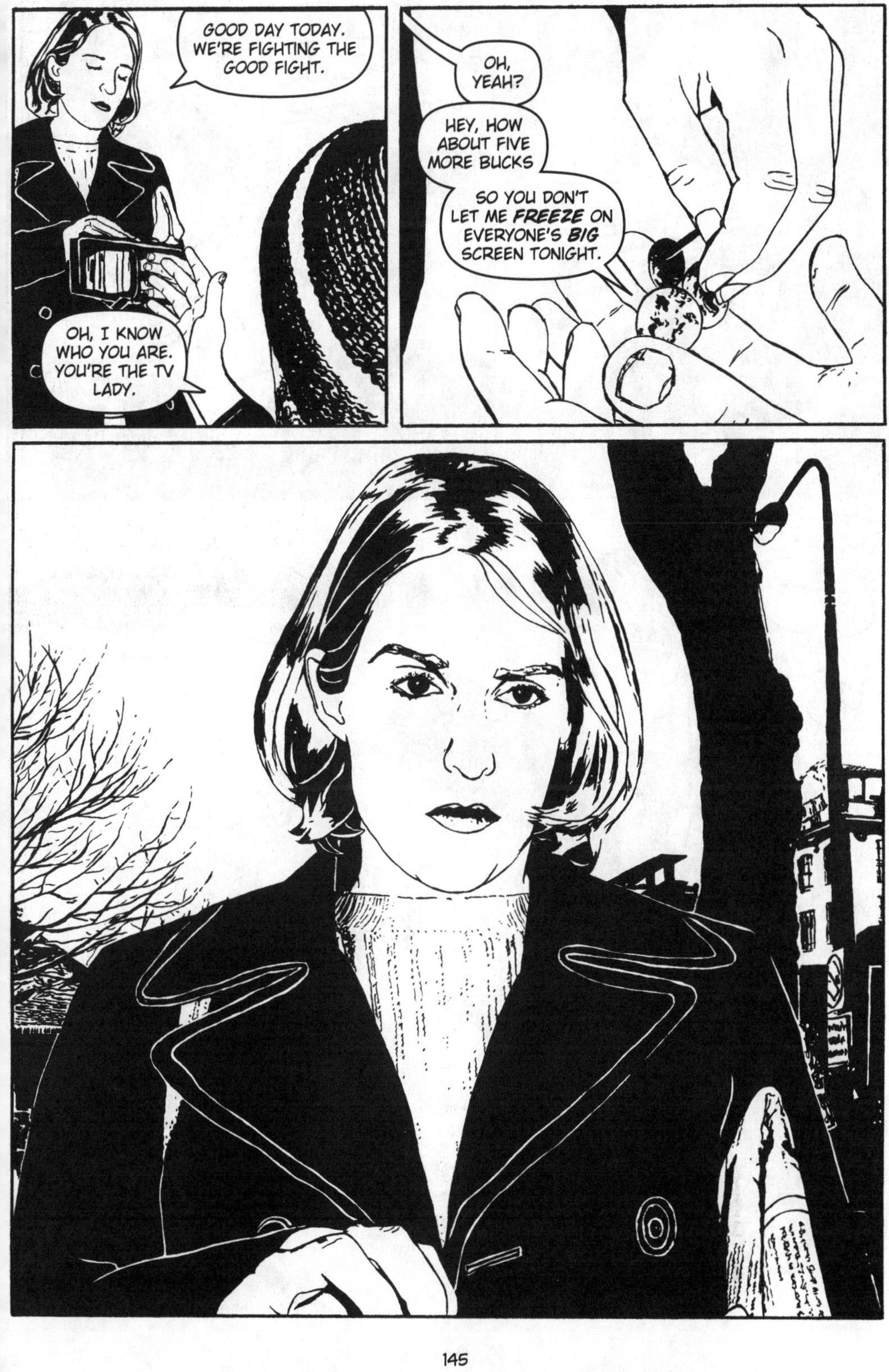
GOOD DAY TODAY. WE'RE FIGHTING THE GOOD FIGHT.
OH, I KNOW WHO YOU ARE. YOU'RE THE TV LADY.
OH, YEAH?
HEY, HOW ABOUT FIVE MORE BUCKS
SO YOU DON'T LET ME FREEZE ON EVERYONE'S BIG SCREEN TONIGHT.

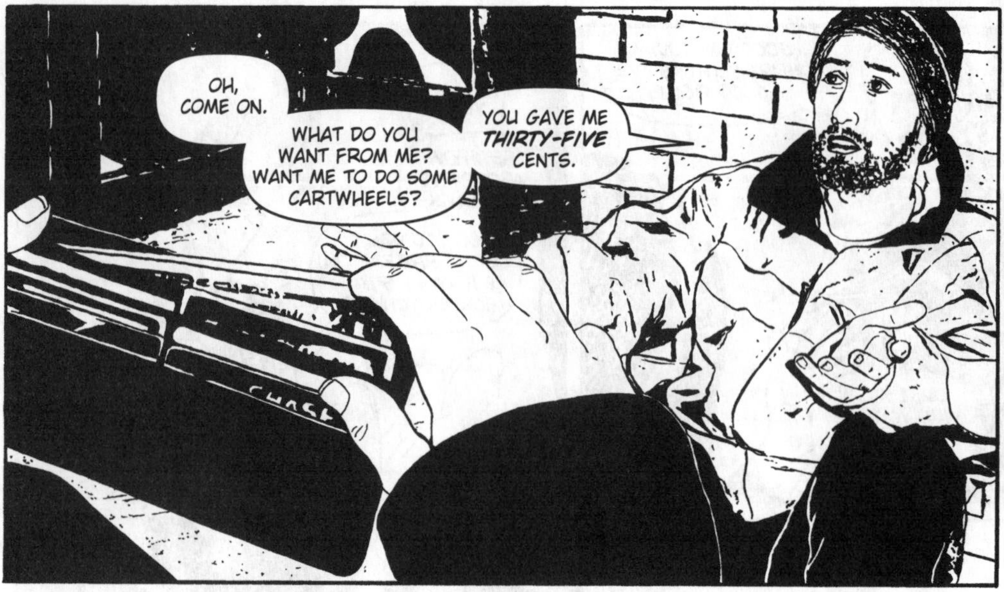
OH, COME ON.
WHAT DO YOU WANT FROM ME? WANT ME TO DO SOME CARTWHEELS?
YOU GAVE ME *THIRTY-FIVE* CENTS.

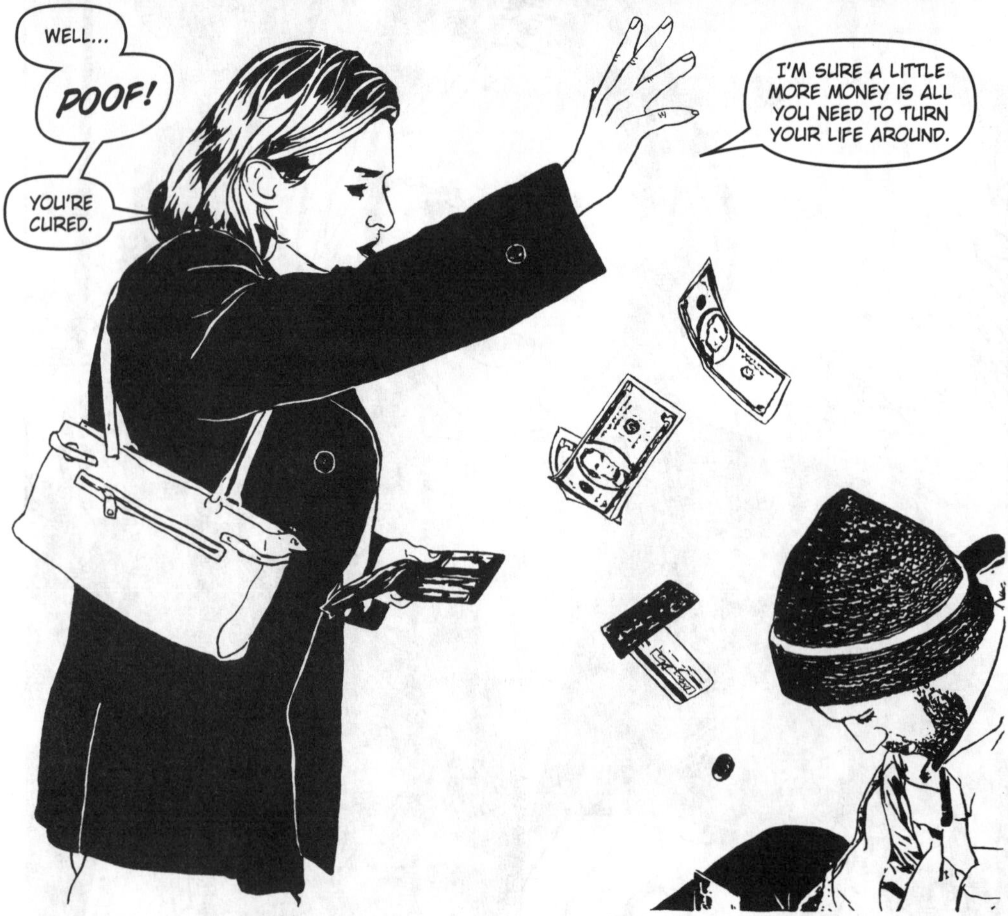
WELL...
POOF!
YOU'RE CURED.
I'M SURE A LITTLE MORE MONEY IS ALL YOU NEED TO TURN YOUR LIFE AROUND.

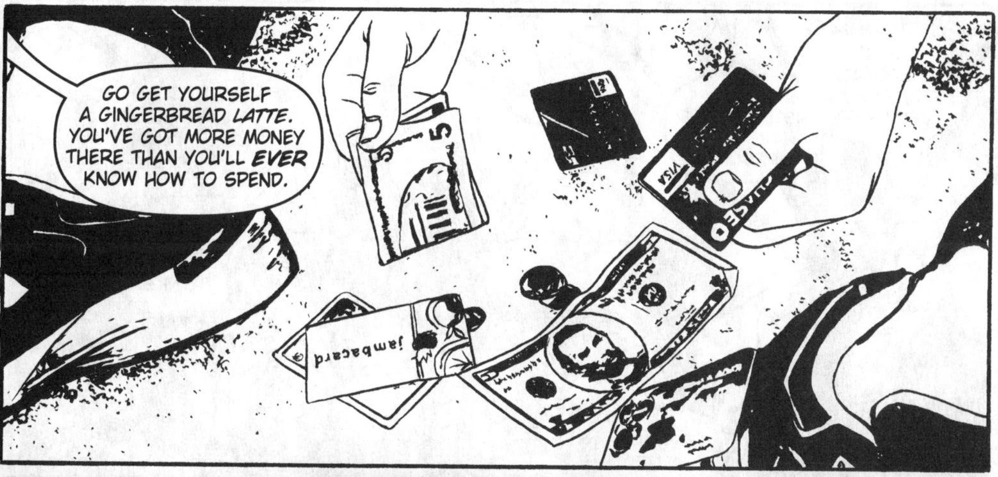
GO GET YOURSELF A GINGERBREAD *LATTE*. YOU'VE GOT MORE MONEY THERE THAN YOU'LL ***EVER*** KNOW HOW TO SPEND.
jambacard

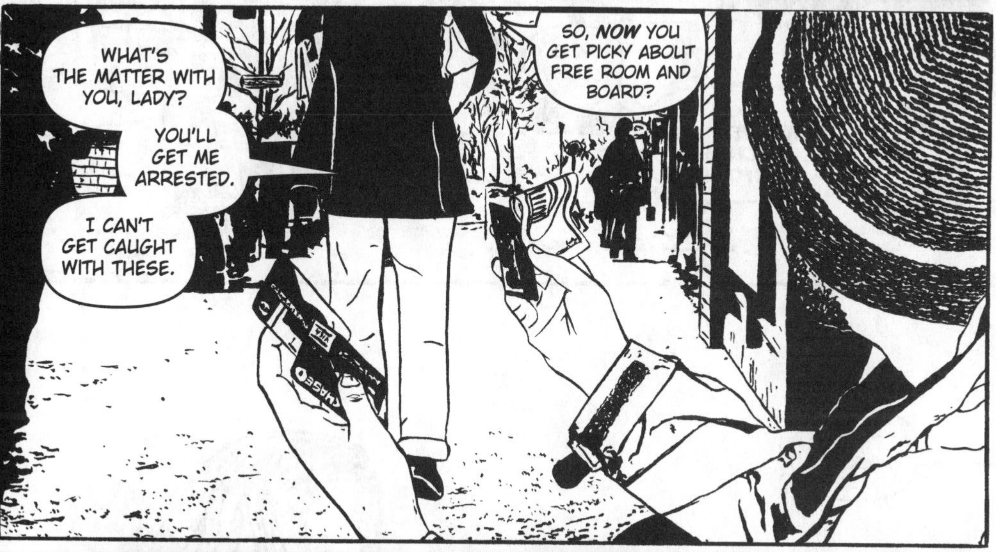
WHAT'S THE MATTER WITH YOU, LADY?
YOU'LL GET ME ARRESTED.
I CAN'T GET CAUGHT WITH THESE.
SO, ***NOW*** YOU GET PICKY ABOUT FREE ROOM AND BOARD?

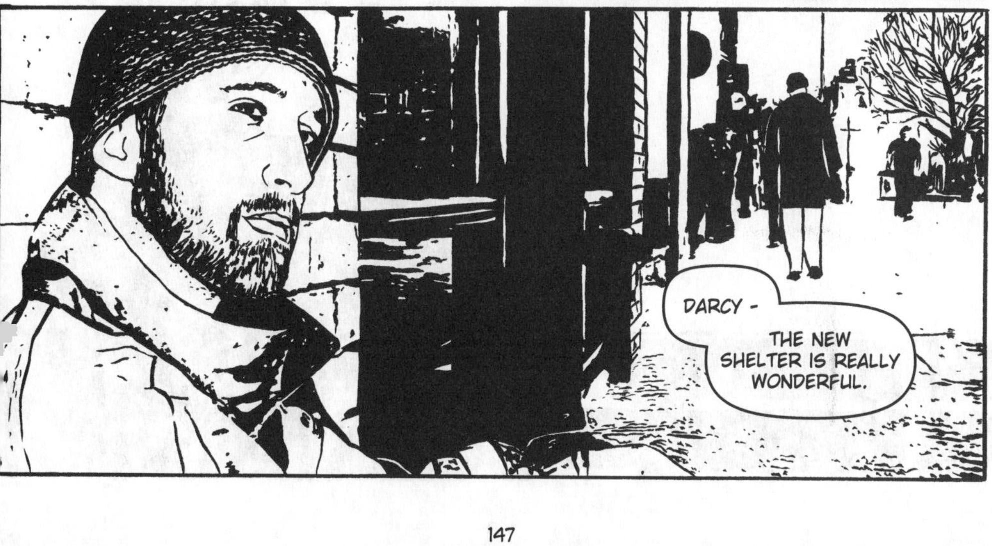
DARCY -
THE NEW SHELTER IS REALLY WONDERFUL.

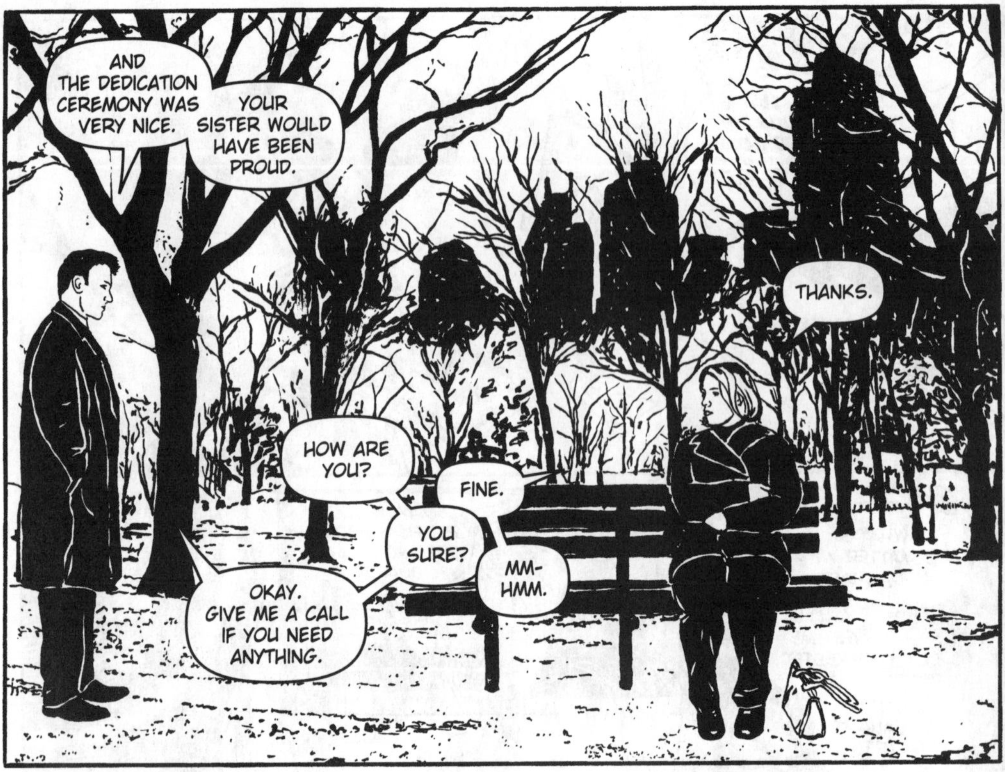
AND THE DEDICATION CEREMONY WAS VERY NICE.
YOUR SISTER WOULD HAVE BEEN PROUD.
THANKS.
HOW ARE YOU?
FINE.
YOU SURE?
MM-HMM.
OKAY. GIVE ME A CALL IF YOU NEED ANYTHING.

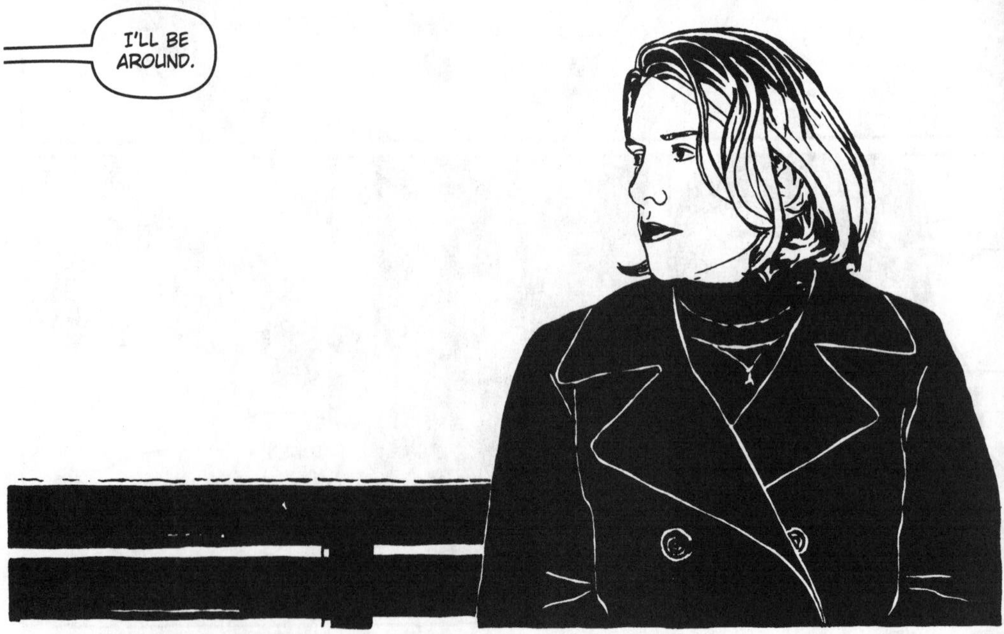
I'LL BE AROUND.

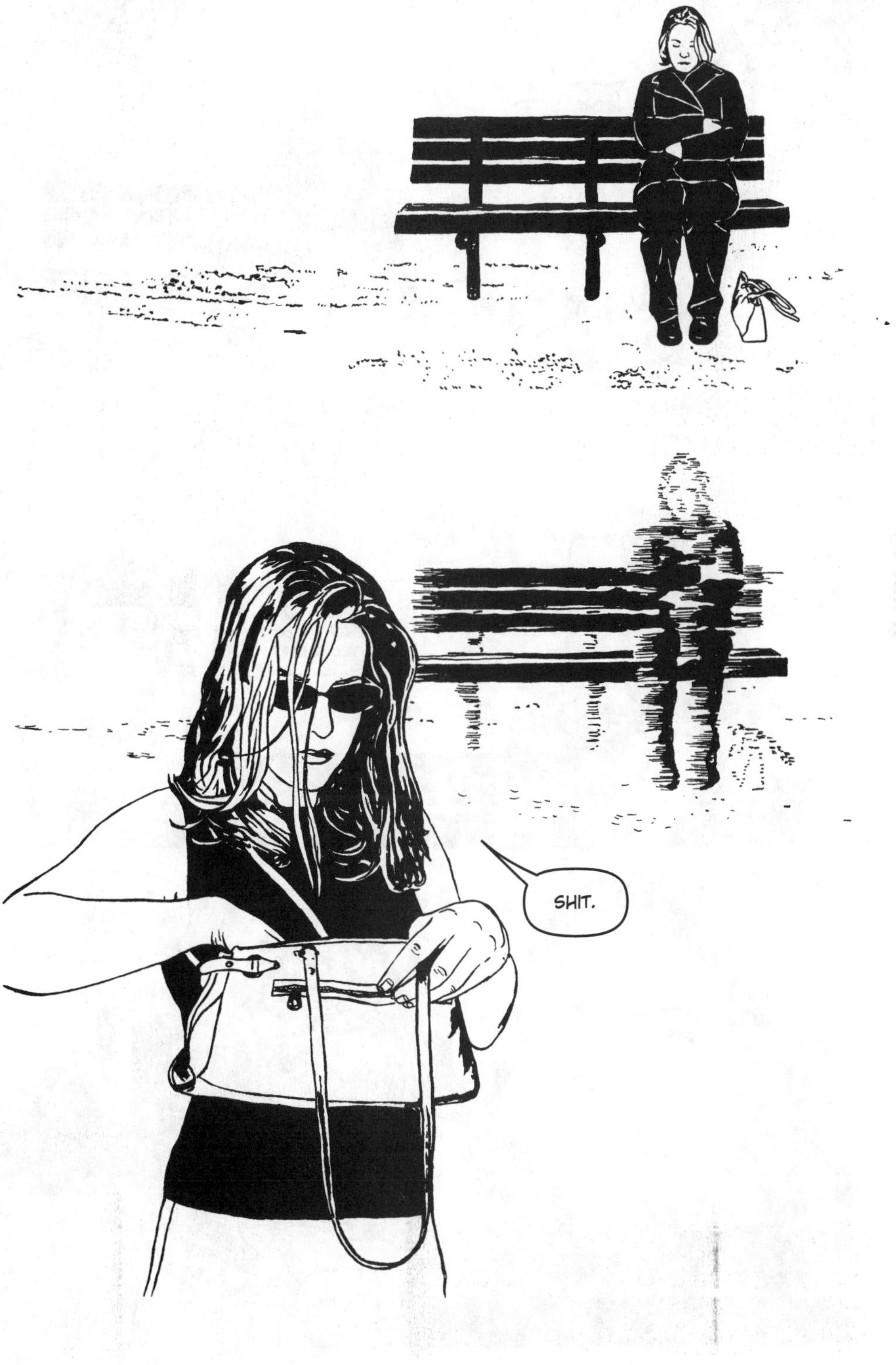
SHIT.

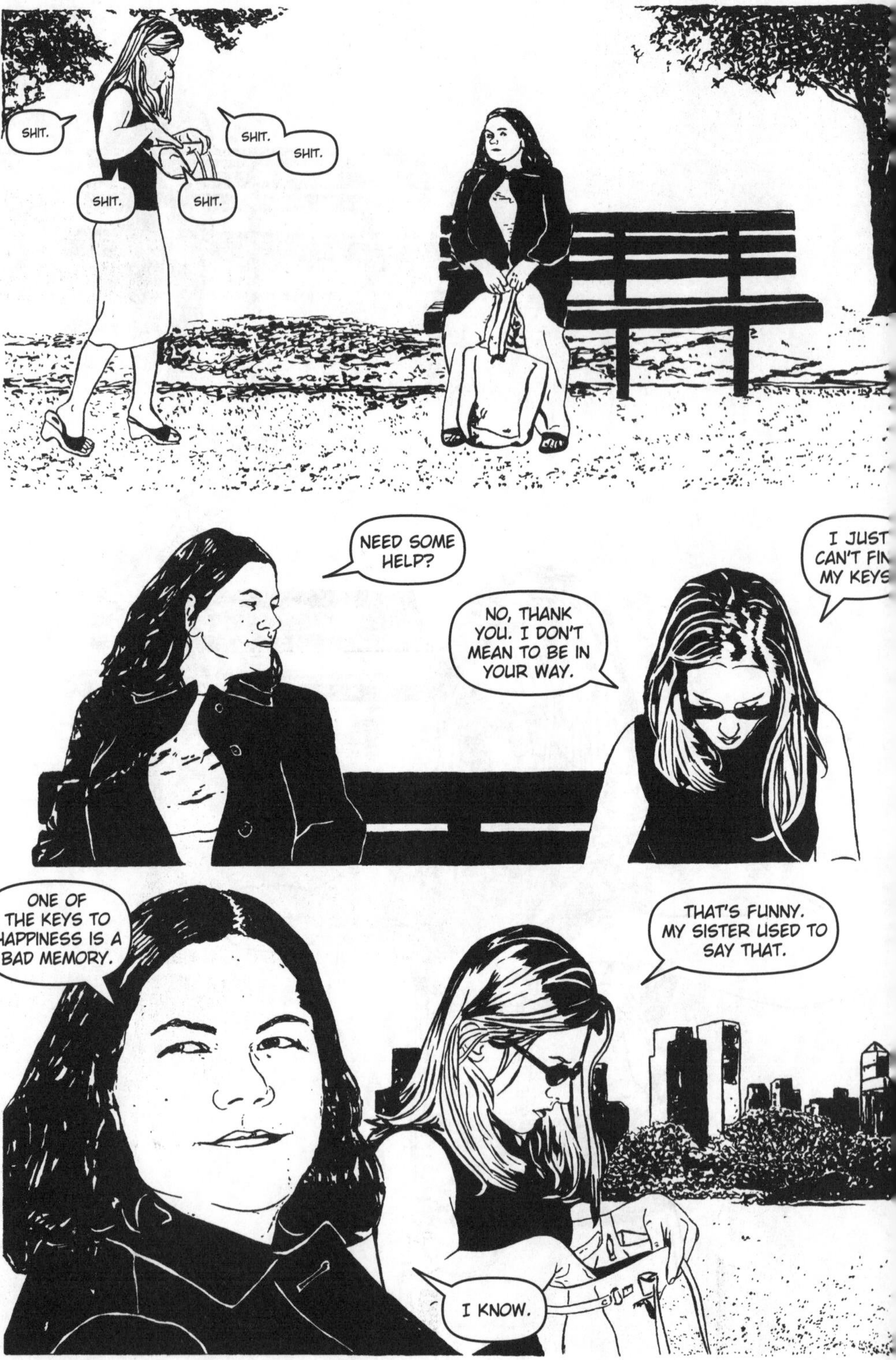
SHIT.
SHIT.
SHIT.
SHIT.
SHIT.
NEED SOME HELP?
NO, THANK YOU. I DON'T MEAN TO BE IN YOUR WAY.
I JUST CAN'T FIN MY KEYS
ONE OF THE KEYS TO HAPPINESS IS A BAD MEMORY.
THAT'S FUNNY. MY SISTER USED TO SAY THAT.
I KNOW.

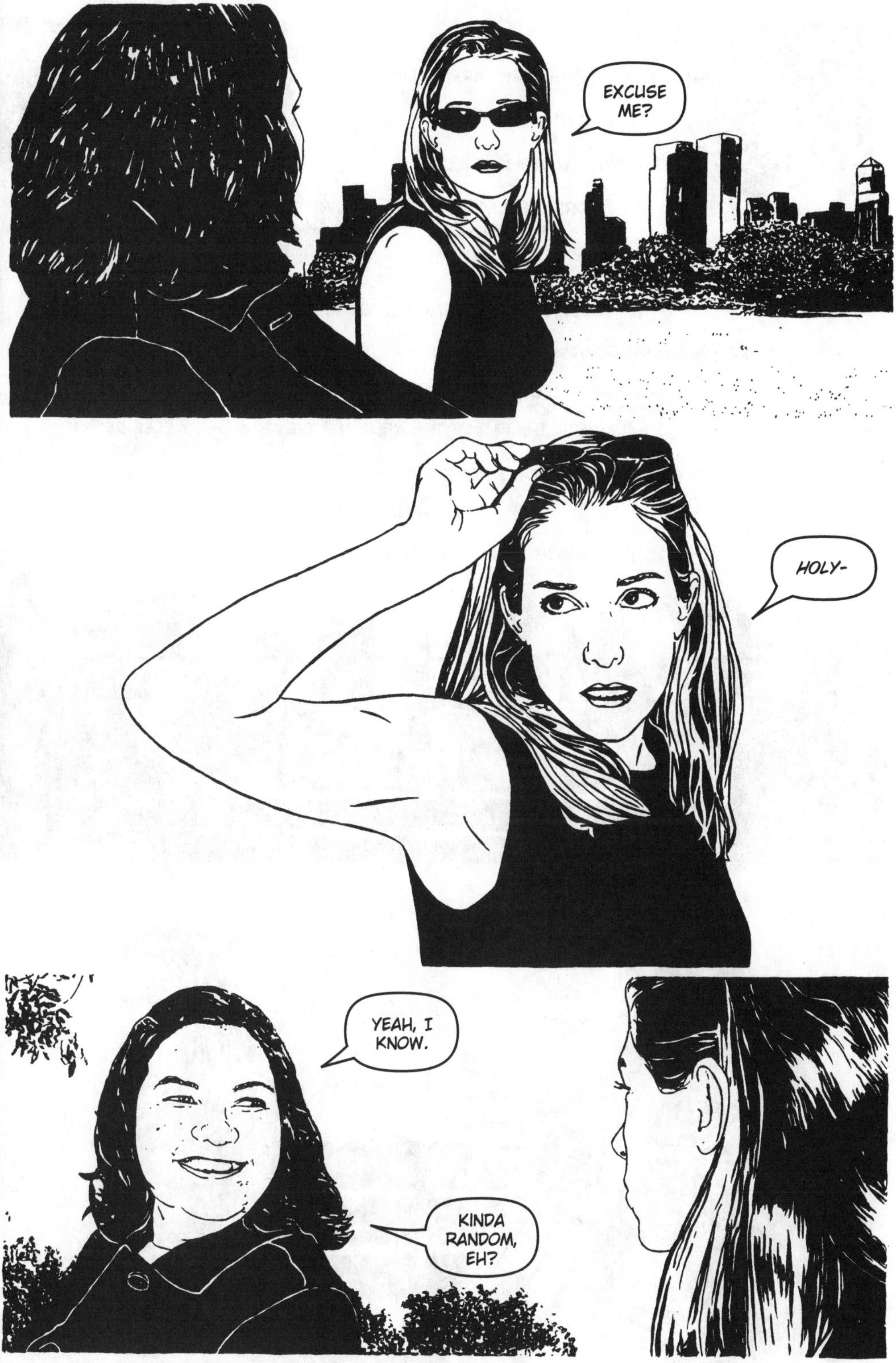
EXCUSE ME?
HOLY-
YEAH, I KNOW.
KINDA RANDOM, EH?

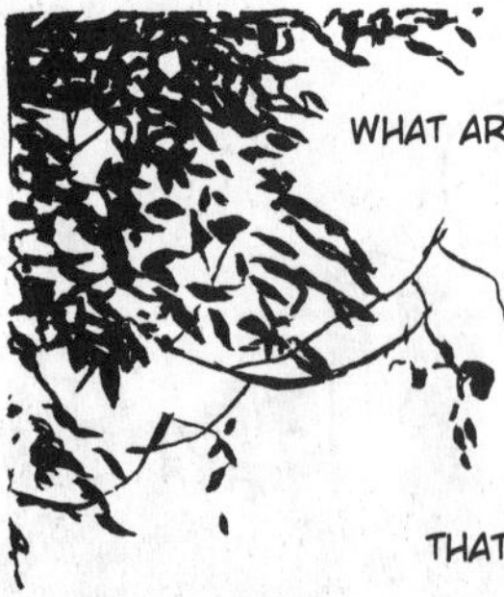

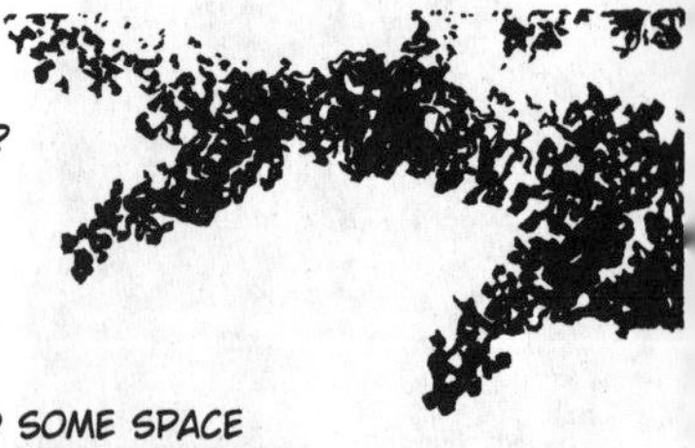

WHAT ARE YOU DOING HERE? ARE YOU IN THE CITY?

I'M VOLUNTEERING DOWN ON BELMONT.

WOW. WHAT- LIKE A JOB?

MORE LIKE LIVING. I GET A COT AND SOME SPACE
AND WE ALL HELP OUT WITH THE CHORES AND STUFF.

THAT'S SOUNDS GOOD.

NOT REALLY. I HAVE TO TURN OVER MY BED AT THE END OF THE WEEK.

WHAT FOR? WHAT DID YOU DO?

NO. CHRIST. IT'S NOT LIKE THAT. THERE ARE JUST TOO MANY
PEOPLE AND NOT ENOUGH BEDS. YOU HAVE TO ROTATE THROUGH.
I HAVE UNTIL THE END OF THE WEEK AND THEN SOMEBODY ELSE GETS IT.

WILL YOU BE OKAY? YOU LOOK KINDA GOOD, BY THE WAY.

WELL, GEE... THANKS.

NO, I MEAN COMPARED TO BEFORE.

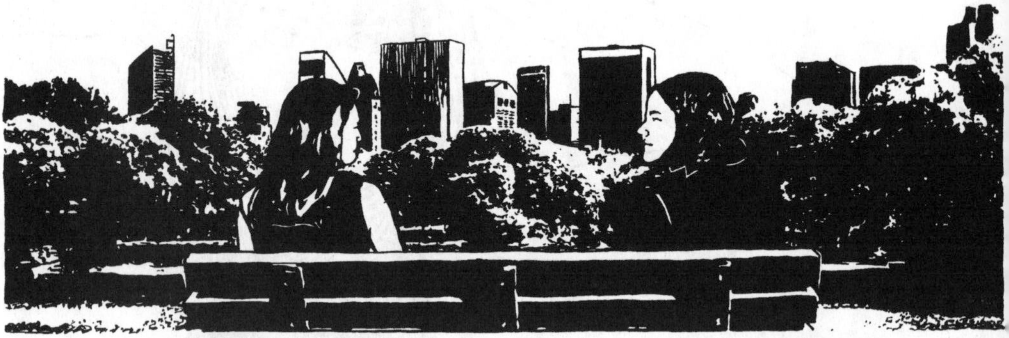

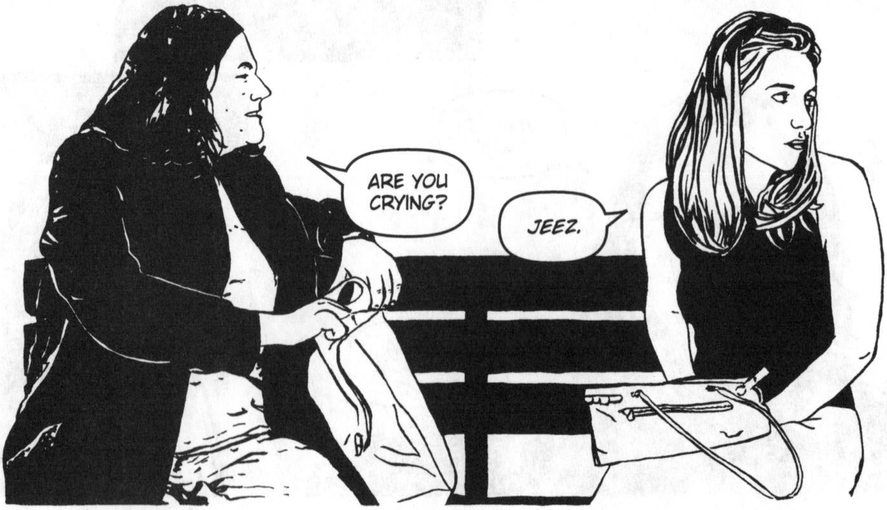
ARE YOU CRYING?
JEEZ.

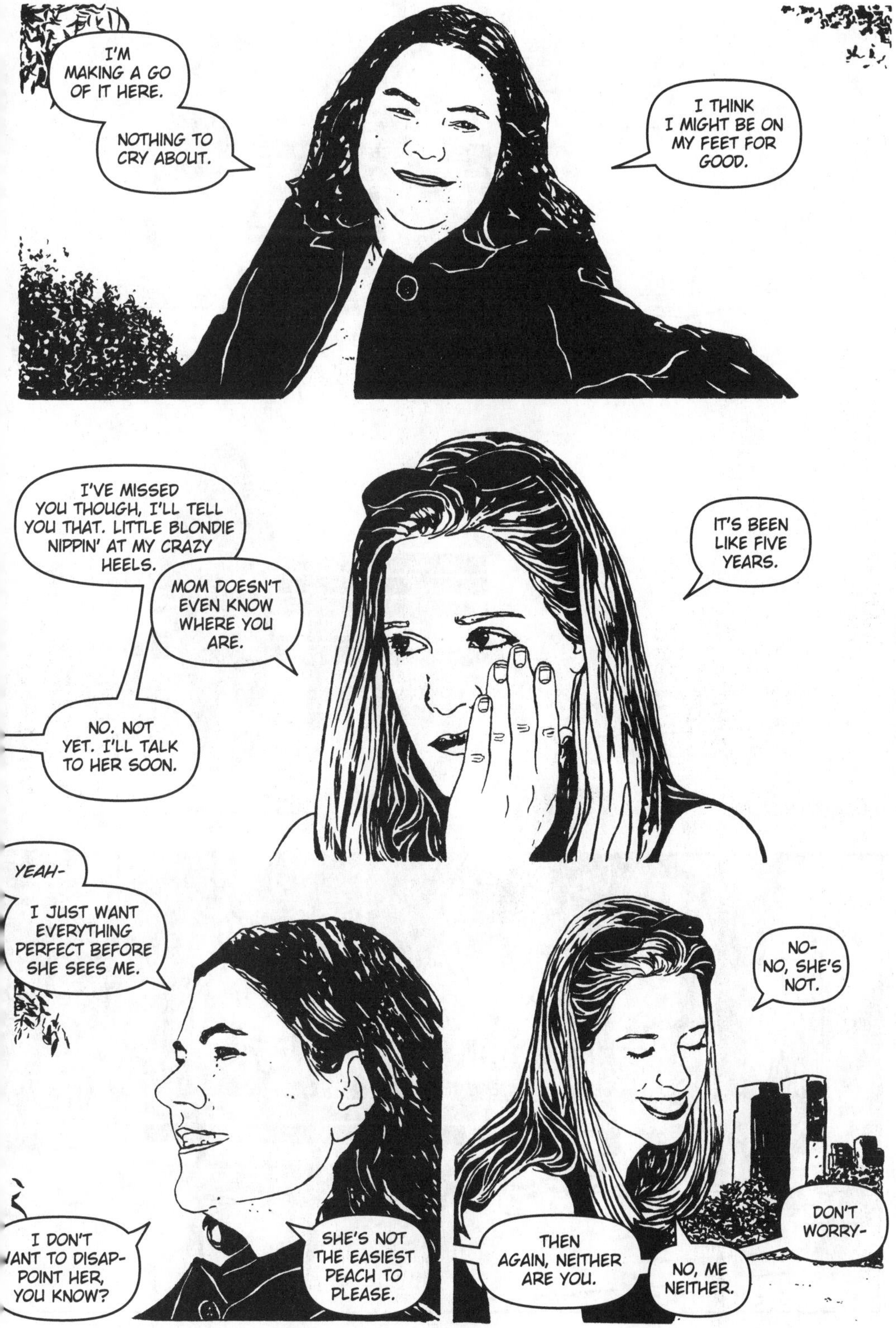
I'M MAKING A GO OF IT HERE.
NOTHING TO CRY ABOUT.
I THINK I MIGHT BE ON MY FEET FOR GOOD.
I'VE MISSED YOU THOUGH, I'LL TELL YOU THAT. LITTLE BLONDIE NIPPIN' AT MY CRAZY HEELS.
IT'S BEEN LIKE FIVE YEARS.
MOM DOESN'T EVEN KNOW WHERE YOU ARE.
NO. NOT YET. I'LL TALK TO HER SOON.
YEAH-
I JUST WANT EVERYTHING PERFECT BEFORE SHE SEES ME.
I DON'T WANT TO DISAP-POINT HER, YOU KNOW?
SHE'S NOT THE EASIEST PEACH TO PLEASE.
NO- NO, SHE'S NOT.
THEN AGAIN, NEITHER ARE YOU.
NO, ME NEITHER.
DON'T WORRY-

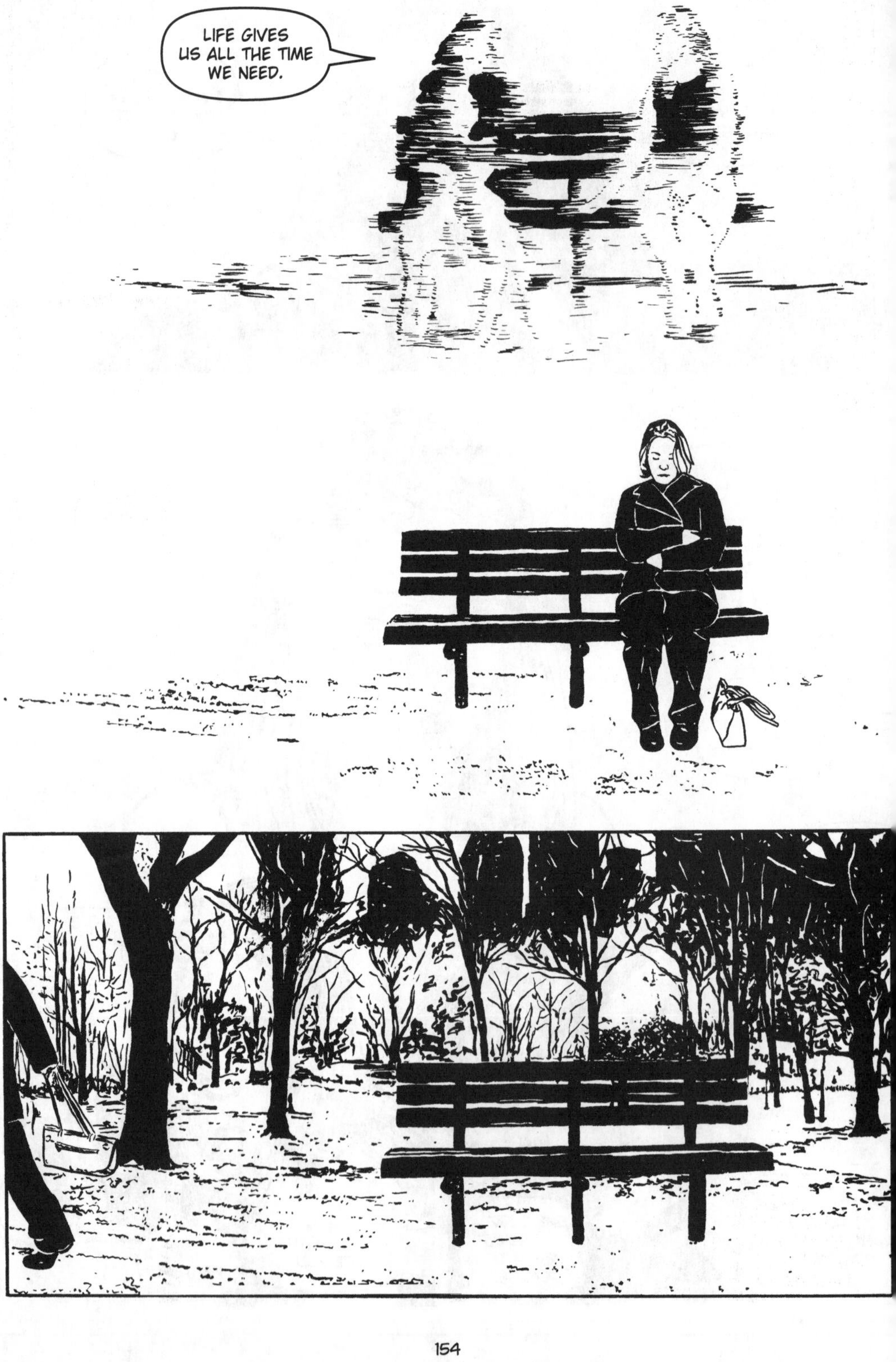
LIFE GIVES US ALL THE TIME WE NEED.

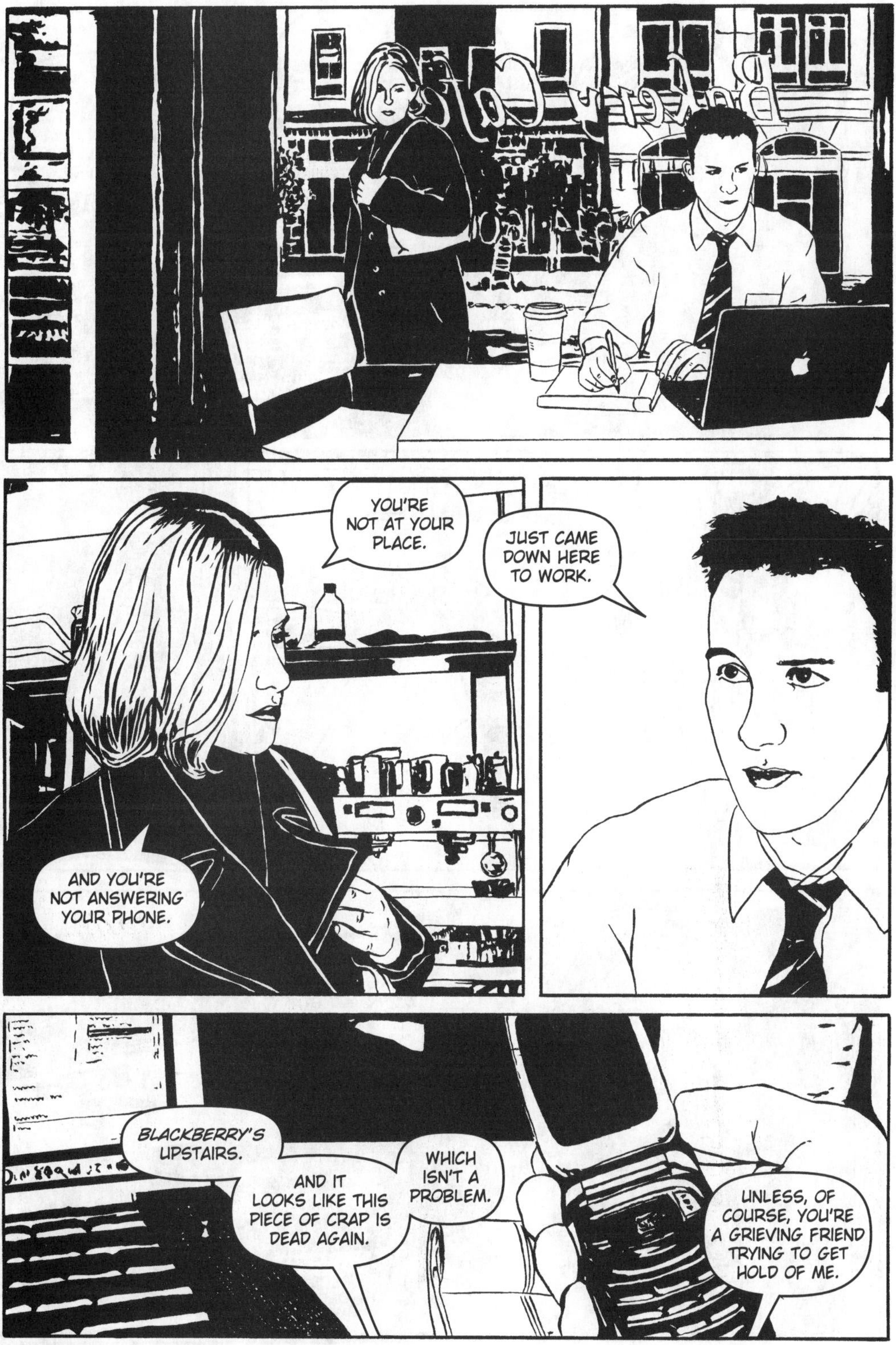
Bakery Café
YOU'RE NOT AT YOUR PLACE.
AND YOU'RE NOT ANSWERING YOUR PHONE.
JUST CAME DOWN HERE TO WORK.
BLACKBERRY'S UPSTAIRS.
AND IT LOOKS LIKE THIS PIECE OF CRAP IS DEAD AGAIN.
WHICH ISN'T A PROBLEM.
UNLESS, OF COURSE, YOU'RE A GRIEVING FRIEND TRYING TO GET HOLD OF ME.

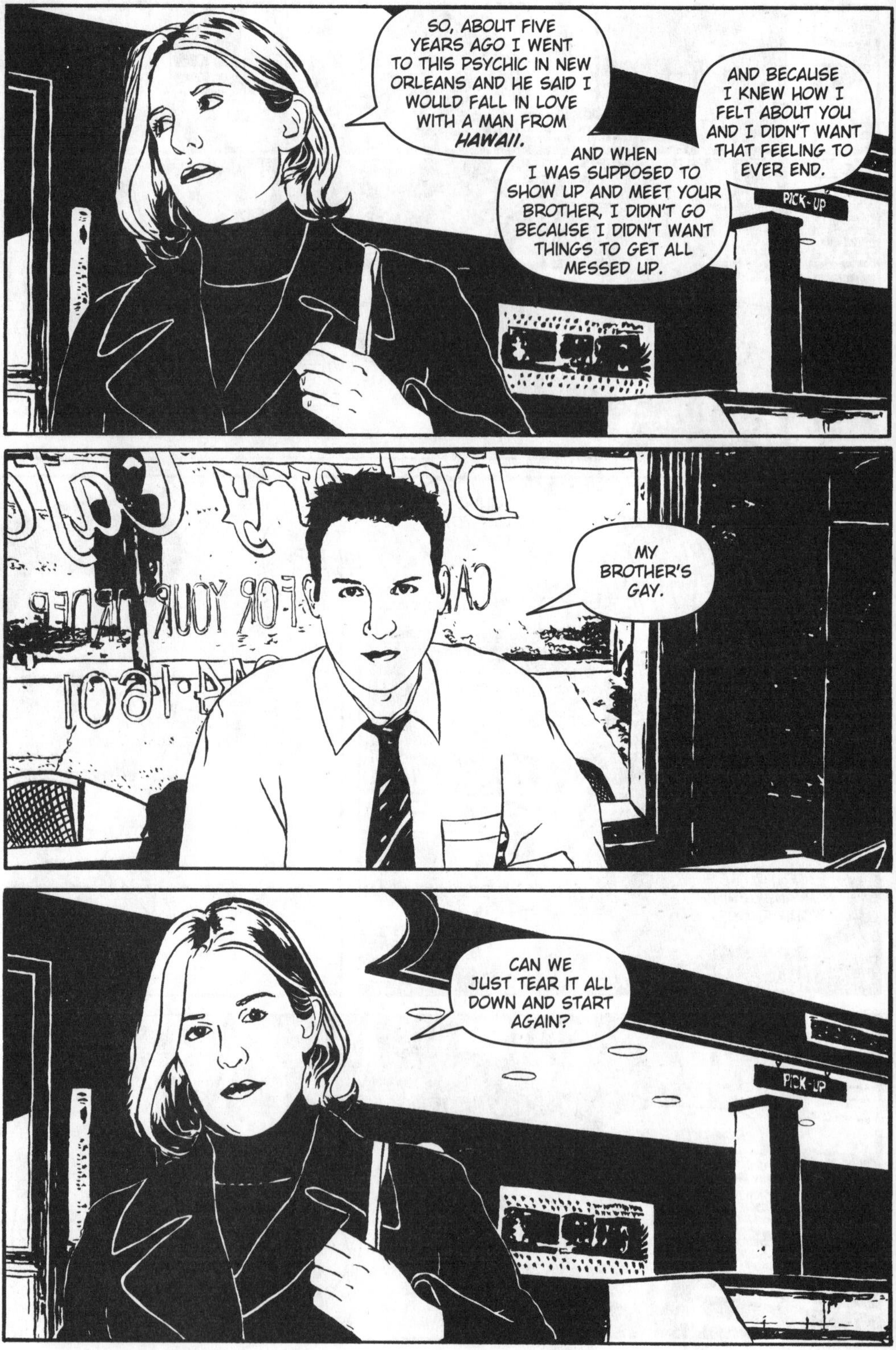
SO, ABOUT FIVE YEARS AGO I WENT TO THIS PSYCHIC IN NEW ORLEANS AND HE SAID I WOULD FALL IN LOVE WITH A MAN FROM *HAWAII.*
AND WHEN I WAS SUPPOSED TO SHOW UP AND MEET YOUR BROTHER, I DIDN'T GO BECAUSE I DIDN'T WANT THINGS TO GET ALL MESSED UP.
AND BECAUSE I KNEW HOW I FELT ABOUT YOU AND I DIDN'T WANT THAT FEELING TO EVER END.
PICK-UP
MY BROTHER'S GAY.
CAN WE JUST TEAR IT ALL DOWN AND START AGAIN?
PICK-UP

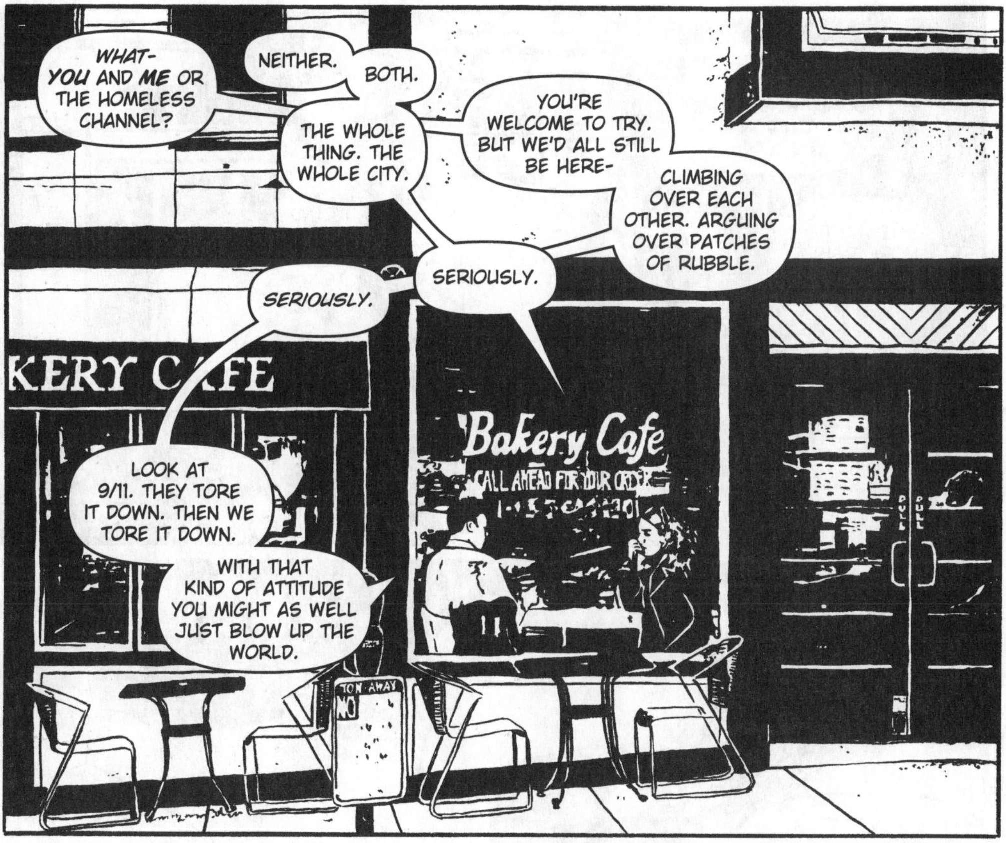
WHAT-
YOU AND ME OR THE HOMELESS CHANNEL?
NEITHER.
BOTH.
THE WHOLE THING. THE WHOLE CITY.
YOU'RE WELCOME TO TRY. BUT WE'D ALL STILL BE HERE-
CLIMBING OVER EACH OTHER. ARGUING OVER PATCHES OF RUBBLE.
SERIOUSLY.
SERIOUSLY.
LOOK AT 9/11. THEY TORE IT DOWN. THEN WE TORE IT DOWN.
WITH THAT KIND OF ATTITUDE YOU MIGHT AS WELL JUST BLOW UP THE WORLD.
KERY CAFE
Bakery Cafe
CALL AHEAD FOR YOUR ORDER
TOW-AWAY
NO
PULL

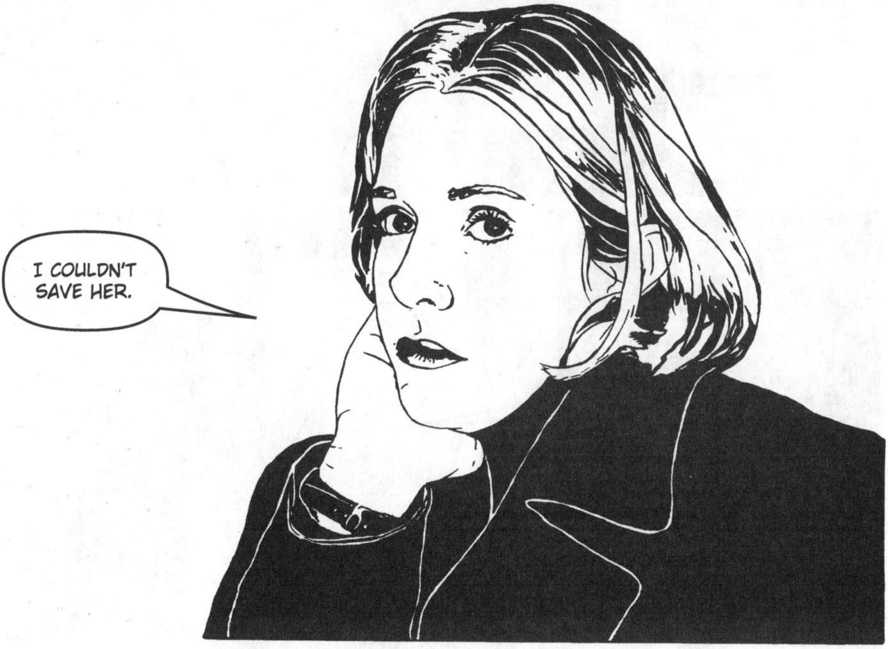
I COULDN'T SAVE HER.

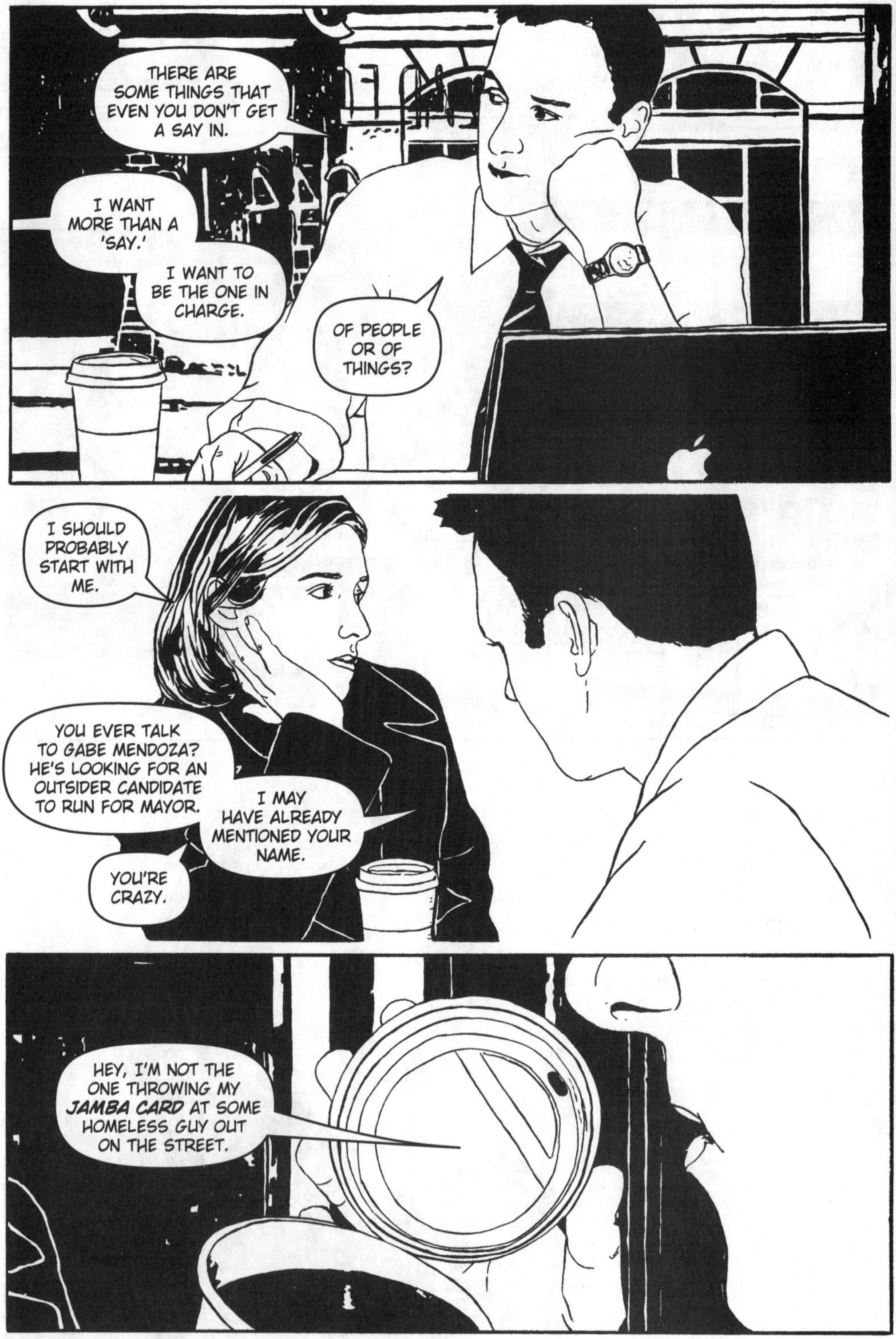
THERE ARE SOME THINGS THAT EVEN YOU DON'T GET A SAY IN.
I WANT MORE THAN A 'SAY.'
I WANT TO BE THE ONE IN CHARGE.
OF PEOPLE OR OF THINGS?
I SHOULD PROBABLY START WITH ME.
YOU EVER TALK TO GABE MENDOZA? HE'S LOOKING FOR AN OUTSIDER CANDIDATE TO RUN FOR MAYOR.
I MAY HAVE ALREADY MENTIONED YOUR NAME.
YOU'RE CRAZY.
HEY, I'M NOT THE ONE THROWING MY *JAMBA CARD* AT SOME HOMELESS GUY OUT ON THE STREET.

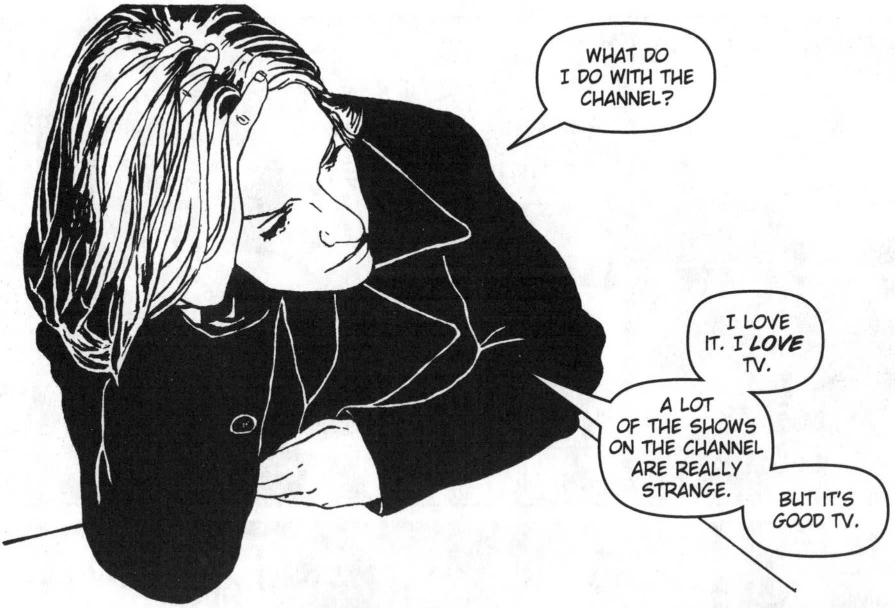
WHAT DO I DO WITH THE CHANNEL?
I LOVE IT. I **LOVE** TV.
A LOT OF THE SHOWS ON THE CHANNEL ARE REALLY STRANGE.
BUT IT'S GOOD TV.

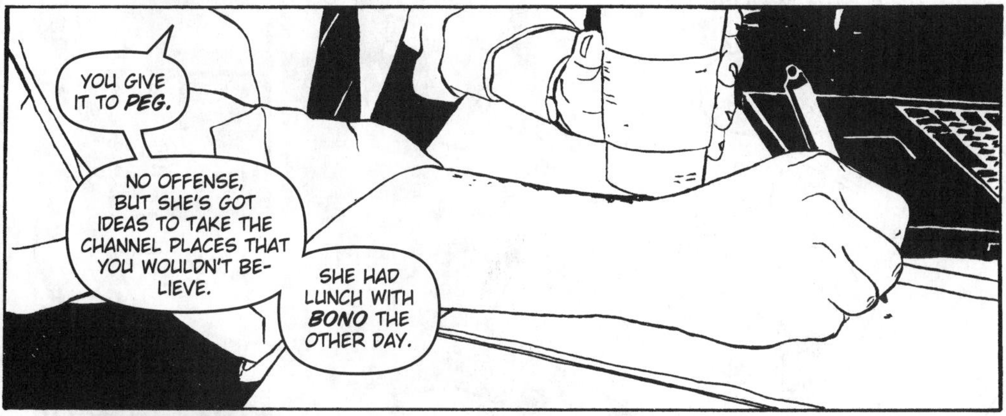
YOU GIVE IT TO **PEG.**
NO OFFENSE, BUT SHE'S GOT IDEAS TO TAKE THE CHANNEL PLACES THAT YOU WOULDN'T BE-LIEVE.
SHE HAD LUNCH WITH **BONO** THE OTHER DAY.

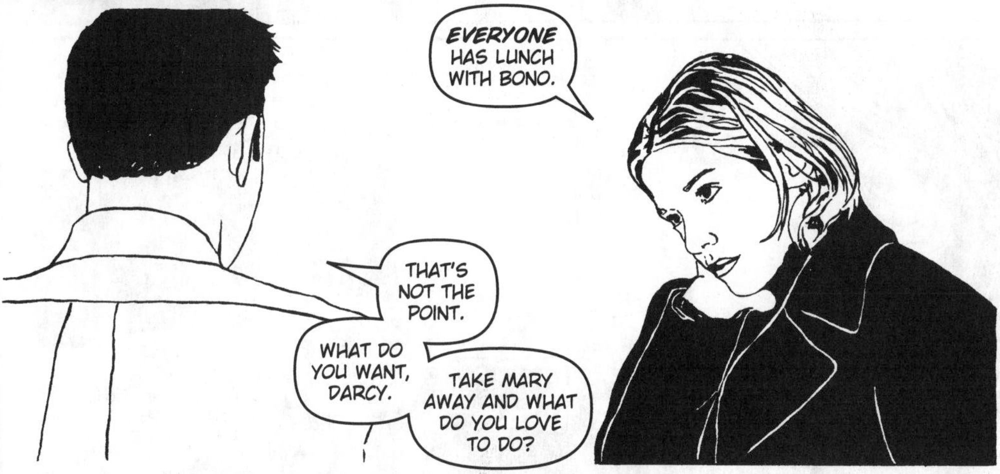
EVERYONE HAS LUNCH WITH BONO.
THAT'S NOT THE POINT.
WHAT DO YOU WANT, DARCY.
TAKE MARY AWAY AND WHAT DO YOU LOVE TO DO?

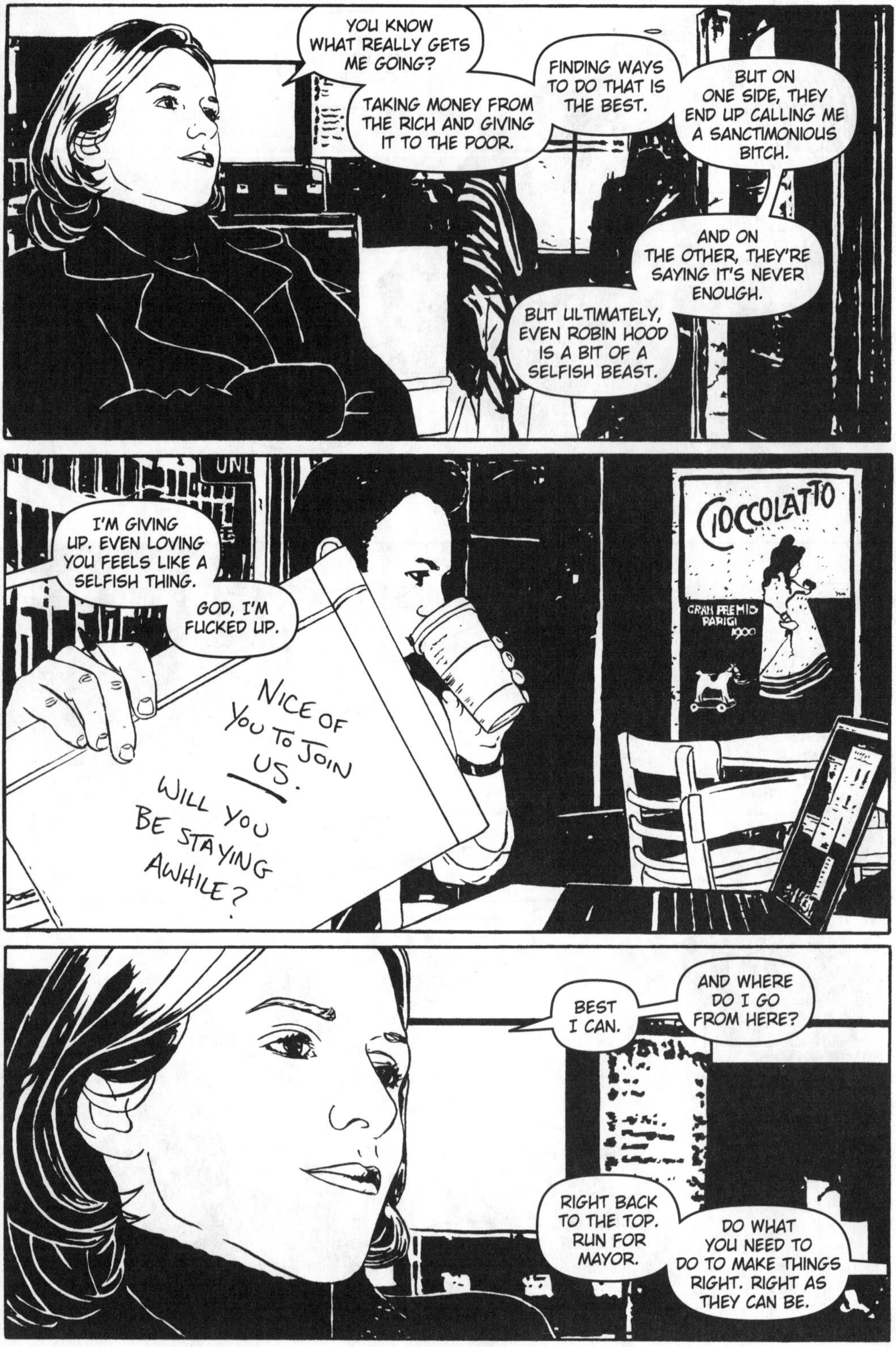
YOU KNOW WHAT REALLY GETS ME GOING?
TAKING MONEY FROM THE RICH AND GIVING IT TO THE POOR.
FINDING WAYS TO DO THAT IS THE BEST.
BUT ON ONE SIDE, THEY END UP CALLING ME A SANCTIMONIOUS BITCH.
AND ON THE OTHER, THEY'RE SAYING IT'S NEVER ENOUGH.
BUT ULTIMATELY, EVEN ROBIN HOOD IS A BIT OF A SELFISH BEAST.
I'M GIVING UP. EVEN LOVING YOU FEELS LIKE A SELFISH THING.
GOD, I'M FUCKED UP.
CIOCCOLATTO
GRAN PREMIO PARIGI 1900
NICE OF YOU TO JOIN US.
WILL YOU BE STAYING AWHILE?
BEST I CAN.
AND WHERE DO I GO FROM HERE?
RIGHT BACK TO THE TOP. RUN FOR MAYOR.
DO WHAT YOU NEED TO DO TO MAKE THINGS RIGHT. RIGHT AS THEY CAN BE.

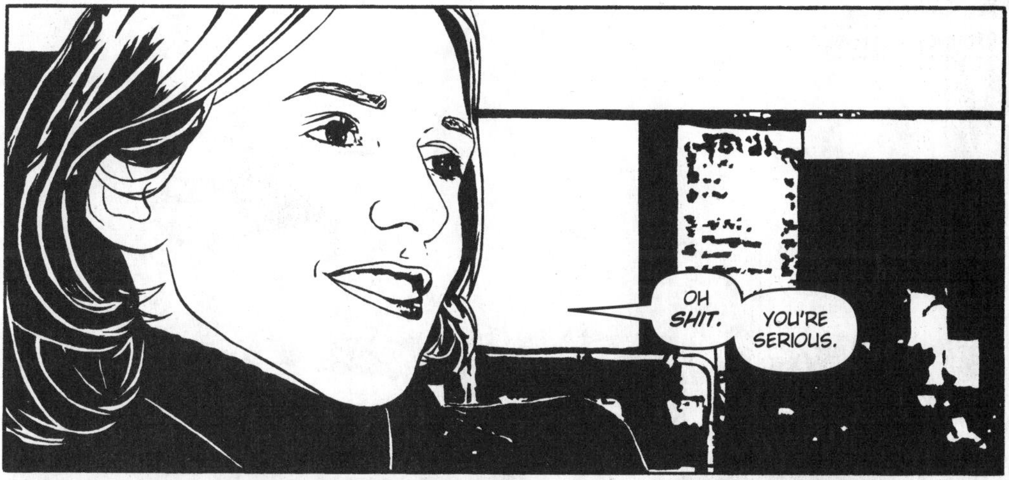
OH *SHIT.*
YOU'RE SERIOUS.

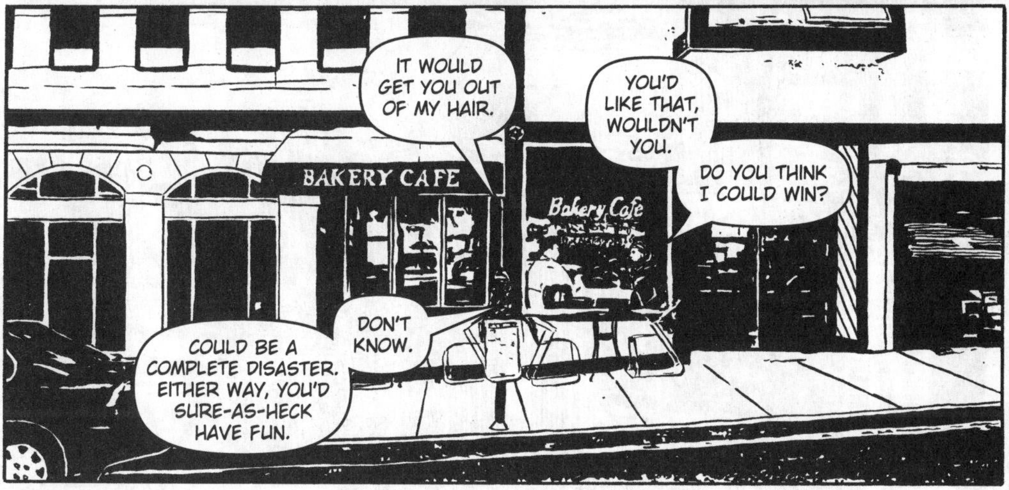
IT WOULD GET YOU OUT OF MY HAIR.
YOU'D LIKE THAT, WOULDN'T YOU.
DO YOU THINK I COULD WIN?
DON'T KNOW.
COULD BE A COMPLETE DISASTER. EITHER WAY, YOU'D SURE-AS-HECK HAVE FUN.
BAKERY CAFE
Bakery Cafe

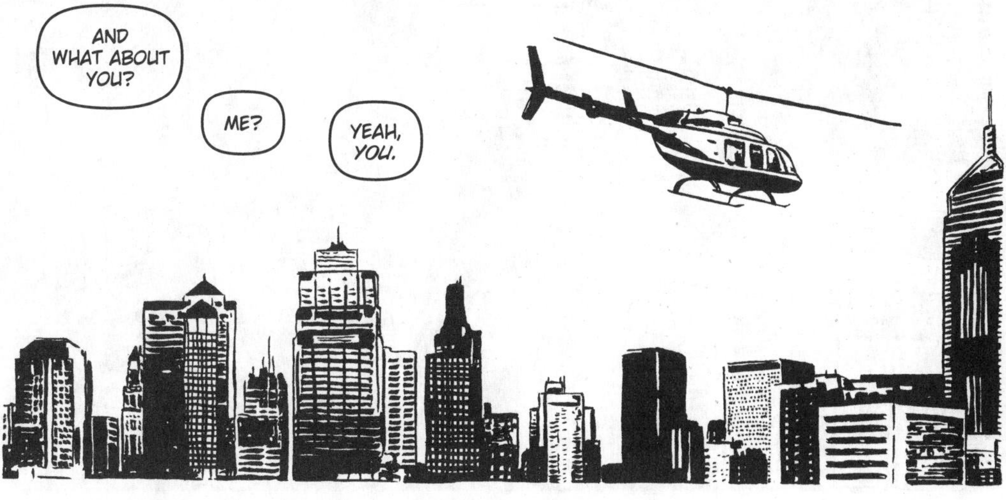
AND WHAT ABOUT YOU?
ME?
YEAH, YOU.

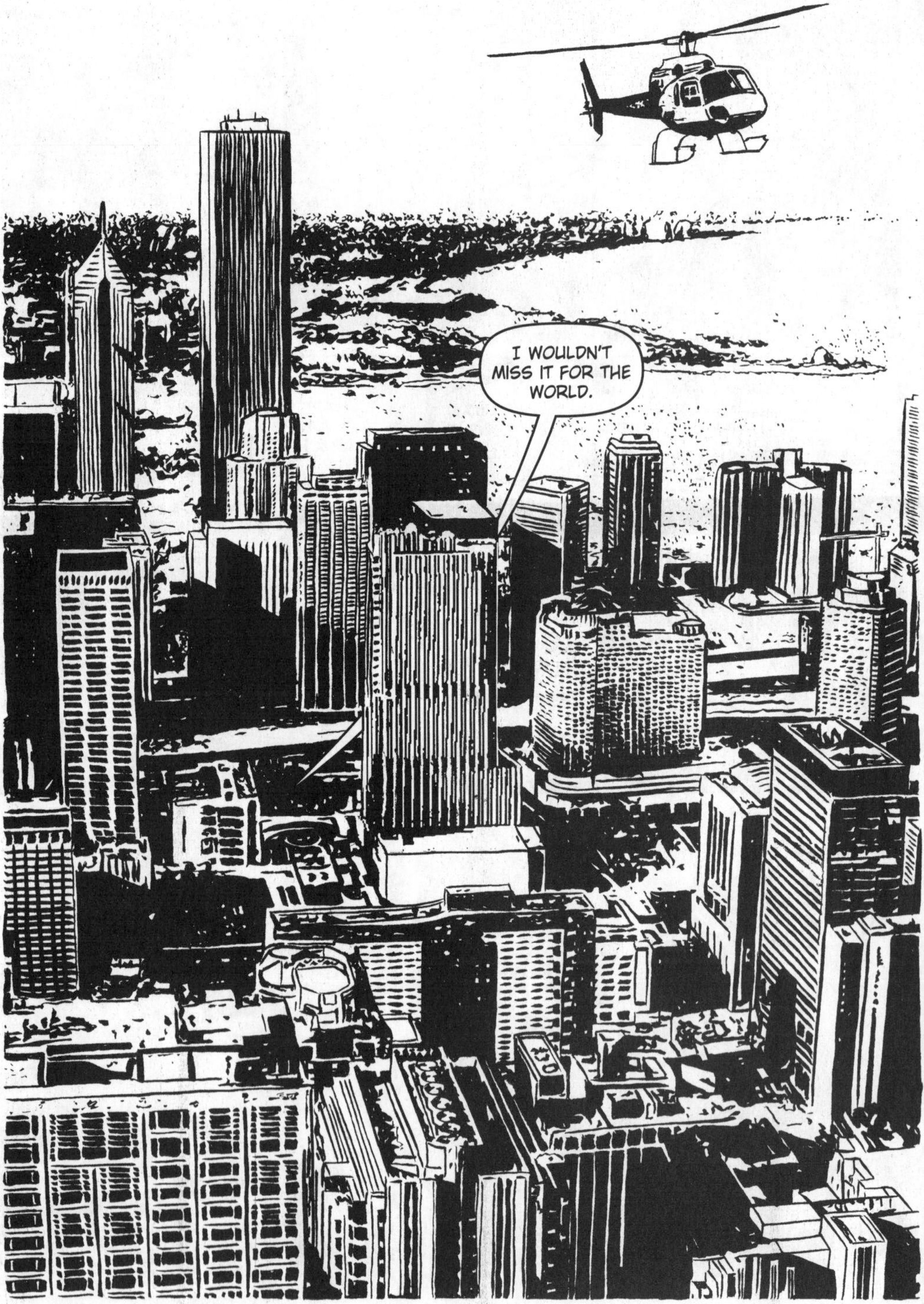
I WOULDN'T MISS IT FOR THE WORLD.

Special Thanks

My sincerest gratitude goes to all
of the friends and family who donated their
time and their energy in an effort to help
me bring this story to life.

In particular, I'd like to thank those who
posed for reference photos
during the creation of this book:

Serena, Megan, Eric,
Sea Min, Kirsten, Karen Jo,
Dr. Krochta, Brendan, Otis, Kate, Sam,
Sarin, Tony, Chris, Melanie, Nathan,
Mandy Dawn, Catie, Angie, Mom & Dad,
Loren, Grace, Alex, and Michelle.

Additional models were referenced from the
the pages of Mark Simon's Facial Expressions.

I'd also like to thank Terri, Peter, Jan,
Claire, Dana, and Hannah for their love
and support. The Isotope Gang: James,
Kirsten, Jared, Ian, and Josh. And
AiT's very own: Larry and Mimi.

Tegan and Sara appear courtesy of
Piers Henwood & Nick Blasko, Artist Management.

About the Author

Matt Silady grew up in the suburbs of Chicago.
In 1997, he received a bachelor's degree in education
from the University of Illinois, Urbana/Champaign and
spent the next six years teaching eighth grade
in the local public schools.

In the summer of 2003, Matt relocated to the
University of California, Davis where he continued to
teach while completing a Master's degree in fiction.

He now resides in Berkeley.